2/26/91

D0148206

# Mastering VMS

### By David W. Bynon

Published By
Professional Press, Inc.
Book Division
101 Witmer Road
Horsham, Pennsylvania 19044

For information, address Professional Press, Inc.
101 Witmer Road, Horsham, PA 19044

Library of Congress Cataloging in Publication Data

Bynon, David W., 1959-
    Mastering VMS / by David W. Bynon
        p.    cm.
    Includes bibliographical references (p.    ).
    ISBN 0-9614729-7-9
    1. VAX/VMS (Computer operating system)    I. Title.
QA76.76.063D965   1990
005.4'44--dc20                                          90-30250
                                                        CIP

The information in this book is subject to change without notice and should not be construed as a commitment by the author or publisher. The author and publisher assume no responsibility for any errors that may appear in this book.

The following are trademarks of Digital Equipment Corporation:

| | | | | |
|---|---|---|---|---|
| ALL-IN-1 | CDD | DATATRIEVE | DDCMP | DEC |
| DECconnect | DECmail | DECnet | DECserver | DECsystem-10 |
| DECSYSTEM-20 | DECUS | DECwindows | DELNI | DNA |
| EVE | FMS | HSC | LAN Bridge | LA100 |
| LSI-11 | MASSBUS | MicroVAX | PDP | PDP-11 |
| Q-bus | Rainbow | Rdb/VMS | RSTS/E | RSX |
| RT-11 | ULTRIX | VAX | VAXBI | VAXcluster |
| VAXserver | VAXstation | VMS | VT | XUI |

MS-DOS is a trademark of Microsoft Corporation.
UNIX is a registered trademark of AT&T.
X Window System is a trademark of MIT.
CP/M is a trademark of Digital Research, Inc.

In 1984, I was thrust from a job managing several PDP-11 systems into a job managing more than 40 VAX systems. If only I had known then what I know now!

Like most people in the same kind of situation, I had to learn quickly just to keep my head above water. The learning didn't come without a struggle. There was too much to learn in too little time. This period in my MIS career sparked the idea for *Mastering VMS*.

As you read *Mastering VMS*, you'll learn what I discovered during the daily management and operation of VAXs, MicroVAXs, VAXstations, VAXclusters, and DECnet. This book comes from hundreds of hours living with VAX computers and the VMS operating system. *Mastering VMS* is not for beginners; it's for VMS professionals.

After reading the first four chapters, you'll understand why the VAX was the most successful computer design of the 1980s. You'll also realize why it will continue to fill computer centers in the 1990s. The VAX's expansion capabilities, software compatibility, and connectivity are legendary. Chapters 1 through 4 explain the interactions of the major components of VMS, i.e., the VAX, clusters, and DECnet. The information won't make you a VAX GURU (Good Understanding, Relatively Useless), but it will help to get the big picture.

The remaining chapters provide necessary background information and step-by-step how-to examples that are helpful to all VAX system managers, operators, and programmers. You won't be introduced to commands and utilities you'll never use, only what's needed to get you going and to keep you going.

The only thing you're not likely to learn from *Mastering VMS* is what your SYSTEM account password is, but I'll show you how to get in if you forget it...

## Acknowledgments

*The list of individuals who contribute to a project of this magnitude would fill several pages. My thanks go to those who have been generous with their time, effort, and skill. Special kudos are sent to Tamela Bynon for her endless hours of editing and to Bill Shipman for his expertise in PageMaker and Designer.*

*I am indebted once again to Dave Mallery and Carl Marbach for getting involved in one of my projects. Their trust and confidence are appreciated. The management and staff of Professional Press have, as usual, worked above and beyond the call to produce a quality product. I would also like to thank Linda DiBiasio and Karen Detwiler for their patience when deadlines were more than a year off schedule.*

*This book would not exist without the United States Navy. The experience I gained working for the Naval Security Group Activity, Skaggs Island, and the Naval Security Group Support Activity, Washington, D.C., is invaluable. So, to all my shipmates, I say "Fair winds and following seas."*

*Finally, many thanks go to Ken Olsen for his "Just say no!" attitude toward complex, impersonal, batch-oriented computing. Your vision, Ken, has swept through every major corporation in the United States. I'm proud to be part of the revolution.*

*David W. Bynon*
*September, 1989*

# Contents

# CHAPTER 3 — DECnet

# CHAPTER 5 (continued)

# CHAPTER 6 — DECwindows                                                     6-1

## CHAPTER 6 (continued)

## CHAPTER 7 — Command Procedures    **7-1**

# CHAPTER 7 (continued)

## CHAPTER 10 (continued)

## APPENDICES    A-1

## GLOSSARY    G-1

## INDEX    I-1

## ANNOTATED BIBLIOGRAPHY    J-1

# The VAX

The first electronic digital computer was built in the early 1940s by J.W. Mauchly and J. Presper Eckert at the University of Pennsylvania. The 30-ton machine was called the Electronic Numerical Integrator and Computer (ENIAC). ENIAC used 18,000 vacuum tubes to form its logic gates and accumulators, and patch-panel wire connectors were used to establish its data paths. By 1940 standards, the ENIAC blazed through problems; it could add or subtract two 10-digit numbers in 200 microseconds. By today's standards the machine was very slow; the original IBM PCs can add or subtract two numbers of that size in about 2 microseconds.

## The von Neumann Machine

In the mid 1940s, the first digital electronic stored-program computer, called the Electronic Discrete Variable Automatic Computer (EDVAC), was built. From its design, John von Neumann published the first known paper on the "stored-program computer" concept, which stated:

1. Program instructions and data are stored in common memory. Previous machines used separate memories for instructions and data.

2. The computer addresses memory linearly, i.e., memory locations are addressed using consecutive location numbers. Memory address begins at 0 and ends at some power of 2. In this layout, data and program instructions are indiscernible to the computer.

von Neumann also designed a method of reading from and writing to linear memory under program control.

3. The linear organization of memory led von Neumann to another new concept, the Program Counter. The Program Counter (PC) is a special register used to hold the memory address of the next instruction to be executed. Each time an instruction is fetched from memory, the PC is updated with the address of the next unit of information (instruction or data) to be fetched.

Most modern computers are based on these von Neumann concepts.

## Limitations of the von Neumann Machine

Since 1951, when the first commercial computer, the UNIVAC 1, became available, computer designers have had a common problem: memory. Memory is expensive and limited.

The first stored-program linear memory computers used single contiguous memory allocation. This memory management scheme requires no special hardware; the program and its data must fit in available memory to run. This technique is still used in most personal computer systems.

The problem with the single contiguous memory allocation technique is that only one job can be run at a time, so memory and the computer are not used fully. Ken Olsen, and other engineers, recognized the limitations of standalone and batch-oriented systems that operated in this manner. To implement his ideas about small multiprogramming systems, Olsen left his job at Massachusetts Institute of Technology (MIT) and started Digital Equipment Corporation.

## A LOOK AT THE BIRTH OF DEC AND THE VAX

Digital Equipment Corporation has deep roots at MIT. There, in the 1950s, the three Digital founders, Ken Olsen, Harland Anderson and Stan Olsen, worked together on some of the first transistorized computers. While building computers for MIT, Ken, Harland, and Stan had a vision of building smaller, less expensive, interactive computers for the mass market. The idea came after a new transistor computer developed by Jay Forrester and Bob Everett was working. The computer was unique at the time because it was simple, fast, and interactive. Most computers of the time were complicated machines developed by professors. The only problem with the vision was that no one at MIT would pay attention. So, as young entrepreneurs, the three men decided to form a company. That was in 1957.

## Digital, The Early Days

Ken, Harland and Stan went to the American Research and Development Corporation, a venture capital company in Boston, for financial support. The men were engineers, not businessmen, and no one at the time had made any money on computers; according to *FORTUNE* magazine and other industry experts, no one would.

The Digital founders didn't let those business perceptions stop them. In their proposal to American Research, Ken and Harland used the word *module* instead of *computer*. After all, these were the pieces they had to make first to build their computers. They made another bold move in their plan: they promised 10 percent profit, when the standard was five percent, in the first year.

Their proposal worked. American Research gave them $70,000 start-up capital. Said Ken Olsen, "The nice thing about $70,000 — there are so few of them you can watch every one." By the way, Digital Equipment Corporation did make a profit in its first year, but it was very small.

With the money, the three new businessmen rented space, hired a lawyer and an accountant, and purchased a parts inventory and supplies. They rented 8,680 square feet in an old woolen mill in Maynard, Massachusetts, for $0.25 per square foot per year. The mill, which dates back to the 1840s, was founded by Amory Maynard to produce carpet. The carpet company failed in the business panic of 1857. In 1862, Maynard helped to form the Assabet Manufacturing Company, which prospered by producing blankets, flannels, and woolens for the army from the start of the Civil War through World War II.

In 1950, the mill again closed. This time, it had succumbed to foreign and Southern competition and the popular use of synthetic materials.

In 1953, 10 businessmen bought the mill and began leasing its space. After only 17 years in business, Digital bought the whole mill complex.

The first Digital products were electronic modules, which would be used to build computers. The three men did everything themselves. The circuit board photography was done in Ken's basement, and silk screens were used to transfer the circuit image to the blank circuit boards. The printed circuits were etched in fish aquariums, purchased from a thrift store. The modules were built using some of the techniques learned at MIT but with a new transistor design. The first modules went to market in 1958, and, for a while, Digital had a monopoly on a small market.

## PDP, The First Generation

In 1960, Digital introduced its first small computer, the Programmable Digital Processor-1 (PDP-1). The PDP-1 operating system was finished in 1963. It was the first Digital timesharing system put into production. Later that same year, Digital unveiled another first, the PDP-5, the world's first minicomputer.

Digital's first timeshare operating system addressed many of the inefficiencies of the single contiguous memory allocation system. It was basically a simple multiprogramming system that allowed the fixed resources of a PDP computer to be matched to varying resource demands. This was accomplished, quite simply, by allowing multiple programs to run on the system at one time. Each program occupied a portion of the system's memory and received increments of the CPU's processing time, called round-robin scheduling.

The memory management technique used in the first multiprogramming PDP systems was called static partition allocation. Static partitioning means that memory is divided into partitions at bootstrap time. No special hardware was required to implement partitioned allocation memory management; however, a memory protection mechanism was invented to prevent one program from disrupting another. Over the next several years, Digital produced new machines at an amazing rate. In 1964, Digital offered its first large-scale computer, the PDP-6. It served as the foundation for the first mass-produced minicomputer, the PDP-8, which was announced in 1965. In

1966, Harland left Digital over a disagreement with Ken and Stan about the PDP-6. Stan remained with Digital until 1980.

Both the PDP-6 and the PDP-8 were victims of the same problems: available memory and operating system memory management. The static partitioning scheme worked well when the size and frequency of jobs were well known. However, if job-to-partition sizes were mismatched, considerable memory was wasted. This problem led to the development of dynamic partition allocation systems, i.e., partitions are created at program runtime.

Many algorithms were developed to allocate and deallocate memory dynamically, but they all had memory fragmentation problems. Fragmentation is the development of many separate free areas, created when partitions of various sizes are allocated and deallocated. In a badly fragmented system, some programs would not execute because there isn't enough contiguous memory. An obvious solution to the fragmentation problem was to periodically combine all the free areas into contiguous space. This would be done by moving all of the allocated partitions. Although this might seem simple, moving a program's memory partition usually guarantees it won't continue to run. Most programs have items which are location sensitive, such as data, lists, memory reference locations, and stacks. To be moved successfully, all location-sensitive items must be modified with the new memory offset.

In 1967, Digital came up with a hardware solution to this problem in its PDP-10 computer. Two special registers, called the base relocation register and the bounds register (available to the operating system only), were implemented. On every memory reference, the contents of the base relocation register is added to the effective address; the result is the final address. The technique is known as relocatable partitioned allocation.

The PDP-10 was the last of the first-generation PDP systems. Digital engineers realized, with the PDP-11 and the PDP-12, that a new memory allocation concept would be needed to move them into the next generation of computers. The new concept was known as mapped memory. The memory address space seen by a program is not necessarily the physical address space being used.

## PDP-11, The Second Generation

By 1970, Digital's technology had advanced from 8- and 12-bit machine architectures to a 16-bit design. A 16-bit machine was needed to meet the increasing demands of memory and floating-point operations. That year saw the birth of the first commercially available PDP-11 computer (Digital's second generation machine), the PDP-11/20 and the UNIBUS.

The UNIBUS was Digital's first general purpose peripheral adapter (computer bus). UNIBUS systems are still in production today, two decades after their inception.

Another first was introduced in 1970, the RSTS operating system. RSTS was the first general purpose, multiuser operating system with generalized device handling. This was a significant feature for Digital, because it allowed its customers to migrate to new Digital CPUs. Many of the features of this operating system are available in VMS. RSTS offered another first for Digital as well: paged memory management. Paged memory management allowed designers to avoid the contiguity problems of earlier systems by dividing each job's address space into equal segments, called pages. Likewise, physical memory is divided into segments of the same size. The memory segments are called blocks.

By providing hardware mapping capability to the PDP-11s, any program page could be placed into any memory block. To the program, the pages remain logically contiguous. However, the corresponding memory blocks can be scattered throughout available memory. A memory data structure called the page map table is used to keep track of pages in memory. Another Digital operating system, called RSX-11, also used this feature of the PDP-11s.

Even with paged memory management support, the PDP-11s (and other paged memory systems) fell short on one mark: sufficient memory to load and run any program. As a result, jobs either waited to be run until there was enough free memory, or programmers wrote them in small, independent segments called overlays. Both of these situations wasted valuable time.

By 1974, Digital had shipped 30,000 computers. Number 30,000 was a PDP-11/35, a model announced in 1971 along with the 11/45.

Few other systems were announced between 1971 and 1974, as Digital engineers were hard at work designing their first microprocessor.

The new microprocessor technology was offered to the public in 1975, when the first large scale integration computer was introduced, the LSI-11. That same year, Digital's most powerful PDP-11 was introduced, the PDP-11/70. The PDP-11/70, which had a 22-bit address bus, was one of Digital's fastest and most popular computers for many years. It was sold into the mid-1980s, until FCC regulations forced it out of production. By the end of 1975, computer system number 50,000 was delivered. It was a PDP-11/50.

Between 1975 and 1978, Digital jumped another hurdle by introducing its first large-scale time-sharing systems, the DECsystem-10s and DECsystem-20s. The DECsystems, which have a unique 36-bit architecture, became the lowest-priced general purpose time-share systems on the market.

Memory limitations continued to plague Digital's computers. It was time for the third generation, virtual memory.

## VAX, The Third Generation

From the lessons learned in building previous machines, Digital's engineers set out to design a computer architecture that would break the physical memory barrier. Much work in this direction had been done by other companies and institutions. The idea of virtual memory (the illusion of an extremely large memory) began in 1969 and was implemented by IBM, Honeywell, and Sperry in large mainframe systems by 1972. The technique used is called demand-paged memory management.

Digital, however, had more than memory management in mind for its new machine. The company was designing a computer architecture for a family of computers that would span several decades, the Virtual Address Extension (VAX) architecture. Digital's goal was to develop a totally new computer family architecture.

The primary criteria was to extend and protect its customers' investment in PDP-11 computers, while at the same time extending address space to a degree that would eliminate program overlays. Four other major goals were achieved: high-bit density, operator and data type extensibility, a systematic yet elegant instruction set, and a single architecture that would apply to any family member, independent of the hardware technology being used. The VAX architecture features the ability to execute the same software on any VAX family member.

Since 1977, Digital has developed six  VAX product lines (VAX-11/700, MicroVAX II and 2000, VAX 8000, VAX 6000, and  MicroVAX 3000) and more than 20 VAX processors, some with several variations. The VAX-11/7xx family was current until the mid-1980s, when Digital phased it out in favor of the newer 8000 systems. The VAX architecture is so robust that it will serve well into the 1990s.

## PREMIER FEATURES OF THE VAX ARCHITECTURE

The VAX's memory addressing capability is determined by its base register size. As an example, an 8-bit microcomputer (using register enhancement) can address 64K of memory directly, whereas the 32-bit design of the VAX allows it to address more than four billion locations.

### Virtual Address Extension

In Digital's PDP and PDP-11 computers (and other nonvirtual memory machines), memory is limited both by the physical addressing capability of the computer (by design) and the amount of memory the customer can afford. With the giant address space of a VAX, the physical addressing problem (for most practical purposes) is solved. Filling a VAX with four gigabytes of physical memory, however, is cost prohibitive, but that's the beauty of the VAX architecture.

The giant address space of the VAX is virtual. In other words, the physical memory doesn't need to be four gigabytes for the VAX to process data and instructions whose addresses are scattered throughout the four gigabyte address space. The term virtual memory is used because the large memory is only an illusion. Something that is virtual appears to be present but really isn't.

Where Digital's PDP and PDP-11 computers (and other multiprogramming computers) attempt to get 100 percent memory use through various memory management techniques, the VAX logically can attain more than 100 percent. In other words, the sum of all address spaces of the jobs (called processes on the VAX) being multiprogrammed can exceed the amount of physical memory on the machine. The VAX accomplishes this feat with special hardware and a memory management technique known as demand-paged memory management.

At the heart of the demand-paged memory management is the VAX's virtual memory addressing capability, an idealized address space where 512-byte pages of memory are made to appear contiguous. To a VAX programmer, addresses generated by his program appear to be in contiguous memory. VAX programs and data are located in memory as 8-bit bytes. Each byte is identified by a 32-bit virtual address. The virtual address of each memory location is translated by the processor to real addresses using special hardware registers and operating system software. Without knowing it, a programmer's program addresses are segmented and dealt out to physical pages of memory, which might or might not be contiguous.

Unlike a physical memory address, a virtual address is not a unique location. For instance, two or more programs in memory can access the same virtual addresses, but the actual physical memory addresses used would be different. The virtual address mechanism provides another important feature: storage of program segments in both physical memory and on disk. When a program segment is not actively in use, it can be stored on disk to free physical memory.

Demand-paged memory management removes the requirement that a process' entire address space (i.e., a whole program) be in memory at one time. Instead, only portions of the address space, called pages, must be loaded.

When a process starts on the VAX, its pages (of instructions and data) are loaded (i.e., paged) into memory until there are enough to begin execution. The physical memory in use by a process is known as its working set. A process executes a program until it references a location that's not in physical memory. At this point, a page interrupt is generated.

The page interrupt (called a page fault in VMS) is a hardware condition that must be handled by the operating system software. The operating system responds to the condition by loading the required page and adjusting page table entries (PTEs) accordingly. When a page interrupt occurs, the required page is loaded on demand. Thus, the name of the memory management scheme is demand-paged memory management.

The demand-page concept raises an important question: From where are a process' pages loaded when demanded? A copy of a process' entire address space is made when the process is created and subsequently is updated each time a program image is run. When a page is needed in physical memory, it is read from a file on disk called a page file.

The demand-page memory management scheme works fine until physical memory becomes filled with pages. After this happens, it is possible to load another page only by first removing one presently in memory. The page file again is used for this purpose; the pages being replaced are copied to the page file before the new ones are read.

## Process Context and Virtual Memory

Another interesting aspect of the VAX architecture is how it provides a multiprogramming environment. Many programs can be loaded for execution at one time, although only one is being processed at any given time. To keep track of each program loaded, the VAX establishes an environment called a process.

A process is the basic entity that can be scheduled for execution by a VAX. It consists of a hardware context, software context, and an address space. The hardware context is defined by a data structure called the process control block (PCB), which is illustrated in Figure 1-1. The PCB contains replications of the 14 general-purpose registers, the program counter, the processor status longword (PSL), process virtual memory (as defined by four base and length registers), several minor control fields, and the four per-process stack pointers.

The PCB stores the last known information about the process while it's not executing. When a process is scheduled to execute, the majority of the PCB is moved into internal registers. This is known as a context switch. Context switching occurs continuously, as one process after another is scheduled for execution.

| |
|---|
| Kernel Mode Stack Pointer |
| Executive Mode Stack Pointer |
| Supervisor Mode Stack Pointer |
| User Mode Stack Pointer |
| Register 0 |
| Register 1 |
| Register 2 |
| Register 3 |
| Register 4 |
| Register 5 |
| Register 6 |
| Register 7 |
| Register 8 |
| Register 9 |
| Register 10 |
| Register 11 |
| Register 12 |
| Register 13 |
| Register 14 |
| Register 15 |
| Processor Status Longword |
| Program Region Base Register |
| Program Region Length Register |
| Control Region Base Register |
| Control Region Length Register |

**Figure 1-1: Hardware process control block**

System virtual memory is divided into two distinct areas: system space (addresses with the most significant bit set) and process space (addresses with the most significant bit cleared). System space is used to maintain the operating system software and systemwide data structures, and to facilitate system service routines and interrupt handling. The system area is shared by all processes.

Process space, which is defined separately for each process, is subdivided further into P0 space, in which the program image and data reside, and P1 space, in which the system allocates stack space and areas for process-specific data. P0 and P1 combine to form a process' working memory. Each process has its own process space, independent of other processes in the system.

A process' address space is administered by VAX memory management logic. This logic serves several principal purposes:

1. Many processes can occupy memory at the same time, all freely using process space addresses, while referencing (independently) their own programs and data.

2. The VAX operating system can scatter pieces of a process' programs and data wherever space is available in memory.

3. The VAX operating system can keep selected parts of a process and its data in physical memory, bringing other parts in as needed, without intervention of the program or process.

4. Cooperating processes share memory through a controlled structure.

5. The VAX operating system controls access to status, control, and data registers of peripheral devices and their controllers (as these registers are part of the physical address space).

6. The VAX operating system limits access to memory through process privileges.

Figure 1-2 illustrates the virtual address space of several processes and the system in a multiprogramming environment.

A fascinating relationship exists between each process, memory, and the VAX memory management hardware. For the purpose of memory

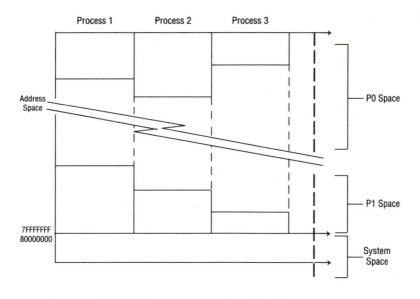

**Figure 1-2: Process virtual address space**

management, memory is segmented into 512-byte pages. Because a process' address space is virtual, all physical addresses must be accessed using a 32-bit virtual address. Fortunately, this translation is performed by the operating system and is of little concern to the programmer.

A virtual address has three distinct components, as shown in Figure 1-3. Bits 30 and 31 of the virtual address select the system, P0 or P1 space. Bits 9 through 29 are used to locate the PTE longword. Bits 0 through 8 select a byte within a page. In theory, a PTE is obtained on every memory reference. If this were true, the processor would spend an inordinate amount of time translating virtual to physical addresses, and it wouldn't get much work done. In reality, the processor has a translation buffer (a high-speed cache of recently used PTEs) that will contain most of the PTEs for virtual addresses used by the process.

All virtual addresses are translated to physical addresses by using PTEs. Their usage is different for system, P0, and P1 space. System virtual address space is defined by the system page table (SPT), which

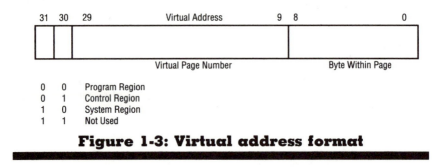

**Figure 1-3: Virtual address format**

is a vector of PTEs. P0 address space is mapped by the P0 page table (P0PT), and a base translation register (P0BR), and the P0 length register (P0LR).

The P0BR contains a virtual address in system space that is the base address of the P0 page table. The P0LR holds the size of the P0 page table, i.e., the number of PTE entries. The PTE to which the P0BR points maps the first page of the P0 virtual address space, i.e., virtual address zero.

P1 virtual address works similarly, except that P1 space grows from its highest address to lower addresses. Unlike P0 space, the P1 space base register and length register describe that portion of P1 space that is not available. Figure 1-4 illustrates how a P0 virtual address is translated to a physical address using the process virtual address, base register, and PTE.

When designing its new computer architecture, the Digital engineers thought of a machine in terms of attributes. How the architecture would be implemented in hardware would come with the design of each new machine.

The VAX architecture attributes consist of those that make up the user architecture and those that make up the operating system architecture. The user architecture consists of:

- Four gigabyte vitual address space
- Instruction set format
- Data types

- Addressing modes
- The processor status word (low word of PSL)
- User mode instructions
- User mode exception handling
- PDP-11 compatibility mode instructions

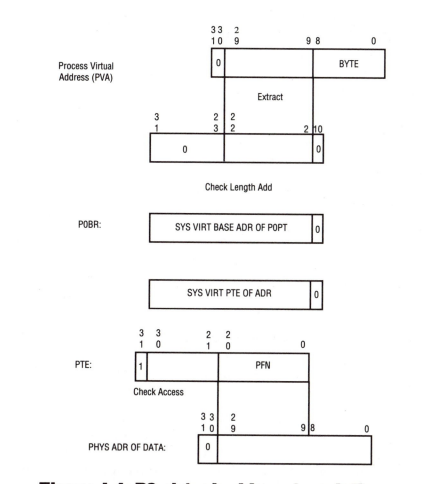

**Figure 1-4: P0 virtual address translation characteristics of the VAX architecture**

The operating system attributes comprise:

- Memory management

- The structure of a process

- Interrupt exception handling

- Privileged instructions

- Processor status longword (high word of PSL)

How the VAX architecture is implemented in hardware is determined by the hardware engineers and their design goals, i.e., size, performance, cost, and so on. VAX processors now span a range from personal desktop systems to mainframe-class systems.

## VAX BUS ARCHITECTURES

One of the most fundamental components of a computer system is its bus and bus adapters. A bus is the mass of wires that connects a processor and its memory to the system's input/output components. It provides communication paths for addresses, data, and control information.

One of the many important design steps that Digital has taken over the years is to build processors that link to standard bus adapters. For instance, the UNIBUS, MASSBUS, and Q-bus are general purpose, proprietary buses used to link peripherals, such as disk and tape controllers, to a central processor and main memory.

Traditionally, with the design of each new CPU class, Digital has built a private, high-speed bus for the CPU and memory. The first VAX, the VAX-11/780, uses the synchronous backplane interconnect (SBI), and the VAX-11/750 uses the memory interconnect.

The concept of separating the central processor from the system's peripherals has a favorable impact on Digital's customers. Primarily, peripherals can be moved from CPU to CPU as the organization grows. It was quite common to see customers who started with a small PDP-11, like the PDP-11/45, move up to a PDP-11/70, then upgrade again to a VAX-11/780. Their peripherals, such as the disk drives, tape drives, network adapters and communication adapters were, quite literally, unplugged from the old CPU and plugged into the new. Furthermore,

Digital's commitment to PDP-11 and VAX-11 compatibility meant that little time was spent converting software.

Digital's present engineering strategy is to get away from its traditional bus designs of the past: UNIBUS, Q-bus, and MASSBUS. The current trend, which seems to be very successful, is to build compatible computer interconnects. For example, let's look at some of Digital's system offerings: VAX Bus Interconnect (VAXBI), Network Interconnect (NI or Ethernet), Computer Interconnect (CI), and Storage Interconnect (SI).

## The VAX Bus Interconnect

The VAX Bus Interconnect (VAXBI) is Digital's most recent bus adapter. It is the interconnect around which Digital is building future generations of VAX systems. It will most likely remain current well into the 1990s. Unlike Digital's past bus adapters, the VAXBI is capable of supporting multiple processors and other bus adapters. The VAXBI acts as a network for computer components, such as CPUs, memory, and peripheral controllers.

The VAXBI is a fully specified 32-bit synchronous bus. A single ZMOS interface chip, the Bus Interface Interconnect Chip (BIIC), provides the interface between the VAXBI bus and the user interface on each of the system components, called nodes. This single chip is responsible for all bus transactions: interrupts, multiprocessing commands, error checking, and distributed arbitration. The BIIC's arbitration scheme ensures fair access for all nodes on the bus.

The BIIC, together with a custom clock receiver and a handful of discrete components on one end of the edge connector, make up the VAXBI Corner. A second VAXBI component, the VAXBI Chip Interface (BCI), provides a synchronous interface bus to link the BIIC and the user interface of each node.

A VAXBI node is one or more VAXBI modules, which can be a mix of three fundamental types of options, i.e., CPUs, memories, and adapters. CPU nodes process machine instructions, access memory nodes, and control the action of adapters. Memory nodes temporarily store instructions and data for CPUs and adapters. They are active devices that respond to read and write transactions issued by a CPU or adapter.

Adapter nodes move data to and from memory and take control instructions from CPUs.

There are several types of adapters: mass storage, communication, and bus. Mass storage adapters provide high-speed data transfer between storage devices and VAXBI memory nodes. Communication adapters provide interfaces to LANs, other computer systems (cluster nodes), and terminal devices. And finally, the bus adapter enables the use of UNIBUS devices. As many as 16 VAXBI nodes can be supported on a single VAXBI bus.

The VAXBI performs synchronous operations. This simply means that all operations are clocked. Events occur on the bus at 200-nanosecond intervals (in Grace Hopper terms, that's about 196.66 feet of light speed), with all address, data, arbitration, and error checking being time-division-multiplexed over all 32 transmission lines. The addressable range of a VAXBI bus is 1 GB (30-bit addressing). The address space is divided evenly between I/O devices and memory. VAXBI data transfers are performed at fixed lengths of 4, 8, or 16 bytes. The maximum data transfer rate is 13.3 MB per second for 16-byte transfers. Compare this with the UNIBUS at 1.1 MB per second or the Q-bus at 3.3 MB per second. For Digital, the VAXBI is a quantum leap in performance.

VAXBI bus arbitration is evenly distributed between the nodes. When the bus is idle, any node can arbitrate. The node with the highest priority will always win control of the bus. When a node gains bus control, it is then the master for one command transaction. Using this technique, no single node can take control. When it is the master, a node sends its command and address information onto the bus. This begins a VAXBI transaction. The node that responds to the master's transaction is called the slave.

One of the most important features of the VAXBI is that it uses multiple processors to their maximum. Of the 13 possible VAXBI transactions, nine fully support multiprocessing. Two of these instructions support interlocked communication between nodes, and another provides interprocessor interrupts.

Let's look at the way Digital builds computer systems around the VAXBI bus. A single processor system can use the VAXBI bus as a combination memory and I/O bus (see Figure 1-5). Multiprocessing systems with two CPUs and a common memory node can use the VAXBI as a shared memory bus (see Figure 1-6). The VAXBI bus also will support single board computers with a private memory bus. This scheme is used to build a high-end system, where the full bandwidth of the VAXBI is required for I/O (see Figure 1-7).

In these high-end systems, which can support multiple processors, a high-speed memory bus is used. A VAXBI adapter is used to connect one or more VAXBI buses to the system.

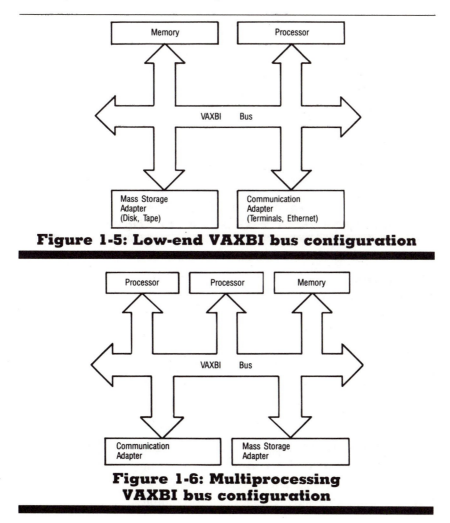

**Figure 1-5: Low-end VAXBI bus configuration**

**Figure 1-6: Multiprocessing VAXBI bus configuration**

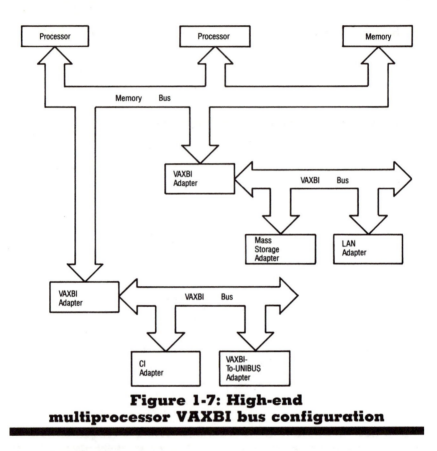

## Figure 1-7: High-end multiprocessor VAXBI bus configuration

## The Q-bus

The Q-bus was designed to meet the demands for small minicomputer
and high-performance microcomputers systems. Over the years,
Digital has modified the Q-bus to produce three basic models. The
first two were designed for large scale integration (LSI) and MicroPDP
systems. They used 16- and 18-bit addressing. The third model,
designed for MicroVAX II and MicroVAX 3000 systems, required 22-
bit addressing and therefore employs an extended Q-bus design. The
Q-bus used with MicroVAX I, II, and 3000 systems is called a Q22 bus.

The Q-bus consists of two unidirectional and 42 bidirectional signal
lines incorporated into a backplane. The backplane, which houses the
signal lines and physical connectors for each module, is divided
into four rows (A-D) and eight or 12 slots (columns). As a special

design for the MicroVAX II and 3000 processors, the Q-bus is wired so that some of the C and D backplane rows are interconnected. This C and D row interconnection is known as the MicroVAX Memory Interconnect or CD. Depending on the backplane, three or more slots can be wired this way.

All communication on the Q-bus is performed asynchronously, which allows devices to transfer data at varying data rates. The bus operates in a master/slave relationship. If more than one device requests use of the bus, the one with the highest priority gets it. When a device takes control of the bus, it is then said to be the master. The master device can control data transfers until it decides to release the bus. In performing the data transfers, the master addresses another device which is designated as its slave.

The bus master is generally a processor or a DMA device which initiates a bus transaction. The slave acknowledges the transaction by receiving data from or transmitting data to the master. For example, a disk drive controller as master could transfer data into memory as the slave.

The Q-bus supports two methods of device priority: distributed arbitration and position-defined arbitration. Using the distributed arbitration method, priority levels are implemented in the hardware. When two or more devices of equal priority interrupt the system at the same time, the device electrically closest to the primary CPU is granted priority. Position-defined arbitration grants priority based solely on the electrical position of the device on the bus. The device closest to the CPU has the highest priority. MicroVAX systems use the distributed priority method.

Q-bus performance is enhanced on the MicroVAX II and MicroVAX 3000 systems through the use of a Private Memory Interconnect (PMI). By putting main memory data transfers on a private bus, the main bus can be freed for device I/O operations. MicroVAX 3300 and 3400 CPUs go one step further by removing memory, disk, and Ethernet input/output from the Q-bus. These functions are contained locally on the CPU board.

Figure 1-8 shows how the MicroVAX II and MicroVAX 3000 systems use the Q-bus.

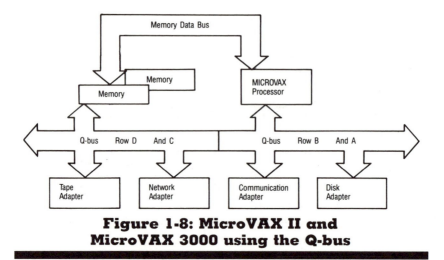

## Figure 1-8: MicroVAX II and MicroVAX 3000 using the Q-bus

### Single-board Computer Designs
In an attempt to build smaller VAX systems cost effectively, Digital has designed single-board computers based on existing CPU chip sets. For instance, the MicroVAX 2000 uses the same CPU and floating point processor as the MicroVAX II, and the VAXstation 3100 contains the ever-popular complimentary metal-oxide semiconductor (CMOS) chip set found in the MicroVAX 3300 and 3400 processors.

These single-board computers have all the primary functions of their larger cousins repackaged onto a single multilayer printed circuit board. A private bus (local to the CPU board) is used to connect additional memory, graphics coprocessors, communication devices, and external storage devices.

These microcomputers are said to be busless, because they lack the backplane or bus adapter typically associated with other Digital computer systems. Still, this does not mean the system is without a bus and thus isn't expandable. Figure 1-9 displays a block diagram of the MicroVAX 2000 single-board computer.

### Computer and Network Interconnects
From the beginning, Ken Olsen has had unique ideas about interconnecting multiple small and medium size computers to build a large

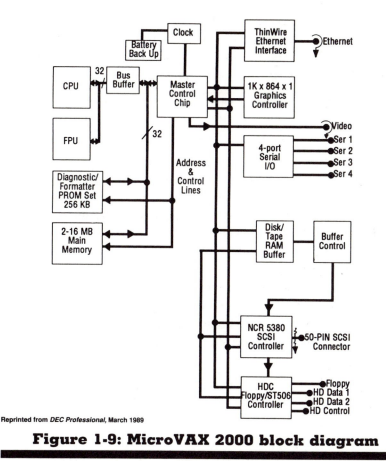

Reprinted from *DEC Professional*, March 1989

## Figure 1-9: MicroVAX 2000 block diagram

system. His ideas have been adopted as a corporate philosophy and have made Digital the world's largest network vendor.

Presently, Digital uses networks in two of its bus strategies: the Computer Interconnect and the Network Interconnect. These are both high-speed processor-to-processor interconnect channels used to form VAXclusters. Processor interconnects are needed to pass information and data between the cluster members, i.e., member connection messages, cluster transition state information, and user files.

Large VAXcluster systems use the CI, which is a high-speed coaxial network. Each node has an Input/Output processor (CI780, CI750, or CIBCI) which connects two communication channels to a central passive hub called a Star Coupler. The Star Coupler forms a star-shaped network between the processors.

To implement the VAXcluster technology on a broader scale, Digital uses Ethernet as its communication medium. It refers to this medium as the Network Interconnect.

Unlike the VAXBI and Q-bus designs, the Computer Interconnect and Network Interconnect are not priority-ruled bus designs. They work on the principle of contention. For instance, Ethernet is a broadcast-based network. It uses an access method known as carrier sense multiple access with collision detection (CSMA/CD).

## CONCLUSION

Digital's history, products, and success are (at least to this user) remarkable. The VAX, a design now entering its second decade, continues to revolutionize the computer industry and business. It's the Porsche 911 of computers; the VAX architecture is a rich and timeless design.

# Chapter 2

# A Look Into the VMS Operating System

The purpose of this chapter is to help you understand the fundamentals of the VMS operating system. The material presented here won't make you an expert on the subject or go into great detail; other books have been dedicated to that task. However, by having a general understanding of the operating system, you'll be prepared to use and manage its capabilities. VMS is a hands-on operating system. It must be understood before it can be mastered.

## A Computer Operating System

VAX computer systems are powerful, but without software to make them readily usable, they are almost useless. VMS, the native VAX operating system, is a collection of software programs that use the power of the raw VAX hardware. Without VMS, the VAX would be awkward and difficult to use.

An operating system consists of software programs that direct the control of the equipment's resources, such as the processor, main memory, file storage, and input/output devices. These programs control the computer, simplify its use, and attempt to optimize its performance. The operating system (i.e., VMS) acts as a translator between the user and the physical hardware, i.e., the VAX.

The VMS operating system is a group of programs that control the overall operation of a VAX computer system. For instance, VMS controls the scheduling of the central processing unit (CPU), the management of main memory and file operations. Most sophisticated operating systems, including VMS, increase the efficiency of a computer system. For instance, it supports multiple users concurrently performing interactive tasks, like word processing or database queries. This multiuser support uses the VAX hardware efficiently.

## SYSTEM OVERVIEW

This section introduces the basic concepts and major components of VMS.

### The Functions of the VMS Operating System

VMS performs duties at many different levels so that user programs

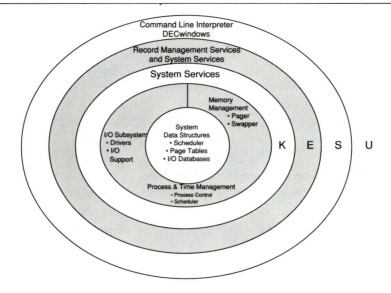

**Figure 2-1: VMS layers**

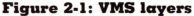

run with ease and efficiency. For example, the user interface or command line interpreter (CLI) is the outer layer of VMS. The layered structure of the operating system is displayed in Figure 2-1.

## The VMS Systems Kernel

At the heart of VMS is the operating system kernel, which consists of an input/output (I/O) subsystem, the job scheduler and memory management. These three components of VMS perform the majority of the operating system's resource-oriented tasks.

The I/O subsystem is a collection of device drivers (low level, hardware specific programs) and several key system services, most notably $QIO, which read/write physical devices on behalf of software requests. The $QIO system service is used by all outer layers of the operating system to access the device drivers. The I/O subsystem has the additional responsibility of servicing device interrupts, and logging device time-outs and errors.

The busiest VMS mechanism is the job scheduler, which is responsible for selecting processes for execution or processing. It synchronizes processes for execution by continuously checking process state transitions and process priorities. In addition, the scheduler performs many duties at timed intervals, such as waking hibernating processes and switching in a new process to be executed when another's quantum of time has elapsed.

The most complex mechanism of the VMS kernel is memory management, which comprises the swapper and the page fault handler. The swapper and page fault handler have four basic responsibilities:

- To distribute physical memory among all processes.
- To translate virtual memory addresses to physical addresses.
- To permit selective sharing of information among processes.
- To protect process information (memory) from other processes.

The swapper's primary job is to help the system fully use the available physical memory, while the page fault handler implements the software virtual memory support.

## System Services

System services are a collection of procedures that the operating system uses to perform basic functions, such as coordination of I/O, to control resources available to processes and to provide interprocess communications. Most system services are used primarily by VMS on behalf of processes running on the system, but there are still many available for general programming use.

## The Record Management Services

The VAX record management services (RMS) is a set of generalized procedures that provide data management services to user programs. Some of these are creating, deleting, reading, and writing files. These services are provided at two distinct levels, the RMS routines themselves and through disk/tape ancillary control processes (ACPs). The ACPs, which are separate processes running on the system, perform the actual mass storage transactions to avoid access conflicts among processes.

## The Command Line Interpreter

The outermost functional layer of VMS is the command line interpreter (CLI). The CLI is the user's direct interface to the operating system and its facilities. Services provided by the CLI call system services, RMS, or external images, including VMS utilities and user-written programs. The most popular CLI used with VMS is the Digital Command Language (DCL); however, other CLIs might be developed by DEC or other software engineers.

## THE VMS PROCESS

The primary unit of VMS is a conceptual body known as a process. The process is the entity selected by the scheduler for execution and the body from which all useful work is accomplished. When a process creates or spawns one or more subprocesses unto itself, the parent process is called the creator, and its subprocesses are called descendants. The collection of the creator, descendants and its subprocesses, is known as a job. The programs that run within the context of a process to accomplish useful work are called executable images.

**Job "SHIPMAN"**

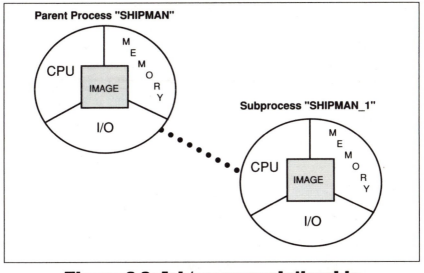

**Figure 2-2: Job/process relationship**

## Process Context

A process is supported by a VMS system in two contexts: hardware and software. The hardware context includes the general purpose machine registers (R0-R11, PC, AP, and FP), four stack pointers, and the processor status longword (PSL). The software context describes the process' quotas, privileges, user identification code (UIC), username, process ID, and the process' scheduling priority.

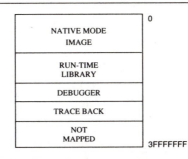

**Figure 2-3: P0 virtual address space**

A process is further represented by its virtual address space description that's divided into three distinct regions: program (P0) shown in Figure 2-3, control (P1) as in Figure 2-4, and system (S0) illustrated in Figure 2-5. A process' virtual address space defines the virtual memory allocated to it. The process itself is concerned only with the P0 and P1 page tables that are stored in the process header. The process' virtual address space is changed during image execution and termination.

| |
|---|
| User Stack |
| Per-Process Message Sections |
| CLI Symbol Table |
| Files-11 XQP |
| Image I/O Segment |
| Process I/O Segment |
| Process Allocation Region |
| Channel Control Block Table |
| P1 Window to Process Header |
| RMS  Data Pages |
| Per-Process Common Data |
| Compatibility Mode Data Pages |
| VMS User Mode Data Page |
| Security Audit Data Pages |
| Image Activator Context Page |
| Debugger Context |
| Message Vectors |
| Image Header Buffer |
| KRP Lookaside List |
| Kernel, Executive, and Supervisor Stacks |
| System Service Vectors |
| P1 Pointer Page |
| Debugger Symbol Table |

**Figure 2-4: P1 virtual address space**

| | |
|---|---|
| System Service Vectors | |
| Executive Code & Data | • Scheduler<br>• System Service Code |
| File System Routines | • RMS |
| Error Messages | • SYSMSG.EXE |
| Physical Memory Description | • PFN Database |
| Shared Dynamic Data Structures | • Paged Pool<br>• Global Section Descriptors |
| Drivers | • Nonpaged Pool<br>• Lookaside Lists |
| Interrupt Stack | |
| Hardware Vector Table | • System Control Block |
| Process Header Storage | • Balance Set Slots |
| Virtual Address Map | • System Header   - System Working Set List<br>                        - Global Sect ion Table |
| System Virtual Address Map | • System Page Table |
| Global Page Table Map | • Gobal Page Table |

**Figure 2-5: S0 virtual address space**

To get a quick look at your own process context, use the DCL command SHOW PROCESS/ALL. A sample output of this command is displayed in Screen 2-1.

## Process Controls

VMS places controls on a process with privileges, quotas, and identifications. To prevent an operation from performing a process that could destroy data or system integrity, VMS requires processes to have the privilege to execute potentially dangerous instructions. VMS has 35 privileges, divided into seven general categories.

VMS quotas, also known as quotas and limits, are a means for the operating system to control allocation of systemwide resources, such as CPU, memory, and input/output. Quotas must be placed on processes to permit even distribution of resources to all the processes of a running system. Imagine the chaos that would arise if VMS didn't limit the amount of memory you could use or the number of concurrent input/output requests that could be issued.

To keep track of processes, VMS uses two simple identification methods: the UIC and the process identification (PID). The UIC

```
10-APR-1989 09:01:46.40  OPA0:              User: BYNON
Pid: 00000037          Proc. name: _OPA0:        UIC: [BYNON]
Priority:  4 Default file spec: USER$DISK:[BYNON]

Devices allocated: BIFF$OPA0:

Process Quotas:
 Account name:  BYNON
 CPU limit:                          Infinite      Direct I/O limit:        50
 Buffered I/O byte count quota:        35904       Buffered I/O limit:      50
 Timer queue entry quota:                 30       Open file quota:         59
 Paging file quota:                    19063       Subprocess quota:         6
 Default page fault cluster:              64       AST quota:               78
 Enqueue quota:                          600       Shared file limit:       30
 Max detached processes:                   0       Max active jobs:          0

Accounting information:
 Buffered I/O count:          169       Peak working set size:      381
 Direct I/O count:             52       Peak virtual size:         2040
 Page faults:                 806       Mounted volumes:              0
 Images activated:              8
 Elapsed CPU time:    0 00:00:04.63
 Connect time:        0 00:01:20.23

Process privileges:
 TMPMBX        may create temporary mailbox
 NETMBX        may create network device

Process rights identifiers:
 INTERACTIVE
 LOCAL
 SYS$NODE_BIFF

Process Dynamic Memory Area
 Current Size (bytes)      25600     Current Total Size (pages)       50
 Free Space (bytes)        22416     Space in Use (bytes)           3184
 Size of Largest Block     22096     Size of Smallest Block           56
 Number of Free Blocks         3     Free Blocks LEQU 32 Bytes         0

Processes in this tree:
 _OPA0: (*)
```

## Screen 2-1: The SHOW PROCESS display

identifies a process in terms of access to system objects, such as files
and devices. The PID identifies the active process on the system.

### Process Creation

Process creation combines the efforts of several VMS components,
namely a creator process, the swapper, and the Create Process system
service. The Create Process system service ($CREPRC) is called by the
creator process, but the swapper performs the critical task of
establishing the new process.

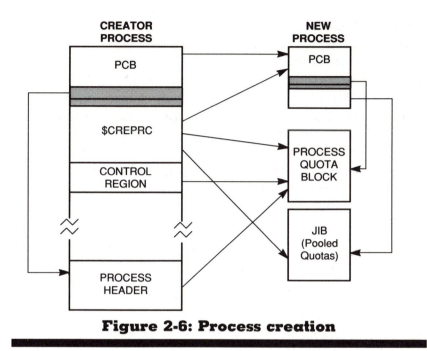

**Figure 2-6: Process creation**

When a creator process calls SYS$CREPRC, the system service makes quota and privilege checks, and loads the process control block (PCB) and process quota block (PQB) with explicit or implicit parameters taken from the creator process. It then puts the new process in the scheduler's database. The state of the new process is computable-outswapped (COMO). This allows the swapper to deal with it outside the balance set, i.e., execution is suppressed.

When the swapper discovers the new process in its database, it inswaps a template process, called the shell. This is a paged portion of the system executive image SYS$SYSTEM:SYS.EXE. The shell contains a minimal process header and P1 space. Finally, the swapper calls the routine SWP$SHELINIT to configure the newly created process header. After this operation is completed, the new process is swapped into the balance set for execution with other processes.

## Process States

After a process is created, it goes through a cycle of states for its entire life. A process' state defines its readiness to be scheduled for CPU execution and indicates if the process is memory resident or outswapped. The three typical states in which a process can be are current, computable, or waiting. When a process' state is current, it's being executed by the CPU. A computable state indicates that the process is waiting for its turn in the CPU. A process that's in a wait state is tied up in a condition that must be fulfilled before the process can become computable again.

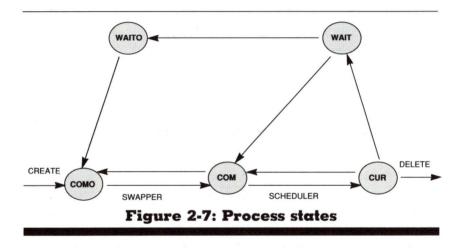

**Figure 2-7: Process states**

## Process Deletion

Processes delete themselves after they have performed their appointed tasks. They also can be instructed to delete themselves by another process, which must have group or world privilege.

The Delete Process system service, $DELPRC, is used to remove a process from the system. This job is accomplished in two procedures. First, the process is marked for deletion and a kernel mode asynchronous system trap (AST) is queued to the appropriate process. The Delete Process AST is executed by the processes being deleted, so that a process always will delete itself, regardless of the process that called $DELPRC.

## VMS PROCESS SCHEDULING

Scheduling defines the events that take place to order processes into CPU execution and incidents that occur based on time. Process scheduling (called scheduling) is the job of the VMS scheduler. It identifies the memory-resident, computable process with the highest priority and updates its process control block (PCB) so that it can be executed. Scheduling is accomplished on the basis of time, process priority, and process state.

### Scheduling Time

Scheduling time is based on the system parameter QUANTUM. It's a value measured in 10-millisecond increments. The value of QUANTUM  defines the round-robin scheduling period of time-share processes on the system. When a new process is scheduled for execution, the value of QUANTUM is placed in the quantum-remaining field of the process header. Every 10 milliseconds, this value is decremented by the VMS clock interrupt service routine. When the quantum-remaining value reaches zero, quantum end is signaled, and a new process is scheduled.

### Scheduling Priority

VMS executes processes on the basis of relative precedence, called software priority. In other words, a computable process with a higher priority will execute before a computable process with a lower priority. Software priorities have an integer range of 0 to 31, with 31 being the highest priority. This range of priorities is divided between two distinct classifications: 0 to 15 for time-share (normal) processes and 16-31 for real-time processes. A process' CPU scheduling is affected by its priority.

Time-share processes make up the majority of processes running on a VMS system. They include interactive users, batch jobs, network tasks, and most system processes, except the swapper. The swapper executes at priority level 16.

A time-share process doesn't necessarily execute at its assigned or base priority. Instead, priority boosting occurs: VMS raises a process' priority above its base, to assist it, when it has been waiting for a resource. Priority boosting can be as high as six priority levels. In general, I/O-bound processes tend to operate with a priority boost, while CPU-bound processes operate near their base priority.

Most time-share processes operate at a base priority of four, which allows them to be scheduled in a round-robin fashion. Therefore, a time-share process has control of the CPU until either it's pre-empted by a higher priority process, it enters a wait state, or its QUANTUM expires.

Unlike the time-share processes, real-time process priorities don't get boosted. However, because real-time processes are in the minority on a VMS system, they get scheduled like jobs in a normal real-time system. Real-time processes are pre-emptive with no regard for QUANTUM. Real-time processes are removed from the CPU when they are pre-empted by a process with higher priority, or the process enters a wait state.

Process states scheduling also involves the swapper. It comes into play when the processes running on the system have exceeded available physical memory or when the process balance set has been reached. The swapper outswaps memory-resident processes to free memory or to comply with the system balance set parameter. The scheduler and swapper work in tandem to move computable processes into the CPU for execution. Much of this scheduling action is based on process states.

All processes are in a wait state except for the process currently being executed. Thus, they are divided into two categories: those that are readily computable and those that must wait for a resource to become available. Furthermore, computable processes are divided into those that are memory resident (COM) and those that are outswapped (COMO). Each computable process is queued-up to one of 32 priority queues as directed by its current processing priority. The computable outswapped processes have a similar set of queues.

Wait states, or resource wait states, have several classifications. The most common are voluntary wait, memory management wait, and miscellaneous wait.

A voluntary wait state occurs when the process willingly takes itself out of the processing loop to hibernate (HIB) or to wait for a local event flag (LEF) to be set. Processes hibernate for a specified period of time. The scheduler awakens them when their timer expires.

Memory management wait states are associated with a process' memory activity. For instance, a process waiting for a page to be brought into physical memory from the page file enters a page fault wait (PFW). A collided page wait state (COLPG) occurs when two or more processes simultaneously cause page faults on the same shared page. A free page wait state (FPG) commences when a process requests a working set increase, but there are no free pages of memory available. The FPG is generally solved by swapper trimming activity.

A miscellaneous wait state (MWAIT) identifies a process waiting for a system resource not managed by other wait state facilities. For example, a process waiting for a resource that's allocated to another process or a process waiting for a depleted resource is forced into an MWAIT state.

As with the computable process, all wait state processes can be memory resident or outswapped. Outswapped processes are indicated with an O appended to the state name.

## VMS MEMORY MANAGEMENT

The memory management functions of a VMS system are concerned with management of the VAX's physical memory. Specifically, VMS memory management is responsible for:

- Allocation of memory
- Deallocation of memory
- Keeping track of the status of each memory location
- Memory allocation policy

VMS memory management is handled by two system mechanisms, the pager and the swapper. The pager, or page fault handler as it's also known, is an exception service routine that responds to page faults. It brings a process' virtual pages into memory (the process' working set) on behalf of a process. The swapper's function, in memory management, is to keep computable processes with the highest priority in memory. The swapper is also responsible for trimming process working sets to maintain a balance of free memory.

## Virtual Memory

The VAX is capable of addressing more than four billion address locations, a vast amount by any standard. Because the memory can be virtual, there's no need to have physical memory anywhere near that size for the VAX to process data whose addresses are scattered throughout the address range. In other words, virtual memory is the ability of the VAX to address more memory than the system physically contains. Virtual memory is an illusion.

How does the VAX and its VMS operating system make use of a four billion byte storage capability if it only has, for instance, 16 million bytes of memory? The answer is simple and clever.

A VMS system does essentially the same thing you do each time you read a book. Regardless of the length of the book, you read it one page at a time. VMS memory management does the same thing. It processes program instructions and data one page at a time.

To the VAX and VMS, a program is similar to a book in that it can be divided into many pages and an index of these pages. These instruction or data pages are stored on a disk drive to be accessed at the program's request.

When a process executes a program, VMS first scans the entire program, breaking it into pages to form an index. The pages can then be read into memory as needed. When finished with a page or segment, VMS can put it back on disk into the system page file to make room for other pages.

When a new page is required in memory to continue processing the program, a page fault is generated. The word fault is an expression for the word interrupt. A page fault doesn't indicate that anything is wrong, only that the process requires a page not available in memory. The page fault is analogous to turning the page in a book. This paging scheme is known as demand-page memory management.

## The Pager

The VMS operating system can logically attain more than 100 percent memory use. Demand-page memory management removes the requirement for a process' entire address space to be in physical memory at one time. The pager loads only those pages of memory currently needed. This type of memory management is feasible, because most programs use only a small amount of their address space at any point during execution.

When a process needs a page of the program that it's executing but that isn't in memory, it generates a page fault. VMS processes this interrupt by having the pager load the required page and adjusting the page table entries accordingly. The process demands the page of memory, and the pager responds to this request. When the page of memory is loaded, program execution is restarted.

When a process runs a program, only the first page is loaded. Other pages needed by the program are loaded on demand, thus guaranteeing that unnecessary pages won't be loaded. Note that when a program first executes, it page faults heavily, i.e., heavy I/O activity to the system and page file disks. This heavy page faulting occurs until enough pages of the program have been loaded into the working set to allow it to operate in some cycle, or until it must perform an input/output operation.

During execution, a program's pages are maintained in pager storage, which is a combination of main memory, called the page file cache, and disk storage, called the page file. The location of the program in the pager storage is mapped by the pager. Thus, when a page is needed in main memory, its location is found on the map and loaded.

The page file cache is a relatively small amount of memory used to maintain pages most recently paged out of or removed from a process' working set. This helps to resolve the problem of temporal locality. When a program accesses a location, either instruction or data, it's usually referenced again soon. Pager activity to the page file cache is called a soft page fault, as it consumes less system time and resources, while pager activity to the page file is referred to as a hard page fault.

When memory is filled completely, or a process has reached its working set quota, another page can be loaded only by first removing one of the pages currently in memory. The target page (i.e., the page being replaced) is written back to the page file before the new page is loaded.

The pager doesn't work alone. There is close interaction between the VAX hardware and the pager software. Figure 2-4 displays this special relationship between the VAX and pager.

## The Swapper

VMS doesn't correlate the amount of physical memory with the number of concurrent processes. To make this arrangement possible, the swapper controls the number of processes maintained in physical memory. In general, the swapper is a systemwide memory manager. Unlike the pager which is part of the system image, the swapper is a separate process in the operating system.

The swapper has two primary memory management duties:

- To maintain the subset of executable processes with the highest priority in physical memory.

- To maintain the number of pages on the free page list above the low limits set by the system parameters, FREELIM and FREEGOAL.

The VMS swapper tries to maintain as high a number of resident processes as possible, as the function of swapping resident and outswapped processes is resource intensive. To do so, the swapper first trims resident working sets in an attempt to free memory. Processes are only swapped if there's a need for memory that can't be fulfilled by working set trimming or flushing the modified page list. An outswap candidate is selected by imposing criteria for a process to remain resident. This selection occurs in several passes in which the residence criteria increases in strictness. For instance, the swapper checks process priorities and activity. If a process is in the middle of disk I/O, it's a poor candidate, as it soon will become computable requiring it to be inswapped again.

Selection of inswap candidates is linked directly to the scheduling process. After it determines that a process can be inswapped, the swapper follows the same criteria as the scheduler. In other words, the swapper searches the COMO queue for the outswapped process with the highest priority. If a computable outswapped process with a higher priority than resident computable processes is found, it will be inswapped and scheduled for CPU execution.

The pager and swapper are similar in the following ways:

- The pager and swapper both perform conventional I/O.

- The pager and swapper work from common databases.

- The pager and swapper both try to read and write as many blocks of data in a single I/O operation as possible.

The pager and the swapper differ in these ways:

- The swapper supports a large number of concurrent processes with a limited amount of physical memory, while the pager supports programs with potentially large address spaces.

- The unit of paging is a page, and the unit of swapping is the process working set.

- The swapper is a systemwide process that moves processes in and out of memory, while the pager is a processswide function of VMS that moves pages of memory in and out of process working sets.

- The pager is an exception service routine that executes in the context of the process that incurs a page fault interrupt, whereas the swapper is a separate process that hibernates until it's awakened by another process for swapper activity.

## VMS SYSTEM DEVICE MANAGEMENT

This section focuses on the operating systems' control and management of I/O devices, such as disk drives, tape drives and, terminals. The basic functions of the I/O system are:

- Device allocation — Physically assigning a device to an active process and allocation policy. In other words, it defines  which process gets a device, the duration and when.

- Device deallocation policy.

- Keeping track of system devices, which requires a number of special mechanisms. The two primary VMS mechanisms that control I/O devices are the channel control block (CCB) and the unit control block (UCB). Each device has a CCB and UCB associated with it.

- Device drivers — The software programs that control the physical hardware.

Of the many tasks performed by an operating system, device management is the most intricate, as the computer must deal with each device at the hardware level. Each device connected to the VAX has its own protocol, which is the language that makes it do its job. Software drivers enable VMS to communicate with the many different devices that can be connected to it. Drivers implement the low-level hardware control needed for each type of device and present a uniform interface to the rest of the operating system.

An understanding of how devices are classified might shed some light on why certain devices act as they do. For the most part, devices are managed in three categories: dedicated, shared, and virtual.

A dedicated device is allocated to a process (or job) until the process releases it or terminates. Most devices fall into this category, as they simply don't lend themselves to multiuser access. It's difficult, for instance, to share terminals, tape drives, and printers.

Shared devices can be used concurrently by multiple processes. The most common of these is a direct access storage device, such as a Winchester disk drive. Managing a shared device is complicated, particularly when high efficiency is desired.

Virtual devices were developed to make up for the shortcomings of dedicated devices. The most common of these is called simultaneous peripheral operation on line (spooling), which buffers I/O requests to a device. This technique is used widely so that printing devices can be shared.

## Device Assignment and Allocation

A process must identify a device to a VMS system before it can issue an I/O request to it, such as READ or WRITE. The identification is accomplished through a device channel, which is associated with each device. Channel assignment is accomplished through the system service $ASSIGN.

After a device has a channel assigned to it, it must then be allocated for use. This is accomplished through use of the $ALLOC system service. A process deallocates a device with the $DALLOC system service.

When a process allocates a device, the device is reserved for its exclusive use. No other process can use that device until it has been deallocated. How are devices shared on a VMS system? Shared devices are allocated by ACPs. All I/O requests to shared devices are handled by an ACP on behalf of the requesting process.

When a process is finished using a device, the system service $DASSGN deassigns the I/O channel. This system service clears the linkage and corresponding CCB control information. If a file was left open, it's closed, and outstanding I/O operations are canceled. If the device is marked for dismount, it's dismounted. If the process is deleted from the system prior to device deassignment, it's deassigned automatically as part of the process deletion.

## Device I/O

Device I/O operations are performed using the $QIO system service. A process calls $QIO to queue an I/O request to the device's driver. After the I/O operation has been initiated, control is returned to the process, which must then synchronize the I/O completion. Synchronization can be accomplished by process hibernation, by issuing an AST routine to be executed, or by testing the associated I/O status block.

A simpler method of programming is to use an alternative system service, $QIOW. $QIOW is identical to using $QIO and $WAITFR in that it waits for I/O completion before returning control.

The following FORTRAN code segment demonstrates how to assign, allocate, and queue an I/O request to a disk device:

```
C Subprogram
C
        INTEGER*2    STATUS,CHANNEL,IOSB(4)
        INTEGER*4    SYS$ASSIGN,SYSQIOW,LOGICAL_BLOCK
        INTEGER*4    BUFFER(512)
        .
        .
        .
```

```
C Assign a channel to DUA0
C
        STATUS=SYS$ASSIGN('DUA0:',CHANNEL,,)
        IF (.NOT. STATUS) CALL LIB%SIGNAL(%VAL(STATUS))
C
C Allocate DUA0
C
        STATUS=SYS$ALLOC('DUA0:',,,,)
        IF (.NOT. STATUS) CALL LIB%SIGNAL(%VAL(STATUS))
C
C Read from logical block 1024
C
        LOGICAL_BLOCK=1024
        STATUS=SYS$QIOW(,%VAL(CHANNEL),    ! Disk I/O channel
     2       %VAL(IO$_READLBLK),           ! read function
     2       IOSB,,,                        ! I/O Status block
     2       BUFFER,                        ! Read buffer
     2       %VAL(512),                     ! Bytes to be read
     2       %VAL(LOGICAL_BLOCK))           ! Logical block
C
C Check for errors
C
        IF(.NOT. IOSB(1)) CALL LIB$SIGNAL(%VAL(IOSB(1)))
        IF(.NOT. STATUS) CALL LIB$SIGNAL(%VAL(STATUS))
        .
        .
        .
        END
```

## Getting Information About Devices

VMS, like most operating systems, maintains information about the devices it controls. In VMS, this device information is provided by the get device/volume information ($GETDVI) system service. $GETDVI provides device-independent information about a device, including the device class, owner, and protection.

$GETDVI can be demonstrated using the DCL lexical function F$GETDVI(). For instance, the following command returns the number of free blocks:

```
$ WRITE SYS$OUTPUT F$GETDVI("DUB3","FREEBLOCKS")
167382
$
```

The $GETDVI system service is often used in programs to get information about a device before calling $ASSIGN, $ALLOC, or $QIO.

## Device Drivers

A device driver is low-level code and tables used to control I/O operations on a system device, including reading, writing, and formatting. The tables are used to provide a VMS system with information and present a standard interface between the I/O system and driver. The low-level code converts the commands issued by the I/O system into commands understood by the physical device.

VMS maintains a myriad of drivers. Each is a separate file located in the directory SYS$SYSTEM. Each driver is distinguished by its two-letter identification, i.e., TTDRIVER, DUDRIVER, TSDRIVER, and PUDRIVER.

Starting with VMS Version 3.0, device drivers were developed in two layers: the communication layer called the class driver, and the device function layer known as the port driver. A class driver implements a specific VMS protocol, like mass storage control protocol (MSCP) or system communication architecture (SCA). The port driver implements the device-specific properties, such as managing a UDA50 port device.

## CONCLUSION

The VMS operating system makes a VAX processor a unique and powerful computer system. Without VMS, a VAX processor has few advantages over any other computer system. The ability to operate on the entire range of processors, from desktop workstation to mainframe, has made VMS one of the most popular operating systems in the world.

# Chapter 3

# DECnet

During the 1970s, the user's demand to have computing power closer to where the work was being done firmly established the use of minicomputers. Minicomputers, like mainframes, support multiple users, although at a much smaller scale and cost. During this era, the range of computer applications that required users to share files, programs, storage, and other resources grew. A new requirement emerged: communication among computers.

As soon as the early networks were deployed, distributed minicomputer systems were being used successfully to off-load the central mainframe. In many cases, these systems replaced central mainframe systems, as they could collectively provide more economical processing power than a single computer.

In the 1980s, the benefits of distributing and networking systems were further recognized by the advent of the personal computer. PCs brought computing capability to the user's desk or workbench. It's now quite normal for systems to be located at the application site and for these systems to communicate over local and long distances based on telephone communication technologies.

This chapter presents DECnet as a computer networking capability. We'll discuss the type of networks that DECnet supports, various media, configurations, and the basic internal workings of the DECnet network software.

## WHAT IS A COMPUTER NETWORK?

A computer network is defined as two or more autonomous computers connected for the express purpose of sharing resources. Resource sharing is the definitive attribute of a computer network.

A computer's resources are anything you value that allows you to accomplish tasks in your daily work. This includes your files, the machine's computing ability, or possibly a program, like electronic mail. Networking permits you to share these things.

A computer network is simple to understand because it's similar to other, more familiar, networks. Let's consider the telephone and railway networks.

The public telephone network provides you point-to-point communication access to another party. In the same way, a computer network allows computers and their users to communicate.

The railway network is analogous to computers sharing files. Just as the railway network transports cargo and people between cities, a computer network furnishes a means to move files and other types of data between computers.

### DECnet Networking Capabilities

DECnet brings together as one the power of many machines. This is especially unique when you consider that DECnet doesn't care what hardware or operating system you're using, as long as DECnet has been implemented for it.

The DECnet network can be used for simple chores, such as sending electronic mail and file sharing. It can also be used for complex tasks, such as loading a remote computer with its operating system. DECnet allows personal computer and terminal users to connect to any computer in the network and use it as if it were their local system.

One of the most useful functions of DECnet is its ability to allow programs running on separate systems to communicate with one another. This is the heart of many DECnet functions, such as electronic mail. When you send electronic mail to someone on another system, the MAIL programs on each system must communicate cooperatively to deliver your message. In its most rudimentary form, DECnet is an extension of the VAX file system. To get a better understanding, let's take a look at a VMS system file specification:

BIFF::MYFILE.DAT

Here, the full location and name of the file MYFILE.DAT is specified on a computer system called BIFF. Used in this context, any file operation, such as EDIT, DELETE, RENAME or APPEND, can be performed over DECnet, on the remote machine, BIFF::. The file can also be opened for reading and writing records. To the user, the file appears as if it's on the local machine.

## TYPES OF COMPUTER NETWORKS

Computer networks vary widely in type and purpose. However, they can be grouped into two specific geographic categories: local area and wide area. They can be topological too, but that deals more with design than classification.

### Local Area Network

A local area network (LAN) is a network that spans a relatively small geographic area. Generally, LANs are used within an office, building, or building complex. With existing technology, a LAN can extend to an area of about 35 square miles. Because LANs use high-speed communication media, they're unable to span wide areas.

### Wide Area Network

A wide area network (WAN) has almost no geographic limitation based on present communication technology. The public phone system, radio, and communication satellites permit communication throughout the world. However, a WAN can't provide the same high-speed throughput as a LAN. In addition, wide area networks can be very costly.

## NETWORK TOPOLOGIES

Networks are formed by a collection of computers, called nodes or hosts. The nodes are connected by a transport system called a subnet or link. The nodes use network links to send and receive information called traffic or messages. For consistency, all computers in a network will be called nodes, and the transport system will be called a link. The information exchanged by the nodes will be called messages.

Network topology is the geometric arrangement of nodes and links that make up a network. Broadly speaking, there are two types of network links that allow the formation of various topologies: point-to-point and broadcast. Point-to-point links are used most commonly in wide area networks, while most local area networks take advantage of broadcast methods.

A point-to-point network is made up of many cables, leased lines, or dial-up lines; each one connects a pair of nodes. If two nodes that don't share a link want to communicate, the messages must be passed, or routed, by one or more of the intermediate nodes. Figure 3-1 displays some of the possible point-to-point topologies.

The important design issue with point-to-point networks is what the node interconnection should look like. For example, in a star network, where a central node is used to route all messages to the nodes in the

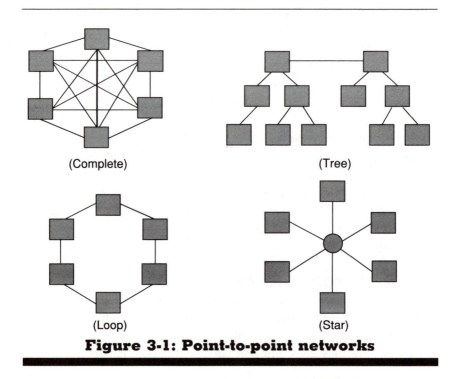

(Complete)          (Tree)

(Loop)          (Star)

**Figure 3-1: Point-to-point networks**

network, the maximum number of hops (i.e., number of intermediate links to the final destination) to the next node is two. In a loop topology where each node routes messages, the average number of hops is one-half the number of links in the network.

As one computer wag says, "A routing node is a tired node." Routing, which is the process of sending a message from node A to C via node B, consumes resources. Within the design of your networks, strive to keep routing to a minimum.

A broadcast network uses a single link shared by all nodes in the network. A message sent to one node is received by all. Messages in a broadcast network must specify the intended node. In this way, nodes not specified ignore the message being broadcasted. Figure 3-2 displays some of the possible broadcast topologies.

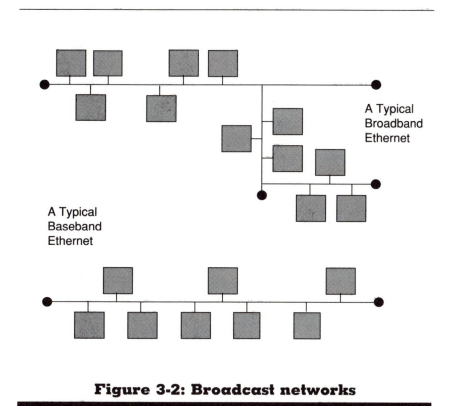

A Typical
Broadband
Ethernet

A Typical
Baseband
Ethernet

**Figure 3-2: Broadcast networks**

## NETWORK CONTROL AND ACCESS METHODS

Many access methods have been invented to control the use of a network link. They all, however, come under two umbrellas: centralized control or distributed control.

Using centralized control, access to the network is governed by a single node, the master. The master node is a dedicated communications processor or a switch. Distributed control gives each node the ability to establish connections and access the network independently.

Examples of these two access methods are polling and contention. In a polling network, a master node queries the other nodes, called tributaries, to find messages waiting for transmittal. If the node has nothing to send, the master moves on to the next node. In a contention network, each node is free to send a message whenever the link is not busy. The contention method is controlled by a set of rules implemented by each node.

Both polling and contention access methods contain limitations. Polling is time consuming and leads to poor performance characteristics when network traffic is heavy. Contention networks experience high data collision rates, caused when two or more nodes try to send a message at the same time. These basic problems were solved through the invention of token and carrier sense multiple access/collision detect (CSMA/CD) access methods.

A token network, which is an efficient variation of polling, uses a special bit pattern called a token. The token is passed from node to node. If a node doesn't have a message to send, the token is passed along to the next node. If the node does have a message to send, it puts the message in front of the token, then reinserts the token into the network.

A CSMA/CD network is the best known distributed access method for broadcast networks. Using this method, a node listens to the link before transmitting. If nothing is heard, the node begins to transmit. If it hears a collision where two or more nodes begin transmitting at the same time, the transmitting node pauses for a random period of time, then begins the process again. It's like a polite group conversation.

## NETWORK MEDIA

Network media provide the physical connection used to send messages between nodes in a network. Media can be classified as bounded as in wire or optical fiber, and unbounded as in radio, microwave, or infrared transmissions. Understanding the various types of media and their attributes is important, because media characterize a network's performance.

Networks can be constructed using many combinations of topology, access methods, and transmission media. For instance, Ethernet, that was originally implemented on coaxial cable, can now be run on common twisted-pair wire or optical fiber.

### Twisted-Pair Wire

The original computer network medium was twisted-pair, the wire used in most telephone communication systems. Twisted-pair is still the most common medium, because it's inexpensive and easy to install. Twisted-pair gets its name from the way it's made. Pairs of copper wire are twisted together to minimize interference created by adjacent cables and broadcast signals. Each wire is individually covered with insulation, usually Teflon™ or polyvinyl chloride (PVC). The copper conductors are typically 22 or 24 gauge.

The shielding properties of twisted-pair are important in differential transmission methods where data is conveyed by the variation of voltage between the two wires. Wire releases and absorbs high amounts of electrical magnetic interference (EMI) and radio frequency interference (RFI); this results in high error rates. (These properties also pose a significant problem where security is important.) If interference is a problem, shielded twisted-pair can be used. Shielded twisted pair is available with each wire or pair shielded, or with an overall shield.

The typical data transmission rate over twisted-pair medium is 2.4 to 9.6 KBps, depending on the type of line, i.e., circuit switched or leased. It's interesting to note, however, that twisted-pair now is commonly used to connect low-speed data equipment (1.2 to 19.2 KBps), such as terminals and printers, and to implement medium-speed networks (1 to 10 MBps), such as Ethernet and token ring.

## Coaxial Cable

Coaxial cable has been the medium of choice for most LANs. It offers high bandwidth and the ability to handle high data rates without the interference problems that plague twisted pair. It has been used for many years in telephone networks to multiplex many calls onto a single cable, thereby reducing the need for thousands of long-distance cables.

This same capability is widely used by organizations for multipurpose networks. For instance, in a broadband network application, a single coaxial cable can be used for data, voice, TV, and other transmissions.

A coaxial cable consists of a center copper conductor surrounded by insulation (Teflon™ or PVC), which is enclosed by a braided wire mesh or an extruded aluminum sleeve. An outer insulation sheath is optional. The outer layer and the center conductor share the same axis, thus the name coaxial cable. It is often referred to simply as coax.

A coaxial cable has a bandwidth range of 300-400 MHz. In terms of channels, that amount of bandwidth has the capacity to carry thousands of voice or low-speed (i.e., 9.6 to 56 KBps) data lines.

Because of its widespread use, coaxial cable is readily available and moderate in cost. Additionally, the methods of installation and connection are well developed. Coaxial cable is almost as simple to use as twisted pair.

There are several varieties of coaxial cable used for LANs. The type employed depends on the signaling technique used, either baseband or broadband. A baseband transmission uses the full capacity of the cable to transmit a single baseband signal at very high data rates. Data rates of 10 MBps are typical. The broadband transmission method uses the cable's capacity to create a large number of subchannels on which many networks can be implemented.

## Fiber Optics

Optical fibers serve as the ultra-high-performance network medium. They combine the compactness of twisted pair with a bandwidth that exceeds any coaxial cable. Its most appealing characteristic is its resistance to most forms of electrical interference.

Optical fibers are made from strands of plastic or glass. A light source is used to transmit data signals, while a light detector is used to receive them. Using this method, data rates of more than 1 GBps are possible. Several optical fibers have the signal carrying capacity of hundreds of twisted-pair wires.

The fiber's inability to transmit voltages limits its practical use in LAN applications. Networks based on the CSMA/CD transmission method use the presence of a DC voltage to detect collisions. Therefore, optical fibers are used most commonly to couple bus segments of large Ethernet systems and in high capacity point-to-point networks.

## THE DECNET NETWORK ARCHITECTURE

What's the difference between DECnet and Ethernet? The use of an Ethernet LAN has become synonymous with DECnet. However, they're not the same.

DECnet is a family of software and hardware communication products that allow Digital computers, and select computers of other manufacturers, to participate in a network. Ethernet, DEC's standard LAN protocol, is one of the three protocols that DECnet supports. The other two are the Digital Data Communications Message Protocol (DDCMP), the original DECnet protocol, and X.25, the standard public network protocol.

DECnet's configuration flexibility makes it unique. A DECnet network can start with two nodes, connected by a twisted-pair cable. It can grow to more than 64,000 nodes. Best of all, DECnet doesn't care about the physical link among the nodes. The link can be Ethernet, fiber optic, satellite, leased line, or another available communication medium. You can have a 10-node Ethernet LAN in Washington, D.C., connected to a single node in San Diego, California through leased or dial-up lines, connected to a packet-switched network in London via satellite. The connection method is undetectable to the network users. The nodes in London, San Diego, and the District appear to be next door.

All DECnet networks feature a peer relationship among the nodes. Any node in the network can communicate with another without consulting a master or controlling node. DECnet control is fully distributed.

The advantage of distributed control is that each node can be equally attentive to user requests. Furthermore, because the exchange of messages isn't routed through a master node, overall network efficiency is increased.

The nodes in a DECnet network can operate under many different operating systems: VAX/VMS, ULTRIX-32, RT-11, RSTS/E, RSX-11, VAXELN, TOPS-10, TOPS-20, P/OS, MS-DOS, PC-DOS, and Macintosh. In fact, the type of computer or operating system makes little difference. DECnet, operating on any system, provides the same outward interface: the Digital Network Architecture (DNA).

## DNA and the OSI

All network designs are built on a set of standards or rules. DEC chose to pattern DECnet after the International Standards Organization's Open Systems Interconnect (OSI) model. The International Standards Organization is the group chartered to provide industry standards, i.e., recommendations.

The DNA and OSI models both specify a network architecture in terms of layers or tiers. Each layer performs a specific function, which corresponds to the same layer on other nodes. The layered network architecture defines two important intercomponent relationships: protocols and interfaces.

The differences between the DNA and OSI model are mostly syntactical. At the time of this writing, DEC was working to bring DECnet into full compliance with the OSI. Figure 3-3 shows the parallels between the ISO and DNA. For continuity, the OSI model will be used to explain the functions of DECnet. The seven layers of the OSI model are:

**Physical layer (hardware)** — Defines the characteristics for the physical connection, i.e., controllers and device drivers.

**Data Link layer (hardware)** — Defines a bit- or byte-oriented protocol for information exchange, acknowledgment, error-detection, and retransmission on the data link.

**Network layer (software)** — Defines a higher-level protocol to provide the multiplexing functions required to route messages between the local and a remote node through the data link. This module also provides network congestion control.

**Transport layer (software)** — Creates logical to physical links and ensures integrity of the data transfer, including all required error recovery not handled at lower levels.

**Session layer (software)** — Handles establishment and termination of the virtual connections between two nodes.

**Presentation layer (software)** — Handles data format translation of the user's data format and the network's data format for such functions as remote file access, file transfer, and virtual terminal functions.

**Application layer (software)** — Allows users and applications to communicate with (i.e., use) the network.

| OSI | DNA |
|---|---|
| Application | User |
| | Network Management |
| Presentation | Network Application |
| Session | Session Control |
| Transport | End-to-End Communication |
| Network | Routing |
| Data Link | Data Link |
| Physical Link | Physical Link |

**Figure 3-3: The OSI and DNA architecture layers**

## DECNET PROTOCOLS

A protocol is a set of rules. Each network layer communicates with the corresponding layer of other nodes in the network through a set of rules established to exchange messages. Network protocols are very specific. They provide information needed by nodes in a network to understand the others' role in the message exchange. Figure 3-4 shows the relationship between the layers.

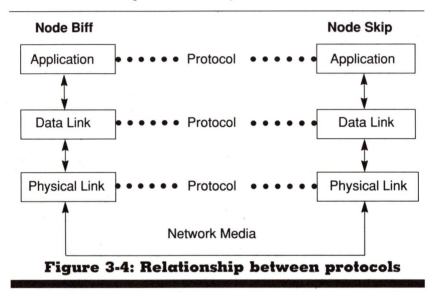

**Figure 3-4: Relationship between protocols**

The journey of a network message begins at the Application layer of the sending node and ends at the Application layer of the receiving node. On the sending node, each network layer encapsulates the message with its protocol. Conversely, each layer of the receiving node peels off the Protocol layer, so it can see what it needs to do with the message.

Let's use Biff, Skip, and Liz as an example. The three nodes are connected by a point-to-point link between Skip and Biff, and an Ethernet link between Biff and Liz. Biff is the designated router. See Figure 3-5.

If a user on Skip wants to copy a file to Liz, each network message must go through node Biff. Here's the beauty of using Protocol layers: When Biff receives a message designated for Liz, the message starts up the layers. When the Network layer peels off the protocol capsule, it sees that the message isn't for Biff but for Liz. Being smart about the network topology, Biff puts a Network layer capsule back on and directs the message to the Data Link layer module that handles Liz's physical link.

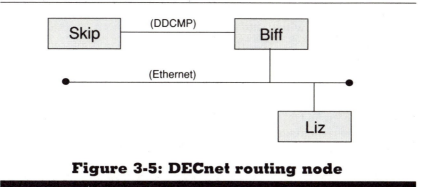

**Figure 3-5: DECnet routing node**

The Data Link layer is the only one that has more than one protocol. Each data link protocol is used to support a different type of physical hardware link. DEC supplies three data link protocols: DDCMP, X.25, and Ethernet. You can supply your own Data Link protocol module for hardware not supported by DEC.

## The DDCMP Protocol

The Digital Data Communications Message Protocol is generic and byte-oriented. It can be used with asynchronous, synchronous, full- or half-duplex, serial, or parallel communication hardware systems. The simplest example is two nodes sitting side-by-side connected by a twisted-pair cable.

A byte-oriented protocol, such as DDCMP, tracks the number of bytes sent in the data portion of each message packet. A bit-oriented protocol frames data in undefined lengths by using flags. A character-oriented protocol uses special ASCII characters to signal the start and end of a message and its text. Neither the bit- nor character-oriented protocol has provisions for checking if a message ever reached its final destination.

DDCMP sends and receives data grouped into blocks called data messages. Each block provides a mechanism that allows the receiving node to detect an error and ask for the message to be sent again. The end result is error-free data, no matter how bad the physical line is when transmitting data.

The protocol works like this: The sender assigns a one-up number to each message beginning with one. Also, it maintains a counter of the last good message received by the other node. This counter is updated each time a message is received that's one higher than the previous message. The count is included in the Response field of the message being sent. It tells the receiver the highest message the sender thinks it has received. To detect data errors, DDCMP places a 16-bit cyclic redundancy check (CRC) code (i.e., polynomial) at the end of each message.

The receiver checks each message for errors by trying to recreate the CRC code and, if there are none, returns an acknowledgment (ACK) that it has received the message. When a node receives a message with errors, it sends back a negative acknowledgment (NAK); this tells the sender to retransmit the message. The receiving node doesn't need to acknowledge each message sent, because the number in the Response field of the message header specifies the number of the last good message received.

If the receiving node gets a message out of sequence, it ignores that message to force a time-out. When the transmitting node times out, it sends a Reply to Message Number (REP) message that contains the sequence number of the most recently unacknowledged message. The REP is a request for the receiving node to reply to the message number just sent, or to send the last message number received.

The DDCMP protocol uses five control messages: Acknowledge (ACK), Negative Acknowledge (NAK), Reply to Message Number (REP), Start Message (STRT), and Start Acknowledge (STACK). The DDCMP message format is displayed in Figure 3-6.

## DDCMP Physical Links

The DDCMP data link protocol is compatible with any of DEC's standard terminal communication interfaces, including DHV11,

DHQ11, DZV11, DMF32, and DMZ32, and with the high performance network specific devices, such as the DMB32, DMV11, DPV11, or DMR11.

| SOH | COUNT | FLAGS | RESPONSE | SEQUENCE | ADDRESS | CRC1 | DATA | CRC2 |
|-----|-------|-------|----------|----------|---------|------|------|------|
| 8 | 14 | 2 | 8 | 8 | 8 | 16 | 8N | 16 |

SOH ............................. Start of header (data message identifier)
COUNT ........................ Data byte count
FLAGS ......................... Link flags
RESPONSE ................. The response number
SEQUENCE ................. The transmit sequence number
ADDRESS .................... The station address
CRC1 ........................... CRC code of the header information
DATA ........................... Data being transferred
CRC2 ........................... CRC code of the data

**Figure 3-6: DDCMP message format**

You can choose the media that connects to the physical interface. The most common methods are standard phone line using a low-speed modem (1,200 bps to 2,400 bps), leased line using high-speed modems (4,800 bps to 19,200 bps), twisted-pair wire (using short-haul modems if the distance is more than 400 feet), and fiber optics.

## The X.25 Protocol

In most countries, the Postal Telephone and Telegraph Authorities (PTT) and private companies offer packet-switched data networks (PSDNs) to any organization that wishes to subscribe. The network links are owned by the network vendor, but conform to the X.25 recommendation of the Comite Consultatif International Telephonique et Telegraphique (CCITT), France. It recommends standards for host computers and terminal equipment to interface with packet-switched networks.

PSDN systems are often called public networks, as they are analogous to, and often part of, the public telephone system. Services such as CompuServe, The Source or Telenet™ are or have access to an X.25 network that provides nationwide or worldwide network services.

## PSDN Service in the United States

There are many PSDNs in the United States. Some of these include Telenet™, TYMNET®, Uninet™, and Autonet™. Most of the U.S. carriers charge by the volume of data sent, connect time, or both, but not by the distance. The PSDN vendor arranges a subscriber's messages into a number of discrete packets. The packets then are interleaved with packets from other subscribers over a shared link. This uses a link's bandwidth efficiently, reducing the cost of networking.

## X.25 Configurations

Each PSDN is set up as a group of geographically separated switching nodes that are connected by high-speed links. Organizations leasing a circuit on the PSDN physically connect their own computer to one of the switching nodes. The switching nodes are called Data Circuit-terminating Equipment (DCE). The user's computer connected to a switching node is called Data Terminal Equipment (DTE). Each node in this type of network has a DTE/DCE connection. The differences between DTE and the DCE are found primarily in the Link layer protocol.

At the Link layer, X.25 uses a form of the standard high-level data-link control (HDLC) protocol. HDLC provides link layer functions, such as link connect, link reset, link disconnect, information exchange, frame acknowledgment, information flow control, frame sequence number generation and checking, CRC-16 generation and error detection, frame rejection, and frame retransmission. The content of information exchanged on the link is unknown at this level and doesn't affect the link operation.

At the Network level, X.25 provides a method for establishing a logical channel (a circuit or data path) between two stations, on different computers, in the network. A station can be a software process, task, terminal, or a terminal device. The data exchange on each logical channel (there can be multiple logical channels on a single physical link) is unaffected by that on any other channel.

## X.25 Physical Links

The X.25 Physical layer protocol, called X.21, specifies the physical, electrical, and procedural interface between each point in the network. X.21 is essentially an asynchronous serial interface that's compatible with RS-232, a common serial interface used on most computers and terminal equipment. Multiple X.21 circuits can be used on a single host. Each circuit provides a point-to-point link to another node in the network.

Most of DEC's serial communication devices are X.21 (DEC RS-232 and RS423) compatible. However, some, such as the DMV11 and DMR11, are designed specifically as intelligent, high-performance communication processors. These communication processors enhance performance, while relieving the host CPU of a heavy I/O burden.

## The Ethernet Protocol

The Ethernet local area network specification is the result of a collaborative effort among DEC, Xerox, and Intel Corporations. The consortium, organized in the early 1980s, developed and published a standard, now known as the *Ethernet Blue Book*. The standard was based on Xerox Corporation's original Ethernet development in the Xerox Research Center in Palo Alto, California.

The original *Ethernet Blue Book* prescribed the techniques in which Ethernets would be developed and implemented. The *Book* specified how the Ethernet physical layer and data-link services would work. Further development produced a cooperative standard known as Ethernet version 2.0. Ethernet is now the most popular local area network technology.

Ethernet was billed by Xerox as the "ultimate network that would tie everything on the network together." Its name is derived from an old theoretical substance called lumineferous ether, an electromagnetic matter once thought to be the key element binding the universe and all its parts.

## Ethernet Configuration and Characteristics

Ethernet LANs are configured using a bus topology. A backbone, which is normally a coaxial cable, is used as the communication media. Computers and peripheral devices can exchange data at speeds up to 10 MBps. As many as 1,024 nodes can be connected to a single

Ethernet LAN. Each node must be separated by at least 2.8 meters of cable distance.

Nodes are connected to the backbone using taps. Ethernet taps can be intrusive or nonintrusive. An intrusive tap requires that the cable be cut to install connectors. Nonintrusive taps connect to the Ethernet by drilling a hole in the outer layers of the coaxial cable, so the tap's probe can touch the center conductor. Most baseband Ethernet LANs use nonintrusive taps, while most broadband Ethernets require intrusive taps. Ethernet LANs have a limitation of about 100 taps per main segment of cable.

Local repeaters are used between cable segments to extend the LAN. A tap is connected to a device that broadcasts and receives data from the cable, called a transceiver. It transmits and receives data simultaneously. The transceiver connects to a host computer through a transceiver cable, which transfers the data between the computer's Ethernet controller and the transceiver. Transceivers are active electronic devices that get their power and ground from the Ethernet controller through the transceiver cable.

## Types of Ethernets

There are two Ethernet media variations: baseband and broadband. Baseband Ethernet uses the entire bandwidth of the backbone for Ethernet data transmissions, whereas a broadband Ethernet divides the cable into many different channels.

A baseband Ethernet transmits data in a manner known as the Manchester-encoded digital signaling method. Digital data (1s and 0s) is represented as timing intervals rather than a series of high and low transitions, i.e., a sine or square wave signal. Each end of the backbone must be terminated with a 50 ohm load, called a terminator. The media can be ThickWire (i.e., .395" shielded) coaxial cable, ThinWire (i.e., RG58) coaxial cable or twisted-pair (i.e., AT&T type C&D or Northern Telecom 3-pair). ThickWire coaxial cable has a distance limitation of 500 meters, while ThinWire runs can be up to 1,000 meters. The larger coaxial cable has better shielding properties. Twisted-pair Ethernet segments can be up to 70 meters long. Broadband Ethernet uses an analog base transmission method. Here, radio frequency modems are used to broadcast and receive signals from the backbone. The bandwidth of the cable is divided (using frequency division multiplexing) into numerous channels for transmitting voice, video or data. Broadband networks can be extended to lengths up to 50 miles.

### Ethernet Protocol at the Data Link

The functions of the Ethernet data link are few when compared to DDCMP and X.25. Data encapsulation/decapsulation and link management are the Ethernet protocol's primary tasks. Much of this work is accomplished by the Ethernet hardware. For example, link traffic is detected by the transceiver.

Data encapsulation/decapsulation  is the process of framing and addressing message packets, and detecting errors. A frame defines the format of a message packet, as in the DDCMP protocol. The addressing function makes sure source and destination addresses get added, and error detection senses any physical media transmission errors. Errors are detected using a 32-bit cyclic redundancy check code. Figure 3-7 illustrates the format of an Ethernet message frame.

Link management involves allocation and access of the physical link, for which the CSMA/CD method is used. CSMA/CD is easy to understand by comparing it to a group of people having a conversation. The conversation is open to anyone who has something to say, and the Ethernet cable is available to any computer that needs to transmit a message or data. Before speaking, people wait until someone else is finished. Each computer listens to the Ethernet and transmits data only when the line is clear. If two people begin to speak at once, each stops and allows the other to go ahead; when a transceiver detects a transmission collision, it tells the Ethernet controller to stop sending. The controller will wait a random period and then try to send again.

| DESTINATION | SOURCE | TYPE | COUNT | DATA | PAD | CRC-32 |
|---|---|---|---|---|---|---|

DESTINATION ................A 48-bit destination address
SOURCE .........................A 48-bit source data link address
TYPE .............................Used by higher level protocols
COUNT ...........................A 16-bit count of the number of data bytes
DATA ..............................The data being transmitted, 0 to 1498 bytes
PAD .................................If the data is less than 1498, the leftover
                                         bytes are filled with nulls to pad the frame
CRC-32 ...........................32-bit polynomial used to detect errors

**Figure 3-7: Ethernet message frame format**

## ROUTING

If all nodes were adjacent to one another, such as the nodes in a single Ethernet LAN, the function of the network would be greatly simplified. But most networks form a series of point-to-point links between nodes or point-to-point links between groups of adjacent nodes. This presents the network with the problem of how to route messages between two nodes that don't share a physical link.

Routing is the function of choosing a path or route along which a message packet travels to its destination. A path is a series of links, called circuits, between the source and destination. The routing function allows a user to specify the name of a remote node with which to communicate. The path taken is completely transparent to both the sender and receiver, regardless of the number of links in the circuit.

Figure 3-8 displays a simple requirement for routing between two Ethernet LANs.

### Routing Nodes

DECnet is an area-based network. Areas logically group nodes and allow one or more routing nodes to provide links outside the area. The term router is generic for any node that receives and forwards messages addressed to other nodes in the network. DECnet has two router types: Level 1 routers, which route messages within an area, and Level 2 routers, which transfer messages between areas.

A Level 1 router controls routing within its area and keeps itself
informed of the state of the other nodes in its area. It's not concerned
with nodes outside its area. All message traffic between areas must
take place through a Level 2 router. Level 2 routers find the least-cost
path to the destination and determine the state of the nodes in their
area.

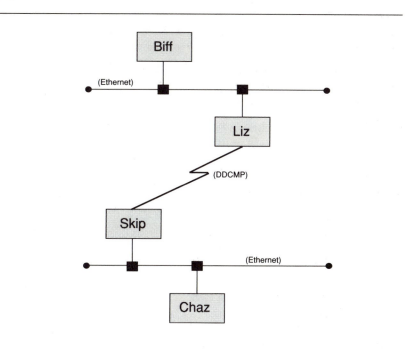

## Figure 3-8: Routing between LANs

A router selects a path based on the network topology and assigned
circuit costs. A cost is assigned to circuits to give them a selection
weight. In other words, if there are two possible paths from node A to
node E, A-C-E or A-B-E, and the circuits A-C and C-E each had a cost of
two, but circuits A-B and B-E had a cost of one, the A-B-E route would
be taken. Circuit cost is assigned on the basis of bandwidth. The
greater the bandwidth of a circuit, the lower its cost.

The total circuit distance between a source and destination node is
called the path length. The path length is measured in hops, which are

the logical distances between adjacent nodes. A network manager has control over routing activity, in that he can assign a value for the maximum number of hops in a path. This prevents the routers from bouncing a message packet endlessly around a large network with many possible circuits.

## Miscellaneous Routing Functions

The Routing layer has other duties in addition to determining message packet paths, path cost, and path length. They include passing message packets to the local node, topology adaptation, circuit queue control, updating routing information on other nodes, and returning packets addressed to unreachable nodes.

The ability to adapt to change is important for a network. For instance, if a circuit or node fails, can the routing nodes find alternate paths?

DECnet can adapt to changes in topology, including the addition of new nodes and circuits, and to different kinds of circuits, such as DDCMP point-to-point and multipoint links, Ethernet, and X.25 virtual circuits. It's a routing node's responsibility to detect changes in the network and to update other routing nodes with that information.

## DECNET LOGICAL LINKS

DECnet deals with physical links only at its lower layers, one through four. The lower layers collectively provide a transport service, shielding the upper layers from the technicalities of how communication between nodes is achieved. All DECnet functions above the Transport layer reference logical links rather than physical ones. The Transport layer bridges the gap between the physical and logical links.

## Network Services Protocol

The layers of local and remote nodes communicate through DEC's network services protocol (NSP). NSP is responsible for the creation of logical links, delivery of data, and control messages (in order), breaking up normal data messages that can be broken up and transmitted, and managing the movement of messages (i.e., flow control).

NSP has three types of messages that it can send or receive: control, data, and acknowledgment. The network services protocol establishes, maintains, and destroys logical links by exchanging control messages with itself (if the processes are on the same node) or other NSP modules.

## Creating a Logical Link

To a program or process running on a DECnet system, the link to another node appears to be direct, no matter how many circuit hops there might be. The link is logical.

A logical link is created when two cooperating programs make calls to DECnet facilities to start a handshake procedure. DECnet calls are passed between the programs that establish an agreement to communicate. Both programs must agree to form the logical link. This point is very important to system security.

The so-called handshake procedure takes place in a specific order. First, the source program issues a call to request communication with a target program. This sends an NSP message, CONNECT INITIATE, to the target node. The program on the target node can accept or reject the request. If the process accepts the request, NSP returns a CONNECT CONFIRM message. When the link is established, the NSPs send and receive data and acknowledge messages for the cooperating programs, until one of the programs requests that the link be broken.

After a logical link is established, both programs can make calls to send and receive data. It's like opening a disk file. After it's open, you can read and write to it. The beauty of this mechanism is that multiple logical links can be created over a single physical link. Figure 3-9 illustrates communication between the Transport layers of nodes Liz and Chaz.

## TASK-TO-TASK COMMUNICATION

The Session layer is the first layer in the OSI model considered to be system dependent. The software in this layer provides process-to-process communication functions, better known in DECnet as task-to-task communication. This function is needed to bridge the gap between the Presentation layer and logical links.

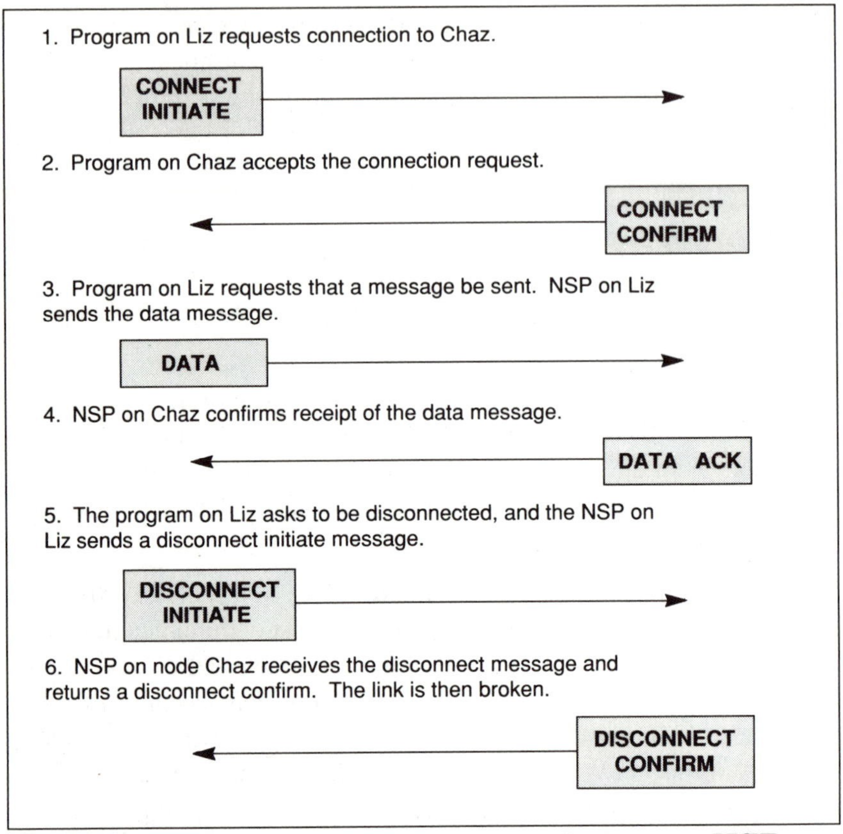

1. Program on Liz requests connection to Chaz.

   CONNECT INITIATE ──────────────────────►

2. Program on Chaz accepts the connection request.

   ◄────────────────────── CONNECT CONFIRM

3. Program on Liz requests that a message be sent.  NSP on Liz sends the data message.

   DATA ──────────────────────►

4. NSP on Chaz confirms receipt of the data message.

   ◄────────────────────── DATA  ACK

5. The program on Liz asks to be disconnected, and the NSP on Liz sends a disconnect initiate message.

   DISCONNECT INITIATE ──────────────────────►

6. NSP on node Chaz receives the disconnect message and returns a disconnect confirm.  The link is then broken.

   ◄────────────────────── DISCONNECT CONFIRM

**Figure 3-9: Message exchange between NSPs**

Task-to-task functions include requesting logical links for processes, receiving connect requests for processes, sending and receiving logical link data, disconnecting and aborting logical links, monitoring logical links, identifying processes, creating processes for incoming connect requests, and mapping node names to node addresses.

## Process Connection

Task-to-task communication makes a connection between two processes. When a DECnet node initiates a connect request to a remote node and process, it performs the following tasks:

- Identifies the destination node through the use of the DECnet node-name mapping table.

- Formats connect data for the Presentation layer.

- Issues a connect request to the Presentation layer.

- Optionally starts a connection abort timer. The timer is used to abort the link if the processes have not completed before it expires.

When a DECnet node receives an incoming connect request, it performs these tasks:

- Parses connection information to obtain the source and destination, the remote process name, and access control information if available.

- Validates access control information in the local SYSUAF.DAT file.

- Activates or creates a destination process.

- Links the source node's address to the node name.

- Transfers the incoming connect request to the destination process.

- Optionally starts a connection abort timer.

## DECnet Objects

A program on a remote node makes itself known to the local session layer software by declaring an object type and name. A program must have an object type and name declared before it can accept a connection request.

A source program identifies an object in the connect request to specify the target program with which it wants to communicate. Object types can be either a type zero object or a nonzero object. To address a target program, a source program's connect request must specify an object type or an object name, but not both.

Objects with a zero object type are usually user-defined images for user-written applications. These objects have a text name that identifies them.

Nonzero objects are known objects that provide standard network functions, such as File Access Listener (FAL), or MAIL. The object type is assigned an integer value from 1 to 255, while the object name is blank.

## Access Control

At the user level, DECnet uses two access control mechanisms: embedded access control and proxy login. Embedded access control means that the security information, i.e., username and password, is embedded in the user's DECnet request. For example:

```
$ COPY BIFF"BYNON NEVERTELL"::-
_$USER$DISK:[BYNON]NAMES.TXT *.*
```

The username, BYNON, and password, NEVERTELL, are embedded directly in the command to the remote node. The session access control mechanism matches this information against entries in the system authorization file.

The second method, proxy login, allows the destination node to determine access eligibility based on the source node and username. A database, called NETUAF.DAT, contains entries for each proxy account user. The database has three pieces of information: the source node name, the source username, and the destination username. For instance, if a node's proxy database had the entry "SKIP::WILLIS WILLIS", then user Willis, requesting connections from node Skip, would be permitted access to the WILLIS account.

DECnet can also provide link-level access control. When a DECnet circuit is started, it attempts to initialize with the DECnet software on other nodes. As a part of the initialization, a remote node can ask for a password before it completes the operation.

## FILE AND TERMINAL SERVICES

All the network functions discussed to this point are needed for the correct operation of a DECnet network. The others are icing on the cake.

The Presentation layer is a collection of useful, but not always essential, services. Among these are the programs and interfaces DEC builds into DECnet to provide transparent file and record access, virtual terminal services, and more.

### Remote File and Record Access

Using DECnet, a user on one node can access files on another. The remote file access capability of DECnet allows DCL or a user-written program to create and delete remote files, open and close remote files, and read from and write to records of remote files.

Like task-to-task and logical link functions, remote file access requires the cooperation of two DECnet programs: a source and a target. The target program is always a version of the FAL, whose purpose is to receive remote file access requests.

FAL translates incoming access requests into calls to the local file system (RMS on a VMS system). FAL then returns the resulting file information to the source program. The operating system running the source program reformats the data to conform to the local file system.

The FAL and the source program communicate through the data access protocol (DAP). DAP is part of the Presentation layer, but it uses the logical link functions of the Transport layer to perform its work.

### Virtual Terminal Services

The virtual terminal capability of DECnet allows a user to logically connect a terminal to a remote node. This facility permits programs to run interactively on the remote node. For example, if your local node doesn't have a word processor, but a remote node does, you can log into the remote node and use the word processor.

### THE NETWORK IS THE SYSTEM

Most computer users and organizations discover that no single computer system is adept at every application. This results either in not getting the job done (because you don't have the right tools), or in a menagerie of standalone computers which aren't compatible with one another.

Ethernet LAN products have turned this problem into a solution. Ethernet forces you to look at the local area network as a system.

By standardizing on a network system, rather than a computer system, you can take advantage of many computers, peripheral devices, and software applications. The network solves many computer compatibility problems.

DEC and other hardware and software vendors have developed a vast array of Ethernet-based products to tie computer hardware together and make all parts work as a system.

## Disk, File, and Print Servers

One of the common systems now found on Ethernet LANs is a server. A server is a VAX that provides connectivity services to its disk, file, and print queue resources for microcomputers. A server process runs on the VAX host to make the resources available, and client software runs on the microcomputers so the microcomputer can access the resources. DEC's server software, called VMS Services for MS-DOS, ties MS-DOS and PC-DOS microcomputers into the VAX resources. Several third-party software vendors have similar systems for PCs and Macintoshes.

A disk server provides transparent use of its storage to a client system. Most disk servers make storage available through a file formatted to the client system's disk structure specifications. In other words, a VMS file called PC_DISK.DAT could be used by a client PC as disk H:. The client PC can use the drive as if it were a local floppy or hard disk.

Disk servers have some inherent limitations. For one, client files within the server disk file aren't compatible with the VMS file system. There's no way to get at them from the VAX. Second, file and record locking is difficult, limiting the use of each server disk file to a single user. These problems are solved by file servers.

A file server is similar to a disk server in its basic function, because a client system uses the VAX to store its files. They differ in method: A file server provides storage services in the server's native format, i.e., client PC files are stored in VAX RMS file format. The benefit of this is twofold: File and record locking is accomplished by VMS, and the files are accessible to both VAX and client systems.

Most vendors who build microcomputer-to-host integration packages provide print server functions as a standard feature. A print server, like disk and file servers, allows a client system to use VAX printers as if they were local.

## Terminal Servers

One of the most useful network devices is the Ethernet terminal server. A terminal server is like an intelligent switching device that uses the Ethernet LAN to connect X to Y.

The terminal server hardware has a single port, used to connect it to the LAN, and from eight to 100 or more terminal device ports, depending on the make and model. At the terminal device port, you can connect ASCII terminals, printers, microcomputers, or any other device that conforms to the RS-232 serial communication standard.

The terminal server allows devices or computers connected to the LAN or terminal server to be accessed by others. For instance, a terminal or microcomputer connected to a terminal server can connect to any multiuser computer, or a printer connected to the terminal server can be accessed by all computers on the LAN.

A device or computer is made accessible by defining it as a service. A VAX, for example, isn't accessible to a terminal server until the VAX has been defined as a service, using the LATCP. Conversely, a device on a terminal server, such as a printer, can't be reached by a VAX or other computers on the LAN until it has been defined as a service on the terminal server.

The connectivity between a terminal server port and a host is made by a DEC virtual circuit protocol called local area transport (LAT). DEC terminal servers use the LAT protocol to allow connected terminals to establish a logical link to a host. The host supports the LAT protocol through a LAT port driver (LTDRIVER), which creates virtual terminal circuits and acts as a multiplexer/demultiplexer of the terminal traffic.

## Ethernet Repeaters

The limitations of an Ethernet LAN restrict the network size, i.e., the number of nodes or distance you can build. To get around the nodes-per-segment and distance restrictions, you can use Ethernet LAN repeaters.

A repeater receives the traffic from one Ethernet LAN segment and sends it to another. There are several different types of repeaters, such as local, remote, and multiport, depending on the application or problem. To the Ethernet, the repeater looks like any other node. The difference is that the repeater operates in promiscuous mode, allowing it to listen to all network messages.

A local repeater is used to connect two Ethernet LAN segments. The connection is made by simply connecting a transceiver cable from a tap on each segment to the repeater. Transceiver cable lengths of up to 50 meters can be used, limiting the distance between segments to 100 meters.

Remote repeaters solve the 100-meter distance problem by forming a point-to-point link between two Ethernet segments. Two repeaters are used, each connected to a segment through a transceiver cable. Fiber optic or twisted-pair cable is used to connect the two repeaters. The point-to-point link can be up to 1,000 meters long.

The multiport repeater is suited to a network that requires multiple legs, such as one per office, area, or floor. A multiport repeater is configured like a local repeater, but outputs to multiple Ethernet segments, instead of just one. Each segment of the multiport repeater is electrically isolated. If a segment fails, it won't affect the other nodes.

## CONCLUSION

Although computer networking is still a young technology, it has firmly entrenched itself as a necessity, not a luxury. DECnet networks allow us to communicate easily. They permit us to share resources, and they help us to be more productive through the use of workstations. For all of these reasons, and others, it's difficult to look at DECnet as just a communication medium. DECnet is an organizational lifeline.

# Chapter 4

# VAXclusters

The true power of VAX systems is realized in their various networking capabilities. The focus here will be on a special form of networking called clustering. A VAXcluster system is a multipurpose computing environment. Clustered VAXs (i.e., minicomputers) can provide the power and data storage capabilities normally associated with mainframe-class systems.

A VAXcluster is a group of cooperating VAX computers and their peripherals, configured using a method of interconnecting that permits resource sharing and a flexible growth potential. Let's look at the methods of interconnection, the hardware and software components used, the various configurations possible and system management issues that relate to VAXclusters.

## THE PURPOSE AND
## BENEFITS OF A VAXCLUSTER

A VAXcluster provides two or more VAX computers with the best attributes of a network and multiprocessor system (shared communications and resources), while maintaining the independence of each VAX. System resources can be shared throughout the cluster, including data storage, printers, print and batch queues, software products and user-written programs, the operating system (i.e., VMS) and user files. You can access your data from any node in the cluster. Plus, it's economical for the system to share expensive peripherals. Figure 4-1 displays a mixed cluster of VAX and MicroVAX systems.

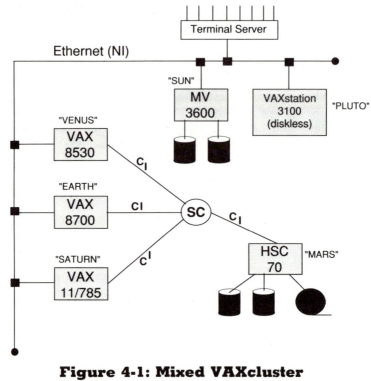

**Figure 4-1: Mixed VAXcluster using VAX and MicroVAX systems**

## Improved System Management and Security

Shared resources and hardware make a cluster feel and act like a single system. For this reason, a single system manager can easily manage a large VAXcluster, but not the same number of individual systems with any efficiency. Security for all cluster members, or nodes, can be controlled by one manager. This is because a cluster, through its data sharing capabilities, can use a single security database. Standalone VAX systems use individual security databases. Each security database must be maintained separately by the system manager.

## High Availability of Resources

Through a cluster's redundant hardware capability, in the form of multiple CPUs, hierarchical storage controllers (HSCs), and shadow disks, a VAXcluster can be equipped to provide a reduced service capability at all times. In other words, in a properly configured cluster, if a CPU or disk fails, the capability of the system as a whole is reduced only by the faulty unit.

When a cluster node fails, users can continue to work using other CPUs in the cluster. Simple cluster features, such as automatic system fail-over support, ensure that large batch jobs won't be interrupted and that users are shifted to an alternate CPU, if one is available.

## Flexible Configurations

VAXclusters have a unique quality not found in other systems. They offer incremental expansion to meet the needs of your organization. You can start off with a small cluster, say two or three nodes, and grow into a very large cluster with as many as 26 nodes.

Additionally, your cluster can be a mix of configurations. VAXs can share system disks, authorization files, and software, or they can be independent, sharing only vital resources.

## VAXCLUSTER HARDWARE

Clusters emanated from the need to share resources and to build larger, more capable computer systems. A VAXcluster is primarily a software system. It doesn't matter which VAX processors you have or what hardware you use to connect the VAX computers, as long as it provides the needed performance characteristics.

VAXcluster software is a set of resource managers and drivers. Cluster drivers comprise port and class drivers. This strategy facilitates device independence. It doesn't matter what medium you use to connect your cluster members. Simply write a port driver to support it.

Let's consider the DEC hardware components that can be used to form a VAXcluster system.

## VAXcluster Processors

According to Digital's documentation, any VAX processor can be clustered, except the VAX 11/730, VAX 11/725, and the MicroVAX I. However, I have successfully used MicroVAX I processors in a cluster. MicroVAX computers, including VAXstation systems based on a MicroVAX processor, can only be clustered using Ethernet. All other VAX processors can be clustered using either Digital's Computer Interconnect (CI) hardware or Ethernet. Systems operating under VAX/VMS V5 can form a cluster using a combination of CI and Ethernet hardware. A cluster using both communication mediums is called a mixed VAXcluster.

The number of nodes in a cluster varies with cluster hardware and operating system versions. At this writing, Computer Interconnect clusters support two to 16 nodes, while Ethernet clusters support two to 26 members. Cluster members don't need to be alike. You can have big, small, old, and new processors in your VAXcluster.

## Processor-to-Processor Communication Channels

The primary hardware component used to form a VAXcluster is the cluster communication path, that is, a processor-interconnect bus. The processor-interconnect is needed to pass information and data among the cluster members, including member connection messages, cluster transition-state information, and user files.

The connection must be high speed. A low-speed link would never be sufficient, because of the volume of information that must be moved and the timeliness of the interprocessor messages. Imagine the poor response of a system where file and record locking tables were updated at, say, 9,600 baud. A high-speed link is mandatory.

Large VAXcluster systems, based on non-MicroVAX processors, use DEC's CI, a high-speed coaxial network. Each node has an input/output processor, either CI780, CI750, or CIBCI, that connects two communication channels, A and B, to a central passive hub called a Star Coupler. Although this technology could have been implemented on MicroVAX systems, the cost would have been prohibitive.

To cluster MicroVAX and other low-end VAX computers, DEC chose to use a more common (and less expensive) medium, Ethernet. When used to connect processors, the Ethernet is referred to as the Network Interconnect (NI). Digital calls these low-end clusters Local Area VAXclusters (LAVc), as they are based on local area network (LAN) technology.

Like a CI processor, an Ethernet controller, such as a DEQNA or
DESVA, is a high-speed communication device that uses a coaxial
cable as its medium. Small differences exist, such as the CI's 70
megabit bandwidth compared to Ethernet's 10 and, of course,
Ethernet's single channel.

By using Ethernet as the interconnect, a LAVc can forego the
expensive hardware components such as the Star Coupler, CI
processor, and an HSC. Furthermore, multiple LAVcs can use the same
Ethernet, and the Ethernet can continue to serve its original purpose
as a LAN.

### Star Coupler

A Star Coupler, a network hub used to connect CI channels, is a
required component for a CI-based cluster. Each cluster node, VAX or
HSC, connects to the Star Coupler with two pairs of CI cables, A and B.
Cluster nodes can be as far as 45 meters away from the Star Coupler.

### Hierarchical Storage Controller

The hierarchical storage controller is a mass storage control
subsystem. As a self-contained, intelligent disk and tape controller, it
removes the need for individual storage devices on each VAX
processor. An HSC permits VAX systems to share disk and tape storage
devices. By using one or more HSCs, VAX systems in a cluster can
operate without local disks. System startup, or booting, and data
transfer take place over the CI.

The HSC makes continuous data access possible. If a VAX system fails,
the other cluster members will continue to have access to the disks
and tapes connected to the HSC. This would not be true if storage
devices were connected directly to individual VAX processors.

Another feature makes HSC redundancy possible. It's called dual
porting. Digital designed its disk and tape drives with dual access
ports, A and B. When two HSCs are used, with one connected to port A
and the other to port B of a storage device, device control fails over to
the alternate HSC if the primary HSC goes down.

An HSC isn't a required component of a VAXcluster. Cluster nodes can
share disk storage through cluster software without using an HSC.

This technique is called mass storage control protocol (MSCP) serving.

The HSC is a passive node in the cluster. Although each HSC is recognized by the other members of the cluster, the HSC processor provides no compute capability. It simply processes storage device access requests. A maximum of 15 HSCs can be connected to the cluster. Each supports multiple disk and tape interfaces made up of any combination of the standard disk interface (SDI) or standard tape interface (STI).

The HSC supports only Digital storage architecture (DSA) disks, such as the RA81, RA82, or RA90, and Digital TA series tape drives, such as the TA78. As of this writing, several OEMs have developed disk interconnect modules that permit non-DEC disk drives to be used with an HSC or other DSA controllers.

See Figure 4-2 for a diagram of an HSC-based VAXcluster.

## Local Disks

VAXclusters can share local storage devices. A local VAX storage device can be configured for cluster access through the use of the MSCP server, a cluster software component. This is how local area VAXcluster processors share disks where an HSC can't be used.

Just as diskless VAX systems can boot from HSC controllers, diskless MicroVAX systems can boot from a VAX processor which has an MSCP-served system disk. This system is known as a LAVc boot node. All other nodes in the LAVc are called satellites.

To facilitate redundancy of resources, such as that found with HSCs, two boot nodes are used. Unlike HSC-based cluster systems, however, local area VAXcluster disks can't be dual ported, and data availability isn't always guaranteed. If one of the two boot nodes goes down, the storage maintained by that system will be unavailable to the cluster.

Using two boot nodes also improves I/O performance. In a large LAVc with, say, eight or more nodes, a second boot node relieves the heavy disk I/O activity that plagues a single boot node.

## Ethernet Terminal Servers

With the multiple CPU design of a VAXcluster, a flexible method of

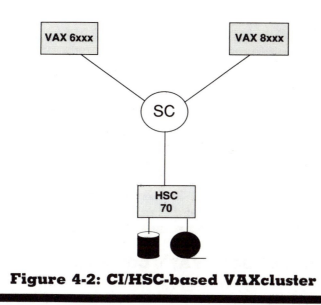

**Figure 4-2: CI/HSC-based VAXcluster**

terminal connection is mandatory. If a user's terminal is connected directly to a VAX processor, his system access will be tied to the availability of that node. That's not an ideal situation, especially when other processors might be available.

By using Ethernet-based terminal servers, virtual point-to-point connections can be made between a terminal device and any node on the network. This way, if one node goes down, the user simply connects to another and continues processing. Digital terminal servers provide automatic fail-over support. When a node fails, the user is connected to another system automatically.

Another benefit of the terminal server to a VAXcluster system is its ability to load balance at user login time. A special algorithm is used to connect users to the cluster member with the lightest load.

See Figure 4-3 for an example of a LAVc using an Ethernet terminal server.

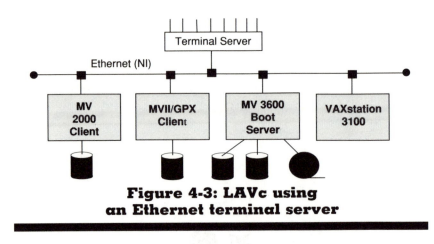

## Figure 4-3: LAVc using an Ethernet terminal server

## VAXCLUSTER SOFTWARE COMPONENTS

A VAXcluster is a distributed computing system whose characteristics are shaped by its software. It uses hardware components, but they change with new technology.

In a distributed system, computing tasks are dispersed among two or more processing elements. It has a systemwide operating system, where services are requested directly by name, not by their location, as in a network. The allocation of resources and processing of jobs is completely transparent to the user. A distributed system looks like a single computer system. A VAXcluster fits the description of a distributed system.

VMS is the unifying operating system. It runs on every processor in the cluster except the HSC. Although you can direct your jobs to a specific node in the cluster, you don't need to know this is happening.

All VAXcluster resources are accessible by name. For instance, local disk device names always begin with the cluster node name, like BIFF$DUB0: or SKIP$DUA1:. This ensures their uniqueness in the cluster. Print and batch queue names, another shared cluster resource, are left to the imagination of the system manager.

Let's take a look at the primary software components of a VMS system that turns ordinary VAX processors into super distributed computer systems, VAXclusters.

## System Communication Services

The VMS system communication services (SCS) provide the most important function of clustering: unified interprocessor communication. SCS facilitates communication between all cluster members. Its basic function is to provide message formatting for other cluster software components. SCS implements its functions based on Digital's system communication architecture (SCA).

Cluster communication, with the present hardware technology, goes through the CI port driver (PADRIVER) or the NI port driver (PEDRIVER) to active VAX nodes or HSCs in the cluster. Information transmitted over the cluster medium comes from system applications or SYSAPs, including the disk and tape class drivers (DUDRIVER and TUDRIVER), the DECnet class driver for the CI (CNDRIVER), the MSCP server, and the connection manager. User-written SYSAPs can use SCS as well.

SYSAPs communicate with one another. In other words, the MSCP SYSAP on one node communicates with the MSCP SYSAPs on other nodes in the cluster. The SYSAP communication messages are formatted by system communication services and passed along to the respective port driver and vice versa.

## Port and Class Drivers

The VAX/VMS operating system has dozens of device drivers. It must support VAXBI, MASSBUS, UNIBUS, and Q-bus devices, which is a formidable task for a single operating system. Information must flow from one system to another with no regard to the physical configuration of the other system. This is accomplished through the use of port and class drivers, which separate form from function. A port driver supports a specific hardware device, such as an Ethernet controller, CI processor, or disk controller. The port driver represents the lowest level interface to a hardware device. A class driver, on the other hand, implements a protocol like the MSCP, used to control disk access. A class driver presents a standard interface for the operating system, regardless of the hardware used.

Port and class drivers pass information to each other through system communication services. They format the information (i.e., messages) to be exchanged by two pieces of software. For example, when a VMS process requests access to a remote disk (i.e., one not connected to its local computer bus), the request must be routed to the appropriate class driver, converted to MSCP format, sent to the correct port driver, and decoded by the disk controller.

After the request is decoded, the disk controller passes the data back through the port driver to the process requesting it. The final transaction is an MSCP message, sent through the SCS to the class driver, to complete the request. This process is the same to the local system, whether the disk is connected to an HSC or local to another cluster member.

## Mass Storage Control Protocol

MSCP is actually two components: the MSCP server and MSCP implemented by the disk class driver.

The MSCP server provides a link between SCS, the local VAXBI, MASSBUS, UNIBUS or Q-bus disk driver, and the disk class driver. The MSCP server makes a local disk device name unique to the cluster, by preceding the physical device name with the node name, as in node$device:. Then it makes these devices available to the other cluster members through SCS and the CI or NI port drivers.

When a process from a remote cluster node requests access to a local disk, the MSCP server decodes the MSCP I/O request and sends it to the local disk driver. The MSCP server acts as a bridge to move data between the local disk, the cluster communication path and the requesting process. The server must be executing on the local node to permit clusterwide access to local disks.

## Connection Manager

To coordinate cluster activity, especially the coming and going of cluster members, a single point of control is needed. It's called the connection manager.

The connection manager coordinates VAXcluster membership. Each time a cluster member joins or leaves a cluster, the cluster is said to be in a state transition. During a state transition, connection managers on each node of the cluster adjust their quorum values and communicate their status to the other members. "Yo, Biff, I'm ready." "Okay Skip, so am I."

The connection manager allows each node to know the cluster membership, i.e., who's playing ball. Further, through the quorum scheme, the cluster manager prevents data corruption by preventing cluster partitioning. Cluster partitioning occurs when two clusters, unaware of each other, access the same storage devices.

Quorum is a clusterwide value of processor votes that must be met before cluster activity can take place. Each cluster member is assigned a number of votes that it applies to quorum. If there aren't enough votes to meet quorum, the cluster hangs (i.e., suspends processing activity), waiting for additional votes.

The minimum value for quorum is two, which means you can never have a cluster of one node. To solve this problem, a disk, available to the cluster, can be used to provide a single vote. The disk is said to be a quorum disk, as it's used to preserve quorum if all but one node leaves the cluster.

The quorum value is initially taken from the system parameter EXPECTED_VOTES (in v5 or QUORUM in V4). It's possible, however, to adjust quorum using the $SET QUORUM command. An anomaly of quorum is that it's not reduced when a node leaves the cluster, but it's adjusted when a processor boots into the cluster.

A processor is rejected from joining the cluster or even forced to crash if it tries to specify a quorum value that would cause the cluster to suspend activity. Data integrity is serious business.

## Distributed Lock Manager

To ensure resource integrity, you need a mechanism that controls access to all data elements. In a VAXcluster, this is the job of the distributed lock manager.

The distributed lock manager synchronizes access to shared resources to prevent collisions and guarantee data integrity. Access is synchronized at the device, file, and record level. The distributed lock manager is accessed primarily by record management services (RMS), the VAX file system, the job controller, and user-written cluster applications.

The distributed lock manager runs on each cluster member. It accomplishes its task by maintaining lock tables for each node in the cluster. It uses both the connection manager and system communication services to send and receive lock information from the other cluster members. If a node in the cluster fails, the connection manager notifies the distributed lock manager, and that node's locks are released.

## Distributed File System

The distributed file system makes access to files 100 percent transparent, even when the files are scattered about the cluster. It activates when a user or process wants to access files on disks connected to remote systems. It's not used when accessing local files.

The distributed file system allows transparent access to RMS disk files among nodes whose disks are MSCP served and to HSC-based disks and tapes. HSC tapes are available to all nodes in the cluster, but, only one process at a time can use the tape. The distributed file system and RMS use the lock manager to accommodate this clusterwide file access.

## Distributed Job Controller

In a VAXcluster, a user can submit a batch job for execution or send a file to a printer without knowing that another node in the cluster is processing the work. This distribution of jobs is the function of the distributed job controller.

The distributed job controller uses the distributed lock manager to signal other cluster members to check their print and batch queues for work to be processed. Stated simply, this software permits users to submit batch and print jobs to queues established on another node in the cluster.

This functionality distributes the batch and print workload to the nodes best equipped to handle the work. For example, a user might queue a file to be printed on a laser printer connected to a remote node. He doesn't need to know which system has the laser printer. Only the queue name is required, for instance, SYS$LASER.

## VAXCLUSTER ENVIRONMENTS

VAXclusters, being akin to networks, are very flexible in their configurations. There are only two basic types of cluster environments: homogeneous and heterogeneous. All others are hybrids.

## Homogeneous VAXclusters

In a VAXcluster, homogeneous means that there's a single operating environment. The same operating system is used by each node of the cluster, and members boot from a common system disk on which these files are shared. Furthermore, users log in via a common SYSUAF file, and the nodes share application software. Thus, it doesn't matter to which processor a user actually logs in, as the system will look the same.

Additional commonalty and sharing takes place with respect to common print and batch queues, and fully shared mass storage devices. In this environment, users can continue to work if a processor in the cluster fails. Because the user environment is common, either processor can provide the same services.

A homogeneous VAXcluster is almost as easy to manage as a single VAX. In essence, the members of the homogeneous cluster become one large, easy-to-maintain system, without the failure catastrophes that could plague a single machine.

## Heterogeneous VAXcluster

A heterogeneous VAXcluster is a processing environment where each member provides a unique service. Each node is set up differently. Applications between these systems differ, and users might be restricted from individual systems.

Generally speaking, heterogeneous cluster members boot from their own (i.e., individual) system disk. The resources of each system might or might not be available to the other cluster members, at the discretion of the system designer. As an example, print and batch queues can be strictly local, or shared among some or all the cluster members.

System management of a heterogeneous VAXcluster is more complex than it is with a homogeneous VAXcluster system. In some cases, particularly if you must protect resources from users of another node, system management can be a nightmare.

## VAXcluster System Disks

VAXcluster system disks can be a single common volume or individual volumes. As a single common system disk, each node is assigned a root directory, i.e., [SYS0] or [SYS1]. Systems booting from a common disk share most operating system files, such as drivers, utilities, and libraries. Individual system disks maintain operating system files for a single system only.

Using a common system disk reduces the number of system disks to manage, and simplifies operating system upgrades, product installations, and backups. Independent system disks increase potential performance and system management chores. The only down side to using a common system disk is that the disk is prone to becoming an I/O bottleneck or a single point of failure.

## Storage Device Names

Shareable devices in a cluster must have unique names so they can be accessed by any member. If two or more of the VAX systems have a disk device named DUA0, for instance, it would be impossible to specify the one you wanted to access. Therefore, in a cluster, shareable storage devices are named using the node name with the device, like node$device, or in the case of an HSC-based system with the allocation class and the device name, as in $class$device.

For instance, if node BIFF has disks that are MSCP-served to the cluster, these disks would have the name BIFF$ before them. When the cluster has one or more HSCs, each HSC is given an allocation class of from one to 255. That class forms the unique device names and precedes the disk or tape device name. In addition, HSC disks and tapes can be accessed using the HSC node name, as with a drive connected locally on a VAX cluster member. Here are some common examples:

**$1$DUA0:** — Dual-pathed MASSBUS or HSC disk (allocation class 1).

**HSC001$DUB1:** — Disk connected to HSC node HSC001 .

**BIFF$DUA2:** — MSCP-served disk on VAX node BIFF.

**LIZ$MUA0:** — Tape drive connected to HSC node LIZ.

## System Disk File Coordination

A little background information helps with understanding the directory structure of a common system disk. Although homogeneous cluster members share most files, they don't share all. Each node has a handful of files that are unique to that member, such as a node-specific start-up procedure. So, to make a single disk both common and specific, a little mirror magic is used. Figure 4-4 presents a graphic description of the structure.

According the VAX/VMS documentation set, logical names are used to represent physical devices and directories. Three are defined for each member:

**SYS$SPECIFIC** — A node's system root device and directory, for instance, $1$DUA0:[SYS0.].

**SYS$COMMON** — A common root device and directory tree shared by all cluster members, as in $1$DUA0:[VMS$COMMON].

**SYS$SYSROOT** — An RMS search list that points to both the system root and the common root. Therefore, SYS$SYSROOT always points to two directory structures, e.g.,

- SYS$MANAGER: =
  SYS$SPECIFIC:[SYSMGR],SYS$COMMON:[SYSMGR]

- SYS$SYSTEM: =
  SYS$SPECIFIC:[SYSEXE],SYS$COMMON:[SYSEXE]

Files specific to a cluster member should be stored in the node's SYS$SPECIFIC directory structure. These can include network databases, authorize databases (if heterogeneous), software products to be run on that node only, and node specific start-up and login procedures. Files common to all cluster members should be stored in the cluster common directory structure, SYS$COMMON. To name a

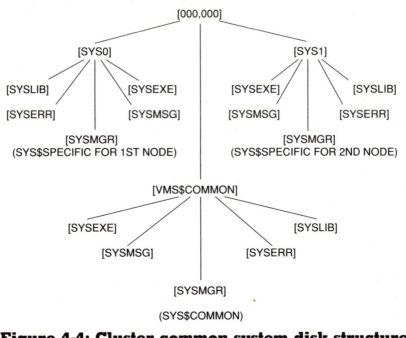

## Figure 4-4: Cluster common system disk structure

few, drivers go in SYS$COMMON:[SYSEXE], help files are contained in
SYS$COMMON:[SYSHLP], library files are stored in SYS4$COMMON:
[SYSLIB], and the authorize databases are maintained in
SYS$COMMON: [SYSEXE].

### CONCLUSION
Clustering is a powerful VAX/VMS feature. The capability exists to
start with single a MicroVAX computer, when your needs are small.
Later, it can grow to a powerful mainframe-class system, but still be
easily maintained by a single system manager.

# Chapter 5

# Utilities and Commands

This is an important chapter, even if you're a seasoned VMS professional. The Digital Command Language and VMS utilities are so robust that it's difficult for anyone to fully recall every command, its purpose, and its syntax. So, this chapter is a source of reference on the tools we use to make a VAX work for us. When reading this chapter, you also might discover subtle features that you forgot or never knew.

## DIGITAL COMMAND LANGUAGE OVERVIEW

The Digital Command Language (DCL) is an interpretive computer language. It can be compared to a language such as BASIC. The DCL command interpreter accepts human readable commands (e.g., PRINT, TYPE, etc.), interprets them, then performs the intended operation. DCL can accept commands from several sources: the user's keyboard, a file, or a combination of the two.

DCL maintains more than 200 commands called verbs. Each DCL verb acts on a parameter or assumed parameter. The action of these verbs and the scope of their parameters may be modified with qualifiers. The use of qualifiers makes DCL extremely flexible.

As a computer language, DCL has a set of rules governing the proper use of its commands, parameters, and qualifiers. We call this the DCL syntax. DCL commands, parameters, and qualifiers must be entered in a way that is understandable to the command line interpreter (CLI).

The following line shows the format of a DCL command. The items in brackets ([]) are optional components. The ellipsis (...) indicates that more than one item (where valid) may be specified.

$ [LABEL:] VERB [/QUAL...] [PAR...][/QUAL] [!COMMENT]

## Label

A label is an optional user-specified character string with a maximum length of 255 characters. It's commonly used in command procedures to mark a block of commands or a control point for such commands as GOTO, GOSUB, CALL, and ON. When used, the label precedes the command verb and is separated from it by a colon (:). In our example, the label START: is used as an iteration control point:

```
    .
    .
    .
$   COUNT = 0
$   START:
$   COUNT = COUNT + 1
$   WRITE SYS$OUTPUT COUNT
$   IF COUNT .NE. 10 THEN GOTO START
    .
    .
    .
```

## Command Verb

The command verb (also known as the command) defines the action VMS will take when the command line is interpreted. The command verb may be a DCL command or a symbol. The DIRECTORY verb, for instance, produces a file directory listing on the default output device.

## Parameters

Parameters specify the object or a list of objects on which the command verb will act. Multiple parameters may be specified with a single command line, but the parameters must be separated from the command verb and other parameters by a space, multiple spaces, or a tab.

Most DCL commands accept or require parameters. Parameters must be positioned in a specified order within the command; however, you don't need to memorize them. This is because DCL makes extensive use of default values and prompts. As an example, if you enter a DCL verb that requires a parameter, but omit it, you will be prompted for it. The COPY command illustrates how this feature works:

```
$ COPY
$_From: LOGIN.COM
$_To: LOGIN.SAV
```

The _From: and _To: prompts are provided by DCL to guide us through entering the command parameters. Once learned, however, you can enter the command on a single line without prompting:

```
$ COPY LOGIN.COM LOGIN.SAV
```

Many DCL commands accept a list of parameters. You will commonly use this technique when working with files. The following print command shows you how a parameter list is specified:

```
$ PRINT MENU.FOR,REPORT.FOR,PARSE.FOR
```

Not all DCL commands accept lists. The commands that do not will give you an error message if you specify more than one parameter.

## Qualifiers

Qualifiers further define or modify the function of a DCL command verb. A qualifier is a keyword, or a keyword followed by a value or list of values. The qualifier keyword is always preceded by a slash (/). Three classes of qualifiers exist: parameter qualifiers, positional qualifiers, and command qualifiers. Multiple qualifiers may be specified with a single DCL command, provided that each qualifier is preceded with a slash. Qualifiers are usually not required.

Qualifiers allow us to control specific built-in attributes of DCL commands. Most DCL commands have one or more qualifiers associated with them, but most commands do not require a qualifier to execute correctly. For this reason, you'll never be prompted for a qualifier if you don't specify one that's required. Instead, you'll get an error message.

Qualifiers can be command, position, or parameter oriented. A command qualifier applies to the whole command. General practice suggests that these qualifiers should be placed after the command verb, although in most cases a command qualifier may be placed anywhere in the command string. The following command displays a full listing of two directories, using the /FULL qualifier of the DIRECTORY command:

$ DIRECTORY/FULL SYS$MANAGER:,SYS$SYSTEM:

A positional qualifier takes on a different meaning based on its location in the command. If a positional qualifier is placed after the command verb but before the first parameter, the qualifier will affect the entire command. If the same positional parameter is placed after a parameter, only that parameter will be modified. The following two PRINT commands demonstrate:

$ PRINT/COPIES=3 MVAX1.TXT,MVAX3.TXT
$ PRINT MVAX4.TXT/COPIES=2,MVAX10.TXT

The first PRINT command will print three copies of each file. The second PRINT command prints two copies of the first file but only one of the second.

A parameter qualifier modifies the parameter it follows. In the next example, file SYSTARTUP.COM is sent to queue SYS$LASER to be printed, and file ACCOUNTING.RPT is sent to queue SYS$FAST for printing:

$ PRINT SYSTARTUP.COM/QUEUE=SYS$LASER -
_$ ACCOUNTING.RPT/QUEUE=SYS$FAST

Qualifiers have several formats. They are classified as value qualifiers, positive/negative qualifiers, qualifier lists, and default qualifiers. A value qualifier is one that accepts a value. You've seen an example of value qualifiers in the PRINT commands given above, where the /COPIES qualifier is used to specify the number of copies to be printed. A value qualifier is one that uses the equal sign (=) to specify a key word or value.

With some value qualifiers, you can specify a list. The list must be enclosed in parentheses, with each element separated by a comma. In this example, three batch jobs are deleted from the SYS$BATCH queue:

$ DELETE/QUEUE/ENTRY=(119,123,124) SYS$BATCH

Positive/negative qualifiers take on a true or false value. The qualifiers are positive by default. You explicitly negate them by prefixing NO. The example commands show how terminal broadcast would be turned on and off:

$ SET TERMINAL/BROADCAST
$ SET TERMINAL/NOBROADCAST

Default qualifiers are qualifiers that do not affect the command if they are not specified. For instance, a default qualifier of the DIRECTORY command is /BRIEF.

## Comments

A comment is an optional, user-specified, remark about the command. It is used in command procedures to document the command for future reference. Although comments can be used at the end of interactive commands, they are most commonly used in command procedures.

## DCL COMMAND ENTRY

DCL commands may be entered in uppercase, lowercase, or a combination of the two. The DCL command line interpreter changes all commands to uppercase characters automatically. Multiple spaces or tabs may be used where a single space or tab is legal. Excess spaces are discarded.

A command line may be one to 265 characters long and may have up to 128 elements (i.e., verb, parameters, qualifiers, and so on). For your convenience, you may continue a command to one or more new lines. To continue a command, simply enter a hyphen after a complete command element and press <RETURN>. The CLI will respond with your prompt preceded by an underscore.

All DCL commands may be abbreviated to their shortest unique length, which is generally no more than four characters. A classic example is the DIRECTORY command, which consists of nine letters. The shortest unique length for this command is three letters, because of the DIFFERENCES, DISMOUNT, and DISCONNECT commands. If we specify only the first two characters of the DIRECTORY command, the CLI cannot determine which command to execute, as the following example illustrates:

```
$ DI
%DCL-W-ADVERB, ambiguous command verb-supply more characters
 \DI\
$
```

Proper abbreviation saves time and keystrokes. These two commands are equivalent:

```
$ SHOW CLUSTER/CONTINUOUS
$ SH CL/C
```

DCL assumes default objects and values; i.e., device, directory, file name, or value automatically used by DCL when you do not explicitly supply a value yourself. We use most of the defaults without ever giving them a second thought, such as our default device and directory. The defaults make DCL commands easier to use.

## Command Line Recall and Editing

One of the many convenient features of DCL is command recall and editing. The command line interpreter stores the last 20 commands that you've entered in a command buffer.

To recall a previous command line, press <UP ARROW> or <CTRL/B>. The RECALL/ALL command may be used to list the commands you have stored in the command buffer. The output from the command looks like:

```
$ RECALL/ALL
 1 DIR
 2 FORTRAN MENU.FOR
 3 EDIT MENU.FOR
$
```

To recall a specific command from the command buffer, you would use the RECALL command again, this time with a command line number as the parameter.

```
$ RECALL 2
$ FORTRAN MENU.FOR
```

When you recall a command line, you then may use the arrows and other editing keys to modify it.

Another method of recalling a command with RECALL is to specify part of the command you want to recall. For instance, if you specify ED (from the examples above), the last edit command is recalled:

$ RECALL ED
$ EDIT MENU.FOR

Table 5-1 displays the control and function keys that may be used to enter and edit DCL commands.

### Command Buffering

Another handy feature of the command line interpreter is the type-ahead buffer. It permits you to enter commands while the VAX is processing an existing command. Commands are stored in the type-ahead buffer until the operating system is ready to accept them. The type-ahead buffer enables you to enter a series of commands or program responses as rapidly as you wish, even though the computer system might not be ready to act on them yet.

## CONTROLLING DCL COMMANDS

After you enter a DCL command, you may interrupt its execution and control its output to your display with control-key commands. The keys that interrupt an executable program image are <CTRL/Y>, <CTRL/C>, and <CTRL/T>. Screen control is handled by <HOLD SCREEN>, <CTRL/S>, <CTRL/Q>, and <CTRL/O>.

### Temporarily Interrupting a Command

When you use <CTRL/Y>, whatever program image is currently executing will be interrupted, and control will return to DCL, i.e., you will get your prompt back. The program image is temporarily suspended so that one or more built-in DCL commands (SPAWN, ATTACH, and CONTINUE) can be used. If you enter any command other than SPAWN, ATTACH, or CONTINUE (the built-in commands), the interrupted program image will be canceled, i.e., the image will be run down.

## Table 5-1: Terminal Function Keys

| Key | Function |
| --- | --- |
| <CTRL/A>, <F14> | Toggle overstrike/insert mode. |
| <RUBOUT>, <DELETE> | Deletes the character to the right of the cursor. |
| <CTRL/B>, <UP ARROW> | Recalls the previous command in the command buffer. |
| <CTRL/D>, <LEFT ARROW> | Moves the cursor one position left. |
| <CTRL/E> | Positions the cursor at the end of the line. |
| <CTRL/F>, <RIGHT ARROW> | Moves the cursor one position right. |
| <CTRL/H>, <BS>, <F12> | Positions the cursor at the beginning of the line. |
| <CTRL/I>, <TAB> | Moves the cursor to the next tab stop. |
| <CTRL/J>, <LF>, <F13> | Deletes the word to the left of the cursor. |
| <CTRL/U> | Deletes the command line. |
| <CTRL/X> | Deletes the current line and the contents of the type-ahead buffer. |

The <CTRL/Y> control key has several special purposes. First, it allows you to abruptly cancel a command. The STOP and EXIT commands may be used with <CTRL/Y> to shut down the interrupted program image. The EXIT command executes cleanup procedures before terminating; STOP does not. For example:

```
$ RUN DOIT
<CTRL/Y> *INTERRUPT*
$ EXIT
$
```

When you use <CTRL/Y> to suspend program image processing, your process will wait until the CONTINUE command is entered to resume execution. You will find this useful if you forgot to set something up, such as mounting a tape, and need to suspend processing without aborting the command. For example:

```
$ @FULL_BACKUP
<CTRL/Y> *INTERRUPT*
$ CONTINUE
$
```

Finally, many times you will want to stop what you're doing, start something else, then come back to what you were originally doing. The <CTRL/Y> control key allows you to do this too. After suspending a program image, you can use the SPAWN and ATTACH commands to create and access subprocesses. When you return from the subprocess (i.e., back to the interrupted one), use the CONTINUE command to resume the interrupted program image:

```
$ FORTRAN @ORDER_ENTRY
<CTRL/Y> *INTERRUPT*
$ SPAWN MAIL
%DCL-S-SPAWNED, process BYNON_1 spawned
%DCL-S-ATTACHED, terminal now attached to process BYNON_1

You have 1 new message.

MAIL> READ

  .

  .

  .
MAIL> EXIT
%DCL-S-RETURNED, control returned to process BYNON
```

```
$ CONTINUE
$
```

## Canceling a Command

The <CTRL/C> command key interrupts the execution of built-in commands and most program images. Program images, however, may define what action is taken when you press <CTRL/C>. Many program images treat a <CTRL/C> interrupt as if <CTRL/Y> were pressed. Others, such as the TYPE command, define <CTRL/C> as a cancel command. In the case of the TYPE command, pressing <CTRL/C> tells TYPE to quit displaying the file it's currently processing and move on to the next. Control is not returned to DCL until the last file is processed.

## Checking Program Status

It is often necessary to get statistical information about your process while a program image or command procedure is executing. The <CTRL/T> command key performs this function.

When you press <CTRL/T>, the executing command or DCL is interrupted, and a line of statistical information is displayed. The status line provides information about your current process: node name, process name, system time, current program image, CPU time used, page faults, number of I/O operations, and your working set size. The example shows how <CTRL/T> interrupts a command procedure, prints a status line, then resumes command procedure processing:

```
$ @DAILY_REPORT
<CTRL/T>
LIZ::BILL 14:51:10 (DCL) CPU=00:00.28 PF=891 IO=78 MEM=756
$
```

## Controlling Screen Output

Many times, you will execute a command or run a program that sends large quantities of information to your display. There are three control keys that allow you to control the flow of this information: <CTRL/O>, <CTRL/S>, and <CTRL/Q>.

Pressing <CTRL/O> toggles screen output off and on for the program image currently executing. The messages "Output off" and "Output on" are displayed, as appropriate. When you press <CTRL/O> to turn display output off, the program image continues to process, and the display information is lost. The <CTRL/O> control key command is useful if large quantities of messages are being sent to your display; shutting off the display output will decrease the processing time.

If you want to suspend terminal output, so that you can read what's on your screen, use <CTRL/S> and <CTRL/Q> (or the <HOLD SCREEN> key). The <CTRL/S> control key command suspends program output, and <CTRL/Q> lets the output resume. No output information is lost.

## DCL MESSAGES

When you enter a command that's incorrect or results in an error, VMS displays a message. Also, in some cases, such as with the PRINT, SUBMIT, MOUNT, and other DCL commands, a success message is generated. Most system messages come from the VAX/VMS MESSAGE facility, which always generates messages in the same format.

Most DCL commands do not provide an informational message when they are invoked. Generally, the only notification you'll receive when a DCL command executes successfully is your prompt. If you make an error when you specify a DCL command or if the system is unable to process the command, it will return an error message.

Both error messages and informational messages follow a standard format. The MESSAGE facility will report the source of the error or message, its severity, a mnemonic abbreviation of the error or message, and an explanation of the error or message. The format of a message is:

%FACILITY-L-IDENT, TEXT

The percent sign (%) at the beginning of the message identifies the first message issued from a facility. Subsequent messages issued for the same error are prefaced with a hyphen (-).

The FACILITY indicates the source of the error. The source can be the DCL command line interpreter, one of the various VMS utilities, or a program image.

The severity LEVEL indicator (L) will have one of the following values: S (successful completion), I (information), W (warning), E (error), or F (fatal or severe error). Success and information messages merely let you know that the system has completed the function that you have requested. Warning messages indicate that some, but not all, of the functions requested by your command have been performed. Error messages tell you that the command is incorrect. Fatal messages indicate that your command has failed; the system cannot continue to process the command or request.

IDENT is an abbreviation of the error message text. It can be used to look up the error and possible recovery procedures in the *VAX/VMS System Messages* manual. In most cases, the ident and text will provide you with enough information to correct the error.

The TEXT provides an explanation of the error message. For example, "file not found" is displayed when you try to manipulate a nonexistent file.

## DEFINING FOREIGN COMMANDS WITH SYMBOLS

DCL is a table-driven interpreter. A table of commands, contained in DCLTABLES.EXE, defines the commands to which the command line interpreter will respond. From this table, the CLI invokes the appropriate executable image file. Not all executable images have an entry in the DCL tables. There are many reasons for this, ranging from system security to no command line parsing support in the program itself. For these programs, you may define a foreign command using a DCL symbol.

A symbol is a name that represents a character string. When a symbol name is entered at the beginning of a DCL command line, the command line interpreter attempts to translate it as a command. Let's use the INSTALL utility as an example. The INSTALL utility, which is used to install known images, does not have an entry in the DCL tables. To use the utility in its command mode, you must define a symbol:

```
$ INSTALL == "$INSTALL/COMMAND_MODE"
$ INSTALL
INSTALL> LIST
```

.

.

.

INSTALL> EXIT
$

In the symbol definition above, the dollar sign ($) in the string is used in place of the command RUN SYS$SYSTEM or MCR.

The DCL symbol facility also provides a way to define abbreviated commands, as in:

$ KER*MIT == "$KERMIT"
$ KERM
$ Kermit-32>

An asterisk is used to define the minimum number of characters that must be used for the command to be recognized.

## VMS FILES AND DIRECTORIES

Most DCL commands, in some way, deal with VMS files and directories. For this reason, let's investigate the features and tools provided by DCL.

### Files

A file is a computer storage element that contains machine-readable information. A file can contain a letter, a computer program, a mailing list, a graphics image, or a chapter to a book. Anything that can be represented by alphanumeric characters or numeric values can be used to form a file.

Files are organized as groups of logical records. A record is a file element, such as a line of text to a word processor or a row of information to a database manager. Files are recorded on mass storage devices, such as a magnetic disk or tape.

All files have a file type name that indicates the type of data they contain. Typically, it's a three-character abbreviation for the type of file, i.e., .TXT for a text file, .WPS for WPS-PLUS, or .EXE for executable. However, in reality, there is no file type. Information is always stored the same way, although different applications interpret it differently. Therefore, a program which processes a file must know how to handle the file information. For example, a text editor assumes the data in a file is ASCII (text) characters. If you try to edit a non-

ASCII file with a text editor, the information in the file is unintelligible.

Files may be created with one of three record organization characteristics: sequential, indexed, or relative.

Records in a sequential file are arranged one after another, in the order they are entered. To access a particular record, each one before it must be read. To modify a sequential file, all records must be written to a new file along with the modified record.

Records in an indexed file are organized randomly by a key value. A key is one or more fixed locations in the record. A record in an indexed file may be read randomly by specifying a key number and a value for the key. After reading a record randomly, it can then be read sequentially. Indexed records may be added, modified, or deleted without creating a new file.

A relative file contains records with a fixed-length and a cell number. Cell numbers are used to determine the relative position of a record, which is used for direct access. Records in a relative file may also be accessed sequentially.

## Directories

To facilitate organization of related files, VMS supports a special file known as a directory. A directory catalogs files by name and device location. Each directory file contains important information about the files it maintains: file name, file type, version number, and a pointer to the file's header.

Directories are developed in a tree-like structure, as shown in  Figure 5-1.

The names in brackets ([]) represent directories. The other names are files within the directory. Note that more than one subdirectory can reside in a directory.

## File Specification

Because a VAX computer system can contain thousands of files and directories, there must be a way for the VAX, and us, to distinguish between them. This is easily accomplished by assigning a unique

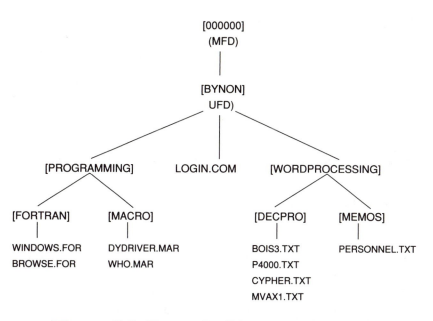

## Figure 5-1: Example Directory Structure

identifier, or name, to each directory and file. The complete name for any file is known as its file specification.

A complete file specification consists of a network node name, a device and directory name where the file resides, the file name, file type, and a version number of the file. This information is everything the operating system needs to locate and identify a file. VMS can find a file anywhere on a single computer or anywhere within a DECnet network with this information.

As shown in Figure 5-2, VMS will use default values for the node, device, and directory names if you do not supply them.

### Node Name
A node name identifies a computer system in a DECnet network. Network node names are one to six characters in length and are terminated by double colons (::). If you do not specify a node name, VMS assumes that the file is located on the local node. Of course, if your computer system is not in a DECnet network, there's no need to include the node name in a file specification.

## Figure 5-2: Full file specification

### Device Name

A device name indicates the physical device where the file is stored. Most commonly, this will be a magnetic disk, magnetic tape, or optical disk drive. The device name is a four character alphanumeric code that identifies the device type, the hardware controller to which the device is attached, and the unit number of the device on the controller. Device names are always terminated with a single colon (:). A VMS device name is specified in the following format:

ddcu

where dd is a device code that represents a device type, c is the controller number, and u is the device unit number. For instance, the device DUB2: specifies the third disk device on the second controller in the system.

If you omit the device name from a file specification, VMS assumes that you are referring to a file on your default device. VMS uses a file in the system account to determine which device is your default.

### Directory Name

A directory name specifies the name of the directory that contains the file. Directory names are always enclosed in brackets ([]). If you omit the directory name from a file specification, VMS will assume that you are referring to your default directory.

### File Name

The file name identifies a file within a directory. It may contain up to 39 alphanumeric characters and select punctuation characters, such as the underscore and dollar sign.

## File Type

A file type is a name or code consisting of up to 39 alphanumeric characters. Generally, it indicates the type of information stored in the file. You may supply a file type of your choice, but some system programs and utilities supply three character default file types.

## Version Number

The file version number is a one- to five-digit number that the system assigns to a file by default. When a file is created, the system assigns it a version number of 1. Each time the file is edited or another version of it is created, the version number is automatically incremented by 1.

## Rules for Assigning File Specifications

The components of a file specification must be separated with punctuation characters recognized by VMS. By observing a few simple rules when you create files, you'll have no difficulty with invalid file specifications. The components and the punctuation separators that must follow them are:

**Node name** .......................... double colon (::)
**Device name** ....................... single colon (:)
**Directory name** ................ left and right brackets ( [ ... ] )
**File name** ........................... period (.)
**File type** ........................... semicolon (;)

No blank spaces are allowed within any portion of a file specification. You can use an underscore (_), hyphen (-), or dollar sign ($) character to simulate a blank space or separator as necessary.

You may use any alphanumeric character within a file specification. However, each element of a file specification cannot exceed the maximum allowable length as indicated below:

**Node name** .......................... One to six characters
**Device name** ....................... Four to seven characters
**Directory name** ................ One to 39 characters
**Subdirectory name** ........... One to 39 characters
**File name** ........................... Zero to 39 characters

**File type** .............................Zero to 39 characters
**Version number** ................Integer from 1 and 32,767

## Creating Files

The most versatile way to create or modify a file is with an interactive text editor, such as EVE or EDT. There are several other methods, such as with the CREATE command.

The CREATE command produces a file from text entered through SYS$INPUT. To use CREATE, specify a file name as the parameter, then enter your text. You must press <RETURN> after each line entered. To end input, press <CTRL/Z>. For example:

```
$ CREATE WHO_FILES.COM
WHO.FOR, GETJPI.FOR, COMMON.FOR
<CTRL/Z>
$
```

When you press <CTRL/Z>, the file will be created, and your prompt will return. This file creation method is quick and easy for making small files, such as the one above, which might be used to assist you with other commands:

```
$ FORTRAN
$WHO_FILES
$ LINK @WHO_FILES
```

The COPY command may also be used to create a file. Unlike CREATE, however, COPY creates a new file from the contents of one or more existing files. In the example, a user's login command procedure is created from a template in the system manager's directory:

```
$ COPY SYS$MANAGER:TEMPLATE_LOGIN.COM -
_$ USER$DISK:[SHIPMAN]LOGIN.COM
```

In the example above, a copy of TEMPLATE_LOGIN.COM is placed in a new directory with a different name.

Also, the COPY command is used to append two or more files to create a new one. To do so, separate the source file names with commas.

## Table 5-2: Create File Commands

| Create File Operation | DCL Command |
| --- | --- |
| Create a file from keyboard input | CREATE file_spec<br>COPY SYS$INPUT file_spec |
| Duplicate a file | COPY source_file dest_file |
| Overwrite an existing file | COPY/OVERLAY<br>COPY/REPLACE |
| Copy files | |
|     By date | COPY/BEFORE[=time]<br>COPY/CREATED[=time]<br>COPY/MODIFIED[=time]<br>COPY/SINCE[=time] |
|     By exception | COPY/EXCLUDE=(file_spec) |
|     By flag | COPY/BACKUP/-<br>BEFORE[=time]<br>COPY/BACKUP/SINCE[=time]<br>COPY/EXPIRED-<br>/BEFORE[=time]<br>COPY/EXPIRED/SINCE[=time] |
|     With protection | COPY/PROTECTION=(code) |

## Modifying Files

The RENAME command defines a new name for a file and optionally relocates it to a different directory. Files may be renamed to any directory on the volume on which they are stored, but not to another volume. The first RENAME example changes the name of the file LOGIN.COM to LOGIN.SAV. The second example moves LOGIN.COM to a new directory:

```
$ RENAME LOGIN.COM LOGIN.SAV
$ RENAME LOGIN.COM [BYNON.PROCEDURES]
```

The APPEND command allows us to concatenate, or string together, files. The source file is appended to the target without creating a new version.

Table 5-3 shows file modification commands.

## Table 5-3: File Modification Commands

| Modify File Operation | DCL Command |
|---|---|
| Change file name | RENAME old_name new_name |
| By date | RENAME/BEFORE[=time]<br>RENAME/CREATED[=time]<br>RENAME/SINCE[=time]<br>RENAME/MODIFIED[=time] |
| By flag | RENAME/BACKUP/BEFORE[=time]<br>RENAME/BACKUP/SINCE[=time]<br>RENAME/EXPIRED/BEFORE[=time]<br>RENAME/EXPIRED/SINCE[=time] |
| By owner | RENAME/BY_OWNER[=uic] |
| Concatenate files | APPEND input_file output_file |
| By date | APPEND/BEFORE[=time]<br>APPEND/CREATED[=time]<br>APPEND/MODIFIED[=time]<br>APPEND/SINCE[=time] |
| By exception | APPEND/EXCLUDE=(file_spec) |
| By flag | APPEND/BACKUP/BEFORE[=time]<br>APPEND/BACKUP/SINCE[=time]<br>APPEND/EXPIRED/BEFORE[=time]<br>APPEND/EXPIRED/SINCE[=time] |
| With protection | APPEND/PROTECTION=(code) |

## Deleting and Purging Files

To remove a file from a directory, use the DELETE command. You must supply a specific file name, file type, and version number when you use this command. If not, the system will return an error message.

There are two exceptions to this rule: You can use the asterisk wildcard instead of the version number and/or file type, and you can delete the most recent version of a file by specifying a semicolon instead of the version number. If you delete many files using wildcard characters, you should use the qualifier /CONFIRM to confirm each deletion.

```
$ DELETE /CONFIRM *.COM;*
SYS$MANAGER:LTLOAD.COM;1 delete? [N]:
    .
    .
    .
SYS$MANAGER:SYSTARTUP.COM;12 delete? [Y]:
$
```

Also, you might want to have the file completely erased from disk. The /ERASE qualifier will perform this function for you.

The PURGE command is used to delete old versions of a file. By default, the PURGE command erases all but the most recent version of a file. Specified without a parameter, PURGE will delete all files:

```
$ PURGE
```

If you provide a file specification parameter, you cannot specify a version number. This example will purge all files in the default directory with a file type of .DAT:

```
$ PURGE *.DAT
```

If you want to retain several of the most recent versions of a file, use the /KEEP qualifier:

```
$ PURGE/KEEP=2
```

The /KEEP qualifier tells PURGE to retain $x$ number of old versions.

Table 5-4 lists deletion commands.

## Table 5-4: File Deletion Commands

| Delete File Operation | DCL Command |
|---|---|
| Delete a specific file | DELETE file_spec |
|     By date | DELETE/BEFORE[=time] |
| | DELETE/CREATED[=time] |
| | DELETE/MODIFIED[=time] |
| | DELETE/SINCE[=time] |
|     By exception | DELETE/EXCLUDE=(file_spec) |
|     By flag | DELETE/BACKUP/BEFORE[=time] |
| | DELETE/BACKUP/SINCE[=time] |
| | DELETE/EXPIRED/BEFORE[=time] |
| | DELETE/EXPIRED/SINCE[=time] |
|     By owner | DELETE/BY_OWNER=(uic) |
| Delete old versions | PURGE [file_spec] |
|     By date | PURGE/BEFORE[=time] |
| | PURGE/CREATED[=time] |
| | PURGE/MODIFIED[=time] |
| | PURGE/SINCE[=time] |
|     By exception | PURGE/EXCLUDE=(file_spec) |
|     By flag | PURGE/BACKUP/BEFORE[=time] |
| | PURGE/BACKUP/SINCE[=time] |
| | PURGE/EXPIRED/BEFORE[=time] |
| | PURGE/EXPIRED/SINCE[=time] |
|     By owner | PURGE/BY_OWNER=(uic) |
| Overwrite data on disk | DELETE/ERASE |
| | PURGE/ERASE |

## Printing and Displaying Files

The PRINT command is used to produce a printed copy of a file. When you issue a PRINT command, your print job is sent to a printer queue for execution. The print queue takes each job, in turn, and sends it to the printer.

There are three types of print queues:

- **Terminal queue** – a print queue assigned to a spooled terminal port.

- **Printer queue** – a queue assigned to a high-speed printing device.

- **Generic queue** – an input queue that distributes jobs to printers with like characteristics. A generic queue holds jobs until an assigned printer queue becomes available.

When you submit a file to a print queue, the system displays an information message. This message indicates the name of the print job, the name of the queue to which it has been submitted, and the queue entry number assigned to your print job. A typical informational message is:

```
$ PRINT STARTQ.COM
 Job STARTQ (queue SYS$PRINT, entry 52) started on SYS$PRINT
```

The default print queue is called SYS$PRINT. If you do not specify a queue name, your job will be sent to the default print queue. A queue is specified with the /QUEUE qualifier:

```
$ PRINT CHAPTER_1.MEM /QUEUE=SYS$LASER
```

After submitting jobs to be printed, you can check the progress with the commands SHOW ENTRY (VMS V5 only) or SHOW QUEUE. For example:

```
$ SHOW ENTRY
```

| Jobname | Username | Entry | Blocks Status |
|---------|----------|-------|---------------|
| CHAPTER_1 | BYNON 53 | 87 | Printing On  SYS$LASER |

```
$
```

The queue entry number is important if you decide to abort the job.

The queue entry number is used with the DELETE command to remove the job from the queue:

$ DELETE/ENTRY=53 SYS$LASER

If your system is part of a DECnet network, you can print on a remote system in two steps:

1. Copy the file you want printed to the remote node.

2. Use the /REMOTE qualifier on your print command. Be aware, however, that remote printing always gets queued to the default print queue.

It's often useful to view ASCII text files on your terminal. The TYPE command provides this function. The TYPE command sends, and optionally pages, text files to your display for viewing. Use the /PAGE qualifier to view a file one page at a time. For example:

$ TYPE/PAGE CHAPTER_1.TXT

Table 5-5 lists print commands.

## Master File Directory and User File Directories

All disk volumes have a main directory structure, called the master file directory (MFD); these are used to maintain user file directories (UFDs) and system file directories (SFDs). Typically, the system manager configures the MFD to suit the needs of the system. The MFD is referenced by the directory name [000000].

For each user account, the system manager establishes a UFD. In most cases, the UFD name is the same as the user's account name, i.e., if your name is WILLIAMS, your UFD is [WILLIAMS]. The UFD and disk volume name, together, are a user's default login area.

## Creating Directories and Subdirectories

Seven subdirectory levels may be created beneath a UFD of SFD; there may be nine directory levels total. The ability to create and use subdirectories allows you to set up many workspaces to organize information.

Each subdirectory has a corresponding directory file. Directory files are identified by the file type .DIR. These files are used exclusively by

VMS FILES-11 to catalog the contents of the directory. You cannot store data in a directory file yourself. Basically, all you can do to directory files is create and delete them.

The CREATE/DIRECTORY command is used to make a new directory or subdirectory. In our example, a SFD called PRODUCTS is created:

$ CREATE/DIRECTORY SYS$SYSDEVICE:[PRODUCTS]

## Table 5-5: Print Commands

| Print File Operation | DCL Command |
| --- | --- |
| Print file | PRINT file_spec |
| Print copies by file | PRINT/COPIES=n |
| By specified file | PRINT file_spec/COPIES=n |
| Print x pages | PRINT/PAGES=n |
| Print with notification | PRINT/NOTIFY |
| Controlled printing | PRINT/AFTER<br>PRINT/HOLD |
| List print jobs | SHOW/ENTRY |
| Abort print jobs<br>and stop queue | STOP/ABORT |
| Abort and requeue | STOP/REQUEUE |
| Delete job | DELETE/ENTRY |
| Display file on screen<br>　With paging | TYPE file_spec<br>TYPE/PAGE |

To create a subdirectory within a UFD or SFD, you must specify the directory path or have the default directory set to the correct path. In this example, a subdirectory called VMS is created in the SFD directory PRODUCTS:

$ CREATE/DIRECTORY SYS$SYSDEVICE:[PRODUCTS.VMS]

## Listing a File Directory

To list files in a directory, use the DIRECTORY command:

$ DIRECTORY SYS$SYSDEVICE:[PRODUCTS]

Directory BIFF$DUA0:[PRODUCTS]

VMS.DIR;1

Total of 1 file.

The DIRECTORY command has many qualifiers that allow us to be selective about the directory listing and the information presented. Some of the most useful DIRECTORY command qualifiers are:

**/SIZE**..............................................Indicates the size of each file in blocks.
**/OWNER** .....................................Shows the UIC of the file.
**/PROTECTION** ..........................Displays the protection code of a file.

## Setting a Default Directory

The DCL command SET DEFAULT is used to specify a new default working directory:

$ SET DEFAULT SYS$SYSDEVICE:[PRODUCTS]

The corresponding SHOW DEFAULT command is used to display your current default directory:

$ SHOW DEFAULT
  SYS$SYSDEVICE:[PRODUCTS]
$

When moving to a subdirectory of the directory you're in, you only need to specify the subdirectory name. VMS will use the default path for the rest:

$ SET DEFAULT [.VMS]

```
$ SHOW DEFAULT
  SYS$SYSDEVICE:[PRODUCTS.VMS]
$
```

To return to the parent directory of your default (i.e., move up one level), use:

```
$ SHOW DEFAULT
  SYS$SYSDEVICE:[PRODUCTS.VMS]
$ SET DEFAULT [-]
$ SHOW DEFAULT
  SYS$SYSDEVICE:[PRODUCTS]
$
```

## Deleting Directories and Subdirectories

When you no longer need a directory or subdirectory, you should delete it from the disk. Directory files are removed in three steps:

1. Delete all the files in the subdirectory, or copy them to another subdirectory.

2. Set the protection code on the target subdirectory so that the owner may delete it.

3. Use the DELETE command to delete the subdirectory file.

For example:

```
$ DELETE SYS$SYSDEVICE:[PRODUCTS.VMS]*.*;*
$ SET PROTECTION=O:RWED
  SYS$SYSDEVICE:[PRODUCTS]VMS.DIR;1
$ DELETE SYS$SYSDEVICE:[PRODUCTS]VMS.DIR;1
```

The file protection code on the subdirectory must be set because, by default, a subdirectory is protected against inadvertent deletion by its owner.

Table 5-6 shows directory commands.

## File and Directory Wildcards

VMS supports the use of wildcard characters in DCL commands that perform file and directory operations. A wildcard is a special character used to match part or all of a file specification. Using

## Table 5-6: Directory Commands

| Directory Operations | DCL Command |
|---|---|
| List directory | DIRECTORY |
| List directory | |
|     By date | DIRECTORY/BEFORE[=time] |
| | DIRECTORY/CREATED[=time] |
| | DIRECTORY/MODIFIED[=time] |
| | DIRECTORY/SINCE[=time] |
|     By exception | DIRECTORY/EXCLUDE=(file_spec) |
|     By flag | DIRECTORY/BACKUP/BEFORE[=time] |
| | DIRECTORY/BACKUP/SINCE[=time] |
| | DIRECTORY/EXPIRED/BEFORE[=time] |
| | DIRECTORY/EXPIRED/SINCE[=time] |
|     By owner | DIRECTORY/BY_OWNER=(uic) |
|     To device | DIRECTORY/OUTPUT=file_spec |
| | DIRECTORY/PRINTER |
| Set default directory | SET DEFAULT device:[directory] |
| Make directory | CREATE/DIRECTORY device:[directory] |
| Alternate UIC | CREATE/DIRECTORY/OWNER_UIC[option] |
| With protection | CREATE/DIRECTORY/PROTECTION=(code) |
| Limited versions | CREATE/DIRECTORY/VERSION_LIMIT=n |

wildcard characters saves you time and keystrokes. It often lets you apply a single DCL command to multiple files and directories at one time.

## File Matching Wildcards

Two wildcard characters are supported for the file name portion of a file specification: the asterisk (*) and the percent sign (%). The asterisk can be used as a substitute for the file name, file type, and slash, or version number portions of a file specification. The percent sign is valid only within the file name and/or the file type. The percent sign acts as a substitute for an individual character position within either of these portions of a file specification.

To see how the asterisk wildcard character works, assume you have a number of files in a directory that you want to delete. Now, instead of repetitively entering a DELETE command for each file, you could enter:

$ DELETE *.*;*

Using this command, all files in the directory would be deleted so be careful! The asterisk wildcard character is a valid substitute for the file name, file type, and the version number.

The % wildcard character allows you be more selective. Use the percent wildcard when you want to specify all files that contain a single character in a given position. The % identifies the position that is to be wildcarded. For example:

$ TYPE/PAGE CHAPTER_%.TXT

Here, the files named CHAPTER_1.TXT through CHAPTER_9.TXT would be paged to the display.

## Directory Searching Wildcards

Two characters are supported as directory search wildcards: the ellipsis (...) and the hyphen (-). The ellipsis wildcard permits you to search down a hierarchy of directories. The ellipsis may be specified:

• After a directory specification:

$ DIRECTORY [SYS0...]*.COM

• Before a directory specification:

$ TYPE [...MACRO]WHO.MAR

• In place of a directory specification:

$ DELETE [...]*.LOG;*

The hyphen wildcard permits you to search up through a directory hierarchy. Each hyphen represents the next higher directory. With hyphens, you can move up a directory and then back down another path:

$ DIRECTORY [-]

The hyphen and ellipsis may be used together, i.e., DIRECTORY [-...].

In addition, the file specification wildcards may be used when specifying a directory name. For instance, to list the contents of an entire directory, you could use this command:

$ DIRECTORY [*...]

## LOGICAL NAMES

A VMS logical name is a substitute name for a full or partial file specification, a character string, or another logical name. After it has been defined, a logical name may be used in place of its equivalence name. Logical names provide two important features: file and device name independence, and file specification shorthand.

### File and Device Independence

The term file and device independence means that you are not bound to a physical device name, e.g., DUA1:, LCA0:, TXC7:. VMS allows you to achieve this independence through logical names associated with input/output operations.

To illustrate why device independence is so important, let's look at an example. Assume that you're the manager of a large VAX system that supports 500 users. As the system manager, it's your responsibility to establish accounts for each user. A VMS account defines, among other things, the disk on which each user will store his files. If you establish an account using a physical device name, such as DUA0: or DJA1:, the user is locked into that device. What happens if a user disk fails?

If you use logical names, the logical name can be reassigned to a new physical device. User files can then be restored to the new device, and the system will be operational again.

On the other hand, if you use physical device names, you must change each user account assigned to the failed disk. On a large system, this would be a long and tedious task.

### Shorthand

If you use files nested deep into subdirectories, with long names, you can define a meaningful logical name to represent the full file specification. Such names are faster to type and easier to remember than the full file specification.

### Defining Logical Names

The DEFINE command is used to create logical names. The following example associates the logical name SYS$PRODUCTS with the equivalence name $1$DUA12:[PRODUCTS].

```
$ DEFINE SYS$PRODUCTS $1$DUA12:[PRODUCTS]
```

You can now use the name SYS$PRODUCTS anywhere you would make reference to the directory specification.

If the logical name is to represent a device, such as a tape or disk drive, indicate so by terminating the equivalence name with a colon:

```
$ DEFINE $MODEM1 TXB0:
$ DEFINE USER$DISK BIFF$DUA2:
```

If you define a partial file specification, it must be the first part (left side), and it must be separated from the rest of the file specification with a colon. For example:

```
$ DEFINE COM USER$DISK:[FRED]*.COM
```

A logical name, such as this one, could be used in conjunction with the DIRECTORY command (e.g., $DIRECTORY COM) to list all command procedure files in the directory USER$DISK:[FRED].

### Displaying Logical Names

The DCL command SHOW LOGICAL displays logical name translations:

```
$ SHOW LOGICAL SYS$LOGIN
  "SYS$LOGIN" = "USER$DISK:[BYNON]" (LNM$JOB_806A6)
```

Here, LNM$JOB_nnn indicates that this logical name resides in job (as opposed to the system or group) logical name table. Use the SHOW LOGICAL command without parameters or qualifiers to list all four logical name tables. To list an individual logical name table, specify the qualifier /SYSTEM, /GROUP, /JOB, or /PROCESS (i.e., default) as appropriate.

Another DCL command, SHOW TRANSLATION, performs a similar function to the SHOW LOGICAL command. This command returns the translation string for a logical name:

```
$ SHOW TRANSLATION SYS$DISK
  SYS$DISK = "USER$DISK:" (LNM$PROCESS_TABLE)
```

Unlike SHOW LOGICAL, however, the SHOW TRANSLATION command displays only the first translation found.

## Deassigning Logical Names

Logical names are deassigned (i.e., deleted from logical name tables) with the DEASSIGN command:

```
$ DEASSIGN SYS$PRODUCTS
```

Logical names in your process and job logical name table are deleted when you log out or when your process is terminated by some other means.

## Logical Name Tables

Logical names are defined by users and the system. When defined, logical names are maintained in one of four logical name tables:

- Process logical name table
- Job logical name table
- Group logical name table
- System logical name table

Unless specified otherwise, the logical names you create in your process (i.e., login session) are entered in your process logical name table. Process and job logical name tables are private and volatile.

The logical names in these tables are accessible only to the process that creates them, and they are deleted when the process terminates. System and group logical name tables are sharable with other system users, and their definitions remain until the system is rebooted.

### The Process Logical Name Table

Your process logical name table (LNM$PROCESS_TABLE) holds logical names that are available to your process and its subprocesses only. The table is created for you by VMS when you log in. Additionally, VMS defines several logical names in your process table, which are used as defaults by your process. These default logical names are described in Table 5-7. The logical name LNM$PROCESS is defined to reference this table.

### The Job Logical Name Table

Your job logical name table, LNM$JOB_nnn (nnn is the job information block address), maintains logical names that are available to all processes in your job tree. Like your process logical name table, the job table receives several logical names defined by VMS when you log in. The default job logical names are defined in Table 5-8. To access your job logical name table, use the logical name LNM$JOB, which is defined by VMS when you log in.

### The Group Logical Name Table

The group logical name table maintains logical name definitions for users of the same UIC group number. Group tables are named LNM$GROUP_nnn, where nnn is the UIC group number. The logical name LNM$GROUP may be used to access your respective group table.

To create and delete names in a group table, you must have the privileges GRPPRV and GRPNAM, or the SYSPRV privilege.

### The System Logical Name Table

The system logical name table maintains public logical names, i.e., they are available to all users of the system. The system logical name table, called LNM$SYSTEM_TABLE, may be referenced by its logical name LNM$SYSTEM. To create and delete entries in this table, you must have the SYSNAM and SYSPRV privileges.

## Table 5-7: Default Process Logical Names

| Logical Name | Description |
|---|---|
| SYS$COMMAND | The initial file from which DCL gets its input, i.e., the input stream. SYS$COMMAND is usually defined as the user's keyboard but may be redirected. |
| SYS$DISK | The default disk established at login time. This logical name is updated by the SET DEFAULT command. |
| SYS$ERROR | The default file or device to which DCL writes error messages. |
| SYS$INPUT | The default file from which DCL gets input. |
| SYS$NET | The logical link established by a source process using the task-to-task communication facility of DECnet. |
| SYS$OUTPUT | The default file or output device to which DCL writes output. |
| TT | The default device name for your terminal line. |

## Logical Name Directory Tables

VMS provides two logical name directory tables to catalog logical name tables:

**LNM$PROCESS_DIRECTORY** — Catalogs process logical name tables.
**LNM$SYSTEM_DIRECTORY** — Catalogs shareable logical name
tables.

Each of these directories contains logical names which translate to
logical name table names, i.e., LNM$SYSTEM_TABLE,
LNM$GROUP_TABLE, etc. You can display the contents of the
directory tables with the SHOW LOGICAL/STRUCTURE command.

### User-defined Logical Name Tables
You can create your own logical name tables, to categorize logical
names, using the CREATE/NAME_TABLE command. When you create a
logical name table, it will be cataloged in one of the two directory
logical name tables (either process or system) as specified by the

## Table 5-8: Default Job Logical Names

| Job Logical Name | Description |
| --- | --- |
| SYS$LOGIN | Your default login device and directory. |
| SYS$LOGIN_DEVICE | Your default login device. |
| SYS$REM_ID | For DECnet initiated jobs, the process ID of the remote process that originated the job. If proxy logins are in use, the logical name will be the process' user name. |
| SYS$REM_NODE | For DECnet initiated jobs, the name of the DECnet node from which the job was originated. |
| SYS$SCRATCH | The default device and directory to which temporary files are written. |

/PARENT_TABLE qualifier. In the example, a logical name table called DATABASES is created under the SYSTEM logical name table:

```
$ CREATE/NAME_TABLE DATABASES /PARENT_TABLE=LNM$SYSTEM
$ DEFINE/TABLE=DATABASES LABELS $1$DUA3:[MAILING]LABELS.DAT
$ SHOW LOGICAL/TABLE=DATABASES LABELS
  "LABELS" = "$1$DUA3:[MAILING]LABELS.DAT" (DATABASES)
```

To delete a user-defined logical name table, specify the logical name table directory that contains it. The following example shows how to delete the DATABASES logical name table:

```
$ DEASSIGN/TABLE=LNM$SYSTEM_DIRECTORY DATABASES
```

## Defining Logical Name Access Modes

The four VMS operating system access modes (i.e., user, supervisor, executive, and kernel) can be applied to logical names. The default access mode is supervisor mode. Kernel mode logical names are defined by VMS and privileged programs only. User mode and executive mode logical names have special characteristics.

Logical names created in user mode are temporary; they exist for the execution of one image only. This feature is useful when redirecting terminal output for a single command:

```
$ DEFINE/USER_MODE SYS$OUTPUT SYSGEN.LIS
$ MCR SYSGEN
SYSGEN> LIST/MAJOR
SYSGEN> EXIT
$ TYPE/PAGE SYSGEN.LIS
  .
  .
  .
$
```

Executive mode logical names are used by privileged images. Privileged images, such as MAIL, PHONE, and LOGINOUT, bypass user and supervisor mode logical names. For this reason, when defining systemwide logical names for devices, they should be defined in executive mode:

```
$ DEFINE /SYSTEM/EXECUTIVE_MODE USER$DISK SKIP$DUA1:
$ DEFINE /SYSTEM/EXECUTIVE_MODE SYS$MODEM TXC0:
```

Defining logical names in executive mode requires SYSPRV privilege. Table 5-9 shows logical name commands.

## RMS Search Lists

A record management services (RMS) search list is a logical name that specifies two or more equivalence names. Typically, the search list defines disks and directories, but it may be any file specification. It is used as a list of places to look. It is not a wildcard.

The most common use of the RMS search list is to define two or more directories as a single logical name. For example:

```
$ DEFINE GUIDES USER$DISK:[BYNON.GUIDES], -
_$ USER$DISK:[SHIPMAN.GUIDES]
$ DIRECTORY GUIDES

Directory of $1$DUA2:[BYNON.GUIDES]

  .
  .
  .

Total of 23 files.

Directory of $1$DUA2:[SHIPMAN.GUIDES]

  .
  .
  .

Total of 37 files.
$
```

This technique is used to define cluster-common system disks, as you can see by examining the logical name SYS$SYSROOT:

```
$ SHOW LOGICAL SYS$SYSROOT
"SYS$SYSROOT" = "LIZ$DUA0:[SYS4.]" (LNM$SYSTEM)
 = "SYS$COMMON:"
1 "SYS$COMMON" = "LIZ$DUA0:[SYS4.SYSCOMMON.]" (LNM$SYSTEM)
```

When using search lists to perform file operations, the first matching file specification found in the search list will be used. The RUN command, however, is an exception. When you use a search list with the RUN command, RUN checks to see if any of the images matching the file specification are installed images. It runs the first file found in the search list that is an installed image.

## Table 5-9: Logical Name Commands

| Logical Name Operation | DCL Command |
| --- | --- |
| Create logical name table | CREATE/NAME_TABLE table_name |
| Create logical name | DEFINE logical_name equiv_string |
| By table | DEFINE/PROCESS (default)<br>DEFINE/JOB<br>DEFINE/GROUP<br>DEFINE/SYSTEM<br>DEFINE/TABLE=table_name |
| By access mode | DEFINE/USER_MODE<br>DEFINE/EXECUTIVE_MODE<br>DEFINE/SUPERVISOR_MODE |
| List logical names | SHOW LOGICAL logical_name<br>SHOW TRANSLATION logical_name |
| By table | SHOW LOGICAL/PROCESS (default)<br>SHOW LOGICAL/JOB<br>SHOW LOGICAL/GROUP<br>SHOW LOGICAL/SYSTEM<br>SHOW LOGICAL/TABLE=table_name |
| Delete logical name | DEASSIGN logical_name |
| By table | DEASSIGN/PROCESS (default)<br>DEASSIGN/JOB<br>DEASSIGN/GROUP<br>DEASSIGN/SYSTEM<br>DEASSIGN/ALL<br>DEASSIGN/TABLE=table_name |

## VMS TEXT EDITORS

A text editor is a utility used to enter text from your terminal into a file. It can also be used to make alterations or corrections to an existing file. A text editor is similar to a word processor in that it allows you to insert, delete, rearrange, and correct text in a file. Files you create and edit with VMS text editors can be used in the following ways:

- To create command procedures

- As input to a compiler or assembler

- To create mail messages

- As a text file to be printed as is

- As a text file to be processed by a text processing utility.

VMS comes with two standard text editors, TPU and EDT. EDT, the standard text editor for many years, is the most widely known. TPU is gaining in popularity because of its advanced programmable features.

## THE EDT EDITOR

EDT is an easy-to-use, general purpose text editor. Its output is a standard ASCII file. EDT gives you the capability to work on multiple files simultaneously.

EDT has three edit modes. It gives you the ability to redefine keys to suit your needs, and the ability to create EDT start-up files. These files will allow you to set the specific editing characteristics you desire before starting an editing session.

The EDT editor also has an automatic backup facility. During an editing session, a journal file is created. This file stores all the keystrokes that you enter during an editing session. It can be used to restore or recover text that was lost because of a system crash or an improperly terminated editing session.

### Starting an EDT Session

To start an EDT edit session, use one of the following commands:

$ EDIT FILENAME
or
$ EDIT/EDT FILENAME

When you do this, EDT will establish a working space for your file called a main buffer (MAIN). A journal file buffer is also opened at this time. Both buffers typically require 80 blocks of disk space, so you must have a minimum of 160 free blocks in your account to use EDT effectively. A smaller buffer called PASTE is opened if the appropriate commands are issued, and you can create additional buffers to store segments of text if desired.

If you are using EDT to create a new file, the editor will respond with:

Input file does not exist
[EOB]
*

The first line of this display informs you that no text was copied to the main buffer. The [EOB] symbol shows you where the end of the file is. The asterisk, on the third line, is the EDT line mode prompt.

If you are editing an existing file, it is not changed by EDT. A copy of the file will be created and loaded into the main buffer. This is where text manipulation takes place. The copy in the main buffer does not become an actual file until you end your editing session with the EDT EXIT command.

You can move the cursor throughout the text using the four arrow keys. Each key moves the cursor in the direction indicated by the arrow: left, right, up, or down. Left and right cursor movement is character by character, while up and down movement is line by line.

## EDT Editing Modes

EDT has three modes: line, keypad, and nokeypad. Because EDT is a full-screen editor, the more powerful editing commands are found in the keypad mode.

Keypad mode is used on DEC (and DEC compatible) video terminals. It involves moving the cursor within a 22-line window of text that is displayed on the screen. In keypad mode, the cursor can be moved to any location in the text window. This allows you to insert, change, or delete text displayed anywhere on the screen.

EDT's nokeypad mode allows you to perform screen editing at a video terminal that does not have a numeric keypad. In nokeypad mode, text appears in the upper portion of the screen, and your editing commands are displayed at the bottom of the screen as you enter them. Pressing <RETURN> causes nokeypad EDT to invoke your commands.

Line mode is normally used on hardcopy (i.e., printing) terminals. It consists of about a dozen commands used to change individual lines of text.

## EDT Keypad Mode Editing

Keypad mode EDT gives you the ability to insert, delete, copy, substitute, and rearrange text at a number of entity levels, including character, word, line, paragraph, page, sentence, and buffer. Keypad mode editing is often referred to as screen-mode editing. This is because keypad mode enables you to edit text anywhere on the terminal screen, not just on a specific line of text.

When you use EDT's keypad mode, text is entered directly into EDT's main buffer as you type. The cursor on the terminal screen indicates exactly where characters will be placed, and the display is constantly updated as text is inserted or deleted.

You can move the cursor around the screen using the keyboard arrow keys, or using the keypad commands TOP, BOTTOM, CHARACTER, WORD, LINE, EOL (end of line), and PAGE.

To enter EDT's keypad mode, invoke the editor and type CHANGE or C at the asterisk prompt. On a Digital VT terminal, the first 22 lines of text will be displayed. If you are creating a new file, the [EOB] symbol will appear in the upper left hand corner of the screen.

Occasionally, you might receive the prompt C*. This is EDT's way of telling you the terminal you're using is not compatible, or that it's not configured correctly. If you're using a DEC VT terminal or a true compatible, you solve this problem by entering one of the following DCL commands:

$SET TERMINAL/INQUIRE

or

$SET TERMINAL VT100

You may now begin inserting text by typing it at the keyboard. Each time you press <RETURN>, you create a new line. As your screen fills, the lines automatically scroll upward. To modify or manipulate text in keypad mode, use the numeric keypad.

If a message is sent (i.e., broadcasted from the system manager) to your terminal screen during an editing session, the message will not be included in your text file. This informational message displayed on your screen will write over a portion of the text you're editing. Although distracting, these messages can be erased by pressing <CTRL/W> to refresh the screen.

If you want to switch from keypad mode to line mode EDT, to enter a series of line mode commands, press <CTRL/Z>. You will receive the line mode asterisk prompt.

## The EDT Keypad

The EDT keypad consists of the numeric keypad, arrow keys, and the editing pad above the arrow keys, on LK201 keyboards only. Different functions are assigned to each key when you are using the EDT editor. Figure 5-3 displays the layout and function names of the EDT keypad for the LK201 (i.e., VT200 and VT300) keyboard. EDT keypad functions and keyboard keys are defined in Tables 5-10 and 5-11. Note that each key (except the <GOLD> key and the <HELP> key) has two functions. To select the GOLD function for a key, press and release the <GOLD> key, then press the desired function key.

In Table 5-10, key names followed by (G) indicate a <GOLD> key sequence. To invoke these keypad commands, the <GOLD> key must be pressed before pressing the keypad key, i.e., press <GOLD><BOTTOM> to go to the bottom of the file.

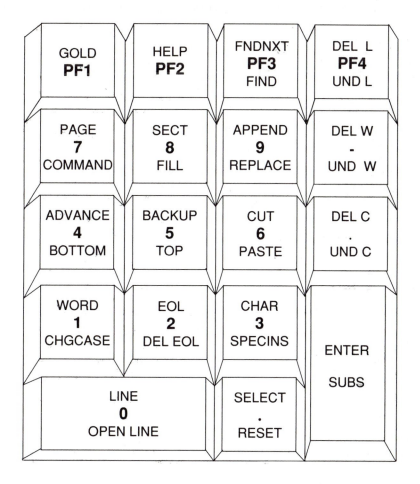

**Figure 5-3: LK201 EDT keypad**

## Table 5-10, EDT Keypad Mode
## Commands and Functions

| Keypad Key | Function |
| --- | --- |
| <ADVANCE> | Sets the cursor in its default mode. When EDT is in the ADVANCE mode, the cursor moves forward by character, word, line, or other entity. ADVANCE is the default mode; BACKUP is the alternate mode. |
| <APPEND> | Allows you to append the selected range to the end of the paste buffer. To use APPEND, SELECT each passage or text entity , then press <APPEND>. |
| <BACKUP> | Sets cursor movement in a backward direction. This is useful if you are at the bottom of a file and want to search for a phrase without first going back to the top of the file. |
| <BOTTOM>(G) | Moves the cursor to the end (bottom) of the file. |
| <CHAR> | Moves the cursor one character position in the current direction (ADVANCE or BACKUP). |
| <CHNGCASE>(G) | Changes the case (upper/lower) of the current character or selected range of characters. |

## Table 5-10, EDT Keypad Mode Commands and Functions (cont'd)

| Keypad Key | Function |
|---|---|
| <COMMAND>(G) | Lets you enter a line mode EDT command while you're in keypad mode. The prompt Command: will appear at the bottom left of the screen. At the prompt, enter a valid line mode command, then press <ENTER> (not <RETURN>). |
| <CUT> | Removes a portion of text previously selected with the SELECT command, and deposits it into the paste buffer. |
| <DEL C> | Deletes the character directly under the cursor. |
| <DEL L> | Deletes the current line to the right of the cursor. |
| <DEL W> | Deletes the current word to the right of the cursor. |
| <ENTER> | Used to terminate Command:, Search for:, and line mode commands. |
| <EOL> | (End Of Line) Moves the cursor to the end of the line on which it is positioned. |
| <FILL> | Formats the selected range of text by filling lines with as many whole words as possible. This may be necessary after changing the line width with the SET WRAP command. |

## Table 5-10, EDT Keypad Mode
## Commands and Functions (cont'd)

| Keypad Key | Function |
|---|---|
| <FIND>(G) | Used to locate text strings. At the bottom of the screen, the prompt Search for: appears. Type in the word or character string you want to find, then press <ENTER> (not <RETURN>). |
| <FINDNXT> | Used to find the next occurrence of a string specified with the FIND command. |
| <GOLD> | Used to initiate a GOLD key function. When pressed before pressing another keypad key, it specifies that key's alternate function. When the <GOLD> key is followed by an integer value, the next function will be repeated the specified number of times. |
| <HELP> | Gives you access to EDT's on-line HELP facility. |
| <LINE> | Moves the cursor to the beginning of the next line. |
| <OPENLINE> (G) | Terminates the line at the current cursor position. |
| <PASTE>(G) | Places the contents of the paste buffer into your text file, starting at the cursor position. The contents of the paste buffer are not affected by the PASTE command. The contents of the paste buffer will be altered by subsequent CUT or APPEND commands. |

## Table 5-10, EDT Keypad Mode
## Commands and Functions (cont'd)

| Keypad Key | Function |
| --- | --- |
| <REPLACE>(G) | Deletes a SELECTed range of text and replaces it with the contents of the PASTE buffer. |
| <RESET>(G) | Cancels the action of a GOLD KEY function, or any other key sequence, and sets EDT to the default (ADVANCE) cursor movement direction. It is also useful for canceling or unselecting a range of SELECTed text. |
| <SECT> | Advances the cursor to the next section (screen) in the file. The direction of the cursor is affected by current mode (ADVANCE or BACKUP). |
| <SELECT> | Specifies a range of text on which the keypad command will operate. To use SELECT, position the cursor at the beginning of the text to be selected, then press <SELECT>. Now move the cursor through the text you wish to select, using <ARROW>, <CHARACTER>, <WORD>, <EOL>, or <LINE> keys. The selected text will be highlighted in reverse video. Now, enter the command that you wish to apply to the SELECTed text. |

## Table 5-10, EDT Keypad Mode
## Commands and Functions (cont'd)

| Keypad Key | Function |
|---|---|
| <SPECINS> (G) | Allows you to enter special characters, such as <ESC>, into your text file. To enter a special character into a file, <ESC> for example, first determine its ASCII equivalent (<ESC> = 27), then enter the following command string: <GOLD> 27 <GOLD><SPECINS> |
| <SUBS> (G) | Replaces a range of selected text, or a text string found using <FIND> or <FINDNXT>, with the contents of paste buffer. |
| <TOP> (G) | Moves the cursor to the top of the file you are editing. |
| <WORD> | Moves the cursor one word forward or backward, depending on whether you're in advance or backup mode. |
| <UND C>(G) | Restores the last character deleted with the <DEL C> key at the current cursor location. |
| <UND L>(G) | Restores the last line deleted with the <DEL L> key at the current cursor location. |
| <UND W>(G) | Restores the last word deleted with the <DEL W> key at the current cursor location. |

EDT also recognizes several keyboard key and control keys. These functions are described in the following table.

## Table 5-11: EDT Keyboard and Control Keys

| Key Name | Function |
|---|---|
| \<F12\> | Moves the cursor to the beginning of the current line. |
| \<F13\> | Deletes all characters between the cursor and the beginning of the word. |
| \<RETURN\> | Inserts a line terminator at the current cursor position. |
| \<TAB\> | Moves the cursor to the next tab stop (inserts a horizontal tab character). |
| \<CTRL/A\> | Resets the current indentation level count. |
| \<CTRL/C\> | Aborts the current EDT command. |
| \<CTRL/E\> | Increments the tab indentation count by one. |
| \<CTRL/H\> | Same as \<F12\>. |
| \<CTRL/I\> | Same as \<TAB\>. |
| \<CTRL/J\> | Same as \<F13\>. |

## Table 5-11: EDT Keyboard and Control Keys (cont'd)

| Key Name | Function |
|----------|----------|
| <CTRL/L> | Inserts a form feed character. |
| <CTRL/U> | Deletes all characters between the cursor and the beginning of the line. |
| <CTRL/W> | Refreshes the display. |
| <CTRL/Z> | Changes the EDT mode from keypad to line mode. |

## Line Mode EDT

When you invoke EDT, you will automatically enter the line mode unless an EDTINI.EDT file is set up to do otherwise. Line mode is indicated by the EDT asterisk (*) prompt. All line mode commands are made at the asterisk prompt and are terminated by pressing <RETURN>. Lines that you input are sequentially numbered by the editor, and you can reference a line or group of lines based on these numbers.

Because EDT is generally used in the keypad mode, we'll briefly review EDT's line mode commands. When you are working with line mode EDT, you issue commands at the EDT asterisk prompt. A list of commonly used line mode EDT commands and their functions is presented in Table 5-12. Each command may be abbreviated to the character or characters shown in the parentheses. Complete information on all EDT line mode commands can be found in Digital documentation or through the use of the line mode EDT HELP command.

## Table 5-12: EDT Line Mode Commands

| EDT Command | Function |
| --- | --- |
| CHANGE (C) | Switches EDT from line to keypad mode. |
| COPY (CO) | Allows you to copy a line or group of lines from one portion of a text file to another. If you enter the command CO 5 to 10, line 5 will be copied to the line immediately preceding line 10. The command CO 5:10 to 20 would copy the contents of lines 5 through 10 into the area immediately preceding line 20. |
| DELETE (D) | Lets you to delete a line or group of lines from a text file. The command D13 would delete line 13 from your text file, while the command D13:30 would delete lines 13 through 30. |
| EXIT (EX) | Terminates your EDT editing session, saving all the changes that you have made to your file during this session. It also creates a new version of the file you have been editing. |
| HELP (H) | Provides on-line HELP on all EDT line mode commands. The HELP messages will not be included in the file that you are editing. HELP will give you more detailed information on the commands discussed in this section as well as those which were omitted, i.e., CLEAR, DEFINE, FILL, and JOURNAL. |

## Table 5-12: EDT Line Mode Commands (cont'd)

| EDT Command | Function |
| --- | --- |
| INCLUDE (INC) | Allows you to copy text from an external file into the file you are editing. This command is valuable if you frequently include stock or boilerplate text in the files you create. When you enter the EDT command INCLUDE filename.type during an editing session, filename.type is copied into the file you are editing. |
| INSERT (I) | Inserts specified text directly before the current position in the file. While you are inserting text (either directly from the keyboard or by referencing another file), you will not receive the EDT * prompt. Press <CTRL/Z> to return to the * prompt when you are finished inserting text. |
| MOVE (M) | Allows you to move a line or lines of text. Text will be moved to the area immediately preceding a specified line. For example, the command M 10:15 to 50 would move lines 10 through 15 to the area  immediately preceding line 50. Note: You cannot cut and paste with a line oriented editor. |

## Table 5-12: EDT Line Mode Commands (cont'd)

| EDT Command | Function |
| --- | --- |
| QUIT (QU) | Lets you exit EDT without saving any of the changes made during the editing session. No new version of the file is created, and the file remains as it was prior to the editing session. If you use the QUIT command on a file that you created during the current editing session, the file will be lost. If you exit EDT with the command QUIT/SAVE, a journal file will be provided. Using this journal file, you can recreate the changes that you made to an existing file. The journal file also permits you to restore a file that was created by an editing session. |
| REPLACE (R) | Deletes a specified line or group of lines, then enters the INSERT mode so you can add text in that space. The command R5:10 would delete lines 5 through 10 and switch to the INSERT mode to permit you to enter new text. To exit the REPLACE mode and receive the * prompt, press <CTRL/Z>. |
| RESEQUENCE (RES) | Renumbers all the lines in the file that you are editing, in increments of 1. This is useful because text insertion, movement, or deletion causes the file to lose decimal numeric sequence. For example, five lines inserted before line 50 would be numbered 49.01, 49.02, 49.03, 49.04, and 49.05. Resequencing eliminates the confusion that can result from numbering changes such as these. |

## Table 5-12: EDT Line Mode Commands (cont'd)

| EDT Command | Function |
|---|---|
| SUBSTITUTE (S) | Lets you substitute a new text element for an old one, in the format S/oldtext/newtext/range. The old and new text elements must be separated with slashes (/), and the range must be specified. |
| WRITE (WR) | Allows you to write a given range of text to a new file. An example of this command is WR HISTORY.TXT 50:100. Lines 50 through 100 of the file that you are editing will be written into a new file called HISTORY.TXT. This command has no effect on the file that you are editing. The command will only replicate the stated range of lines in an external file. |

### Exiting from an EDT Edit Session

To exit from an EDT editing session (to terminate keypad EDT normally), press <CTRL/Z>. This will put you into line mode. At the line mode asterisk prompt, type EXIT and press <RETURN>. EDT will terminate after writing a new output file containing the results of your editing session.

If you finish your editing session with the QUIT command or by typing <CTRL/Y>, the main buffer will be deleted, and you will be left with the original file. This file will not reflect any changes made to it during the editing session.

### EDT Start-up File

You can customize your EDT editing environment by writing a start-up command file. This file can contain any valid line mode commands. The file is read by the editor at the beginning of each editing session. By including the appropriate commands in the file, you can direct EDT to automatically set tab stops, word wrapping, and edit mode for you, as well as define special function keys.

System managers can consider defining a systemwide EDT start-up command file for all users. The EDT editor will search your default directory for your personal EDT start-up file (named EDTINI.EDT by default). If EDT finds a start-up file, it will execute the commands it contains.

Although a start-up command file can contain any commands available in line mode EDT, chances are that your file will consist of DEFINE KEY and SET commands. The following EDT start-up command file demonstrates some of the things you can do:

```
! EDTINI.EDT
!
! Function Key Definitions
!
! Exit and quit commands
!
DEFINE KEY GOLD E AS "EXT EXIT."
DEFINE KEY GOLD Q AS "EXT QUIT."
!
! Replace command
!
DEFINE KEY GOLD S AS "EXT S/?*"REPLACE: '/?*'   WITH: '/WHOLE."
!
! Write and include commands
!
DEFINE KEY GOLD W AS "EXT WRITE ?*"WRITE TO FILE: '."
DEFINE KEY GOLD X AS "EXT INCLUDE ?*"INCLUDE FILE: '."
!
SET QUIET
!
! Define entity delimiters
SET ENTITY WORD ' .,?!;:[]()<>*-+=/\'
SET ENTITY SENTENCE '. ?!'
!
! Set line wrap
SET WRAP 72
SET MODE CHANGE
```

This is an extremely simple example of a start-up command file. To create a more sophisticated EDT initiator, refer to Digital's documentation on the EDT editor.

### EDT Error Recovery

Whenever you're actively editing a file in EDT, a journal file is maintained by the editor. The journal file stores all the editing commands and text you have typed during the editing session. When you exit an editing session normally, your new file is saved and the journal file is deleted.

The journal file is used for recovery when your file is inadvertently lost through system failures or crashes, when you use <CTRL/Y> to exit from EDT, or by exceeding your disk quota while editing. To recover an EDT session using the journal file, enter the command:

$ EDIT/EDT/RECOVER file_spec

EDT will use the journal file to re-edit your file in exactly the same fashion and sequence as you did prior to the problem.  Do not touch the keyboard until the file is restored; just sit back and watch a high-speed replay of your editing session. You may, however, type <CTRL/O> to suppress the video display during the recovery procedure. This will speed the process of file recovery.

### EVE AND THE TEXT PROCESSING UTILITY (TPU)

TPU is a programmable text processing utility. It was designed for developing text editors, such as EDT. In fact, TPU is equipped with two working editors, Extensible VAX Editor (EVE), and an EDT emulator. TPU editors are invoked by defining the logical name TPUSECINI with the name of a SECINI file, such as EDTSECINI. EVE is the default TPU editor.

## Invoking EVE

To start an EVE editing session, invoke EVE with the command EDIT/
TPU. You must include the name of the file you want to edit or create.
For instance, if you want to edit the site specific start-up file, you
would enter the command:

$ EDIT/TPU SYSTARTUP_V5.COM

This command would load the existing file and display the following
status lines at the bottom of the display:

Buffer SYSTARTUP.COM                Insert    Forward

%TPU-S-FILEIN, 77 lines read from file SYSTARTUP_V5.COM;13

When you edit a file, EVE stores it in a work area called a buffer. The
buffer name (i.e., SYSTARTUP_V5.COM) and your current editing
modes are displayed in highlighted status line.

The contents of a buffer are displayed in an area of your screen called
a buffer window. All editing on the contents of the current buffer is
performed through the buffer windows. When you finish editing, you
tell EVE to save or throw away the edited buffer contents.

To save your editing session, use the EXIT command. Press <DO>,
type EXIT at the Command: prompt, then press <RETURN>. Or, you
may press <F10> or <CTRL/Z>, which both duplicate the EXIT
command. If you've made editing changes, EXIT will create a new
version of the file with your modifications. For example:

<DO>
Command: EXIT <RETURN>
$

To quit from an editing session without saving the changes, press
<DO>, type QUIT at the Command: prompt, then press <RETURN>.
EVE will prompt you for confirmation:

<DO>
Command: QUIT <RETURN>
Buffer modifications will not be saved, continue (Y or N)?

To continue quitting, press <Y>, then <RETURN>.

## Using the EVE Keypad

When you're in an EVE session, you may enter EVE commands to manipulate your text. This is done by pressing EVE keypad keys and by entering EVE commands. Figure 5-4 displays the keyboard layout for the VT200's and VT300's LK201 keyboard. Table 5-13 lists the EVE keypad functions.

## Using EVE Commands

In addition to using the EVE keypad, you can enter EVE commands. This is accomplished at the EVE Command: prompt, which is invoked by pressing <DO>. After typing your EVE command, press <RETURN> or <DO>.

Like DCL, EVE allows you to abbreviate and recall commands. EVE will store your last 20 commands and will accept any command that is unambiguous. Also, if you make a typing mistake, you can use the DCL editing keys to correct it, i.e., <CTRL/U> to erase the line, <CTRL/A> to toggle insert/overstrike mode, and so on. Tables 5-14 through 5-16 define the most frequently used EVE commands.

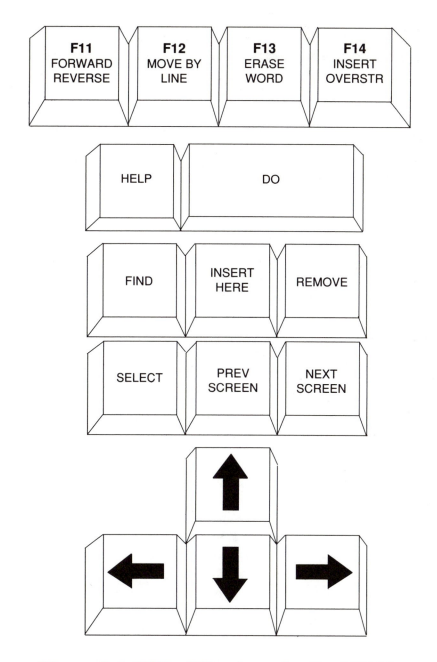

**Figure 5-4: EVE editing keys for the LK201**

## Table 5-13: EVE Keypad Functions

| Key Name | Function |
| --- | --- |
| <EXIT>F10 | Stores the contents of the current buffer into a new file. |
| <FORWARD/REV> | Toggles between forward and reverse mode. |
| <MOVE BY LINE> | Moves the cursor to the end of the next line in the forward mode. In the reverse mode, it moves the cursor to the beginning of the previous line. |
| <ERASE WORD> | Erases the current word or, if the cursor is not on a word, the next word. |
| <INSERT/OVER> | Toggles between text insert and text overstrike modes. |
| <HELP> | Displays a keypad help screen. |
| <DO> | Allows you to enter an EVE command. Press <DO> and then type the command at the Command: prompt. End the command by pressing <RETURN>. |
| <FIND> | Searches for an occurrence of a string. FIND will prompt for the search string. End the string by pressing <RETURN>. To search for the previously specified string, press <FIND> twice. FIND is case-insensitive. |

## Table 5-13: EVE Keypad Functions (cont'd)

| Key Name | Function |
|----------|----------|
| <INSERT HERE> | Used to move and copy text. To copy text, press <INSERT HERE> immediately after hitting <REMOVE>. This will put the text back in its original position. Then move the cursor to the place where you want the text inserted, and press <INSERT HERE> again to make another copy. To move a block of text, press <INSERT HERE> only after you have moved the cursor to the new position. |
| <REMOVE> | Removes the text in the currently selected range. |
| <SELECT> | Marks one end of a select range. A select range is a block of text on which various operations, such as REMOVE, can be performed. To select a range, put the cursor on the first character to be selected, press <SELECT>, then move the cursor to the last character to be selected. |
| <PREV SCREEN> | Moves the cursor vertically through the file, one screen of text at a time. The cursor moves backward, filling your screen with the previously entered lines of text. |
| <NEXT SCREEN> | Moves the cursor vertically through the file, one screen of text at a time. The cursor moves forward, filling your screen with the following lines of text. |

## Table 5-14: EVE Text
## Delete and Restore Commands

| Command | Function |
|---------|----------|
| ERASE CHARACTER | Deletes the character under the cursor. |
| ERASE LINE | Deletes the current line. |
| ERASE PREVIOUS WORD | Deletes the word to the left of the cursor. |
| ERASE START OF LINE | Deletes all characters left of the cursor to the beginning of the line. |
| ERASE WORD | Erases the word the cursor is on or the next word. |
| RESTORE | Restores, at the current cursor location, the character, word, line, or sentence most recently deleted with an ERASE command or editing key. |
| RESTORE CHARACTER | Restores, at the current cursor position, the last character deleted by command or editing key. |
| RESTORE LINE | Restores, at the current cursor position, the last line deleted by command or editing key. |
| RESTORE WORD | Restores, at the current cursor position, the last word erased by a command or an editing key. |

## Table 5-15: EVE Cursor Commands

| Command | Function |
|---------|----------|
| BOTTOM | Moves the cursor to the end of the buffer. |
| BUFFER | Puts the specified buffer in the current window and moves the cursor to the end of the new buffer. |
| END OF LINE | Puts the cursor at the end of the line. |
| LINE | Moves the cursor to the start of a line you specify by number. |
| MOVE BY LINE | Moves the cursor to the start or end of a line, depending on the current direction. |
| MOVE BY PAGE | Moves the cursor to the next page break. |
| MOVE BY WORD | Moves the cursor a word forward or backward depending on the current direction. |
| NEXT SCREEN | Scrolls the next screen's worth of text into the window. The cursor remains at the same relative screen position. |
| NEXT WINDOW | Puts the cursor in the next window on your screen (if another exists). |

## Table 5-15: EVE Cursor Commands (cont'd)

| Command | Function |
|---------|----------|
| PREVIOUS WINDOW | Moves the cursor to the previous window you were editing (assuming one exists). |
| START OF LINE | Moves the cursor to the beginning of the current line. |
| TOP | Puts the cursor at the top of the file. |

## Table 5-16: EVE Text Formatting Commands

| Command | Function |
|---------|----------|
| CAPITALIZE WORD | Capitalizes a word or selected range of text highlighted by the <FIND> or <SELECT>function keys. |
| CENTER LINE | Centers the current line of text. |
| FILL | Reformats the current paragraph or selected range of text according to the margins set for the buffer. |
| FILL PARAGRAPH | Reformats the current paragraph according to the margins set for the buffer. |
| INSERT PAGE | Inserts a form feed character. |

## Table 5-16: EVE Text
## Formatting Commands (cont'd)

| Command | Function |
| --- | --- |
| SET LEFT MARGIN | Establishes a new left margin for the current buffer. |
| SET RIGHT MARGIN | Establishes a new right margin for the current buffer. The right margin must be greater than the left margin. |
| SET TABS AT | Sets tab stops at the columns you specify. |
| SET TABS EVERY | Sets tabs at the specified interval. |
| SET TABS VISIBLE | Displays tabs as visible characters. |
| SET TABS INVISIBLE | Doesn't display tabs on the screen. |
| SET WIDTH | Establishes the width of lines displayed on the screen, i.e., 80 or 132 columns. |
| SET WRAP | Enables word wrapping at the specified column. |
| SET NOWRAP | Disables word wrap. |

## Exiting From an EVE Edit Session

You can use two different commands to exit from an EVE editing session: EXIT and QUIT. When you use the EXIT command, EVE saves your editing session to a new version of the edited file. The QUIT command discards all your edits for the session you are ending. Be careful. There's no way to get the information back after you've quit.

To save your edit session, use the EXIT command. Press <F10> or press <CTRL/Z>. After EVE saves your buffer to a new file, you will be returned to the DCL prompt.

To exit EVE without saving your edit session, use the QUIT command. Press <DO>, type QUIT, then press <RETURN>. You will be returned to the DCL prompt.

## EVE Error Recovery

When you edit a file with EVE, a journal file is maintained for your session. The journal file stores all the editing commands and text you have typed during the editing session. When you exit EVE normally, your new file is saved and the journal file is deleted.

To recover an EVE session using the journal file, enter the command:

$ EDIT/TPU/RECOVER file_spec

TPU will use the journal file to re-edit your file in exactly the same fashion and sequence as you did prior to the problem.  You must recover an editing session using the same type of terminal as the one you used when the journal file was created. When TPU finishes recovering your file, you will have all the text and corrections you typed, except the last few key strokes.

## HELP UTILITY

The VMS HELP utility is one of the most important facilities available to the experienced VMS user. This utility gives you the equivalent of a condensed VAX/VMS documentation set at your fingertips. The HELP utility includes an explanation of each command, most VMS utilities, and end-user software products. HELP has two modes: query and direct.

## Query Mode Help

To use HELP's query mode, type HELP <RETURN> at the DCL command level. HELP will display an alphabetical listing of all DCL commands and other topics for which information is available. After the list, you will be prompted with:

Topic?

If you press <RETURN>, <CTRL/C>, or <CTRL/Z> at this prompt, HELP will exit to DCL. To obtain information on one of the available topics, type the command name followed by <RETURN>. HELP will display details, including how to invoke the command or facility, what it does, and what default values exist.

Most topics have subtopics available. After requesting initial help on a subject, HELP will prompt for a Subtopic:

COMMAND-NAME Subtopic?

At the Subtopic? prompt, you must enter a valid subtopic as listed on the previous screen. For example, if help was requested on the EDIT command, the following information would be displayed:

> The EDIT command performs the following functions:
>
> .
> .
> .
>
> Additional information available:
>
> /ACL    /EDT    /FDL    /TPU

The Additional information available: list displays the subtopics available. You may now select a subtopic that you would like to review, or press <RETURN> to go back to the Topic? prompt. To review all subtopics, enter an asterisk (*) after the topic name. For example:

Topic? SET *

If you'd like to read all the information HELP has about a topic, enter the topic name followed by an ellipsis (...). For instance:

Topic? SHOW ...

## Direct Mode Help

As a VMS professional, you will be most interested in HELP's direct mode. The direct mode gives you instant access to the information you need.

To use the direct mode, enter the HELP command and specify a topic as the parameter. This bypasses the listing of HELP topics and displays the information you request immediately. In the direct mode, you may enter any command, or a command and its qualifiers. For example, to find out about the /SPEED qualifier of the SET TERMINAL command, you would enter:

$ HELP SET TERMINAL/SPEED

If additional information is available, HELP will prompt you for a subtopic.

For further information and details on the HELP command, log into your account and enter the following commands:

$ HELP HINTS
$ HELP HELP/INSTRUCTIONS

## MAIL UTILITY

The VMS personal MAIL utility allows you to send, receive, and store electronic messages on your VAX system. You can communicate with other users of your VAX or the users of any other VAX connected to your system via a DECnet network. The MAIL utility also permits you to file, forward, delete, read, and reply to mail messages that you receive.

When you send someone mail or when someone sends mail to you, the addressee will be notified. This happens in several ways. If the addressee is logged in, a message will appear on his terminal screen, unless the terminal is set to /NOBROADCAST. If not logged in, he will be notified the next time he logs in and when he invokes MAIL.

## Sending Mail Interactively

Mail may be sent by two methods, interactively and directly. In the interactive method, you use MAIL in a conversational fashion. This is done by invoking mail without using parameters:

```
$ MAIL
MAIL>
```

After invoking MAIL, type SEND and press <RETURN>. MAIL will
prompt you for the name of the users (To:) to whom you want to send
your message, and for a subject line (Subj:). After entering the
addressee and subject information, MAIL will give you instructions to
complete or abort the message. For example:

```
MAIL> SEND
To:   T_BYNON
Sub: Financial statement
Enter your message below. Press CTRL/Z when complete, or CTRL/C to quit:

Tamela,

Please mail me a copy of the P&L for Q4, 1988.

Thanks,
David
<CTRL/Z>
```

The mail message is completed by pressing <CTRL/Z>, at which time
it will be sent.

To send the same message to multiple users, supply a list of names at
the To: prompt:

```
MAIL> SEND
To:   ROCK,WILLIS,T_BYNON
```

To send a message to a user on another system, specify the node
name, then the user's name. For example:

```
MAIL> SEND
To:   LIZ::BYNON
```

If you're creating a long mail message or if you're a bad typist, you
can use MAIL's SEND command with the /EDIT qualifier. When you use
SEND/EDIT, your default editor will be invoked. To send the message,
after you have typed it, simply exit normally from the editor. Quitting
the edit session will abort the message and return you to the MAIL
prompt.

## Sending a File as Mail
You can send a file as mail directly from the DCL command level. To

do so, enter a command in the following format:

$ MAIL file_spec addressee /SUBJECT="character string"

File_spec is any valid VAX/VMS file specification, and addressee is the name of a user on your local system or remote system and user. The /SUBJECT qualifier is optional. This MAIL example sends the file CLUSHOSYS.FOR to user SHIPMAN:

$ MAIL CLUSHOSYS.FOR SHIPMAN /SUBJECT="Cluster utility"

## Distribution Lists

If you frequently send copies of messages to the same group of people, you can save time by creating a distribution list. A distribution list is a text file with the names of users whom you want to receive your messages.

Each username in the list must be on a separate line. You can include names of other distribution lists by preceding the name of the list with an at sign (@). Comments may be included by preceding them with an exclamation point. For example:

! MANAGERS.DIS
!
WILLIS
T_BYNON
ROCK

To send a message to the users on a distribution list, you enter @file_spec at the SEND command To: prompt. Each user listed in the distribution file will receive a copy of your message. For example:

MAIL> SEND
To:   @MANAGERS
MAIL>

Create as many distribution list files as you like for different groups of users. Just remember to use a unique filename. The default file type for a MAIL distribution list is .DIS.

## Reading Your Mail

Mail can only be read interactively. When you invoke MAIL, you will be informed if you have new mail:

$ MAIL

You have 3 new messages.

To read your mail, you can either type READ or press <RETURN>. The message will appear on your screen. If the message is longer than one screen of text, MAIL will display the message Press RETURN for more... at the bottom of the screen. To continue reading the message, press the <RETURN> key, or, if you want, you may enter a new MAIL command.

## Replying and Forwarding

Many times, you will receive a message that requires a response, or you'll get one that should also have been sent to someone else. MAIL has the REPLY and FORWARD commands to support these situations.

The FORWARD command sends a copy of the message you have just read to one or more users. MAIL will prompt you for the address names with the To: prompt. You can cancel the FORWARD by pressing <CTRL/C>.

The REPLY command is used to reply to the message you have just read. It works like the SEND command, only MAIL never prompts for an addressee or subject. This information is taken from the message to which you are replying. Use the /EDIT qualifier with the REPLY command to invoke your default editor.

The REPLY and ANSWER commands are interchangeable.

## Mail Folders

The MAIL utility uses folders to store and organize your mail. Three folders are provided, but you can create as many folders as you like. The three default folders are NEWMAIL, MAIL, and WASTEBASKET.

**NEWMAIL:** Stores your new mail messages before you read them, just like the mailbox at your home or office. After you've read a new message, it is automatically moved from the NEWMAIL folder to the MAIL folder (unless you specify a different destination folder with the MOVE command).

**MAIL:** Stores mail messages after you read them, unless you file these messages in specific folders that you have created. Your default mail folder, it always exists.

**WASTEBASKET:** Stores mail messages that you have deleted. Deleted messages remain in this folder until you exit the MAIL utility. At that time, the WASTEBASKET folder is emptied, and your deleted messages are thrown out.

## Creating Folders

You can create folders to permanently store the mail messages you receive. This allows you to organize your messages into specific categories.

To create a folder, select a message and enter the MOVE command. If you attempt to move a mail message to a nonexistent folder, MAIL will inform you that the folder does not exist and ask you if you want to create it. If you respond with Y or YES, MAIL will create the new folder for you.

The following example demonstrates how the new folder facility can be used to create a mail folder in which mail message number 74 will be stored.

```
MAIL> 74
MAIL> MOVE COMPLAINTS

Folder COMPLAINTS does not exist.
Do you want to create it (Y/N, default is N)? Y
  MAIL-I-NEWFOLDER, folder COMPLAINTS created
MAIL>
```

The FILE command works the same way and is interchangeable with the MOVE command.

## Moving Between Folders

The SELECT command is used to move from one folder to another. For instance, if you type SELECT COMPLAINTS at the MAIL prompt, your default folder becomes COMPLAINTS. Then MAIL will respond with a message that lists the number of messages contained in the folder you have selected. For example:

```
MAIL>SELECT COMPLAINTS
      MAIL-I-SELECTED, 1 message selected
MAIL>
```

To list the names of your folders, use the DIRECTORY/FOLDER command, as illustrated in the next example:

```
MAIL> DIRECTORY/FOLDERS
Listing of folders in SKIP$DUB1:[BYNON.MAIL]MAIL.MAI;1
       Press CTRL/C to cancel listing
COMPLAINTS
MAIL
MEMOS
IMPORTANT_STUFF
WASTEBASKET

MAIL>
```

## Deleting Mail and Folders

Use the DELETE command to delete unwanted mail messages. The DELETE command accepts a message number as a parameter, or optionally, deletes the current message.

When you delete a message, it is placed in your WASTEBASKET folder. If you accidentally delete a message, you can retrieve it by selecting the WASTEBASKET folder and refiling the message with the MOVE command. When you exit from MAIL, the WASTEBASKET is emptied.

To delete a folder, simply delete all messages in the folder. To do so, use the DELETE qualifier /ALL. In this next example, the COMPLAINTS folder will be deleted:

```
MAIL> SELECT COMPLAINTS
%MAIL-I-SELECTED, 1 message selected

MAIL> DELETE/ALL
```

## Printing Your Mail

The PRINT command adds a copy of the current message to an output file for printing. The output file is not sent to the designated printer until you exit from mail (unless you specify /NOW). For example:

```
MAIL> PRINT/QUEUE=SYS$LASER/COPIES=3
```

If you do not specify an output queue, the default print queue, SYS$PRINT, will be used. The most commonly used qualifiers of the DCL PRINT command, such as /AFTER, /COPIES, /FORM, /FEED, /QUEUE, and /NOTIFY, are available with the MAIL PRINT command.

## Creating a File From a Message

Often, you will find it necessary, or convenient, to create a file from a mail message. The EXTRACT command is available for this purpose. In this example, message number 94 is selected and extracted:

```
MAIL> 94
MAIL> EXTRACT/NOHEADER CLUSHOSYS.FOR
```

The EXTRACT qualifier /NOHEADER is used to delete the message header information (i.e., From, To, Subj, etc.) added by MAIL.

## Customizing Mail

MAIL has a number of features that you may set to your preference. These MAIL features are established with SET commands. Corresponding SHOW commands let you see the current settings.

## Personal Name

One of the most popular items to customize is your personal name. The SET PERSONAL_NAME command enables you to append a text string to the end of the From: field of outgoing mail. You can fill this field with a nickname, your full name, or any other information you want. Example:

```
MAIL> SET PERSONAL_NAME "ROTH"
MAIL> SHOW PERSONAL_NAME
Your personal name is "ROTH".
```

As the system manager, or a privileged user, you can list the personal name of another user with the command SHOW PERSONAL_NAME /USER=user_name.

## Selecting a Default Editor

The default MAIL editor is EDT. To change the default to TPU, use the SET EDITOR command:

```
MAIL> SET EDITOR TPU
MAIL> SHOW EDITOR
Your editor is TPU
```

Note: This SET command is not available in VMS V4 MAIL.

## Getting Copies of Everything You Send

If you'd like to receive a copy of everything you send using MAIL, use the SET COPY_SELF command. Parameters for this command are [NO]SEND, [NO]REPLY, and [NO]FORWARD. For example:

```
MAIL> SET COPY_SELF SEND REPLY NOFORWARD
MAIL> SHOW COPY_SELF
Automatic copy to yourself on SEND,REPLY.
```

Note: The [NO]FORWARD parameter is not available in VMS V4 MAIL.

## Sending Carbon Copies

A carbon copy facility (i.e., CC:) was added in VMS V5 MAIL. The feature is turned on with the SET CC_PROMPT command:

```
MAIL> SET CC_PROMPT
```

When carbon copy is on, you will be prompted for carbon copy addressees after the primary addressee:

```
MAIL> SEND
To: TOM
CC: DICK
Subject:
```

To turn the carbon copy feature off, use SET NOCC_PROMPT.

## Receiving Mail at an Alternate Location

If you find yourself working between two or more networked machines or accounts and want to continue receiving your mail, you can have it forwarded. The SET FORWARD command allows you to set a forwarding address for your incoming mail:

```
MAIL> SET FORWARD CHAZ::BYNON
MAIL> SHOW FORWARD
Your mail is being forwarded to CHAZ::BYNON
```

To discontinue forwarding, use the SET NOFORWARD command. If you're the system manager, or a privileged user, you can set or show forwarding for another user with the /USER=user_name qualifier.

## Getting Help with Mail

MAIL has a built-in HELP command. It works exactly like the DCL HELP facility.

## PHONE UTILITY

The VAX/VMS PHONE utility allows you to talk to other users on your VAX system through your terminal. It simulates the functions and features of a real telephone system, including call holding, conference calls, and telephone directories.

## Placing a Call

To place a call with the PHONE utility, enter:

$ PHONE username

The username parameter is the VMS username of the person with whom you want to communicate. Your terminal screen will split horizontally into two sections. The screen will indicate that the PHONE utility is ringing the other party. Your part of the conversation will be displayed in the top half of the screen, while the responses of the other party will appear in the lower half.

The PHONE utility may also be used interactively, like MAIL. At the DCL command level, enter:

$ PHONE

Your terminal will enter split-screen mode, and you will be placed at the PHONE prompt (%). You may now enter PHONE commands. For example, you can enter DIRECTORY, and PHONE will display a directory of users available to phone.

If you are having a conversation with another user, you can get back to the PHONE command prompt by entering the percent sign (%). You must do this, in any case, to exit PHONE with the EXIT command.

As with the MAIL utility, PHONE provides an on-line HELP facility.

## Answering a Call

To answer an incoming call, you must be at the DCL command level or at the PHONE prompt. At the DCL command level, the command is:

$ PHONE ANSWER

At the PHONE prompt, enter:

% ANSWER

In either case, you and the caller will be linked and may carry on your conversation.

## CONCLUSION

DCL is a powerful user interface language. It's consistent, flexible, and easy to use, but no amount of reading can match hands-on experience. You must use DCL day after day to become proficient with it.

DCL must be mastered before you can effectively operate or manage a VMS system.

# Chapter 6

# DECwindows

Digital's philosophy of using small, interactive, distributed computers to build a system was instrumental in guiding the computer industry away from batch processing into timesharing. In the early 1980s, Digital recognized the need for high-performance, multitasking workstations for the next evolution of computing, known as the graphical user interface (GUI) or windowing.

Just as interactive timeshare systems gave us the ability to develop applications that were impossible to achieve in the batch environment, windowing provides the same advance over any interactive (command line oriented) method. It offers methods of problem-solving that are far beyond the capabilities of a text-based terminal. For instance, where compendious text statements were once standard for providing information to the user, graphics constructs are now used, and where lengthy (and hard-to-remember) commands were once typed, a single mouse button is now pushed.

Windowing evolved from early research at the famed Xerox Palo Alto Research Center. The first computer to employ windowing was the Xerox Star. Windowing was refined and popularized by Apple, with the Macintosh personal computer, and by Microsoft, with MS-Windows.

This chapter is an introduction to the functions and architecture of DECwindows, Digital's windowing system.

## THE PURPOSE AND FUNCTION OF DECWINDOWS

The purpose of DECwindows is to present a graphical user interface that permits user access to data and applications throughout a network-based computer system. Digital's primary goal in developing DECwindows was to design a common user interface and application support for the three operating systems it supports, namely VMS, ULTRIX-32, and MS-DOS.

Although DECwindows is an implementation of the X Window System from MIT (an industry standard), it's significantly enhanced. DECwindows presents its own look and feel, which sets it apart from other X Window System implementations. Plus, it's an open platform for application development.

All DECwindows enhancements were implemented with industry standards in mind. DECwindows is compatible with MIT's X Window Version 11, Adobe's PostScript(tm) page description language, and DECnet. It is a key component in Digital's own application integration architecture (AIA) and the compound document architecture (CDA).

It's interesting to look at the history of X Window System, especially when you consider how it became the de facto industry standard. X Window System actually began life at Stanford University as W, which was developed by Paul Asente. W became X after it was jointly adopted by the Laboratory for Computer Science at MIT. Development of X was the project of Robert Scheifler and Jim Gettys.

MIT's interest in windowing, and the formation of a project known as Athena, came about in the early 1980s after a study was conducted by the Dean of Engineering and associated faculty at MIT. The study examined the undergraduate computing capabilities to assess if adequate support was being provided for student development. The study revealed that student access to the vast computer resources at MIT was minimal, as it was mostly consumed by research projects. This was viewed as a liability to the undergraduate program.

Project Athena was launched when MIT realized that, in order to get its engineering program back on track, it had to develop a new method of accessing computer resources. The institution needed a distributed computer architecture accessible to all, i.e., students, faculty, and research projects.

To fund and support Athena, MIT sought the assistance of its two largest vendors, DEC and IBM. The primary goal of project Athena was to develop the technology for a new computing environment that would facilitate information sharing, provide a uniform user and programming interface independent of machine architecture, scale to a large number of systems, and be operated inexpensively. In exchange for funding, equipment, and technological assistance from IBM and DEC, MIT agreed to make the source code and technology publicly available.

From Athena came the X protocol. X is built on three main components: the X server, Xlib, and the X toolkit. Together, they form a client/server model that separates the application program and its presentation to the user.

The X Window System is basically a kernel. From this kernel, vendors must implement their own X Window System, specific to the hardware they want to support. DECwindows is Digital's enhanced version of the MIT X Window System.

## X WINDOW SYSTEM BASICS

X Window System is a network-based windowing system. Its architecture is based on the premise that an application will run on one computer, called the client, while the user interface is handled by another, called the server. This client/server relationship is reversed from the traditional role, or at least as we think of it, because most client/server models use a large host as the server for a smaller computer or workstation.

As in other client/server models, the X server provides a resource service to its clients. The X server software runs on the user's workstation, where the graphics display and keyboard are located. The services provided to client systems are low-level graphics, windowing, and user input functions, i.e., mouse, keyboard, graphics tablet, etc. The X server relies on low-level routines, called primitives, that must be written for each workstation platform to be supported. The X server itself does not directly manipulate the hardware.

The X server provides an interface between the user and the application program he wants to run. The application can be remote (running on another CPU) or local. Also, it's not necessary for the application to be running on a compatible system. In other words, an X server running on a VAXstation using VMS can present an application running on a remote ULTRIX-32 or UNIX client. Figure 6-1 shows the relationship between servers and clients.

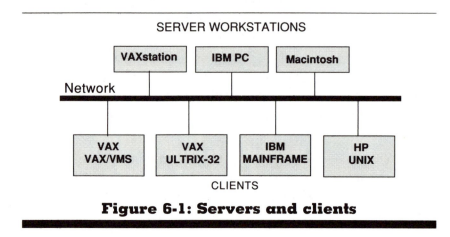

**Figure 6-1: Servers and clients**

The scenario for the X client/server model is actually quite simple. The user of the X server workstation requests application support from a client, the client instructs the server to take actions, such as opening a window or displaying data, and the client does the work requested. The client and server cooperate using a defined protocol X; this allows the client to tell the server what to display and how to do it. The server reports events and screen information back to the client. It should be noted, however, that the server owns the display, not the client, and the workstation user can manipulate the windows at any time.

### The Functions of an X Server

The X server's primary tasks are to implement requests as defined in the X protocol and encoding specification, and to support several hardware dependencies such as the workstation's graphics subsystem, network transport mechanism, and extensions to the base wire protocol. From the workstation user's point of view, the server is simply the windowing program running on his machine.

X servers are event driven, which means that they respond to events, such as keyboard input or mouse movement. After an X server opens a window for a client application, it basically hibernates, waiting for an event to occur. When interrupted for an event, the X server transfers control to the proper routine to handle it. The X server recognizes many events, such as mouse motion, keyboard input, and mouse button transition. In addition, the client application can generate events to which the server process might need to respond.

The X server recognizes only one type of output device: a bit-mapped display. Each server is equipped with a device driver to interface with and support the functions of the display device. Client systems interface only to a server, but have some flexibility in reacting to the server's display device. This is accomplished by the client giving the server hints about how windows or other information should be displayed, i.e., color, size, and position. The window manager (a server component) adjusts the hints to provide the best possible display for the workstation user. Note that the degree to which the server will respond to client requests (contained in hints) will depend on device limitations and the existing state of the server.

## The X Protocol

X clients communicate with an X server through a network protocol known as the X Wire Protocol (X). X defines the semantics by which the server and client will communicate. It allows the server and client to run on different machines and under different host operating systems.

The X protocol is completely independent (or transparent) of any network vendor protocol, i.e., TCP/IP, DECnet, or systems network architecture (SNA). This network transparency sets the X Window System apart from other windowing systems. Its implications are quite profound.

X is an asynchronous packet-based protocol. This means that the client can send a request to a server without having to wait for the completion of previous requests.

X request packets are generated at application run time, by the called routines, which are sent to the network's transport software such as DECnet or TCP/IP. An X protocol request is a fairly generic packet model consisting of a function opcode, the opcode data, and a request length. X protocol requests vary widely in length. So, to reduce network overhead, not all X protocol requests require a response from the receiver, i.e., one-way traffic doesn't generate round-trip overhead. Some operations, however, such as those that require specific pixel addressing, can get very intense. A large number of complicated packets can easily degrade system and network performance. This is a serious problem of the X Window System.

The network supporting the X servers and clients must provide a high, sustained performance level. A 10MBps or better LAN, such as Ethernet, is assumed. X is not expected to work on slow-speed asynchronous communication lines, such as a 9600 or 19,200 baud terminal connection.

### The X Interface Library

To access X and an X server, client applications use Xlib, the X Window library. Xlib is an application call interface. The purpose of Xlib is to standardize the call interface for applications, thus allowing a program to be easily ported to other systems. Using Xlib, program calls on a VAX/VMS system are virtually identical to those of a VAX ULTRIX-32 system or even a PC running OS/2. Figure 6-2 shows the relationship of the client application, Xlib, and the server.

Xlib routines convert calls and parameters into the network wire protocol format and return messages from the server to the application. In essence, Xlib acts as a go-between for the application and the X protocol and X server. Although it's possible for an application to access the server directly through the wire protocol, it's more suitable to use the higher-level Xlib routines.

The Xlib interface is the lowest-level interface that applications should use if the application is expected to be portable. Xlib has more than 300 procedures that are like many other graphics library packages.

The X toolkit (Xtk), also known as the intrinsics library, is an

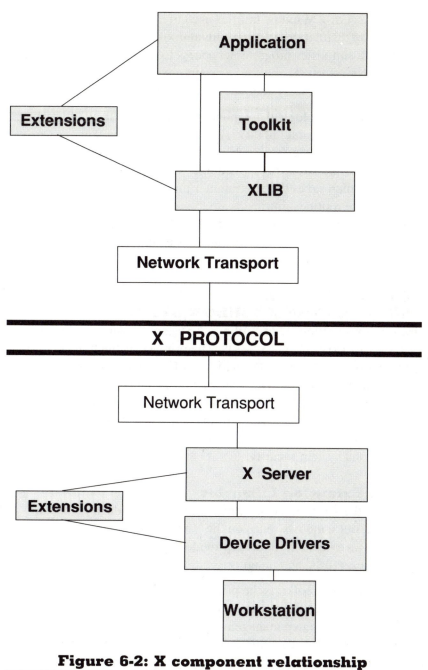

**Figure 6-2: X component relationship**

additional set of X Window utilities used to develop user interfaces. The primary distinction between Xlib and Xtk is that Xtk is a superset of Xlib. Xtk simplifies programmer access to Xlib for most application development efforts. Using Xtk, a programmer can quickly and easily provide an X Window System interface to his application.

Xtk consists of two logical components called widgets and intrinsics, each stored in a separate library. A widget is a routine that implements a user interface such as a dialog box, scroll bars, pull-down menus, and so forth. Applications invoke widgets in their own windows, which saves the programmer the effort of coding his own user interface routines. Intrinsics are the routines used to develop widgets. Intrinsics are fairly well-defined, but widgets aren't. There are many contributed widgets available as examples, but there are no X Consortium standard widgets.

## HOW DECWINDOWS ENHANCES THE X WINDOW SYSTEM

DECwindows is a family of X Window System implementations for VAX/VMS, ULTRIX-32, and MS-DOS. The primary distinction between DECwindows and X is the DECwindows X User Interface (XUI). XUI is implemented via the DECwindows toolkit, which is an extension of the standard X Window System libraries. DECwindows significantly enhances the X Window system in four other ways: the DECwindows Style Guide, base applications programs, a robust programmer interface, and system security.

### Server Extension Libraries

To extend the X server's capabilities and provide industry standard interfaces, DECwindows relies on the X extension library mechanism. DECwindows extension libraries provide support for GKS, PostScript, 3D Graphics, PHIGS, and imaging.

The DECwindows toolkit is the primary X extension provided by DECwindows. It has three major components: widgets, cut-and-paste interfaces, and resource management facilities. These components define the user interface guidelines of windows. The toolkit provides most of the widgets that would be used by applications to interface with users, such as:

- Pull-down and pop-up menus
- Scroll bars
- Help
- Command prompting
- List box
- Message window
- Push buttons
- Dialog boxes
- Work-in-progress box

## Style Guide

DECwindows defines a standard user interface through a set of guidelines for application developers. Known as the DECwindows Style Guide, it's designed to promote a consistent user interface among applications. It emphasizes three areas: user interface consistency, graphic presentation of information, and user interaction with screen objects.

## Base Applications

A set of base applications is included with DECwindows to support the workstation user. The tools include a session manager, a terminal emulator, a window manager, and a VMS user executive.

The session manager is the first application to which a DECwindows user has access. It gets the user logged in, creates a windows session, establishes user preferences (via presaved data files), sets up session parameters for other applications, and initializes the root window that becomes the home for the user's active applications. The session manager also provides some basic functions such as session control, screen printing, customizing the keyboard and screen colors, and creating user executives and terminal emulators.

The terminal emulator (DECterm) allows the DECwindows user to access local or remote applications through standard DEC terminal emulation. DECterm supports all VTxxx terminals and ReGIS emulation, plus full cut-and-paste ability between windows. The cut-and-paste ability allows you to run several applications at once and pass information between them.

In the DECwindows environment, the user owns the screen; it's his real estate. Applications rarely call routines which resize, move, or change the stacking order of a user's windows. Therefore, an agent is needed to perform these functions as the user requests. The window manager is an application that runs as the agent for the workstation user. It's responsible for managing the position and size of all windows on the display, and for setting policy concerning the use of icons.

A VMS user executive (VUE) is a graphically driven command language interface. VUE interfaces with DCL and provides access to the most commonly used command verbs such as TYPE, EDIT, DELETE, COPY, RUN, SET, and SHOW. It allows the user to interface with many DCL commands through widgets. In most cases, the mouse is used to select parameters that would have been typed in through DCL.

## Programming

X Window System supports only a C and Common Lisp interface to Xlib. DECwindows extends this support to include the complete set of VAX standard languages. This means that the programs you currently have written in VAX FORTRAN, BASIC, C, Ada, PASCAL, or any other VAX language can easily be modified to operate under DECwindows.

In addition to full language support, Digital has provided a convenient utility to assist in interfacing with widgets through intrinsic calls in an application. The new utility is a compiler called user interface language (UIL).

UIL, which is analogous to the command definition utility (CDU) in DCL, lets the programmer define widgets, widget hierarchies, callback linkage between widgets, widget creation and destruction, and default values. As with CDU, the programmer creates a definition file, which is identified to the main program, and compiles to create a user interface definition (UID) file. The definition file is then linked with the main program. When the program executes, a component of DECwindows called the digital resource manager (DRM) interprets the UID information and converts it into the appropriate user interface (i.e., widgets). UIL has several advantages: An application can support more than one user interface, applications can be internationalized, and the programmer can quickly modify the interface layout.

The programmer uses the DECwindows toolkit widgets to control the user interface. The user is in charge of the display. It's poor programming practice (in X) to dictate to the user such things as window size and position. The programmer must do whatever the user wants, even if it means more programming effort. For instance, the programmer must be careful not to hard-code values such as display size and color. This is most easily accomplished by calling DECwindows widgets and allowing the server to manage the user's display.

An X program follows eight basic steps:

1. Open a connection to the server.

2. Create the top-level window.

3. Set standard properties for the top-level window, including hints for the window manager.

4. Create window resources that are needed, such as graphics.

5. Create any other windows, possibly widgets.

6. Set up the desired events for each window.

7. Map the windows into application space.

8. Start the server event monitoring loop and user interaction.

## Security

The security features of the MIT X server are minimal. As specified, by default only programs on the local host (or server) can use the display. Additionally, the user can specify a list of hosts that can access the display via an access control list. The access control list can be changed by clients on the local host using the ChangeHost routine.

The ChangeHost routine is protected (though marginally) from misuse through two provisions: The client application calling the ChangeHost routine must reside on the same node as the server, and the client calling ChangeHost must already be a valid (or registered) client.

DECwindows enhances security in several ways. First, DECwindows uses existing VMS and DECnet security features. So, DECwindows is theoretically as secure as VMS. Second, DECwindows provides for discretionary access control to thwart access by unauthorized clients. This control is specified in node/user pairs, like a DECnet proxy login entry. Last, a DECwindows X server has the ability to permit or deny access to clients that use a transport mechanism different from the server's (i.e., DECnet or TCP/IP), or that use an unsupported authentication mechanism.

## GETTING STARTED WITH DECWINDOWS BASE APPLICATIONS

DECwindows' base applications are tools that must be mastered by every DEC workstation user. If you've used other windowing systems, such as MS-Windows or the Macintosh, DECwindows will come naturally to you. All the typical window functions and controls work as you might expect. On the other hand, if this is your first workstation experience, you have a number of new mouse terms to learn.

DECwindows uses the mouse, a simple point-and-select device, to make using your workstation a productive and pleasant experience. In a workstation environment, the mouse is used to point, click, double click, drag, shrink windows to icons, expand windows from icons, and a variety of other highly interactive activities. Although these terms might sound silly, they are quite meaningful.

### Mouse Terms

A mouse is a hand-held device that is attached to your workstation. Digital's corporate mouse has three buttons labeled (from left to right) <MB1>, <MB2>, and <MB3> (you guessed it, MB stands for mouse button). The button order can be reversed using a configuration menu.

When you move the mouse, a pointer on the screen tracks your motion. This pointer, in conjunction with the mouse buttons, is used to choose commands from a menu, cause pop-up menus to appear, expand and shrink windows, and manipulate windows and icons on your screen.

You use the mouse to do the following things:

**Click:** Many operations are initiated by pointing at an object on the screen, then pressing and quickly releasing <MB1>. The click is used most often to press window buttons (such as a shrink to icon button) or select a new input focus window (the window that controls the keyboard).

**Double-click:** Some objects can first be selected and then have other operations performed on them. A common example is selecting, then opening, a mail message. The first click selects the message you point at and the second click opens it. To double click, press and quickly release <MB1> twice in rapid succession.

**Shift Click:** Many applications can perform operations on a list of items: deleting files, for example. To build a list, press and hold the shift key and click on the item. The item will be added to the list.

**Drag:** You drag by pointing to an item, pressing <MB1> and holding it down, moving the pointer, and releasing the button. This mouse action is used to invoke pull-down menus, manipulate window size and placement, and move sliders and other controls.

**Press and Hold:** To perform a continuous operation, such as scrolling through a document using a scroll bar arrow, you move your mouse pointer over a specified region, press <MB1> and hold. The operation will continue until you release the mouse button.

## Widgets

Widgets are DECwindows user interfaces. Some widgets are completely mouse driven, while others accept both keyboard and mouse input. After you understand the functions of, and how to use, the DECwindows widgets, you will be well on your way to mastering DECwindows.

Common widgets you will encounter are:

- Windows
- Pop-up Menus
- Pull-down Menus
- Scroll Bars
- Dialog Boxes
- Control Panels

## Widget Controls

Controls are used in control panels, dialog boxes, windows, and scroll bars. A control is an active object, consisting of graphics, text, or both. When you click on a control, it provides input to the application. Controls are labeled to indicate their purpose. There are four basic types of controls: toggle buttons, radio buttons, push buttons, and scales.

Toggle buttons are switches that can be set in one of two positions, on or off. They allow you to choose whether or not an option is activated. Toggle buttons are always displayed as small squares. If the small square next to the option is highlighted, the option is activated. If the small square next to the option is not highlighted, the option is not activated. To change the setting of a toggle button, move the pointer to the square next to the option and click on it.

Radio buttons, which are round, allow you to activate an option from a list of options. It's like a radio, which has buttons for AM, FM, station, and so on. The radio button selected is a highlighted circle. To change the activated button, move your pointer to the circle next to the option you want to activate and click on it.

A push button is a word that appears in a dialog box within a rectangular frame, such as CANCEL or APPLY. To perform the action indicated by the push button, move the pointer to the push button and click on it. The most commonly used push button in a dialog box has a bold border. This is the default push button. It may be activated by pressing either <RETURN> or <ENTER>, or by clicking on it.

Scales allow you to enter a value from a range of values by adjusting a pointer to the desired position along a line. Scales consist of a label, a line with tick marks that represent the range of the scale from a to z, an arrow which is the analog representation of the selected scale value, and a number directly opposite the arrow that represents the digital value currently selected. To operate a scale, put your pointer on the arrow and drag it up and down on a vertical scale or back and forth on a horizontal scale. Release <MB1> when you reach the desired number.

## Windows

A window is a rectangular area on the screen in which a DECwindows program runs. The top line of each window is the title bar that contains the window title and three square screen buttons. In addition, many windows have a menu bar below the title bar that lists the names of the available pull-down menus.

## Selecting a Window for Input Focus

Your workstation screen can have many windows on it at one time, but only one window has input focus. The window with input focus has control of the keyboard. To select a window for input focus, move the pointer anywhere in the window (except on the menu bar or a screen button in the title bar) and click. The title bar of the window with input focus is highlighted, indicating that the window is active.

## Moving and Sizing Windows

In addition to input focus, you have control of where windows are located on your workstation screen. To move a window from one location to another, move the pointer into the window's title bar (anywhere but on a screen button), then drag the window to its new location. A dotted outline of the window appears. When you release <MB1> after dragging, the window will be repainted in the new location.

You can also change the size of your windows. This is appropriate when you only need to see part of what the window can display. For example, you could reduce a DECterm window from its normal 80 columns by 16 lines to, say, 80 columns by four lines.

To change the size of a window, move your pointer to the right-most screen button, called the sizing button, in the title bar. Then, press and hold <MB1>. While holding <MB1>, move the pointer to the outside of the window (to the right) until a thin frame line appears. To make the window smaller, move your pointer to the left (inside the window) and downward. To make the window larger, move your pointer to the right (outside the window) and upward. When the frame is the size that you want the window to be, release <MB1>. The frame line will disappear, and the window will be repainted to the new size.

## Stacking Windows and Using Icons

After you've created a few windows, they will begin to overlap. You can change the stacking order of windows by moving the window on top to the bottom of the pile. It's like shuffling papers on your desk.

To move the top window to the bottom of the stack, which will make the second one move to the top, click on the push-to-back button. The push-to-back button is the first button to the right of the title in the title bar.

The push-to-back button does not change the input focus. So, to push the top window to the back and change the input focus to the new top window, you must click on the push-to-back button, then click inside the new top window.

To remove the clutter of windows not in active use, you may shrink them to icons. An icon is a small square that contains the name of the window. Icons are held in the window manager's window, called the icon box.

To shrink a window to an icon, simply click the shrink-to-icon button, which is the left-most screen button in the title bar. The window will disappear from the screen and reappear in the icon box as an icon.

To expand an icon back to a window, click on the icon. The window will be returned to the screen location where it appeared before you shrank it to an icon.

## Window Scroll Bars

If a DECwindows window is associated with a file, it will have a scroll bar at the far right, bottom, or both. A scroll bar is used to display information not showing in the window i.e., above or below the present view point.

A scroll bar is an elongated rectangle with triangular arrows called stepping arrows at each end. The region between the stepping arrows is divided into an elongated rectangle called scroll region, and a smaller highlighted rectangle called the slider. The size of the slider indicates how much of the file is showing on the screen. For instance, if the slider takes up 10 percent of the scrolling region, only 10 percent of the file is displayed in the window.

There are several ways to use the scroll bar. The easiest is to move your pointer to a stepping arrow and click on it. This will move the window one line or column in the direction of the stepping arrow. If this is too slow for you, you can click and hold the stepping arrow by holding down <MB1>. This will cause the file to scroll through the window until you release the button.

The slider is used to move quickly through a file. To use it, move your pointer to the slider, then drag the slider through the scrolling region. When you release <MB1>, the file text, relative to the slider position, will be displayed. You may also click in the scroll region (above or below the slider) to move the slider to that location.

## Window Menus

DECwindows has two basic menu types: pull-down and pop-up. Pull-down menus are the most common DECwindows menus and are the only menus with titles. The titles of pull-down menus appear in the window menu bar. A menu bar is located directly under the title bar.

To choose an item from a pull-down menu, position your pointer on the menu title and drag. The menu will appear with a rectangular outline around the menu item you are selecting. When the rectangle is on the choice you want, release <MB1>. If you decide not to choose a menu item, simply move your pointer outside the menu and release <MB1>. Also, some applications can make use of menu accelerators. A menu accelerator is a keyboard shortcut for a click on the menu item. It usually consists of a function key (i.e., F1-F10) or a control key. Accelerators are listed to the right of the menu item.

Some pull-down menus have submenus. If a pull-down menu has a submenu, the submenu icon appears to the right of the pull-down menu. To display a submenu, drag the pointer to the submenu icon. To choose a submenu item, release <MB1> when the rectangle is on the correct submenu item.

Pop-up menus differ from pull-downs by allowing you to keep the pointer in the area where you're working. This eliminates the need to move the pointer back to the menu bar so frequently. The contents of a pop-up menu change because of the location of your mouse pointer and the current selection. Generally speaking, pop-up menus are invoked through pull-down menus or by the application itself because of an event.

## Dialog Boxes

Dialog boxes appear on the screen to request input for a DECwindows application or to display messages. They contain controls and labels that you manipulate. Dialog boxes are displayed in response to some action, such as clicking on a menu item.

Like other windows, all dialog boxes have a title bar (used to move the dialog box from one location to another on the screen) and a push-to-back screen button (used to move the dialog box underneath other windows).

Dialog boxes may contain various controls, such as push buttons, option menus, and list boxes. All dialog boxes will contain at least one push button for acknowledgment. There are six basic types of push buttons, as explained in Table 6-1.

Many dialog boxes will have a default push button assigned. A default push button provides the user with the least destructive response; it may be activated by pressing <RETURN>, <ENTER>, or by clicking on it. A default push button is easily recognized by its bold (i.e., double line) border.

Some dialog boxes have text entry fields, which are locations within a dialog box in which you enter text by typing at the keyboard. You can change the text in a text entry field by deleting the existing text with the <DELETE> key and typing new text.

If a dialog box has more than one text entry field, the cursor is located in the first text entry field when the dialog box appears on the screen. To move the cursor to the next text entry field, either press the <TAB> key or move the pointer to the next text entry field and click on it.

Dialog boxes can also have option menus associated with them. Option menus are a special type of pop-up menu. To make an option menu appear, press <MB2> and move the pointer over the active area of the dialog box. The currently chosen option appears under the pointer. To choose another option, move the pointer through the option menu and release <MB2>.

## Table 6-1: Push Buttons

| Button Name | Button Action |
| --- | --- |
| Apply | Supplies the current dialog box information and settings to the application program. You may continue to alter the settings until you are satisfied. |
| Cancel | Removes the dialog box without applying any changes you might have made. |
| Dismiss | Same as Cancel. |
| No | Supplies a no answer to a question presented in a dialog box. |
| OK | Supplies the current settings and information in the dialog box to the application program, and removes the dialog box. |
| Reset | Returns the dialog box settings to their original state before the dialog box was displayed. |
| Yes | Supplies a yes answer to a question presented in a dialog box. |

### Starting a Session

As a DECwindows user, you log in through a dialog box called Start Session. The dialog box has two input fields: username and password. A VMS account name and password, respectively, must be entered to log in and begin a session. Unlike Digital's other windowing software, VWS, only one account can be logged in at the workstation display.

A narrow cursor, which looks like a vertical bar (I), marks the field in which you're typing (i.e., username or password). Use the mouse to point to the field in which you want to type and click on it. When you have finished entering your account name and password, click on the OK button or press <RETURN>. If you have entered the correct information, your session will begin.

## THE SESSION MANAGER

DECwindows (for VMS) is a VMS-based application. As such, it adheres to the VMS user account and security mechanisms. However, unlike a typical VMS system, where users log in with assistance from the job controller (by interrupting the terminal), the DECwindows users log in through a precreated process called _WSA2. This is the DECwindows' login process.

The DECwindows' login process uses the LOGINOUT image to verify authorization, map the appropriate command line interpreter (CLI), and establish SYS$INPUT and SYS$OUTPUT, as a normal VMS login would. When a user has been verified through the system authorization file, the login process, _WSA2, is renamed to match the account being logged in, i.e., SMITH, JONES, or SYSTEM. Privileges, quotas, and the account user identification code (UIC) are established at this time as well. However, unlike a DCL user, the DECwindows user's parent process does not execute DCLTABLES. Instead, the parent process executes DECW$SESSION, the DECwindows session manager image.

The session manager process, at login time, is responsible for establishing your default environment. It starts the window manager process, which you see on your screen as the icon box, sets up screen colors and default values, then starts VUE and DECterm processes for you. By the time the login is complete, and you can start working, three to seven processes will have been created. Depending on the workstation you're using, and your login options, the login process can take from five to 10 seconds (VAXstation 3100) to a minute or more (VAXstation 2000). Before any useful work begins, the workstation and VMS will have tied up 3.5 to 4 MB of available memory.

After getting you logged in and set up, the session manager has five important functions: session control (quitting and pausing), creating VUE and DECterm processes, customizing the workstation to your preference, screen printing, and displaying system messages.

## Session Manager Menu Bar

DECwindows applications allow you to execute commands by choosing menu items and clicking on controls, rather than by entering commands from the keyboard. Each DECwindows application runs in its own window as one or more VMS processes. DECwindows applications are accessed through the session manager's pull-down menus in the session manager window menu bar. There are five pull-down menu options:  Session, Create, Customize, Print Screen, and Help.

## FileView

The DECwindows FileView application allows you to access other DECwindows applications and work with your VMS files. You can use FileView to copy, compile, edit, print, search and display files, create directories to organize your files, and use the VMS operating system through DCL.

You create a FileView window (a VUE process) by selecting Vue Window from the session manager's Create menu. This is done by positioning your pointer on the Create menu in the session manager's menu bar, dragging the pointer down, and selecting Vue Window option.

## DECterm

To directly access DCL and other VMS applications, select Terminal Window from the Create menu. The Terminal Window option creates a DECterm window, which provides you with the same features as a VT320 terminal. From this window, you can interact with the VMS operating system and use DCL commands. To create a terminal window, position your pointer on the Create menu in the session manager's menu bar, drag the pointer down, and select Terminal Window.

### Session Manager Message Area

Below the session manager's menu bar is a message area. In this area, DECwindows displays messages about tasks that complete successfully or information about problems. For instance, when you start a VUE process, DECwindows displays the message "Starting a VUE process."

### Customizing Your Session Manager

Session manager attributes determine how the screen looks, and how the keyboard and mouse perform when you begin a DECwindows session. To see the current settings, invoke the Customize menu from the session manager's menu bar, and choose one of the seven selections. A dialog box will appear on your screen. Modify the settings as applicable.

After changing settings in a dialog box from the Customize menu, you may save them (i.e., make them permanent) or restore your last-saved settings. To do so, return to the session manager window and pull down the Customize menu again. To disregard the changes you just made and return to the last settings that you saved, choose Use Last Saved Settings. To save your changes, choose Save Current Settings. System default values may be reinstated by selecting Use System Defaults.

### Pausing Your Session and Logging Out

Unless you're in the security of a private office or home, you should always be concerned about leaving your session unattended. If you want to leave the workstation for a short period, you can put your current session on hold. The pause function is invoked from the Session menu in the session manager's menu bar. When selected, pause will clear the screen and put up a password dialog box. To resume your session, simply enter your VMS password.

If you plan to be away from your workstation for a long period, you should end your session. When you end a session, DECwindows stops all applications you have running, clears the screen, and returns the Start Session dialog box to the screen. To end your session, choose Quit from the Session menu.

## DECWINDOWS FILEVIEW

The DECwindows FileView application is your primary interface to VMS commands and other applications. When FileView executes, it creates a VUE process, called the VUE Master, and a FileView window. A VUE Master process is named user_VUEn, where user is the user's account name, and n is a consecutive VUE number for this session. You can create more than one VUE Master.

Each VUE Master will have one or more FileView windows open. A FileView window has three major components:

- User modifiable menu bar
- Default directory and file filter dialog box
- File and directory list box

### FileView Menu Bar

From the FileView menu bar, you can select from the default menus:

- Control
- Customize
- Views

From additional menus you have the option to add or remove:

- Files
- Utilities
- Applications
- Help
- Examples
- Games

### Selecting a View

The directory and file filter dialog box let you choose the directory and the files that will be displayed in the FileView window list box. For instance, you can choose to view only command procedures in SYS$MANAGER.

The directory you select and files you view are specified in two fields: File Filter and Directory. To change either field and activate your new view, click in the field you want to update, enter the appropriate filter (i.e., *.COM) or directory name (i.e., SYS$MANAGER), then click on the update button. Your new view will appear in the list box.

Depending on the directory you select and the filter you apply, the list box may contain one or two lists. Subdirectories, if available and not filtered out, are displayed on the left side of the list box. You can easily select a subdirectory, or its parent, as a new view by clicking on the subdirectory name.

## Selecting Files and Running Programs

When you click on a file in the list box, it becomes selected. When you select a file, you can perform an operation on it, such as DELETE, COPY, or EDIT.

If you double click on a file in the list box, depending on its file type, the VUE master will try to execute a default function for that file's type, i.e., RUN, COMPILE, TYPE, and so on. Of course, this function is only valid for file types that have been associated with a verb. For instance, DCL command procedures and executable images will be executed when you double click on them.

## The Control Menu

The Control menu, accessible from the FileView menu bar, is used to control the environment of the VUE master process. It has the following options:

- New View
- Layout...
- Privileges...
- Menu Bar...
- Logical Names...
- Work in Progress...
- Exit

## Opening a New View Window

The New View option lets you establish a new FileView window with its own view (i.e., default directory and file filter). This is useful if you need to work with files or applications that reside in different directories. You can achieve the same results by creating a new VUE process from the session manager. However, the New View option is quicker and more efficient. You will notice, when the new VUE is created, that the VUE receives its own icon in the icon box. VUEs are siblings. You may delete a VUE without affecting any other VUEs you have open.

### Defining a View's Layout

The Layout... function is used to describe how you want files displayed. You have three category choices from which to choose: Fields, Order, and Versions. Fields contains a list of items, such as node, type, and file owner, which can be toggled on and off. The information associated with each item you turn on will be displayed along with the file name. Order contains a list of radio buttons that  let you decide how you want your file list sorted, for example, by type, by creation date, or by name. Versions contains two radio buttons, letting you choose to display all file versions or just the highest.

### Granting Privileges

The Privileges... option is used to grant or remove privileges for the VUE master process. All VMS processes, except TMPMBX and NETMBX, are listed as toggles. You can individually select privileges by clicking on their toggle buttons, or select All or None by clicking on the appropriate push button. After modifying your privileges, click on the OK push button to update the VUE master process and to put away the Privileges... menu.

### Modifying Your Menu Bar

Use the Menu Bar... function to modify the menu choices in your menu bar. There are two lists: menus listed in the menu bar, and menus not listed in the menu bar. When you click on a menu name, it is added to the other list. After you have made your alterations, click on the OK push button.

### Defining Logical Names

The Logical Names... option is available to help you show, define, and deassign logical names. A dialog box is displayed that contains a name field, definition field, show push button, define push button, and radio buttons to select a logical name table. To show a logical name translation, enter the logical name in the name field, click on the appropriate logical name table radio control, then click on the show push button. The logical name definition will be displayed in the definition field. Defining a new logical name is just as easy, with the additional step of supplying the equivalence string in the definition field.

## Managing Work in Progress

The Work in Progress... function is used to display and stop tasks that are executing or pending execution. To terminate a task, click on the task name to select it, then click on the stop task push button. This menu can also be used to display the output of a task in progress. To put this menu away, click on the dismiss push button.

## THE CUSTOMIZE MENU

The Customize menu is used to save views, tailor menus, and define default actions for file types. There are five menu options:

- Save Startup View
- Save View...
- Unsave View...
- Verbs and Menus...
- File Types...

Each of these menu options modifies your personal FileView profile, which is located in your login directory.

## Saving and Deleting Views

The Save Startup View, Save View..., and Unsave View... options are used to manage established views, i.e., directory and filter combinations. FileView parameters can be saved as a default start-up view or named views, which you can recall through the views menu.

To save the current view as your start-up view, put your pointer on the Customize menu, drag, then select Save Startup View. To save your current view as a named view, select Save View... from the Customize menu. The save view dialog box will appear, which has a name of view field and nine toggle buttons that define the attributes you want saved. You must enter the name you want to identify the view, then click on the OK push button. When you no longer need a view you have saved, use the Unsave View... option to remove it from the list of views.

## Creating and Modifying Verbs and Menus

The Verbs and Menus... function is used to modify FileView menus, create new FileView menus, and add new FileView verbs. FileView menus are simple descriptions containing a menu name, the menu options (called verbs), and the names of verb command procedures executed when you select an option. This information is stored in two VUE profiles:

SYS$LOGIN:VUE$PROFILE.VUE$DATE (personal) and
VUE$LIBRARY:VUE$SYSTEM_PROFILE.VUE$DAT (public).

The public FileView profile cannot be modified. When you make modifications to FileView, they are made to your personal FileView profile. Modify your personal FileView profile with the Verbs and Menus... function. This function opens a window containing three dialog boxes titled Verb Names, Menu Names, and Verbs in Menu. These dialog boxes work together to display information from both your personal and the public FileView profiles, and to help you modify your personal FileView profile.

To create a new menu, first enter a menu name, such as Programming, in the Menu Names dialog box entry field. Then click on the enter push button. The new menu name will be added to the list (and will be highlighted), and the Verbs in Menu list will clear. Next, select the verbs you want listed in the new menu. You must click on each verb you want added, from the Verb Names list. You will have to use the scroll bar to select verbs that are not in view. After you have added your last verb, click on the apply push button under the Verbs in Menu list. Your new menu will be added to your personal FileView profile. To have your new menu displayed in the menu bar, follow the procedures for modifying your menu bar.

In addition to creating your own FileView menus, you can add your own FileView verbs. This is accomplished by adding a Verb name (defined by you) to the Verb Names list, and associating it with a DCL command. For instance, a verb you name Security could be used to execute a command procedure called VUE$LIBRARY: VUE$PRO-TECTION.COM.

To add the new verb (i.e., Security), type its name in the Verb Names entry field, then click on the enter push button. The new verb will be added to the list, in alphabetical order, and will be highlighted. Next, click on the DCL Command for Selected Verb field and enter a DCL command to associate with the verb, i.e., @VUE$LIBRARY: VUE$PROTECTION.

Most often, a verb's associated command will execute a command procedure located in VUE$LIBRARY. However, this is not mandatory. Typically, a command procedure is used so that parameters and options can be queried from the user, and output can be appropriately directed. An example command procedure to implement the Security verb can be found in Figure 6-3.

You'll notice that VUE$PROTECTION.COM has a handful of unique commands, that are all preceded with VUE$. The VUE master, which controls all FileView activities, extends the DCL environment with its own set of commands (i.e., DCL symbols). These commands are required to successfully integrate DCL into the DECwindows environment. The command symbols are created for you (by a procedure called VUE$INIT_SUBPROCESS) when you click on a verb from any of the FileView menus.

## Defining File Type Actions and Pop-up Menus

The File Types... option lets you define the action taken when you double click on a file displayed in the FileView list box. Action is described by file type from a list of known FileView verbs.

As with the Verbs and Menus option, a window is displayed with three dialog boxes titled File Types, Verb Names, and Pop-up Menu. File Types is a list of known file types, i.e., .FOR, .DIR, .TXT, .LOG. You may add or delete file types from your personal profile. Each file type may be associated with a default verb (executed when you double click) and a pop-up menu (displayed when you press <MB2>). For example, to support a file type of .FOR, .BAS, .H, or any other language

```
$! VUE$PROTECTION.COM
$! Security—FileView Verb Procedure
$!_____
$ ON WARNING THEN GOTO PROTECTION_ERROR
$ FILE_LIST=""
$!
$! Count = number of files selected in view
$!
$ VUE$GET_SELECTION_COUNT
$ VUE$READ COUNT
$!
$! If files were selected in the view, pull
$! up the first file in the selection list.
$!
$ IF COUNT .NE. 0
$ THEN
$ VUE$GET_NEXT_SELECTION
$ VUE$READ SELECTION
$!
$! If no files selected, then pop open a dialog window
$!
$ ELSE
$ CURRENT_DEFAULT = "''F$ENVIRONMENT("DEFAULT")'"
$ VUE$INQUIRE ""     File:" "''CURRENT_DEFAULT'"'"
$ VUE$READ SELECTION
$!
$! If the user doesn't enter a file name, then exit
$!
$ IF "'SELECTION'" .EQS. "" THEN EXIT
$ ENDIF
$!
$! Pop open a task output window
$!
$ VUE$POPUP
$!
$BUILD_LIST_LOOP:
$!
$! We're here to build the directory list..."FILE" is the
$! file name and type from a full file spec.
$!
$ FILE = -
  "''F$PARSE(SELECTION,,,"NAME")'''F$PARSE(SELECTION,,,"TYPE")'"
$ FILE_LIST = "''FILE_LIST'" + "'FILE'"
$!
$! Get next file from the view list... when "" we'll quit
$!
```

## Figure 6-3: Verb Command Procedure

```
$ VUE$GET_NEXT_SELECTION
$ VUE$READ SELECTION
$ IF "'SELECTION'" .NES. ""
$ THEN
$ FILE_LIST = "'FILE_LIST'" + ","
$ GOTO BUILD_LIST_LOOP
$ ENDIF
$!
$! The list is complete, display the directory
$!
$ DIRECTORY/NOTOT/NOGRAND/SECUR/VERS=1 'FILE_LIST'
$ EXIT
$!
$ PROTECTION_ERROR:
$ VUE$SET_ERROR_STATUS
$ EXIT
```

## Figure 6-3: Verb Command Procedure (cont'd)

source file type, you might associate the Compile verb. While in the pop-up menu, you could add the verbs:

- Edit
- Compile
- Purge
- Print
- Copy

## THE VIEWS MENU

The Views menu is used to select a new view. The menu has five permanent selections:

- Login Directory
- Show All Versions
- Show Highest Version
- Show Normal
- Show Size and Date

If you have saved any views, such as a start-up view or a named view, they will also be listed in the menu.

If you select Login Directory, the FileView window will be modified to display the file you have in your login directory (SYS$LOGIN). This is the fastest way to get back to your login directory after you have nested FileView down several directory levels.

The Show All Versions, Show Highest Version, Show Normal, and Show Size and Date options are used to tailor information that FileView displays about files. The normal FileView display lists the highest version of a file with no size and date information.

## TERMINAL EMULATION

DECwindows-based applications include a VT terminal emulator called DECterm. DECterm lets you:

- Create a VT emulation window to access DCL
- Customize DECterm characteristics
- Copy and paste information between windows
- Change DECterm windows
- Compose special characters
- Exit from a DECterm window

### Creating a DECterm Window

To create a DECterm window, choose the terminal window menu item from the session manager's Create menu. After the window is displayed, give it input focus by pointing to the window and clicking on it. The title bar will be highlighted when the window has input focus.

### Customizing a Window

You can change DECterm's window features, such as the size of the window, by choosing Window... from DECterm's Customize menu. DECterm will display a dialog box.

The highlighted toggle buttons in the dialog box indicate the current settings. Click on a toggle button or its label to change the setting (on or off), then click on the OK button to apply your changes and close the dialog box.

From the Window dialog box, you can change any of the following window features:

**Record Lines Off Top:** Normally, lines that are scrolled off the top of the display are not saved. To save lines, click the Record Lines Off Top button on.

**Vertical Scroll Bar:** Unless you specify otherwise, a DECterm window will not have a vertical scroll bar. Click on Vertical Scroll Bar to add a vertical scroll bar to the right-hand side of your DECterm window.

**Horizontal Scroll Bar:** This button turns the horizontal scroll bar on or off. Click on Horizontal Scroll Bar to display a horizontal scroll bar on the bottom of your DECterm window.

**Auto Resize Terminal:** By default, when you use the Window Set-Up dialog box to change your terminal size, the window size changes to conform to it. Clicking on Auto Resize Terminal causes the terminal size to conform whenever you modify the window size.

**Auto Resize Window:** By default, when you modify the terminal size, the window size conforms to the new size. Disabling Auto Resize Window means that if your terminal characteristics cause more characters to be displayed than your current window size can accommodate, those characters will be truncated.

**Big Font/Little Font:** Unless you specify otherwise, the Little Font option is the default which causes DECterm to display a 12-point font. Clicking on the Big Font option displays an easy-to-read 18-point font.

**Normal Font/Condensed Font:** Clicking on Normal Font causes DECterm to use the normal font (80 columns). The preset option for font size is normal font/80, condensed/132.

**Terminal Size:** By default, terminal size is set to 24 rows by 80 columns. By clicking on the size you want, you can change the row setting to 48 or 72, and the column setting to 132 or to any setting from 1 to 254.

## Customizing your Display

You can modify DECterm's display features, such as the type of cursor, by choosing the Display... option from the Customize menu.

DECterm will display a dialog box, from which you can customize any of the following display features:

**Auto Wrap:** Normally, when the cursor reaches the right margin, each new character you type will delete the previous character. Clicking on Auto Wrap causes new characters to be displayed on the next line.

**Display Cursor:** Unless you specify otherwise, a cursor is displayed in your DECterm window. If you disable Display Cursor, your cursor will become invisible.

**Cursor Blink:** By default, your cursor blinks. Disabling Cursor Blink causes a nonblinking cursor to be displayed.

**Block Cursor/Underline Cursor:** By default, a block-shaped cursor is displayed. Clicking on the Underline Cursor option causes an underline cursor to be displayed.

**Dark Text, Light Background/Light Text, Dark Background:** You can change the default of dark text with a light background by clicking on the Light Text, Dark Background option.

## Customizing General Features

You can change general features, such as the terminal type, by selecting the General... option from DECterm's Customize menu. DECterm displays a dialog box, from which you can set any of the following terminal features:

**New Line:** Normally, pressing the <RETURN> key does not move the cursor to start a new line. Clicking on this option causes the cursor to move to start a new line when you press <RETURN>.

**Lock UDKs:** Your keyboard has keys that you can define for your own use. Unless you specify otherwise, after you have defined a key, the host system can change the function of the key back to the system default. Clicking on this function locks your user-defined keys so that the host system cannot change them.

**Lock User Features:** DECterm allows you to change two user features: Auto Repeat and Foreground, and Background Display. The host system can change these functions to the system default unless you click on this option to prevent it from doing so.

**Normal Cursor Keys/Application Cursor Keys:** By default, the Normal Cursor Keys option is on, which causes the arrow keys to move the cursor up, down, left, and right. By clicking on the Application Cursor Keys option, you can override the Normal Cursor Keys default and set the arrow keys to application-specific functions.

**Terminal ID:** You can set the device attributes response (i.e., terminal ID) by using the Terminal ID menu item. The device attribute response lets the host system know specific attributes of the terminal. The default is DECterm ID.

**Numeric Keypad/Application Keypad:** Unless you specify otherwise, the Numeric Keypad option is set, which means that pressing the numeric keypad produces the characters that appear on the keycaps. You can override the Numeric Keypad default by clicking on the Application Keypad option, which causes the numeric keypad to function as a set of user-defined keys.

## Customizing your Keyboard

You can set keyboard features, such as turning the warning bell on or off, by selecting Keyboard... from DECterm's Customize menu. DECterm will display a dialog box, from which you can set the following keyboard features:

**Warning Bell:** By default, the keyboard warning bell is set to ring when errors occur. You can disable this function by turning off the Warning Bell option.

**Margin Bell:** By default, the margin bell does not ring when the cursor reaches the right margin. You can enable the margin bell by clicking on Margin Bell.

**Keyclick:** Unless you specify otherwise, the keyboard keys click (through the keyboard speaker) when you press them. You can disable this function by turning off the Keyclick option.

**Auto Repeat:** By default, characters repeat when you hold a key down. To disable this function, click off the Auto Repeat option.

## Selecting a National Character Set

You can pick a National Replacement Character Set (NRCS) that corresponds to the chosen keyboard dialect by choosing the 7-Bit NRCS Selection... menu item on the Customize menu. DECterm displays a dialog box, from which you can select the following character sets:

- Austrian/German
- Belgian/French
- Dutch
- Italian
- Norwegian
- Portuguese
- Spanish
- Swedish
- Swiss (French)
- Swiss (German)

## Saving and Restoring DECterm Features

After modifying DECterm settings, you must save your changes to make them permanent. When you save your changes, DECterm uses these settings each time you create a DECterm window. If you change your mind and want to use the settings that came with your system, you can restore the original defaults.

To save your DECterm settings:

- Choose the Save Current Settings option from DECterm's Customize menu. This is for routine saving of customized features.

- Select the Save Current Settings As... option from DECterm's Customize menu when you want to save the current customized features under a different file name. DECterm displays a dialog box that prompts you for the name of the file you want to use to save your customized features.

To restore customized settings:

- Choose the Use Last Saved Settings option from DECterm's Customize menu to restore an existing file.

- Select the Use System Defaults option from DECterm's Customize menu to restore the system defaults.

- Choose the Use Saved Settings From... option from DECterm's Customize menu to restore previously saved settings.

## Cutting and Pasting Information

You can copy part or all of a file using the Edit menu.

To copy information:

1. Select the text you want to copy by pressing and holding MB1, dragging the pointer over the text, and releasing MB1. The selected area is highlighted.

2. Choose the Copy menu item from the Edit menu to store the copied text.

3. Click on the area where you want to place the text.

4. Choose the Paste menu item from the Edit menu. The selected text is copied to the new location.

## Exiting from DECterm

To exit from DECterm and close the DECterm window, choose the Quit menu item or type logout.

## CONCLUSION

The X Window System is revolutionary. It has the unique capability of separating form from function, which frees users from the confines of any one manufacturer's hardware or software. DECwindows is Digital's standard implementation of the X Window System.

# Chapter 7

# Command Procedures

DCL commands allow you to manipulate files and directories, manage system resources, and run application programs. Interactive DCL is effective, but often slow and tedious, especially if you're entering repetitive commands.

As a VAX system professional, you must learn to develop command procedures to realize the full potential and flexibility of a VMS system. System managers, operators and programmers rely on command procedures to make their jobs easier.

In this chapter, you'll learn how to develop DCL command procedures and understand the many useful features of DCL symbols, lexical functions, and logical names. In addition, this chapter demonstrates the use of the VMS batch processor, a feature that allows you to run jobs without tying up your terminal. When you complete this chapter, you will be able to develop and invoke useful, time-saving command procedures.

## DCL SYMBOLS

It would be difficult to write programs in any language without variables in which to store character strings or numeric values. DCL command procedures are no different.

A symbol is a DCL variable that you can use to temporarily store a string of characters, numeric value, or logical value (true or false).

You can use a symbol anywhere the value it represents is used. The symbol names you create can be one to 255 characters in length, and they must begin with a character, dollar sign, or underscore. If you use lowercase characters, they will be translated to uppercase. Table 7-1 defines some of the DCL commands used to create, manipulate, and delete symbols.

## Table 7-1: Commands to Define, Modify, or Delete Symbols

| DCL Command | Command Function |
| --- | --- |
| := | Defines a symbolic name for a character string value. |
| = | Defines a symbolic name for a character string or integer value. |
| DELETE/SYMBOL | Deletes a symbol from the local symbol table. To delete symbols from the global symbol table, the /GLOBAL qualifier must be used. |
| INQUIRE | Prompts for input at SYS$COMMAND and assigns the value to the specified symbol. |
| READ | Reads a record from a file or device and assigns it to a symbol. |
| SET SYMBOL/SCOPE | Masks local or global symbols at the specified command level. |
| SHOW SYMBOL | Displays the contents of the specified local or global symbol. |

## Creating Symbols

Symbols are created when you assign a value to them using one of the assignment operators, which are = and ==. Symbols can be local to a DCL command level or global to all levels of a login session. They are created in one of the following ways:

symbol_name =[=] value

or

symbol_name[bit_position,size] = value

A local symbol (=) can only be used at the command level in which you defined it, while a global (==) symbol can be used at any command level. For instance, if you define both a local and global symbol in a command procedure, the local symbol will be deleted when the command procedure exits, but the global symbol will still remain.

Let's consider this symbol assignment example:

$ HOME = "SET DEFAULT SYS$LOGIN"

Here, the DCL command SET DEFAULT SYS$LOGIN is assigned to a symbol called HOME. Now, anytime you type HOME at the command prompt, your default directory will be changed. In this example, the symbol is being used as a form of shorthand. You could go a step further, using two or more symbols in a single command. This is demonstrated in the next example, where the global symbols GO and HOME are created and used to set the default directory to SYS$LOGIN:

$ GO == "SET DEFAULT"
$ HOME == "SYS$LOGIN"
$ GO HOME

Symbols have many applications, of which command substitution is the most basic.

You can also use symbols in simple integer math operations. In the following sample command, the symbol RESULT will be assigned the outcome of a math problem:

$ RESULT = 9 * (199 - 23)

Use the DCL command SHOW SYMBOL to display what's in your symbol:

$ SHOW SYMBOL RESULT
RESULT = 1584   Hex = 00000630  Octal = 00000003060

Each process maintains two symbol tables, one for local symbols and another for global symbols. When you use the SHOW SYMBOL command, the process looks for the symbol in your local symbol table by default. To display a symbol from your global symbol table, use the /GLOBAL qualifier. Also, you can use the handy qualifier /ALL to display all local symbols or /GLOBAL/ALL to list your global symbols.

## Deleting Symbols

In some cases, it might be necessary to delete a symbol explicitly. To do so, use the DCL command DELETE/SYMBOL. If the symbol is global, add the /GLOBAL qualifier to the command. Here's how you delete the global symbol HOME:

$ DELETE/SYMBOL/GLOBAL HOME

All symbols, global and local, are deleted when a process is deleted, i.e., when you log out.

## DCL Symbol Translation

When a DCL command is executed, symbols in the following positions are automatically translated:

- At the beginning of the command.
- In a lexical function.
- In a WRITE, IF, EXAMINE or DEPOSIT statement.
- On the right side of an = or == statement.
- Inside brackets on the left side of an assignment statement when you're performing string substitution.

If none of these situations is met, you must force translation of the symbol by enclosing it in apostrophes. In the following illustration, the symbol BUDGET is assigned a full file specification. You must then force translation to use it alone with DCL commands.

$ BUDGET = "DJA2:[ACCOUNTING]BUDGET.DAT"
$ DIRECTORY 'BUDGET'

Without the apostrophes, the result would have looked like this:

```
$ DIRECTORY BUDGET
%DIRECT-W-NOFILES, no files found
```

If you need to force translation of a symbol within a character string, enclose the symbol in double apostrophes, as in this example:

```
$ PB = "PURGE "BUDGET""
```

You might also discover that only a single apostrophe is needed at the end of the symbol as in ''BUDGET''.

## Additional Symbol Uses

Although the most common use of symbols is DCL shorthand, symbols can also be used effectively to produce mnemonics. For example, let's assign values to three symbols that will be used to clear the display of a VTxxx terminal:

```
$ ESC = "<ESC>"! ASCII <ESC> character
$ CLEAR = "[J"    ! VT clear to end of display
$ HOME = "[H"    ! VT home cursor
$
$ WRITE SYS$OUTPUT ESC,HOME,ESC,CLEAR
$
```

You can go one step further and assign the whole command to a symbol, like this:

```
CLR :== WRITE SYS$OUTPUT ESC,HOME,ESC,CLEAR
```

Note that you can omit the quotations around a string substitution if you precede the assignment operator with a colon, as shown above. Be careful, though. Sometimes the results are unpredictable.
Another common use of symbols is to execute command procedures. For example, here's a symbol called VMSINSTAL used to execute the VMS software installation procedure:

```
$ VMSINSTAL == "@SYS$UPDATE:VMSINSTAL"
```

Better yet, you can use symbols to define foreign commands for executable images that don't have a DCL command table entry. In the following example, you define the symbol KERMIT as a command to run KERMIT.EXE, which is located in the SYS$SYSTEM directory:

```
$ KER*MIT == "$KERMIT"
```

The asterisk used in the KERMIT symbol is a wildcard character. When specified, DCL will accept the characters before the wildcard as the command as well as any of the characters after it. Thus, you could use KER, KERM, KERMI or KERMIT as the command. This lets you abbreviate your foreign commands, just like you're used to doing.

The dollar sign ($), used in the KERMIT symbol assignment above, is another handy DCL notation. It causes the image named to be run from the SYS$SYSTEM directory. The DCL command MCR will accomplish the same thing, so $MCR KERMIT is the same as $RUN SYS$SYSTEM:KERMIT.

## DATA REPRESENTATION

When you create a file of any kind, the computer stores the file contents as a representation of the type of data with which you're working. The computer only stores binary values (1s and 0s). The operating system and application software interpret the binary values that allow you to use different types of data, such as characters or numbers.

VMS stores data in several formats:

**Bit** — The basic unit of storage. A bit can only represent a value of zero or one, the digits in the binary counting system.

**Byte** — Equal to eight bits. A byte can range in magnitude from zero to 255 (unsigned number) or -128 to 127 (signed number). Each ASCII character is stored in one byte.

**Word** — Equal to two bytes (16 bits). A word can represent a signed integer value of -32,768 to 32,767 or an unsigned value of 0 through 65,353.

**Longword** — Equal to four bytes (32 bits). The longword can represent a signed integer value of -2,147,483,648 to 2,147,483,647 or an unsigned value of 0 through 4,294,967,295.

**Binary number representation** — A series of eight, 16, or 32 bits, read right to left, with the rightmost bit representing the low-order value.

**Binary character representation** — A series of eight bits, read left to right, with the leftmost bit representing the low-order value. A standard code, known as the ASCII code, defines the value to character association.

To understand this a little better, let's look at how an ASCII character is represented by the VAX:

| **Char** | **ASCII** | **Binary representation** |
|----------|-----------|---------------------------|
| A | 65 | 01000001 |
| B | 66 | 01000010 |
| C | 67 | 01000011 |
| D | 68 | 01000100 |
| E | 69 | 01000101 |
| . | | |
| . | | |
| . | | |
| Y | 89 | 01011001 |
| Z | 90 | 01011010 |

## DCL Expressions

DCL expressions are formed when you combine data elements with DCL operators. There are two categories of DCL operators: names and characters. Operator names are Boolean operators used in most programming languages (.EQ., .AND., .OR. and others). Character operators are those used in common mathematical statements, i.e., plus (+), minus (-), multiply (*) and divide (/).

DCL expression data elements, called operands, can be literal values (1,2,3 ... "COW","PIG" ...) or symbols. All DCL expressions take one of two basic forms: logical comparisons or operations.

A logical comparison evaluates the relationship between operands as true or false. A logic TRUE is equivalent to a numeric 1, and FALSE equals a numeric 0. Consider the following:

```
$ RESULT = 20 - 10
$ TRUE_FALSE = RESULT .EQ. 10
$ SHOW SYMBOL TRUE_FALSE
TRUE_FALSE = 1  Hex = 000001   Octal = 000001
```

The first command assigns the value 10 to the symbol RESULT. The second command says, "If RESULT is equal (.EQ.) to 10, then assign the value of TRUE (TRUE=1) to the symbol TRUE_FALSE; if not, then make it FALSE (FALSE=0)."

A DCL operation assigns a value to a symbol, based on some mathematical evaluation. In this example, two values are multiplied and assigned to a symbol called RESULT:

```
$ RESULT = 23 * 2
$ SHOW SYMBOL RESULT
RESULT = 46    Hex = 000002E   Octal = 0000056
```

It's interesting to note that DCL also will perform character string addition, called concatenation. In the commands below, two literal strings are added together to describe the night.

```
$ THE_NIGHT = "The night " + "was sultry."
$ SHOW SYMBOL THE_NIGHT
THE_NIGHT = "The night was sultry"
$
```

It's also possible to combine data types in a DCL expression, such as integer and character string. DCL will convert one of the two data types to that of the other. Here's how DCL handles this type of expression:

```
$ RESULT = 12 + "12"
$ SHOW SYMBOL RESULT
RESULT = 24    Hex = 0000018   Octal = 0000030
```

## LEXICAL FUNCTIONS

Lexical functions are special VMS routines that return process, system, and device information, or manipulate user-supplied data. Lexicals are unique in that the result is returned in the name of the lexical function, just like a function in a compiled programming language. This allows you to use the result of a lexical function in the same context as a symbol.

Lexical functions are invoked when you force DCL to evaluate them. All lexicals begin with F$ and take the general format:

```
F$function_name([argument, argument...])
```

The argument list must be enclosed in parentheses, and each argument must be separated by a comma. If the lexical doesn't require an argument, you must specify an empty list, i.e., F$TIME().

Let's look at a simple example of the F$SEARCH lexical function that returns a full file specification for the given argument:

```
$ LGICMD = F$SEARCH("SYS$LOGIN:LOGIN.COM")
$ SHOW SYMBOL LGICMD
FILE = "BIFF$DUA3:[BYNON]LOGIN.COM;4"
$
```

If the file specification could not be found, a null string "" would have been returned. F$SEARCH is an example of a lexical function that returns system information. Other lexical functions, such as F$EDIT, manipulate user-supplied data:

```
$ TAXES = "All    I have to do is    die and pay              taxes!"
$ TAXES = F$EDIT(TAXES, "COMPRESS, UPCASE")
$ SHOW SYMBOL TAXES
TAXES = "ALL I HAVE TO DO IS DIE AND PAY TAXES!"
$
```

## Nesting Lexical Functions

Because the result of a lexical function acts like a symbol, lexicals can be used as parameters to other lexical functions. In this example, the F$EXTRACT lexical is used to extract the month field from a time and date string provided by F$TIME:

```
$ MONTH = F$EXTRACT(3,3,F$TIME())
$ SHOW SYMBOL MONTH
MONTH = "AUG"
$
```

There's no practical limit to the depth you can nest the lexical functions. However, each lexical used as an argument to another adds a new level of complexity to your statement. For instance, if you only wanted the time from F$TIME, you could use this statement:

```
$ TIME = F$EXTRACT(F$LOCATE(":",F$TIME)-2, -
F$LENGTH(F$TIME()),F$TIME())
$ SHOW SYMBOL TIME
TIME = "10:29:03.07"
```

You can easily see why it becomes difficult to read and understand.

A VMS system supports lexical functions that:

- Return information about the system
- Convert data types
- Return information about your process
- Manipulate text strings
- Translate logical names
- Supply information about queues
- Return information about files and devices
- Return information about symbols

## COMMAND PROCEDURES

A command procedure is a file containing a sequence of DCL commands. Command procedure files can be processed interactively or as a batch job. Typically, you use command procedures to perform repetitive or complex tasks and to save time. With a command procedure, you can execute many DCL commands with one simple statement. Command procedures aren't bound by simple lists of DCL commands executed one after another. Through command procedures, you can take advantage of all DCL features, such as labels, lexical functions, symbols and relational operators, to build sophisticated procedures that perform like programs.

Command procedures are flexible. You can write a command procedure that will take specific actions based on a response to a question or even one that will perform a particular function depending on the time of day. Even if you know little about conventional programming, you'll find it easy to program in DCL.

Command procedure development is generally fast, because DCL is an interpreter. Procedures are easily tested as you develop them.

For the system manager, command procedures are an absolute necessity. A VMS system uses command procedures to start up and shut down the system. Also, most routine system maintenance is accomplished using procedures. In addition, command procedures are used to control captive and limited user accounts.

Operators make use of time-saving command procedures by creating routines to perform repetitive work, for example, system backup, starting and stopping queues, restarting network circuits, and more.

Programmers make use of command procedures in many ways, too. The most common use of procedures by programmers is to compile and link source programs. Command procedures are also useful when it comes time to test programs.

## DEVELOPING COMMAND PROCEDURES

Command procedures are developed using your favorite text editor, such as EDT or EVE. Whichever text editor you use, the following guidelines apply:

### Naming Convention

Your command procedures should always have a file type of COM. This is the default file type for command procedures. If you use any other file type, you will have to include it when you invoke the procedure.

It's generally helpful if the procedure name tells you something about what it does. For example, if you write a personal phone book procedure, you might name it PHONE_BOOK.COM.

### Command Lines

Each line in a command procedure must begin with a dollar sign ($). Multiple spaces or tabs can be included after the $ to increase readability. DCL will ignore them.

You can extend your commands past a single line by using a hyphen (-). Often, this will make your procedures easier to read, especially if many parameters or qualifiers are used.

```
$ SET TERMINAL -
  ADVANCED_VIDEO -
  /REGIS -
  /WIDTH=80 -
  /PAGE=24 -
  /INSERT
$
```

### Program Input

To supply input to programs, such as YES or NO responses, specify each element on its own line without the dollar sign ($). The data lines will be used by the running program (remember, input has been redirected to the procedure file), not by the DCL command line interpreter (CLI).

Figure 7-1 invokes the MAIL utility and enters commands and responses.

```
$ MAIL                          <- Invokes the MAIL utility
SEND                            <- MAIL SEND command
WILLIS,PENDLETON,T_BYNON        <- In response to "TO:" prompt
System schedule...              <- In response to "Subj:" prompt
Good day,                       <- MAIL message

The system will be down on
Monday, 24 August, from 6 a.m.
to 1 p.m. for normal system
maintenance.
David
$                               <- Terminates the MAIL program
$ EXIT                          <- Terminates the procedure
```

### Figure 7-1: Invoking the MAIL Utility

## Comments and Documentation

You can comment your command procedures by preceding the line with an exclamation point (!). Everything to the right of it is ignored by the DCL command line interpreter. If you take the time to document your command procedures, they will be easier to debug or modify at a later date.

As a side thought to your documentation and remarks, consider not abbreviating commands. It's not a good practice to abbreviate DCL commands in your command procedures. By spelling out commands, your command procedures will be more readable and nearly self-documenting.

## Labels

Labels are markers used by the DCL command line interpreter for conditional processing and repetition loops. They're used by commands that transfer control, such as GOTO and ON.

Although not required, you should put labels on separate lines. Doing so makes the labels easier to find and serves as another form of commenting, if you use descriptive labels. Your label names can be one to 255 characters long but must not contain blanks. Labels are always terminated with a colon (:).

## Command Procedure Debugging

After you write a command procedure, you should test it and change any statements that cause errors. Use the DCL commands SET VERIFY and SHOW SYMBOL to locate problem commands.

The SET VERIFY command tells DCL to display each command as it is processed. This allows you to see where an error is generated and how symbols in strings are translated. The command SET NOVERIFY turns off the verify mode. The SHOW SYMBOL command displays the contents of a symbol. In a command procedure, you can use the SHOW SYMBOL command after you define or manipulate a symbol to see its contents.

## INVOKING COMMAND PROCEDURES

There are two methods of invoking command procedures: as an interactive program or as a batch job.

## Interactive Command Procedures

To run a command procedure interactively, use the EXECUTE command (@) followed by the procedure name. If the file type isn't .COM, you must include the file type. Command procedures can be invoked at the DCL prompt or within another command procedure.

The purpose of the DCL EXECUTE command (@) is somewhat misleading. The EXECUTE command doesn't cause a procedure to be executed like a VMS image file. Instead, the EXECUTE command merely tells DCL to get its input from the specified file. Like any other DCL command, it accepts parameters and qualifiers. The format of the EXECUTE command is:

$ @procedure [P1 P2...P8] [/OUTPUT]

This example invokes a command procedure called FUNCTION_KEYS.COM, which is in the user's default login directory.

```
$ @SYS$LOGIN:FUNCTION_KEYS
```

The EXECUTE command will interpret any valid file specification.

### Batch Command Procedures

You can invoke a command as a batch job, which will run as a separate process from your interactive login session. To do so, use the DCL command SUBMIT.

The SUBMIT command places your job in a batch queue with other jobs waiting to be run. Command procedures are submitted as batch jobs if you want them to execute at a specific time, if they will take a long time to execute, or if the job must run at a reduced priority.

The following command submits the command procedure STARTNET.COM to be executed by the VMS batch processor:

```
$ SUBMIT SYS$MANAGER:STARTNET
Job STARTNET (queue SYS$BATCH, entry 106) started on SYS$BATCH
```

The queue SYS$BATCH is used by default, unless you specify another queue using the /QUEUE qualifier. When VMS executes the procedure, it creates a process with your rights and privileges, and executes the procedure. In fact, the batch processor even runs through your login procedure, LOGIN.COM.

## SYMBOLS AND LEXICAL FUNCTIONS USED IN COMMAND PROCEDURES

Our earlier discussion of symbols and lexicals was limited to their basic usage. Here, we'll discover the true power of these useful tools.

### Using Symbols in Command Procedures

Symbols can be local or global. A local symbol is accessible by DCL at the command level at which it was defined and from within procedures called after its creation. A global symbol is recognized at any DCL command level.

We use local symbols when the symbol is only necessary for the duration of the command procedure using the symbol. If your symbol must survive between command procedures or for the duration of your login session, define it as a global symbol.

## Using Lexical Functions in Command Procedures

Lexical functions allow you to obtain much of the same information
that you get from DCL SHOW commands. As an example, the F$TIME
lexical and DCL command SHOW TIME are almost identical:

```
$ SHOW TIME
  23-AUG-1988 14:28:17
$
$ WRITE SYS$OUTPUT F$TIME()
  23-AUG-1988 14:28:19.37
$
```

In a command procedure, however, it's easier to get and manipulate
information from lexicals. Consider the following procedure,
DATE.COM:

```
$ DATE = F$TIME()
$ DATE = F$EXTRACT(0,11,DATE)
$ WRITE SYS$OUTPUT DATE
```

When invoked, this procedure displays the date portion of the string
returned by the lexical function F$TIME. The lexical function
F$EXTRACT is used to extract a string segment from the supplied
string. In this example, the string segment is the first 11 characters of
the string contained in the symbol DATE. The date string then is
extracted and reassigned to the same symbol.

```
$ @DATE
23-AUG-1988
$
```

If you had used the SHOW TIME command instead of the lexical
function, you wouldn't have been able to assign the output to a
symbol. Also, extracting the desired string segment would have been
cumbersome at best.

## PARAMETERS

It's often useful to be able to pass parameters to a command
procedure. Parameters are used to supply information to the
procedure.

DCL reserves eight global symbols, called P1 through P8, that you
can use in your command procedures to pass and receive information.
Through the use of these parameter symbols, you can specify

different data each time the procedure is run.

P1 through P8 parameters are specified on the command line that invokes the procedure. Unless you specifically design a command procedure to do so, you aren't prompted for the parameters, as you are with DCL commands. Instead, you must know what parameters the procedure is looking for and their order before invoking it. Parameters can be character strings, integers or symbols. You separate parameters with a space.

You can specify all eight parameters on a command line. Each is assigned to the next higher P symbol. For example, if you supply two parameters, A and B, they will be assigned to the symbols P1 and P2 respectively. The remaining parameter symbols (P3-P8) will be assigned null strings (""). If you wish to skip over a parameter, you must specify a null string:

```
$ @COMMAND_PROCEDURE P1 P2 "" P4 . . .
```

If you include more than eight parameters on a command line, VMS will return an error message, and the command procedure will abort.

The following command procedure, ADD.COM, illustrates the use of parameters. If you supply two numbers on the command line, the procedure will return their sum:

```
$! ADD.COM
$! Command procedure to demonstrate passing parameters
$!
$ IF ((P1 .EQ. "") .OR. (P2 .EQ. "")) THEN GOTO ERROR
$ WRITE SYS$OUTPUT P1 + P2
$ EXIT
$ ERROR:
$ WRITE SYS$INPUT "ERROR — PARAMETER(S) MISSING"
$ @ADD 99 1
100
```

If your command procedure requires literal text, such as multiple letters or words, you must enclose the parameter in quotation marks. A string enclosed in quotes is treated as a parameter. Lowercase characters won't be converted to uppercase.

## FLOW CONTROL AND CONDITIONAL PROCESSING

To this point, we've created command procedures and procedure segments that perform a consecutive series of DCL statements. However, it's also possible to write command procedures that execute statements based on a particular condition or that repeat statements a given number of times.

Before we proceed, let's define some terms used in traditional programming:

**Variable** — A symbol that can be changed each time you perform a task, for example, a symbol being used to hold a count.

**Iteration** — A command or group of commands that are repeated. The iteration is the repeat count or, more precisely, the number of times the group of commands has been executed.

**Conditional** — A command or group of commands that can vary each time the task is performed, for example, a statement that's performed based on the time of day. Time is the condition.

### Conditional Statements

Most structured programming languages support one or more forms of conditional processing. DCL is no different.

To test and take action on a particular condition, a common IF-THEN-ELSE statement is used. VMS versions before V5 only support an IF-THEN statement. The IF-THEN and IF-THEN-ELSE statements cause a command to be executed based on the evaluation of a condition. The basic use is:

$ IF condition THEN command

or

$ IF condition THEN command ELSE command

The condition is a Boolean expression (i.e., a statement that evaluates to true or false) and the command is any legal DCL command. In the IF-THEN-ELSE format, if the condition isn't true, the ELSE command is processed.

The following command procedure, GOOD_DAY.COM, demonstrates

## Table 7-2: DCL Boolean Operators

| OPERATOR | FUNCTION |
|----------|----------|
| .EQ./.EQS. | Determines if the two numbers/ character strings are equal. |
| .GE./.GES. | Tests to see if the first number/ character string is greater than or equal to the second. |
| .GT./.GTS. | Determines if the first number/ character string is greater than the second. |
| .LE./.LES. | Tests to see if the first number/ character string is less than or equal to the second. |
| .LT./.LTS. | Determines if the first number/ character string is less than the second. |
| .NE./.NES. | Tests to see if the two numbers/ character strings are not equal. Combines two numbers with a logical AND, i.e., Boolean algebra addition operation. |
| .OR. | Combines two numbers with a logical OR, i.e., Boolean algebra multiplication operation. |
| .NOT. | Logically negates a value. |

the IF-THEN statement:

```
$!GOOD_DAY.COM
$!
$TIME = F$TIME()
$HOUR = F$EXTRACT(12,2,TIME)
$IF (HOUR .LT. 12) THEN -
  WRITE SYS$OUTPUT "Good morning!"
$EXIT
```

In the above example, the IF-THEN statement says, "If the hour is less than (.LT.) 12, then say 'Good morning!'" The acronym .LT. is the Boolean operator LESS THAN. Boolean operators supported by DCL are shown in Table 7-2.

When you write an expression with two operands, you must ensure that the two values are the same data type: integer or character string. If you mix data types, DCL will convert the values to the same data type. Character strings that represent numeric values will be converted to an integer value when mixed with numeric values.

### Transfering Control to a Label

Often, you'll need to execute multiple commands or go around a segment of commands based on a condition. To do so, use the DCL command GOTO. The GOTO command transfers execution control to a specified label, as in this example:

```
$IF condition THEN GOTO GO_AROUND
  .
  .
  .
$GO_AROUND:
  .
  .
  .
$EXIT
```

You can expand the GOOD_DAY.COM procedure using this technique:

```
$GOOD_DAY.COM
$!
$        TIME = F$TIME()
$        HOUR = F$EXTRACT(12,2,TIME)
$        IF HOUR .LT. 12 THEN GOTO MORNING
```

```
$       IF HOUR .LE. 17 THEN GOTO AFTERNOON
$       IF HOUR .GE. 18 THEN GOTO EVENING
$       GOTO END
$MORNING:
$       WRITE SYS$OUTPUT "Good morning!"
$       GOTO END
$AFTERNOON:
$       WRITE SYS$OUTPUT "Good afternoon!"
$       GOTO END
$EVENING:
$       WRITE SYS$OUTPUT "Good evening!"
$END:
$       EXIT
```

## Execution Loops

If you want to repeat a statement or group of statements until a given condition is met, write an execution loop. There are two kinds: the DO WHILE and the DO UNTIL.

The DO WHILE loop tests for the condition before executing any commands. It takes the form:

```
$LOOP:
$       IF .NOT. condition THEN GOTO END
 .
 .      !Statements to be executed go here.
 .
$       GOTO LOOP
$ END:
$       EXIT
```

The DO UNTIL loop executes the statements and then tests the condition:

```
$LOOP:
 .
 .!Statements to be executed go here.
 .
$       IF condition THEN GOTO LOOP
$       EXIT
```

## Subroutines

Subroutines are useful in complex command procedures, where you need to use the same series of commands in different parts of your procedure.

Subroutines also make your procedures easier to read and more compact. The DCL commands CALL and GOSUB are used to build subroutines.

GOSUB command transfers execution control to a label. A RETURN command terminates subroutine execution, returning control to the statement below the GOSUB command. Here's an example of the GOSUB and RETURN commands. Please note that GOSUB and RETURN aren't supported in VMS versions prior to 4.4.

```
    .
    .
    .
$ OPEN/WRITE OUTPUT_FILE PERSINFO.DAT
$!
$! Collect info
$!
$ INQUIRE RECORD "Enter your name"
$ GOSUB WRITE_TO_FILE
$ INQUIRE RECORD "Enter your address"
$ GOSUB WRITE_TO_FILE
$ INQUIRE RECORD "Enter your phone number"
$ GOSUB WRITE_TO_FILE
$ CLOSE OUTPUT_FILE
$ EXIT
$!
$! subroutine WRITE_TO_FILE
$!
$ WRITE_TO_FILE:
        WRITE OUTPUT_FILE RECORD
$       RETURN
```

The CALL command provides the same functionality as its GOSUB counterpart. However, the CALL command creates a new command level. When you issue a CALL command, it's the same as executing another command procedure within your current procedure. The purpose of CALL is to make command procedures easier to manage.

There are two special commands used in conjunction with CALL: SUBROUTINE and ENDSUBROUTINE. The SUBROUTINE command is

specified on the command line after the CALL label. The
ENDSUBROUTINE command is used after the subroutine's EXIT
command, which returns control to the main routine.

## TERMINAL INPUT AND OUTPUT

Most command procedures executed interactively do some form of
text input and output with the terminal. DCL supports terminal I/O with
the READ, WRITE, INQUIRE, TYPE and COPY commands.

### Terminal Output

The WRITE, TYPE and COPY commands can be used to output data to a
terminal. TYPE and COPY are used to display the contents of a file or
input stream on the user's terminal. Their use is limited to text output,
because DCL can't translate symbols in the output streams of these
commands. The following examples show the basic use:

```
$ TYPE WELCOME.TXT

$ COPY SYS$INPUT SYS$OUTPUT
WELCOME TO VAX/VMS V5.1
```

The WRITE command is more flexible than TYPE or COPY, because the
output of a WRITE command is processed directly by DCL. Therefore,
expressions, symbols, and lexical functions are evaluated and
translated before the data is sent to the terminal.

When using the WRITE command, you must direct output to a logical
device. Usually, this will be SYS$OUTPUT. The output expression
must translate to a string. The data, however, can be a string, lexical
function, symbol, or any combination thereof.

These examples illustrate some of the many ways you can use the
WRITE command to output text strings to a terminal:

```
$!
$! Writing a simple text string
$! $ WRITE SYS$OUTPUT "I/O, I/O, out to the terminal I go..."
$! $ USER = F$GETJPI("","USERNAME")
$ HOWDY = "HELLO " + "THERE "
$ WRITE SYS$OUTPUT HOWDY, USER
$!
$! Tired of "WRITE SYS$OUTPUT" yet? Don't forget symbols!
```

```
$!
$ SAY = "WRITE SYS$OUTPUT"
$!
$! Writing the value of a lexical function to your terminal
$!
$ SAY "YOU ARE IN DIRECTORY " F$DIRECTORY()
$!
$! Writing a string that contains a symbol or lexical function
$!
$ SAY ""HI' ''USER' YOU ARE IN DIRECTORY ''F$DIRECTORY()'"
$!
```

## Terminal Input

Most of your command procedures would be rather useless if you couldn't get input from the user. To do this, you use the INQUIRE and READ commands.

The DCL INQUIRE command is special, because its default input source is the terminal keyboard. The INQUIRE command saves a step, because you don't have to tell it from where to get input. The READ command, on the other hand, must be told what the input stream is.

INQUIRE prompts for input, waits for the user to enter data, then assigns it to a symbol of your choice. All INQUIRE data is accepted as a character string. The characters are converted to uppercase and compressed, i.e., extra blanks and tabs are removed for you. The next example typifies the use of INQUIRE:

```
$ INQUIRE YES_NO "ARE YOU READY [Y/N]"
$ IF (YES_NO) THEN . . .
```

There are two useful INQUIRE qualifiers: /NOPUNCTUATION and /GLOBAL. The /NOPUNCTUATION qualifier tells DCL not to put a colon (:) at the end of the prompt, and the /GLOBAL qualifier instructs DCL to make the symbol receiving input a global symbol.

The READ command prompts for input if the /PROMPT qualifier is used, accepts the data from a specified source, and assigns it to a symbol. Data is accepted as is; no string conversion or compression takes place.

These READ examples show some of the many ways you can use READ to get input from the terminal:

```
$! With the READ command, you must specify the source. In many
$! cases, this will be SYS$INPUT. Notice in this example that
$! we evaluated an expression in the WRITE statement, while
$! using the expression as a list element.
$!
$ READ /PROMPT="First value: " SYS$INPUT VALUE_1
$ READ /PROMPT="Second value: " SYS$INPUT VALUE_2
$ WRITE SYS$OUTPUT -    VALUE_1," + ",VALUE_2," =
",VALUE_1+VALUE_2
$!
$! READ is often preferred over INQUIRE because of additional
$! control. The /END_OF_FILE and /ERROR qualifier will
$! transfer control if the user enters <Ctrl/Z> or if an error
$! occurs.
$!
$ LOOP:
$ READ /PROMPT="ARE YOU READY [Y/N]: " YES_NO -
        /END_OF_FILE=LOOP /ERROR=LOOP
$ YES_NO = F$EDIT(YES_NO,"TRIM, UPCASE")
$ IF (YES_NO .NES. "Y") .AND. (YES_NO .NES. "N") -
        THEN GOTO LOOP
$
```

The READ command has another handy qualifier, /TIME_OUT, of
which you might want to take advantage. The TIME OUT qualifier lets
you specify, in seconds, the amount of time to wait for user input.
When the time is up, the procedure will continue to the next
statement.

## FILE INPUT AND OUTPUT

If you program in a high-level language, such as FORTRAN, or in a
low-level language, such as MACRO, you know how tedious it can be
to read and write files. This is not the case with DCL.

DCL supports four basic commands to perform file input and output:
OPEN, READ, WRITE and CLOSE. The steps required to read from and
write to files in a command procedure are:

1. Use the OPEN command to open a file. If the file doesn't exist,
   the OPEN command will create it for you.

2. Use the WRITE or READ commands to write or read records.

3. Use the CLOSE command when you're finished to close the file.

## Opening Files

A file must be open before records can be read or written. To perform this operation, use the DCL OPEN command. Two parameters must be specified. The first is a logical name for the file being opened. All READ and WRITE operations will use this name. The second parameter is the name of the file itself. You can use any valid file specification, including a logical name which translates to a file name. Also, DCL wants you to specify the operations you will be performing on the file. There are three valid file operations: READ, WRITE and APPEND.

## WRITE and APPEND Access

You can write to a file only if it has been opened for WRITE or APPEND access. Use the OPEN command qualifiers /WRITE or /APPEND as appropriate. Only one of these qualifiers can be used in an OPEN statement.

The /WRITE qualifier creates a new file each time it's used, even if the file already exists. The record pointer will be placed at the beginning of the file.

This example shows the correct use of the OPEN command with the /WRITE qualifier:

$ OPEN/WRITE OUTPUT_FILE TIME.DAT

The /APPEND qualifier is used to add records to the end of an existing file. The file must already exist to use this qualifier. When the file is opened, the record pointer is positioned at the end of the file:

$ OPEN/APPEND OUTPUT_FILE TIME.DAT

## READ Access

To open a file for READ access, use the /READ qualifier, which is a default qualifier of the OPEN command. When you open a file for reading, you can only read. The record pointer will initially be located at the first record in the file. Each time a record is read, the pointer is moved down to the next record:

$ OPEN/READ INPUT_FILE TIME.DAT

## SHARED Access for Multiple Users

If the file you're reading or writing is to be used by more than one
user at a time, you must open it for SHARED access. This is done
easily using the /SHARED qualifier:

```
$ OPEN /READ/SHARED NUMBERS -
    SYS$SYSTEM:PHONE_BOOK.DAT
```

Here, both READ and WRITE access are granted to other users wanting
to access the file at the same time. To allow only SHARED READ or
WRITE access, specify /SHARED=READ or /SHARED=WRITE as
appropriate.

## Reading Records From a File

Records are read from an open file with the DCL command READ. The
two most common qualifiers used with READ are /ERROR to detect and
trap errors, and /END_OF_FILE to detect when you've read the last
record in the file.

The following example opens the PHONE_BOOK.DAT file and reads a
record from it:

```
$ OPEN  /READ/ERROR=OPEN_ERROR -
            NUMBERS SYS$SYSTEM:PHONE_BOOK.DAT
$!
$! In this READ statement, "RECORD" is a symbol that
$! contains the record read from the file.
$!
$ READ  /ERROR=READ_ERROR/END_OF_FILE=EOF - NUMBERS
            RECORD
    .
    .
    .

$ EOF:
$ CLOSE NUMBERS
$ EXIT
$ OPEN_ERROR:
$ WRITE SYS$OUTPUT "ERROR OPENING THE PHONE BOOK!"
$ EXIT
$ READ_ERROR:
$ WRITE SYS$OUTPUT "ERROR READING THE PHONE BOOK!"
```

## Writing Records to a File

To write records to a file, open it for WRITE or APPEND access and start writing. Remember, to create a new file, open it for WRITE, and to add to an existing file, open it for APPEND.

```
$ OPEN/WRITE/ERROR=OPEN_ERROR OUTPUT_FILE TIME.DAT
$ WRITE/ERROR=WRITE_ERROR OUTPUT_FILE F$TIME()
$ CLOSE OUTPUT_FILE
  .
  .
  .
$ EXIT
$ OPEN_ERROR:
$ WRITE SYS$OUTPUT "ERROR OPENING THE OUTPUT FILE!"
$ EXIT
$ WRITE_ERROR:
$ WRITE SYS$OUTPUT "ERROR WRITING TO THE OUTPUT FILE!"
```

Note that errors are trapped through the use of the /ERROR qualifier on the OPEN and WRITE commands. The output record can be any valid combination of literal text, symbols, and lexical functions.

## Modifying a Record

To modify an existing record, use the WRITE command with the /UPDATE qualifier. To do so, the file must be open for both READ and WRITE access. Use the READ command to select the record you want to modify, then WRITE to it again as in:

```
$ OPEN  /READ/WRITE/ERROR=OPEN_ERROR -
        NUMBERS SYS$SYSTEM:PHONE_BOOK.DAT
$ READ_LOOP:
$ READ /END_OF_FILE=EOF NUMBERS RECORD
$ IF (F$EXTRACT(0,12,RECORD) .NE. NAME) THEN -
        GOTO READ_LOOP
$ WRITE /ERROR=WRITE_ERROR PHONE NEW_RECORD
$ CLOSE PHONE
```

When you open a file for both READ and WRITE, the record pointer will be placed at the first record in the file. A drawback to this method is that you can only overwrite the record you most recently read. Also, the new record must be the same length as the original record.

## Reading and Writing Indexed Files

A problem with the file input and output methods discussed so far is that they're slow and clumsy to use. This is because all records are processed sequentially (one after another). Using the sequential access method, if you have a file with 10,983 records and you want record number 10,901, you must read 10,901 records to get to it.

There's a better way.

In a VMS system, files can be created with one or more key fields. The key fields can contain any type of information, but normally it's something that will uniquely identify one record from another, i.e., last name, phone number and so on.

The key fields are used by the record management services (RMS) as indices. When a new record is written to the file, RMS examines both the key fields and the file's index, then inserts the record in the correct location. Conversely, records can be read by specifying a key value. This is known as an indexed sequential access method (ISAM).

Indexed files can't be created with a DCL command. You must use a utility such as the file definition language (FDL).

You use the READ command with the /KEY and /INDEX qualifiers to read records randomly. (After a record has been read randomly, the rest of the records can be read sequentially.) In this way, you can instantly access any record in the file. The example below demonstrates the indexed sequential access method.

```
$ OPEN  /READ/WRITE/ERROR=OPEN_ERROR -
        NUMBERS SYS$SYSTEM:PHONE_BOOK.DAT
$ INQUIRE NAME "Last name"
$ READ/INDEX=0/KEY=NAME-
        /ERROR=NO_SUCH_REC NUMBERS RECORD
    .
    .
    .

$ NO_SUCH_REC:
$ WRITE SYS$OUTPUT "That name is not in the phone book"
    .
    .
    .
```

Notice in the READ statement in the previous example that an index number (the key number) was specified. If you don't specify an index number, the primary index (key 0) will be used.

To delete a record in an indexed file, you can use the READ command with the /DELETE qualifier. After the record has been read, it will be deleted.

## Closing Files

If you don't explicitly close a file when you're finished with it, it will be closed for you by VMS when you log out. To close a file, specify the logical name with which you opened the file as a parameter to the CLOSE command:

$ CLOSE OUTPUT_FILE

The only files you don't need to open explicitly for reading and writing are SYS$INPUT, SYS$OUTPUT, SYS$ERROR, and SYS$COMMAND.

## REDIRECTING INPUT AND OUTPUT

Command procedures can direct or redirect output in various ways. The following section explains several ways to redirect command procedure I/O.

## Redefining SYS$INPUT as Your Terminal

Command procedures are often used to invoke interactive utility programs, such as MAIL or EVE. Because these programs normally obtain input from the logical device SYS$INPUT, invoking them from within a command procedure will cause an immediate exit. This is because the logical name SYS$INPUT is directed to the command procedure itself. That's why you can put command and data lines for a utility or program directly in the procedure.

By default, the logical name SYS$COMMAND represents the name of the terminal from which the command procedure is being executed. By redirecting SYS$INPUT to SYS$COMMAND, you can use utilities and other programs interactively from your command procedures, for example:

```
$ DEFINE/USER_MODE SYS$INPUT SYS$COMMAND:
$ MAIL
MAIL>
```

The /USER_MODE qualifier causes the reassignment to be in effect only for the next command. In this example, it's for the duration of the MAIL session.

## Redirecting Command Procedure Output

Generally, command procedure output is displayed at your terminal. You can redirect output to a file of your choice by using the /OUTPUT qualifier when you execute a command procedure, as the following example demonstrates:

```
$ @SYS$MANAGER:STARTNET /OUTPUT=NET.LOG
```

## Redirecting Messages

Digital command language error and severe error messages are directed, by default, to the file indicated by the system logical name SYS$ERROR. When you execute a command procedure interactively, SYS$ERROR is normally assigned to your terminal. If you want to log these error messages, you can redirect SYS$ERROR to a file. Unfortunately, if you redirect SYS$ERROR without also redirecting SYS$OUTPUT, DCL will send error messages to both SYS$ERROR and SYS$OUTPUT. In effect, you will receive the error messages twice — at your terminal and in the file indicated by SYS$ERROR.

If you want, you can suppress error messages completely. There are two ways to accomplish this. The first method is to redirect both SYS$ERROR and SYS$OUTPUT to the null device NL:. Anything sent to the NL: device gets dumped into the proverbial bit bucket:

```
$! Command procedure segment to suppress error messages.
$!
$ DEFINE/USER_MODE SYS$ERROR NL:
$ DEFINE/USER_MODE SYS$OUTPUT NL:
$!
$! Error messages will be suppressed for the next command.
```

The second method is to use the SET MESSAGE command to turn off all message output. For example, the SET MESSAGE command will suppress messages generated by the DCL PURGE command:

$ SET MESSAGE/NOTEXT/NOIDENTIFICATION/NOFACILITY/
    NOSEVERITY
$ PURGE *.DAT

When you use the SET MESSAGE command to disable messages, don't forget to turn them back on:

$ SET MESSAGE/TEXT/IDENTIFICATION/FACILITY/SEVERITY

## DCL ERROR PROCESSING

When DCL processes a command, a code is generated that describes the condition. The code indicates success or failure of the command. After each command is executed, the command interpreter examines the condition code. If an error occurred, the command interpreter prints the message indicated by the condition code.

Unless otherwise directed, with the SET NOON command or by other means, the command line interpreter will execute an EXIT command if a severe error occurs. The EXIT command forces the command procedure to terminate. When this happens, control is returned to the previous command level (DCL or command procedure). To prevent this from happening, you can use the DCL ON command to specify an action for the CLI to take.

The ON command supports three keywords: WARNING, ERROR and SEVERE_ERROR. To override error handling for procedure warnings, use an ON command such as the following:

$ ON WARNING THEN EXIT

or

$ ON WARNING THEN GOTO label

The WARNING keyword causes the command procedure to take the specified action if a warning, error, or severe error occurs. The ERROR keyword causes the action to be taken if an error or severe error occurs. The SEVERE_ERROR keyword causes the command procedure to take the specified action only if a fatal error occurs.

## Using $STATUS and $SEVERITY to Control Errors

$STATUS and $SEVERITY are reserved DCL global symbols. Each time a command is executed, successfully or unsuccessfully, DCL assigns values to these symbols.

The $STATUS symbol holds the full condition code of the last command. The $SEVERITY symbol holds an error severity level. This severity level is the degree of success or failure of the condition code held in $STATUS.

The condition code held in $STATUS is a valid VMS message code, i.e., valid to the VMS MESSAGE facility. It can be used in conjunction with the lexical function F$MESSAGE to obtain the actual text message associated with the code. Consider the following:

```
$ SET DEFAULT DUC0:[PHONE_BOOK]
$ WRITE SYS$OUTPUT $STATUS
 %X00000001
$ WRITE SYS$OUTPUT F$MESSAGE(%X00000001)
 %SYSTEM-S-NORMAL, normal successful completion
```

All DCL commands will return a condition code. Unfortunately, not all condition codes have associated text messages. Condition codes without message text will return the message "%NONAME-E-NOMSG, Message number (an eight-digit code)."

## Table 7-3: Status Severity Codes

| CODE | DEFINITION |
|------|------------|
| 0 | WARNING |
| 1 | SUCCESS |
| 2 | ERROR |
| 3 | INFORMATION |
| 4 | SEVERE ERROR |

Although the message text can be useful in many applications, it's not useful for making conditional decisions (IF-THEN-ELSE). It's most useful to use the contents of $SEVERITY, which contains one of five possible values, extracted from the first three bits of $STATUS. Table 7-3 lists the values and their meanings.

Odd values (1 and 3) indicate the two levels of success, while even values (0, 2 and 4) indicate various degrees of failure. This is the secret of DCL error handling. When $STATUS and $SEVERITY are odd, the command was successful. Even values indicate an error.

There are two ways to handle errors using the status and severity codes. The first is to treat $STATUS as a Boolean value (i.e., TRUE or FALSE), as in this example:

```
$ SET NOON
$ command                                    ! Your DCL command???
$ IF $STATUS THEN GOTO NO_ERROR              ! Testing
$ STATUS for T or F

  .
                                             ! Handle error
  .

  .
$ NO_ERRORS:

  .
                                             ! Continue processing
  .
$ EXIT
```

The second method is to trap the error with an ON WARNING command, then use the severity level to determine what needs to be done about the error. For example:

```
$ SET NOON
$ ON WARNING GOTO ERROR_TRAP
$ command                                    ! Your DCL commands???
$ command
$ .
$ .
$ .
$ command
$ EXIT
$!
$! Start of error trap code
```

```
$!
$ ERROR_TRAP:
$ SEVERITY = $SEVERITY                    ! Must save the code
$ IF SEVERITY = 0 THEN command...         ! If warning...
$ GOTO ERROR_TAKEN_CARE_OF
$ IF SEVERITY = 2 THEN command...         ! If error...
$ GOTO ERROR_TAKEN_CARE_OF
$ IF SEVERITY = 4 THEN command...         ! If severe error...
$ ERROR_TAKEN_CARE_OF: . . .
$ EXIT
```

## Processing Interrupts

DCL allows you to process <CTRL-Y> interrupts in the same fashion
as error conditions. Through the use of the ON CONTROL_Y command,
you can specify an action to be performed when <CTRL-Y> is pressed
at the current command level. Pressing <CTRL-Y> causes VMS to
suspend what it was doing for the process and prompt for input. In the
following example, you'll discover how to take control of the default
interrupt processing:

```
      .
      .
      .
$!
$! Set up <CTRL/Y> processing
$!
$ ON CONTROL_Y THEN GOTO MENU
$ MENU:
$ TYPE MENU.DAT
$ INQUIRE CHOICE "Enter your selection then press RETURN"
$!
$! Reset the default <CTRL/Y> condition
$!
$ SET NOCONTROL=Y
$ SET CONTROL=Y
$ IF CHOICE .EQS. "EXIT" THEN GOTO EXIT_PROGRAM
      .
      .
      .
$ EXIT_PROGRAM:
$ EXIT
```

An ON CONTROL_Y command stays in effect until it's superceded by another ON CONTROL_Y or until it's explicitly turned off using the SET NOCONTROL=Y command. Notice in the example that <CTRL-Y> processing is reset after it fulfills its purpose. The reason for doing this is clear. If the process ever got into an endless loop situation, it could not be terminated by the user. Instead, the DCL STOP command would have to be issued from another terminal. There are situations when this is desirable, such as in the design of a captive menu, where you're trying to make it impossible for the user to get to the DCL level.

### Turning Off DCL Error Checking

Error checking can be disabled completely using the SET NOON command. When in effect, the command line interpreter continues to update condition code status but doesn't perform error condition processing. The SET ON command restores error checking to its normal condition. For instance:

```
$ SET NOON
$ RUN MY_PROGRAM
$ SET ON
```

## TERMINATING COMMAND PROCEDURES

To terminate a command procedure correctly, use the EXIT or STOP command. The EXIT command terminates the current command procedure and returns control to the command level from which it was called. The STOP command terminates all command procedures, if nested, and returns control to DCL.

If you terminate a procedure with an EXIT command, you can return a status as a parameter of the EXIT command. The status parameter is an integer value reserved for the global symbol $STATUS.

## CONCLUSION

The command procedure is a valuable and necessary system management and system operations tools. If you master DCL and command procedures, your system chores will be considerably easier.

# Chapter 8

# VMS Operational Management

To manage a VMS system, you must focus on several key areas, including the computing environment, system integrity, system performance, software installation, and setting up a network. In fact, the duties of the typical VAX system manager are so voluminous that it's often difficult to say, "This is what a VAX system manager does."

On the other hand, it's not difficult to explain what the typical VAX system must go through to become operational and to stay that way. So, the purpose of this chapter is to define and explain VAX operational management.

## TYPICAL SYSTEM MANAGEMENT TASKS

The system manager and system operators must know how to use the system in the most effective way to provide the most benefit to the users. Many of the jobs performed by system managers and operators affect the use of the system.

Many different system utilities are used to perform each management function. Often, information is needed (i.e., must be collected) to run these programs. The information can be collected by the system manager or the operator. The following list presents the most common tasks performed by a system manager or operator and the utilities used to accomplish them:

- **Generating the initial system:** STANDALONE BACKUP, SYSBOOT, SYSGEN, and AUTOGEN.

- **Configuring the system:** SYSTARTUP_V5, SYCONFIG, SYLOGICALS, SYPAGSWPFILES, and SYLOGIN.

- **Shutting down the system:** SHUTDOWN and SYSHUTDWN.

- **Adding user accounts:** ADDUSER, AUTHORIZE, and DISKQUOTA.

- **Using memory efficiently:** INSTALL and SYSGEN.

- **Improving system performance:** SYSGEN, AUTOGEN, and MONITOR.

- **Scheduling work on the system:** SUBMIT.

- **Using printers effectively:** START/QUEUE and INITIALIZE/QUEUE.

- **Controlling public volumes:** INITIALIZE and MOUNT.

- **Saving information stored on public volumes:** BACKUP.

- **Creating systemwide logical names:** DEFINE/SYSTEM.

- **Monitoring system activity to note possible problems:** SHOW SYSTEM, SHOW MEMORY, MONITOR, and ACCOUNTING.

- **Ensuring that the system is secure:** SYSGEN, AUTHORIZE, ACCOUNTING, SET PROTECTION, SET ACL, and others.

## BRINGING UP A NEW SYSTEM

This section covers three important topics: what happens when a VAX boots, VAX console systems, and how to set up your start-up files. Naturally, before you can begin any of these steps, the hardware and VMS must be installed. The VAX hardware and the base VMS kit are normally installed by a qualified field service engineer. If your hardware has not been installed, and Digital Equipment Corporation is your installer, then you must log a trouble call with the local Digital Field Service Office. Digital uses trouble calls to dispatch its people.

Before you start your system for the first time, you should familiarize yourself with the VAX console system. There are several console varieties, depending on the machine that you have. Refer to the VAX console documentation, provided with your system hardware, for complete details.

## The VMS Bootstrap Procedure

Prior to becoming operational, a VAX must be initialized with operating software. This process is called booting or bootstrapping the computer, as it's analogous to lifting yourself up by your bootstraps.

Part of the VAX bootstrap operation is specific to each processor's console device. Regardless of the VAX console implementation, the console has four primary tasks in the bootstrap process:

- Initialize the CPU.

- Locate 64K bytes of error free, page-aligned memory.

- Load VMB.EXE into the second page of memory.

- Pass device codes and flags to VMB via registers R0 through R5.

The VMS operating system is booted in six steps:

1. VMB is loaded.

   VMB.EXE is the initial bootstrap program used to provide a bootstrap, independent of the operating system being loaded (i.e., VMS, ULTRIX-32, or ELN). Its primary objective is to size physical memory, initialize the bus adapter and device that contain a secondary bootstrap image, and load it.

2. Secondary VMS bootstrap code is loaded.

   The secondary bootstrap program, for VMS, is called SYSBOOT.EXE. Like VMB.EXE, it runs standalone on the CPU. Its job is to read SYSBOOT (i.e., SYSGEN) parameters and configure virtual address space based on the specified values. It then loads the system image (i.e., SYS.EXE) and the system device driver. At this time, it transfers control to SYS.EXE.

3. Memory management is turned on.

The first task performed by the system image is to turn on memory management. This entails initializing the scheduler and memory management databases. After this has been done, the swapper can be executed.

4. The swapper is started.

As soon as it's running, the swapper performs a number of tasks needed to begin creating processes. After the swapper has completed initialization, it creates a process called SYSINIT.

5. System initialization begins.

The system initialization process executes tasks that must be performed in process context and do not lend themselves to DCL commands. To this point, all other code has executed in system context. These tasks include mapping RMS and Files-11, and initializing the primary page and swap files. When complete, SYSINIT creates the STARTUP process.

6. STARTUP procedures are run.

The STARTUP process executes the STARTUP.COM command procedure to create the JOB_CONTROL, OPCOM, ERRFMT, SMISERVER and other system processes. The second function of the STARTUP process is to execute the VAX's site-specific start-up procedures, which are configured by the system manager.

There are two methods of booting VMS. You can perform a nonstop boot, which is the quickest and easiest method, or a conversational boot. A nonstop boot automatically sets system parameters and invokes system start-up procedures. This is the default method of booting VMS. A conversational boot allows you to change system parameters before the hardware is autoconfigured. Conversational booting is useful for such occasions as bringing up a minimally configured system, or specifying an alternate parameter file.

## VAX Console Systems
Since the inception of the VAX 11/780, VAX processors have

employed four basic console systems: LSI microcomputers, PRO-380 microcomputers, on-board microprocessors, and the VAX or MicroVAX CPU. No matter what type of console a VAX uses, it has five fundamental purposes:

- Diagnose CPU and memory.

- Initialize the CPU bus and adapters.

- Load the VAX registers with bootstrap values.

- Load VMB.EXE.

- Function as a terminal and logging device after the system is booted.

All MicroVAX systems, including the MicroVAX I, II, 2000, and 3000 systems, boot from a MONITOR routine in read-only memory (ROM). The MONITOR routine runs on the MicroVAX CPU and does not require an intermediate load device, such as a floppy disk or tape cartridge. From the MicroVAX console prompt (>>>), the operator can instruct the CPU to attempt a bootstrap from any local disk, mass storage control protocol (MSCP) tape, or from an Ethernet adapter (except MicroVAX I). The following are example MicroVAX boot commands:

| | |
|---|---|
| >>> B DUA0 | – Boot from disk DUA0: |
| >>> B/1 DUA0 | – Conversational boot from DUA0: |
| >>> B ESA0 | – Ethernet boot (MicroVAX 2000) |
| >>> B/100 DUA0 | – Boot from specified file on DUA0: |
| >>> B MUA0 | – Boot from MSCP tape MUA0: |

MicroVAX console commands vary, slightly, due to the differences in supported devices and advances in technology and convenience. For instance, MicroVAX 3000 systems that have RFxx drives use the console to communicate with the controller. A convenient command supported by the MicroVAX 3000 console, SHOW ETHERNET, replaces the B/100...READ_ADDR method on the MicroVAX II.

VAX processors that use a console device to boot, such as VAX 11/780s, VAX 8000 systems, and VAX 6000 systems, are booted by executing a console command procedure. The default boot command procedure is called DEFBOO. DEFBOO is set up, based on the available hardware, to bootstrap the processor for normal processing. If you enter the boot command (i.e., B) at the VAX console, the console processor searches for the DEFBOO command procedure and executes it.

A second console boot procedure, called GENBOO, is used to perform a conversational boot. Because every VAX system is different, the GENBOO procedure must be written for your hardware configuration. New console systems are supplied with example DEFBOO and GENBOO procedures.

## Conversational Boot

There are many occasions when you'll need to conversationally boot VMS. Common situations you can encounter include needing to bypass the system user authorization file (SYSUAF), bypassing system start-up files, and an emergency start-up after modifying system parameters.

If, for whatever reason, you get locked out of the SYSTEM account, you can specify an alternate authorization file. This is done by performing a conversational boot and modifying the UAFALTERNATE parameter at the SYSBOOT prompt::

```
SYSBOOT> SET UAFALTERNATE 1
SYSBOOT> CONTINUE
```

When VMS finishes booting, you can log in at the system console by entering any username and password. The process you log into will have all system privileges. Before you can set a new password for the SYSTEM account, you must restore the UAFALTERNATE parameter:

```
$ RUN SYS$SYSTEM:SYSGEN
SYSGEN> USE CURRENT
SYSGEN> SET UAFALTERNATE 0
SYSGEN> WRITE CURRENT
SYSGEN> EXIT
```

You then can run the AUTHORIZE utility to establish a new password. As a final step, you must reboot the system.

If your system fails to complete its start-up procedures (i.e., hangs or crashes), or will not let you log in, then you can perform a conversational boot to disable the start-up procedures. There are two methods. The first is to perform a minimum start-up, which disables system device configuration and start-up procedures. This is accomplished by setting start-up parameter P1 to "MIN":

```
SYSBOOT> SET STARTUP_P1 "MIN"
SYSBOOT> CONTINUE
```

When the VAX boots, only the system device will be configured. If you need other devices configured, you'll have to configure them by hand with SYSGEN (i.e., AUTOCONFIGURE ALL/SELECT = DU). When you have fixed the problem, reset the STARTUP_P1 parameter to "", and reboot the system.

If you only need to bypass the system start-up and login procedures, then specify the following at the SYSBOOT prompt:

```
SYSBOOT>>> SET/STARTUP OPA0:
SYSBOOT>>> CONTINUE
```

When the system finishes booting, you can log in and fix the problem. Before rebooting the system again, you can test the start-up procedures by entering the command:

```
$ @SYS$SYSTEM:STARTUP
```

Your final step must be to restore the system parameters with SYSGEN:

```
$ RUN SYS$SYSTEM:SYSGEN
SYSGEN> USE CURRENT
SYSGEN> SET/STARTUP SYS$SYSTEM:STARTUP.COM
SYSGEN> WRITE CURRENT
SYSGEN> EXIT
```

Another problem you might encounter comes about when modifying system parameters. In some cases, you can change a parameter that renders the system unbootable. When this happens, perform a conversational boot, and enter the following:

```
SYSBOOT> USE DEFAULT.PAR
SYSBOOT> CONTINUE
```

When the system finishes booting, examine the system parameter changes you've made using SYSGEN, modify MODPARAMS.DAT, and execute AUTOGEN.

After you've loaded VMS onto a new system, there are numerous tasks that still must be accomplished before the system can be declared operational. The most important tasks are:

- Creating or modifying system start-up procedures.
- Initializing print and batch queues.
- Creating a system login procedure.
- Creating user accounts.
- Installing software applications.
- Setting up the network.

Let's look closely at each of these tasks.

## Start-up Procedures

Each time you boot your system, site specific command procedures are invoked:

- **SYPAGSWPFILES** – A procedure used to install page and swap files.

- **SYCONFIG** – Site-specific device configuration commands.

- **SYLOGICALS** – Used for defining systemwide logical names.

- **SYSTARTUP_V5** – Site-specific start-up procedure. These command procedures are located in the SYS$MANAGER directory.

When you install VMS V5, a template SYSTARTUP_V5.COM file is placed in the SYS$MANAGER directory for you. This template file can be used as a guide, or you can write a new one from scratch. Some of the tasks commonly performed in the site specific start-up procedure are:

- Mounting disks
- Setting the characteristics of devices
- Installing secondary page and swap files
- Starting the queue manager
- Initializing and starting queues
- Installing images
- Starting layered products
- Starting DECnet

- Starting LAT and defining LAT services
- Purging log files
- Disabling accounting or starting a new account file
- Defining announcement and welcome messages
- Defining the systemwide login procedure
- Submitting batch jobs that must be run at start-up time
- Limiting the number of interactive users

## Mounting VMS Disks and Tapes

On a VMS system, disks can be mounted for public or private access. In most cases, disks are mounted for public access to make them available to any system user or process. The MOUNT utility is used to mount storage volumes. The only device you don't have to explicitly mount before it can be used is the system disk. The system disk is mounted when VMS boots.

Include MOUNT commands in your site-specific start-up procedure to mount public disks for systemwide access. Use the following command format:

$ MOUNT/SYSTEM/NOASSIST ddcu: volume_label logical_name

The term ddcu: represents the physical device name, such as DUA0: or $1$DUB2:. The expression volume_label refers to the label assigned to the volume, for instance USER$DISK1 or SCRATCH_DISK. The logical_name expression, which is optional, is a logical name that will be assigned to the physical device name. For example:

$ MOUNT/SYSTEM/NOASSIST BIFF$DUA2: BIFF$USERS USER$DISK1

If you don't supply a logical name, the MOUNT utility will create one for you in the format DISK$volume_label.

## Installing Secondary Page and Swap Files

Because page and swap files are used by every VMS process, they're prone to become a bottleneck. To alleviate this problem, install secondary page and swap files on one or more of your nonsystem disks. If your system has more than one disk, it's beneficial to system performance to use secondary page and swap files on disks other than the system disk.

Page and swap files are created and installed using the SYSTEM
GENERATION utility (SYSGEN). To create a secondary page file, you
use the SYSGEN CREATE command:

```
$ RUN SYS$SYSTEM:SYSGEN
SYSGEN> CREATE /SIZE=75000/CONTIGUOUS-
SYSGEN> DUA2:[SYS0.SYSEXE]PAGEFILE1.SYS
%SYSGEN–I–CREATED, DUA2:[SYS0.SYSEXE]PAGEFILE1.SYS
CREATED
SYSGEN> EXIT
```

The /CONTIGUOUS qualifier specifies that the file should be created
from contiguous disk space. The /SIZE qualifier indicates the size, in
blocks, of the new file to be created. Swap files are created using the
same command.

To install a page or swap file, use the SYSGEN INSTALL command:

```
$ DEFINE /SYSTEM/EXEC PAGE$DISK DUA2:[SYS0.SYSEXE]
$ RUN SYS$SYSTEM:SYSGEN
SYSGEN> INSTALL PAGE$DISK:PAGEFILE1.SYS/PAGE/NOCHECK
SYSGEN> EXIT
```

Typically, secondary page and swap files are installed at system
start-up time. You can accomplish this by putting the appropriate
commands directly in SYSTARTUP_V5 or by using the SYPAGSWPFILES
procedure. The commands are the same either way. For example:

```
$ RUN SYS$SYSTEM:SYSGEN:
INSTALL PAGE$DISK:PAGEFILE1.SYS/PAGE/NOCHECK
INSTALL PAGE$DISK:SWAPFILE1.SYS/SWAP
```

If you're setting up a cluster, you should consider adding a few
additional lines to check for the availability of the disk or the page
and swap files before issuing the INSTALL commands:

```
$ IF F$SEARCH("PAGE$DISK:PAGEFILE1.SYS") .NES. ""
$  THEN
$  RUN SYS$SYSTEM:SYSGEN
INSTALL USER$DISK:[SYS0.SYSEXE]PAGEFILE1.SYS/PAGE/NOCHECK
$ ENDIF
```

Make sure that you mount the secondary page and swap file disks
before trying to install the files.

## Disabling Accounting and Purging Logs

Each time the system is booted, system accounting is started and a new version of OPERATOR.LOG is created. You should make a plan for maintaining these files. They contain important information.

If you're not planning to take advantage of the accounting information, you can disable system accounting in your SYSTARTUP_V5 command procedure:

```
$ SET ACCOUNTING/DISABLE
$ IF F$SEARCH("SYS$MANAGER:ACCOUNTNG.DAT") THEN –
   DELETE SYS$MANAGER:ACCOUNTNG.DAT;*
```

If you don't want to save the old operator log files, you can purge them each time the system boots:

```
$ PURGE/KEEP=2 SYS$MANAGER:OPERATOR.LOG
```

You should always keep the last operator log just in case there's a problem.

## Installing Known Images

Programs can be installed as known images to reduce I/O overhead and improve system security. If you have programs that are frequently run, are run by multiple users, or that require special privileges, you should install them as VMS known images to improve system performance and security.

Known images must be reinstalled each time the system is booted. Most of the VMS known images are installed for you by STARTUP through a list of image names. This list is maintained in a file called SYS$MANAGER:VMSIMAGES.DAT. Digital suggests that this file not be modified by the system manager. A new VMSIMAGES file is created each time AUTOGEN is run.

To install known images, include INSTALL commands in your SYSTARTUP_V5 command procedure:

```
$ RUN SYS$SYSTEM:INSTALL
SYS$SYSTEM:WHO.EXE \OPEN\HEADER\PRIV=(WORLD)
```

The INSTALL utility can be used interactively to remove and add known images.

## Modifying Device Characteristics

Before starting queues, starting DECnet, and letting users log in, devices (such as asynchronous terminal lines and print controllers) must be set up. The DCL commands SET TERMINAL and SET PRINTER are used to establish specific device characteristics, such as the baud rate or device type.

When setting characteristics for interactive terminal devices, it's beneficial to have the terminal line detect the baud rate (i.e., speed) of the device connected to it. This is accomplished by specifying the /AUTOBAUD qualifier rather than a fixed baud rate with the /SPEED qualifier. For instance, direct-connected terminal devices could be set up with the command:

$ SET TERMINAL TXA0: /AUTOBAUD/PERMANENT

If the terminal device is a modem, the /MODEM qualifier should be used:

$ SET TERMINAL TXB7: /MODEM/AUTOBAUD/PERMANENT

If you need to control the device speed, for performance reasons, then specify a fixed baud rate with the /SPEED qualifier:

$ SET TERMINAL TXA4: /SPEED=4800/PERMANENT

When establishing characteristics for print devices, you should specify (when possible) the device type, speed, and page information (i.e., lines and width). In the first printer example, an asynchronous terminal line is set up for an LA100; the second example configures a DEC line printer:

$ SET TERMINAL/DEVICE=LA100-
_$/SPEED=9600/WIDTH=132/PERMANENT
$ SET PRINTER/LP11/PAGE=66/WIDTH=80/LOWER LPB0:

## Initializing Print and Batch Queues

Before users can print or submit jobs for batch executing, you must define a print queue and a batch queue. These tasks can be accomplished at start-up time by inserting the appropriate commands in the SYSTARTUP_V5 command procedure.

Print and batch queues are established in three basic steps:

1. Start the queue manager.

2. Set printer device characteristics.

3. Initialize the queues.

The following example shows how to start the queue manager and initialize a print and batch queue:

```
$! Start the queue manager
$!
$ START/QUEUE/MANAGER SYS$COMMON:[SYSEXE]
$!
$! Set printer characteristics
$!
$ SET PRINTER/LOWER/WIDTH=132 LPA0:
$ SET DEVICE/SPOOLED LPA0:
$!
$! Initialize queues
$!
$ INITIALIZE/QUEUE/START/DEFAULT=FLAG/ON=LPA0: SYS$PRINT
$ INITIALIZE/QUEUE/START/BATCH/BASE_PRIORITY=3 SYS$BATCH
```

## Defining Systemwide Announcements

VMS has two facilities that can be used to disseminate information at user login time: the system announcement message, and the system welcome message. The system announcement message is sent to the user's terminal when he initiates a login (i.e., when the user presses the <RETURN> key to get the Username: prompt). The system welcome message is provided after a successful login.

The two system messages are created by defining the system logical names SYS$ANNOUNCE and SYS$WELCOME. For example:

```
$ DEFINE/SYSTEM SYS$ANNOUNCE –
  "For authorized use only. Violators will be prosecuted."
$ DEFINE/SYSTEM SYS$WELCOME –
  "Welcome to node Chaz"
```

To make your messages more attractive, you can include escape sequences in the equivalence string:

```
$ DEFINE/SYSTEM SYS$WELCOME –
  "<ESC>[H<ESC>[JWelcome to node Chaz<CR><LF>"
```

This example SYS$WELCOME message clears the display before putting out the message. The escape characters (<ESC>) are put into the text using the SPECINS function of EDT.

To display messages longer than one or two lines, you can specify a text file as the logical name equivalence string:

```
$ DEFINE/SYSTEM SYS$WELCOME
"@SYS$MANAGER:WELCOME.TXT"
```

The system announcement facilities are useful tools; however, you should consider their security implications before using them.

## Creating a Systemwide Login Command Procedure

It is sometimes useful or necessary to execute one or more commands for all users at login time. VMS provides the system login command procedure for this purpose.

With the system login command procedure, you can set up a common computing environment for all users. To use this procedure, you must define the system logical SYS$SYLOGIN and create the system login command procedure (SYLOGIN.COM). The logical name is defined in your SYSTARTUP_V5 procedure with the following command:

```
$ DEFINE/SYSTEM/EXEC/NOLOG –
SYS$SYLOGIN SYS$MANAGER:SYLOGIN.COM
```

A typical SYLOGIN procedure might include commands such as:

```
$ IF F$MODE() .EQS. "INTERACTIVE" THEN SET CONTROL=T
$ IF F$MODE() .EQS. "BATCH" THEN EXIT
$ IF F$MODE() .EQS. "NETWORK" THEN EXIT
$ WHO :== SHOW USERS
$ E*DIT :== EDIT/EDT/COMMAND=SYS$MANAGER:EDTINI.EDT
$ CLR == "WRITE SYS$OUTPUT "<ESC>[H<ESC>[J"
$ BR*OWSE == "TYPE/PAGE"
$ KER*MIT == "MCR KERMIT"
$ IF F$MODE() .EQS. "INTERACTIVE" THEN SET TERM/INQUIRE
```

The system login procedure does not take the place of the user's own login command procedure. User login command procedures are executed after the system login command procedure.

## Starting DECnet and LAT

The DECnet software must be started before your system can communicate with other computers. Also, if you're using a standalone workstation with DECwindows, DECnet must be started.

Before starting DECnet, the DECnet executor and network databases must be configured. If you're using a standard Digital Ethernet LAN, this configuration is easily accomplished by executing the NETCONFIG procedure. It's located in the SYS$MANAGER directory.

DECnet is easily started by executing the STARTNET procedure:

$ @SYS$MANAGER:STARTNET

If you have initialized and started a batch queue, you can submit this procedure to batch. Digital claims that this will decrease the time it takes your system to boot. Be aware that other software components, such as local area transport (LAT), DECwindows, and personal computer file system (PCFS), require DECnet to be running before they can be started.

If your users use terminal servers to connect to the system, the LAT network protocol must be started. The LAT protocol coexists with other Ethernet protocols, such as DECnet and LAVc.

To configure your system as a LAT service node, you must execute the LTLOAD procedure:

$ @SYS$MANAGER:LTLOAD

LTLOAD issues commands to the LAT control program (LATCP). It can be used as is, unless you want to support remote printers or create dedicated services.

## Limiting Interactive Users

You can define the number of interactive users that the system will permit to be logged in at one time. This is done by creating a symbol in the site-specific start-up procedure:

$ STARTUP$INTERACTIVE_LOGINS == n

Here, n represents the maximum number of users you want logged in at any given time.

The STARTUP$INTERACTIVE_LOGINS symbol is used by the site-independent start-up procedure (STARTUP) with the DCL command $SET STARTUP/INTERACTIVE=n. If you don't define a value for interactive users, STARTUP will use the default established by AUTOGEN.

## SYSTEM SHUTDOWN

A VMS system is correctly shutdown by executing the SHUTDOWN command procedure located in the SYS$SYSTEM directory. This procedure prompts for the following shutdown information:

How many minutes until final shutdown [0]:
Reason for shutdown [Standalone]:
Do you want to spin down the disk volumes [NO]?
Do you want to invoke the site-specific shutdown [YES]?
Should an automatic system reboot be performed [NO]?
When will the system be rebooted [later]:
Shutdown options (enter as a comma-separated list):

>       REMOVE_NODE
>       CLUSTER_SHUTDOWN
>       REBOOT_CHECK
>       SAVE_FEEDBACK
>       Shutdown options [NONE]:

Pay particular attention to the last question regarding shutdown options. Specify REMOVE_NODE when the system you're shutting down is a cluster member. This informs the other cluster members to adjust their quorum value. Specify CLUSTER_SHUTDOWN when you want to shutdown the entire cluster. Use the REBOOT_CHECK if you think critical bootstrap files have been disturbed. The SAVE_FEEDBACK option is used when tuning VMS with AUTOGEN feedback information.

## SETTING UP A VAXCLUSTER

Let's now concentrate on what it takes to set up, or form, a VAXcluster.

### Coordinating Common System Resources

In a homogeneous cluster (i.e., a cluster with a single system disk), users can log into any node and work in the same operating environment. This is because the cluster members share the same disks, most of the same files, and the same queues. Your task in setting up the homogeneous cluster is to coordinate this sharing of resources.

Full resource sharing is accomplished by establishing shared and private directories for the cluster nodes, MSCP serving disk devices, and by creating cluster common print and batch queues. In addition, application software for the users must be installed for shared cluster access.

A common system disk, from which all cluster nodes boot, is set up with two directory structures: a common system root, and a private root for each node. The common system root is used to maintain all files that can or must be shared between the cluster members. A node's private root holds the files that are specific to the member, such as SYSGEN parameters and start-up files.

Figure 8-1 illustrates a common system disk volume set up for two cluster nodes, BIFF and SKIP. The disk's master file directory (MFD) contains the root directories of BIFF and SKIP (SYS0 and SYS1 respectively), and the system common root directory (VMS$COMMON).

Each of the root directories contain, in addition to the normal VMS system directories, a SYSCOMMON directory. The SYSCOMMON directory is an alias for the system common root directory. The alias is created using the DCL command SET FILE/ENTER.

As you prepare your common system resources, you must be concerned with the placement of several files:

- SYSUAF.DAT
- NETUAF.DAT
- RIGHTSLIST.DAT
- VMSMAIL.DAT
- JBCSYSQUE.DAT

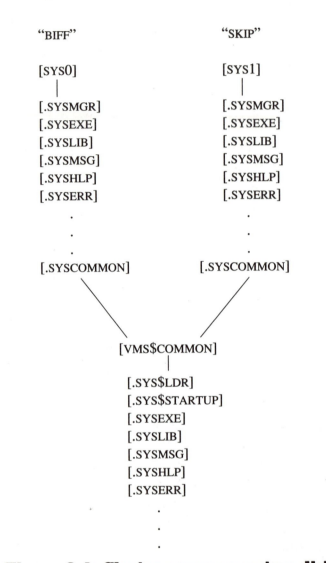

"BIFF"

[SYS0]
|
[.SYSMGR]
[.SYSEXE]
[.SYSLIB]
[.SYSMSG]
[.SYSHLP]
[.SYSERR]

.
.
.

[.SYSCOMMON]

"SKIP"

[SYS1]
|
[.SYSMGR]
[.SYSEXE]
[.SYSLIB]
[.SYSMSG]
[.SYSHLP]
[.SYSERR]

.
.
.

[.SYSCOMMON]

[VMS$COMMON]
|
[.SYS$LDR]
[.SYS$STARTUP]
[.SYSEXE]
[.SYSLIB]
[.SYSMSG]
[.SYSHLP]
[.SYSERR]

.
.
.

**Figure 8-1: Cluster common system disk**

These files, which maintain information about users' accounts,
network access, subject and object identifiers, and queues, define the
user environment of your cluster. In a homogeneous cluster, these
files should be located in SYS$COMMON:[SYSEXE].

## Preparing to Build a VAXcluster

In any distributed processing environment, the most difficult task is figuring out how to make the best use of your resources. Hopefully this planning was done before you bought the hardware.

Your VAXcluster system design will fall into one of three general categories:

- VAXcluster
- Local Area VAXcluster
- Mixed-interconnect VAXcluster

A VAXcluster uses the high-speed capabilities of the Computer Interconnect (CI). The Local Area VAXcluster takes advantage of a standard Ethernet Network Interconnect (NI). A mixed-interconnect VAXcluster uses both CI and NI communication mediums, allowing VAX and MicroVAX systems to share resources. Clusters can be homogeneous or heterogeneous.

No matter what type of cluster you're configuring, the steps you must take are similar. This discussion assumes that your hardware is properly installed, and that you're about to install VMS on the first node of a homogeneous VAXcluster.

Before beginning your VMS installation, you should thoroughly read the installation procedure provided with the VMS V5 release notes. With each release, new information is provided that you will need to know for a successful installation.

During the VMS installation, you will be asked:

Will this node be a cluster member?

Your response should be yes (y). This will start the cluster installation procedure. Next, you'll be prompted for information about your cluster. The questions and appropriate responses are listed in Table 8-1.

## Table 8-1: VMS Installation Questions for VAXcluster

| Cluster Install Questions | Your Response Should Be |
|---|---|
| What is the node's DECnet node name? | Enter a valid DECnet node name, for example, VENUS. The DECnet node name will also be the cluster node name. |
| What is the node's DECnet node address? | Enter a valid DECnet node address, for example, 1.3. |
| Will the Ethernet be used for cluster communications (Y/N)? | If this is a LAVc or mixed-interconnect cluster, enter Y. |
| Enter the cluster's group number. | This question is asked if you are configuring a LAVc. Enter a number between 1 and 4095. |
| Enter the cluster's password: | LAVc clusters use passwords to prevent a nonmember from joining. Passwords are one to 31 alphanumeric characters in length. |
| Will node be a disk server (Y/N)? | In local LAVc configurations, the system disk is always served. Answer Y if this is a LAVc. |

**Table 8-1: VMS Installation
Questions for VAXcluster (cont'd)**

| Cluster Install Questions | Your Response Should Be |
|---|---|
| Will node serve HSC disks (Y/N)? | If you are configuring a mixed cluster, one or more of the CI-based VAX nodes must serve the HSC disks for LAVc access. |
| Enter a value for the ALLOCLASS parameters. | For LAVc configurations, except when using device storage system interconnect (DSSI) drives, the ALLOCLASS parameter should be 0. |
| Does this cluster contain a quorum disk? | In general, a cluster with two nodes should use a quorum disk. |

If VMS has already been installed for a single noncluster system, and you are upgrading to a cluster, you must run the CLUSTER_CONFIG procedure:

```
$ @SYS$MANAGER:CLUSTER_CONFIG
```

After you answer the questions, the CLUSTER_CONFIG procedure will modify MODPARAMS.DAT and run AUTOGEN to make the necessary changes. The system will reboot and come up as a cluster of one node.

## Cluster Start-up Command Procedures

Before adding more nodes into your cluster, it's best to completely configure the first member. For the most part, this entails setting up your start-up command procedures, establishing secondary page and swap files (if necessary), and installing layered software products.

The cluster start-up file differs from that of a noncluster system in two ways: Shared devices must be mounted for cluster access, and a node-specific start-up file must be executed on each cluster member. The site specific start-up procedure (SYSTARTUP_V5.COM) should be located in the SYS$COMMON:[SYSMGR] directory. This will become the site-specific common start-up procedure for the cluster.

Your cluster's SYSTARTUP_V5.COM procedure should perform tasks that are common to each node, such as:

- Mounting cluster disks
- Starting the queue manager
- Initializing queues
- Starting DECnet
- Starting layered software products

At the beginning of the site-specific start-up procedure, you can create a symbol called NODE, which contains the name of the cluster member executing the procedure. The NODE symbol will be used to identify the cluster member that is booting. This is important when defining cluster queues, and for executing the node-specific start-up procedure. The NODE symbol is easily defined with the DCL command:

```
$ NODE = F$GETSYI("NODENAME")
```

In a cluster, disks that are to be shared should be mounted with the /CLUSTER qualifier. Note: The MOUNT qualifier /CLUSTER implies /SYSTEM; therefore, the /SYSTEM qualifier is not required. Each node in the cluster should mount the shared volumes as part of the start-up process.

In a cluster with HSCs, each cluster member should check for the availability of the drives before attempting to mount them:

```
$ IF F$GETDVI("$1$DUA1","AVL") THEN –
    MOUNT/CLUSTER $1$DUA1: USER$DISK1
```

In a local area VAXcluster, each cluster member should check for the presence of the node on which the disk is served and for the disk's availability:

```
$ IF F$GETSYI("CLUSTER_MEMBER","CHAZ")
$ THEN
$ IF F$GETDVI("CHAZ$DUA3","AVL") THEN -
   MOUNT/CLUSTER CHAZ$DUA3: OA$DISK
$ ENDIF
```

After all common start-up functions have been performed, call the node-specific start-up procedure. This procedure should be located in SYS$SPECIFIC:[SYSMGR] (i.e., the node's specific management directory) and have the name node_STARTUP.COM, where NODE is the cluster node name. For instance, cluster member BIFF would use SYS$SPECIFIC:[SYSMGR] BIFF_STARTUP.COM. To call this procedure from SYSTARTUP_V5.COM, use the command:

```
$ @SYS$MANAGER:'NODE'_STARTUP
```

## Adding a Cluster Node

To modify the common system disk to accommodate additional cluster members, use the cluster configuration procedure (CLUSTER_CONFIG.COM). This procedure will only work properly (for adding, modifying, and removing other nodes) if the node on which you're executing it is set up as a cluster.

The cluster configuration procedure performs several useful functions when adding a new node:

- Creates system root directories for the new node.
- Copies node-specific files into the new root.
- Creates boot files for LAVc satellite nodes.
- Serves hierarchical storage controller (HSC) disks for CI-connected VAXs.
- Creates the new node's page and swap files.
- Configures and updates DECnet databases.
- Sets up a cluster quorum disk, if requested.
- Creates system parameter files for the new node.

Before adding a new node, you must know the name of the new cluster member, the DECnet address of the new member, the system root directory, whether or not you want the member to serve its disks, and the Ethernet address of the Ethernet adapter (LAVc nodes only).

The MicroVAX console is used to determine the Ethernet hardware address. On a MicroVAX II CPU, enter the following commands:

```
>>> B/100 XQ
Bootfile: READ_ADDR
```

The MicroVAX 2000 is similar to the MicroVAX II; however, the Ethernet adapter has an electromagnetic storage (ES) device name, not XQ. To get the Ethernet address of a 3000 series MicroVAX, enter this command at the console:

```
>>> SHOW ETHERNET
```

When you have the necessary information to add the new node, execute the cluster configuration procedure. A menu will be presented. Choose ADD and answer the questions. The following is an example of adding a new node, called LIZ, to an existing local area VAXcluster:

```
$ @SYS$MANAGER:CLUSTER_CONFIG

Cluster Configuration Procedure

Enter ? for help at any prompt.

1. ADD a node to a cluster.
2. REMOVE a node from the cluster.
3. CHANGE a cluster member's characteristics.
4. CREATE a duplicate system disk for BIFF.

Enter choice [1]: 1

What is the node's DECnet node name? LIZ
What is the node's DECnet node address? 1.4
Will LIZ be a satellite [Y]?
Verifying circuits in network database...
What is the device name for LIZ's system root [DISK$Biff$V5:]?
What is the name of LIZ's system root [SYS10]? SYS3
Allow conversational bootstraps on LIZ [N]? Y

The following workstation windowing options are available:

1. No workstation software
2. VWS Workstation Software
3. DECwindows Workstation Software

Enter choice [1]: 3
```

Creating directory tree SYS3...
%CREATE–I–CREATED, BIFF$DUA0:<SYS3> created

.

.

.

%CREATE–I–CREATED, BIFF$DUA0:<SYS3.MOM$SYSTEM> created
System root SYS3 created.
Will LIZ be a disk server [N]?
What is LIZ's Ethernet hardware address? FF–0C–2B–10–50–B0
Updating network database...
Size of pagefile for LIZ [10000 blocks]?
Size of swap file for LIZ [8000 blocks]?
Will a local disk on LIZ be used for paging and swapping (Y/N)? N
What is the device name for the page and swap files [DISK$Biff$V5:]?
%SYSGEN–I–CREATED, BIFF$DUA0:<SYS3.SYSEXE>PAGEFILE.SYS;1
    created
%SYSGEN–I–CREATED, BIFF$DUA0:<SYS3.SYSEXE>SWAPFILE.SYS;1
    created
The configuration procedure has completed successfully.

LIZ has been configured to join the cluster.

The first time LIZ boots, NETCONFIG.COM and
AUTOGEN.COM will run automatically.

After the new node has been added, it can be booted into the cluster. The process by which this is done is different for each type of VAX system. Refer to your VAX's *Console Operator's Guide* for complete details.

To boot a MicroVAX into an LAVc, you specify the Ethernet adapter as the boot device. For example:

```
>>> B XQ     — MicroVAX II console
>>> B ES     — MicroVAX 2000 console
```

On large VAX systems, the console boot procedure (DEFBOO.COM) must be configured with information about the CI adapter, HSC CI node number, system root, and the boot device. This information is provided via general registers R0 through R5.

The first time a MicroVAX boots into a LAVc, AUTOGEN is automatically run to size the system. On CI-based VAXs, you must run AUTOGEN by hand after the system boots into the cluster. These details can change with new releases of VMS.

## VAXcluster SYSGEN Parameters

For a VAXcluster system to operate properly, certain SYSGEN
parameters must be established. Table 8-2 lists the most important
SYSGEN parameters specific to VAXclusters.

### Table 8-2: VAXcluster SYSGEN Parameters

| Parameter | Description |
| --- | --- |
| SCSSYSTEMID | Lower 48 bits of the system identification number. The value is computed by multiplying the DECnet area address by 1024 and adding the area number. |
| SCSNODE | Specifies the system communication services (SCS) node name. Must be the same as DECnet node name. |
| VAXCLUSTER | Determines if the system will join or form a VAXcluster. The parameter accepts three values: 0=Node will not join the cluster, 1=Node will join cluster if CI or NI path is present, and 2=Node will boot as a cluster member no matter what. |
| ALLOCLASS | Gives a unique name to dual-pathed disks. The parameter is specified as a value between 0 and 255. |
| VOTES | Total number of votes contributed by this node to cluster quorum. |
| EXPECTED_VOTES | Specifies the total number of votes expected in the cluster. This parameter should be set to the sum of all VOTE parameters, plus any votes provided by the quorum disk. |

## Table 8-2: VAXcluster SYSGEN Parameters (cont'd)

| Parameter | Description |
|-----------|-------------|
| DISK_QUORUM | The name of a disk to supply additional votes when forming a two-node cluster. |
| QDSKVOTES | Specifies the number of votes provided by the quorum disk. |
| NISCS_CONV_BOOT | Controls whether or not a conversational boot is permitted by a LAVc satellite node. When 0, conversational boots are not permitted. When 1, conversational boots are permitted. |
| NISCS_LOAD_PEA0 | Controls whether or not the NI-SCS port driver PEDRIVER is loaded during a system boot. When 0, the PEADRIVER is not loaded (default). A value of 1 loads the driver. |
| NISCS_PORT_SERV | Provides bit flags for the PEDRIVER. When bits 1 and 3 are set (decimal 3), data checking  is performed. The remaining bits are reserved for future use. |
| MSCP_LOAD | Controls the loading of the MSCP server at boot time. If 0, the MSCP server is not loaded. When 1, the MSCP server is loaded, and disks are served as specified by the MSCP_SERVE_ALL parameter. |
| MSCP_SERVE_ALL | Controls the serving of disks during a system boot. If 0, no disks are served (default). When 1, all available local disks are served. If 2, only locally attached disks are served. |

## Booting Nodes into a VAXcluster

Cluster nodes are booted into the cluster in several ways, depending on the type of cluster (NI or CI) and the nodes' function in the cluster.

NI cluster boot nodes must be booted from their local or device storage system interconnect (DSSI) disk before the satellite nodes can be booted. Satellite nodes are booted into the cluster by specifying the network controller as the boot device. For instance:

>>> B XQA0

or

>>> B ESA0

The first boot command boots a Q-bus MicroVAX with a DEQNA or DELQA controller. The second boot command boots a MicroVAX 2000 system. The system image is downline loaded to the MicroVAXs by the boot node.

CI cluster nodes boot from local disks or an HSC. In either case, the machine's DEFBOO console procedure must be set up to define the boot device. The boot device is specified by loading general registers with the correct values, which are defined in the CPU's *Console User's Guide*. The following registers are used:

> R0 – CI boot device type code
> R1 – Boot device bus address
> R2 – CI port number of HSC
> R3 – Drive to boot from (unit number)
> R4 – Not applicable, must be 0
> R5 – Software boot control flags

## QUEUE MANAGEMENT

Most multiuser computer systems have batch-oriented jobs and produce printed material. VMS lends a hand with these tasks by using queues to handle some of the work.

A queue is a list of jobs to be processed. These lists are maintained by the VMS job controller. There are two basic types of queues: batch and print.

Batch queues help to balance the CPU load. Requests made during peak hours can be processed during less active times. Large jobs can be delayed until off-hours, so as not to affect the interactive user's response time.

By associating queues with printing devices, users don't have to wait for the material to be printed. If a user wants to print something, he can send it to a queue and then go off and do other things. Print jobs can be delayed until off-hours, freeing devices for smaller jobs during normal work hours.

VMS queues are ordered by importance, i.e., they are priority ordered. As such, the first job in is not necessarily the first one out. The priority of a queued job is usually the software priority of the process associated with it. VMS first orders the jobs by priority. If there are other jobs with the same priority, they are ordered first-in-first-out within that priority.

The software responsible for the print and batch queues is the job controller. The job controller's process name is JOB_CONTROL. The DCL commands SUBMIT and PRINT interact with the job controller by placing jobs in specified batch and print queues. When these commands are issued, a number is given to the job. The job number is used with other DCL commands to refer to the job.

Jobs in queues can be in one of three states: current, pending, or holding. The job or jobs executing are current. Jobs waiting to be executed are pending. Jobs waiting to be released for executing are holding.

## Queue Types

VMS supports two basic types of queues: execution and generic.

An execution queue is a work queue. Jobs are processed directly from a print or batch execution queue. Batch queues are associated with a specific processor. Print queues are associated with a print device.

A generic queue is a mediator that holds a job until an execution queue becomes available. Users send their print and batch jobs to a generic queue, and the qeneric queue directs their job to the appropriate execution queue with the least load.

Generic queues are most often used with VAXclusters to balance work over the available resources.

## Queue Creation

Typically, you set up your queues by putting the appropriate commands in the SYSTARTUP_V5 command procedure. Another method, which I highly suggest, is to create a separate command procedure, such as STARTQ, to perform the task. By using a separate procedure, you can restart your queues very easily if they become fouled up beyond all repair.

Before a queue can be used, the queue manager must be running, and the queue must be initialized. The queue manager is started using the command:

$START/QUEUE/MANAGER SYS$COMMON:[SYSEXE]JBCSYSQUE.DAT

This command specifies the name of the file to contain information about batch and print jobs, queues, and form definitions. By default, the file JBCSYSQUE.DAT is used, but you can specify any file name. Specifying the exact queue file name is particularly necessary in VAXclusters.

There are several qualifiers that allow you to tailor the queue manager. They are described in Table 8-3.

When the job controller incurs a fatal error, the process aborts and restarts itself, but the queue manager is not restarted. Intervention by a user with OPERATOR privilege is necessary to restart the queue manager and to restore the queues using the START/QUEUE/MANAGER command.

After a queue file has been created and the queue manager is running, execution and generic queues can be initialized and started. Queues are initialized using the INITIALIZE/QUEUE command. For instance, a simple batch queue can be started with the command:

$ INITIALIZE/QUEUE/BATCH/START SYS$BATCH

In this command, the /BATCH qualifier indicates that this will be an execution batch queue, and the /START qualifier tells the queue

## Table 8-3: START/QUEUE/MANAGER Qualifiers

| Qualifier | Purpose |
|---|---|
| /BUFFER_COUNT=n | Specifies the number of buffers in a local buffer cache to allocate for performing I/O operations to the system job queue file. |
| /EXTEND_QUANTITY=n | Specifies the number of blocks by which the system job queue file is extended, if necessary. |
| /NEW_VERSION | Specifies that a new version of the job queue manager file be created to supersede an existing version. The new file contains no information until you issue a subsequent INITIALIZE/ QUEUE command. |
| /RESTART | Specifies that the queue manager be automatically restarted on recovery from a job controller abort. Batch and output queues are restored to the states that existed prior to the interruption of service. |

manager to start the queue. It's possible to hold off starting the queue until later or to start the queue on another CPU, i.e., when the VAX is configured in a cluster.

There are many qualifiers for the INITIALIZE/QUEUE command. They are described in Table 8-4.

## Table 8-4: INITIALIZE/QUEUE Qualifiers

| Qualifier | Purpose |
| --- | --- |
| /BASE_PRIORITY=n | Specifies the base process priority at which jobs are initiated from a batch queue or the base priority of the symbiont for a printer, terminal, or server queue. |
| /BATCH | Specifies that you are initializing a batch queue. |
| /BLOCK_LIMIT=([low,]hi) | Limits the size of print jobs that can be executed on a printer or terminal queue. |
| /CHARACTERISTICS=(char[,...]) | Specifies one or more characteristics for processing jobs in the queue. |
| /CLOSE | Prevents jobs from being entered in the queue through PRINT or SUBMIT commands or as a result of requeue operations. |
| /CPUDEFAULT=time | Defines the default CPU time limit for batch jobs. |
| /CPUMAXIMUM=time | Defines the maximum CPU time limit for batch jobs. |

## Table 8-4: INITIALIZE/QUEUE Qualifiers (cont'd)

| Qualifier | Purpose |
|---|---|
| /DEFAULT=(option[,...]) | Establishes defaults for certain options of the PRINT command. The options are burst, feed, flag, form=type, and trailor. |
| DEVICE[=option] | Specifies that you are initializing an output queue of a particular type. Options are printer, server, and terminal. |
| /DISABLE_SWAPPING | Controls whether batch jobs executed from a queue can be swapped. |
| /FORM_MOUNTED=type | Specifies the form type for a printer, terminal, or server queue. Specify the form type using either a numeric value or a form name that has been defined by the DEFINE/FORM command. |
| /GENERIC[=(queue[,...])] | Specifies that this is a generic queue and that jobs placed in it can be moved for processing to compatible execution queues. For instance, a generic printer queue can feed a mixture of printer and terminal execution queues. |

## Table 8-4: INITIALIZE/QUEUE Qualifiers (cont'd)

| Qualifier | Purpose |
| --- | --- |
| /JOB_LIMIT=n | Indicates the number of batch jobs that can be executed concurrently from the queue. |
| /LIBRARY=file_name | Specifies the file name for the device control library. |
| /ON=[node::]device[:] | Specifies the node and/or device on which this queue is located. |
| /OWNER_UIC=uic | Enables you to change the user identification code of the queue. |
| /PROTECTION=(code) | Specifies the protection of the queue. |
| /SCHEDULE=[NO]SIZE | Specifies whether pending jobs in a printer, terminal, or server queue are scheduled for printing based on the size of the job. |
| /SEPARATE=(option[,...]) | Specifies the job separation defaults for a printer or terminal queue. Separation options are burst, flag, trailer, and reset= (module[,...]). |

## Table 8-4: INITIALIZE/QUEUE Qualifiers (cont'd)

| Qualifier | Purpose |
| --- | --- |
| /START | Specifies that the queue being initialized will start at the conclusion of this INITIALIZE command. |
| /WSDEFAULT=n | Defines a working set default for a batch job. |
| /WSEXTENT=n | Defines a working set extent for the batch job. |
| /WSQUOTA=n | Defines the working set quota for a batch job. |

Some of the more obvious qualifiers you should include when initializing batch queues are /JOB_LIMIT and /BASE_PRIORITY. These qualifiers can seriously affect system performance. For example, the following command initializes a batch queue that allows up to two jobs to concurrently run at a base priority of three:

```
$ INITIALIZE/QUEUE/BATCH/START –
_$ /JOB_LIMIT=2/BASE_PRIORITY=3 SYS$BATCH
```

### Setting Device Characteristics

Before initializing a print queue, the characteristics of the printer port must be established. This is necessary because the device driver has no idea what type of print device you're using or what functions you want to support.

Printer port characteristics are modified using the SET TERMINAL (for terminal queues) and SET PRINTER (for printer queues) commands. After configuring a printer port with the appropriate SET command, it can be spooled. Spooling is a method of virtualizing a slow input or output device through the use of an intermediate storage device and a controlling process.

The following example prepares a terminal line for a generic printer and a printer port for an LP11 line printer:

```
$ SET TERMINAL/SPEED=9600/WIDTH=80/PAGE=66 –
_$ /WRAP/NOBROADCAST/PERMANENT TXA7:
$ SET DEVICE/SPOOLED TXA7:
$ SET PRINTER/PAGE=66/WIDTH=132/LOWER/LP11 LPA0:
$ SET DEVICE/SPOOLED LPA0:
```

When spooling a device, you can specify the queue and the intermediate storage device:

```
$ SET DEVICE/SPOOLED=(SYS$PRINT, SYS$SYSDEVICE) LPA0:
```

## Creating Generic Queues

To create a generic queue, you specify the /GENERIC qualifier and a list of execution queues in an INITIALIZE/QUEUE command. For instance, to create a generic batch queue, called SYS$BATCH, that feeds two execution queues called BATCH1 and BATCH2, you'd issue the command:

```
$ INITIALIZE/QUEUE/BATCH/START –
_$ /GENERIC=(BATCH1,BATCH1) SYS$BATCH
```

## Establishing Cluster Queues

On a standalone VAX system, batch and print queues are confined to the single processor. In a VAXcluster, however, cluster members can share queue resources. This ability to share queues permits better use of printers and allows the cluster workload to be balanced.

Cluster queues are established and controlled using the same commands you'd use on a single VMS system. The primary difference is defining the queue executor node.

Cluster queues are controlled and managed through a single job controller queue file (JBCSYSQUE.DAT). The file, when maintained on an MSCP served disk, makes queues available to all cluster members. You control which nodes in the cluster access the shared job controller queue file when you start the queue manager on each node:

```
$ START/QUEUE/MANAGER SYS$COMMON:[SYSEXE]JBCSYSQUE.DAT
```

## Cluster Print Queues

To establish cluster print queues, you first should determine the type of configuration that best suits your hardware and processing requirements. In a cluster environment, you have several queue alternatives that depend on the number and type of print devices available. For instance, you must decide:

- Which print queues should be assigned to local generic queues.

- Whether to configure generic print queues that are local to each node.

- If clusterwide generic queues should be set up to distribute print jobs.

After you have decided on a print queue scheme, you can proceed by creating a queue start-up procedure, i.e., STARTQ.COM.

The primary difference between defining a queue for a single node and defining a queue for a cluster is the INITIALIZE command /ON qualifier. The /ON qualifier specifies the node and device on which the queue is assigned. For example, the following command initializes a local print queue on node CHAZ:

```
$ INITIALIZE/QUEUE/START/ON=CHAZ::$PRINTER CHAZ_PRINT
```

The command must be executed by node CHAZ only. This is because only the node on which the queue executes can start (/START) the queue. Other cluster members needing access to the print queue must initialize it, but can't start it, i.e., use /NOSTART instead.

A smart command procedure can be written to initialize and start print queues based on the node executing the procedure. The following procedure segment, from STARTQ.COM, is such a procedure:

```
$! Start Queue Procedure
$!
$ NODE = F$GETSYI("NODENAME")
$ BIFF_START = "NOSTART"
$ LIZ_START  = "NOSTART"
```

```
$ SKIP_START = "NOSTART"
$!
$ 'NODE'_START = "START"
  .
  .

  .
$ INIT/QUEUE/ON=BIFF::$PRINTER/'BIFF_START' BIFF$LASER
$ INIT/QUEUE/ON=LIZ::$PRINTER /'LIZ_START' LIZ$LASER
$ INIT/QUEUE/ON=SKIP::$PRINTER/'SKIP_START' SYS$LA100
  .
  .

  .
```

When two or more printers of the same type are available, such as laser printers or line printers, a clusterwide generic queue can be created to distribute jobs:

```
$ INITIALIZE/QUEUE/GENERIC=(BIFF$LASER,LIZ$LASER) –
  /START SYS$LASER
```

With the generic queue defined above, when a print job is queued to SYS$LASER, it is placed in the print queue (i.e., BIFF$LASER or LIZ$LASER) with the least load. In the same way, a generic queue can be used to distribute jobs to multiple line printers on a single node.

### Cluster Batch Queues

As with printer queues, before setting up cluster batch queues, you decide on the best configuration to suit your cluster. How you distribute and configure your cluster batch queues will, to a large extent, define the load placed on each node. You must determine the type of processing that will be performed on each node, set up local batch queues to match those needs, and decide if you need clusterwide generic queues to distribute jobs.

Typically, you set up executor batch queues on each cluster member using the same procedures you'd use for a standalone node. As with a print queue, you assign a name to a batch queue with the INITIALIZE command:

```
$ INITIALIZE/QUEUE/BATCH/ON=SKIP::/START SKIP_BATCH
```

The above command initializes the queue SKIP_BATCH on node SKIP. On a standalone system, you'd name a single batch queue, such as

SYS$BATCH. That's because batch jobs are queued to SYS$BATCH by default. In a cluster, each batch queue must have a unique name. In other words, you can't have a queue named SYS$BATCH on more than one node. To skirt this problem, define a logical name for one of the local batch queues that you want used by default:

$ DEFINE/SYSTEM SYS$BATCH SKIP_BATCH

If you want batch jobs evenly distributed throughout the cluster, you must define a generic batch queue:

$ INITIALIZE/QUEUE/BATCH/GENERIC=(SKIP_BATCH,BIFF_BATCH) –
/START SYS$BATCH

Table 8-5 lists the DCL commands that are used to start, stop, and initialize print and batch queues.

## Table 8-5: Queue Start and Initialization Commands

| Queue Operation | DCL Command |
|---|---|
| Starting the queue manager | START/QUEUE/MANAGER /qual file-spec |
| Stopping the queue manager | STOP/QUEUE/MANAGER |
| Setting a terminal's characteristics | SET TERMINAL/qual device |
| Setting line printer characteristics | SET PRINTER/qual device |
| Spooling a device | SET DEVICE/SPOOLED device |

## Table 8-5: Queue Start and Initialization Commands (cont'd)

| Queue Operation | DCL Command |
| --- | --- |
| Create and start a queue | INITIALIZE/QUEUE/qual queue |
| Pause a queue | STOP/QUEUE |
| Resume a paused queue | START/QUEUE |

### Obtaining Queue Information

To manipulate queues, it's necessary to know what jobs are in queue. The SHOW QUEUE command is used to display information about queues. The SHOW QUEUE command has a single parameter, the name of the queue about which you want information. Table 8-6 lists each SHOW QUEUE qualifier and its purpose.

## Table 8-6: SHOW QUEUE Qualifier

| Qualifier | Purpose |
| --- | --- |
| /ALL_ENTRIES | Displays the names of all job entries in the specified queues. |
| /BATCH | Lists all batch queues and any jobs in those queues that are owned by the current process. |

## Table 8-6: SHOW QUEUE Qualifier (cont'd)

| Qualifier | Purpose |
|---|---|
| /BRIEF | Requests a brief listing of information about job entries in the queue. |
| /BY_JOB_STATUS=(keyword) | Displays jobs with the specified status. Specifies the status with one or more of the following keywords: executing, holding, pending, retained, and timed_release. |
| /DEVICE=(keyword) | Displays a particular type of queue. Specify the type of queue with one or more of the following keywords: printer, server, or terminal. |
| /FILES | Requests a brief listing of information about job entries in the queue with the list of files associated with each job. |
| /FULL | Displays full information about all queues, and about any jobs in the queue that are owned by the current process. |

## Table 8-6: SHOW QUEUE Qualifier (cont'd)

| Qualifier | Purpose |
| --- | --- |
| /GENERIC | Lists all generic queues, and displays any jobs in the queues that are owned by the current process. |
| /OUTPUT=file_spec | Controls where the output of the command is sent. |
| /CHARACTERISTIC | Displays characteristic names and numbers that are available on queues. |
| /FORM | Displays form names and numbers that are available on queues. |

Use the SHOW ENTRY command to get information about individual queue jobs. It can be used to monitor a particular user's jobs, or to determine the status of a particular job.

All jobs in queue have a job status. Table 8-7 lists the 10 possible types of job status returned by SHOW ENTRY and SHOW QUEUE.

### Modifying Jobs

You can modify many job attributes by using the appropriate qualifiers with the SET ENTRY command. SET ENTRY requires a single parameter, a job entry number. For example, the following command puts job number 591 on hold:

```
$ SET ENTRY 591 /HOLD
```

## Table 8-7: Queue Job Status Descriptions

| Status | Description |
| --- | --- |
| Aborting | The executing job is terminating. |
| Executing | The batch job is being executed. |
| Holding | The print or batch job is being held until it is explicitly released. |
| Holding until | The job is being held until the specified time. |
| Pending | The job is waiting for the current job to complete. |
| Printing | The print job is executing on a terminal or printer queue. |
| Processing | The job is being executed in a server queue. |
| Retained on completion | The job remains in queue after completion. |
| Retained on error | The job remains in queue when an error is encountered. |
| Waiting | The symbiont refused the job. |

Job 591 will wait in queue until it is released with the command:

$ SET ENTRY 591 /RELEASE

Table 8-8 describes the qualifiers you can use to modify jobs in queue.

## Table 8-8: SET ENTRY Qualifiers

| Qualifier | Purpose |
| --- | --- |
| /AFTER=time | Used to hold a job until after the specified time. |
| /HOLD | Used to put a job on hold until it is explicitly released. |
| /NAME="name" | Specifies a new name for the job. |
| /PASSALL | Specifies whether the symbiont passes all formatting information to the device driver. |
| /PRIORITY | Specifies the relative scheduling priority, with respect to the priorities of the other jobs in queue. |
| /RELEASE | Releases a job previously put on hold. |
| /REQUEUE | Requests that the specified job be moved to a new queue. |

## Deleting a Job

It is often necessary to terminate a batch or print job; for example, when the printer gets jammed. To delete a job from its queue, you must determine the job entry number, then issue a DELETE/ENTRY command:

$ SHOW QUEUE/ALL/BY_JOB_STATUS

.

.

.

$ DELETE/ENTRY=591

The DELETE/ENTRY command is restricted to the owner of the job and users who have OPER privilege.

## SETTING UP A DECNET NETWORK

If you're the system or network manager, and you're planning to set up your first DECnet network, you will need to understand the mechanics of establishing a network.

## Connecting the Network Hardware

Computers are networked via two mechanisms: communication hardware and communication software. In a DECnet network, each node has one or more communication controllers supported by a DECnet protocol: Ethernet, Digital Data Communications Message Protocol (DDCMP), or X.25.

Each communication controller has one or more ports. A communication port is simply an interface point. Each port provides a single physical connection to the network.

In many cases, a port is connected to another communication device, such as a transceiver or modem, that interfaces with the network. This is because most communication ports handle the raw data only. For example, if the telephone system is used to provide a point-to-point link with another VAX, then modems must be used. Modems modulate/demodulate two tones that ride on a carrier signal. The tones represent high and low transitions, i.e., the individual bits (1s and 0s) that represent binary data.

Using controllers with ports that interface to the raw data has a distinct advantage: It allows you to configure a network in a way that's suitable to the topology of the nodes and the available communication media. For instance, if you have two nodes that sit side-by-side, and each node has a free RS232 port (from a DHV11, DMF32, DMB32, and so on), then a simple null-modem cable between them would suffice. There's no reason to use modems or other expensive communication equipment.

To connect a node to an existing DECnet network, you must have a network controller, communication device, and cables. There are some exceptions, such as with ThinWire Ethernet, where the network controller and transceiver are a single unit. In a ThinWire Ethernet configuration, you simply connect the coaxial cable.

Installation and configuration instructions should be included with your hardware.

## Using the NETCONFIG Procedure

If you're configuring a node into a simple network, such as Ethernet, you can use the NETCONFIG procedure located in SYS$MANAGER. This procedure configures the permanent DECnet databases with the appropriate executor information. NETCONFIG should be used only when bringing a node up for the first time. Modifications must be made by hand.

To invoke NETCONFIG, from the SYSTEM account, enter the command:

$ @SYS$MANAGER:NETCONFIG

You will be prompted as follows:

```
What do you want your DECnet node name to be?
What do you want your DECnet address to be?
Do you want to operate as a router?
Do you want a default DECnet account?
```

Then, NETCONFIG will show you the commands it plans to execute and prompt for approval:

Here are the commands necessary to set up your system:

```
$ RUN SYS$SYSTEM:NCP
PURGE EXECUTOR ALL
PURGE KNOWN LINES ALL

    .
    .
    .

DEFINE EXECUTOR ADDRESS n.n STATE ON
DEFINE EXECUTOR NAME node
DEFINE EXECUTOR MAXIMUM ADDRESS 1023
DEFINE EXECUTOR TYPE NONROUTING IV
DEFINE EXECUTOR NONPRIVILEGED USER DECNET
DEFINE EXECUTOR NONPRIVILEGED PASSWORD DECNET
$ DEFINE/USER_MODE SYSUAF SYS$SYSTEM:SYSUAF.DAT
$ RUN SYS$SYSTEM:AUTHORIZE
ADD DECNET /OWNER="DECNET DEFAULT" –

    .
    .
    .

$ CREATE/DIRECTORY SYS$SPECIFIC:[DECNET] /OWNER=[376,376]
$ RUN SYS$SYSTEM:NCP
DEFINE LINE   QNA–0 STATE ON
DEFINE CIRCUIT QNA–0 STATE ON COST 4
DEFINE LOGGING MONITOR STATE ON
DEFINE LOGGING MONITOR EVENTS 0.0–9
DEFINE LOGGING MONITOR EVENTS 2.0–1
DEFINE LOGGING MONITOR EVENTS 4.2–13,15–16,18–19
DEFINE LOGGING MONITOR EVENTS 5.0–18
DEFINE LOGGING MONITOR EVENTS 128.0–4
```

Do you want these commands to be executed? [YES]:

After you have reviewed the commands that will be executed and are satisfied, respond by pressing <RETURN> or by entering Y and pressing <RETURN>. NETCONFIG will enter the commands, and your node will be configured.

Finally, NETCONFIG will ask you if you want the network started. If you have installed the network key, answer yes to this question. NETCONFIG will start the network by executing the STARTNET procedure. At this point, your DECnet node should be operational.

## Configuring a DECnet Node Manually

The network control program (NCP) is used to configure, control, monitor, and test a DECnet network. With NCP, you can:

- Define the executor name and address.
- Define lines and circuits.
- Define remote node names and addresses.
- Define object names.
- Define monitor events.

To invoke NCP, enter the following command:

$ RUN SYS$SYSTEM:NCP

NCP returns its prompt:

NCP>

To exit from NCP, enter EXIT and press <RETURN>, or press <CTRL/Z>.

To configure a DECnet node, you must:

- Load the correct driver.
- Initialize the device.
- Define the executor's node name, node address, type, account name, and password.
- Define one or more lines and circuits.

If you're bringing up a point-to-point DECnet circuit using an asynchronous terminal port, you must load a special driver and set the terminal characteristics. The driver, called NOA0, is loaded using SYSGEN:

$ RUN SYS$SYSTEM:SYSGEN
SYSGEN> CONNECT NOA0/NOADAPTER

The terminal port is configured using the DCL command SET TERMINAL. For example:

$ SET TERMINAL /PROTOCOL=DDCMP/NOTYPE_AHEAD-
_$ /SPEED=19200/MODEM/PERMANENT TXA7:

The DDCMP protocol is mandatory, and you cannot specify /AUTOBAUD. These commands must be issued before the network is started.

To define executor information (the executor is the local node), issue the following commands:

NCP> DEFINE EXECUTOR ADDRESS area.node STATE ON
NCP> DEFINE EXECUTOR NAME node_name
NCP> DEFINE EXECUTOR TYPE NONROUTING IV
NCP> DEFINE EXECUTOR NONPRIVILEGED USER DECNET
NCP> DEFINE EXECUTOR NONPRIVILEGED PASSWORD DECNET

In the first command, area.node represents a node address, i.e., 1.1, 2.4, 1.8, and so on. Each node must have a unique address that you select in coordination with system or network managers. In the second command, node_name is a one- to six-character node name for the system that you choose. The DEFINE EXECUTOR TYPE command defines the executor as a routing or nonrouting phase III, IV, or V DECnet node. The last two commands define the DECnet account name and password.

After the executor information is defined, you can define circuits and lines. Each circuit and line is associated with a physical device and port. Devices are specified in the format:

device-controller-unit

or

device-controller

For example, to define the line and circuit for the first DEQNA Ethernet controller on a MicroVAX, you'd enter the NCP commands:

NCP> DEFINE LINE QNA–0 STATE ON
NCP> DEFINE CIRCUIT QNA–0 STATE ON

An Ethernet adapter has only one port; therefore, a port number is not specified. To define port 7 on the second DMF32 controller, you'd enter the commands:

NCP> DEFINE LINE TX–1–7 STATE ON
NCP> DEFINE CIRCUIT TX–1–7 STATE ON

Other line and circuit information, such as line receive buffers, line speed, and circuit cost, can be defined when you enter the DEFINE LINE and DEFINE CIRCUIT commands. For example:

NCP> DEFINE LINE TX–0–0 STATE ON RECEIVE BUFFERS 4
NCP> DEFINE CIRCUIT TX–0–0 STATE ON COST 10
NCP> DEFINE LINE SVA–0 STATE ON
NCP> DEFINE CIRCUIT SVA–0 STATE ON COST 4

Before DECnet can be started for the first time, a DECNET account
must exist. A default DECNET account is defined with the following
commands:

```
$ DEFINE/USER_MODE SYSUAF SYS$SYSTEM:SYSUAF.DAT
$ RUN SYS$SYSTEM:AUTHORIZE
ADD DECNET /OWNER="DECNET DEFAULT" -
/PASSWORD=DECNET/UIC=[376,376]/ACCOUNT=DECNET -
/DEVICE=SYS$SPECIFIC:/DIRECTORY=[DECNET] -
/PRIV=(TMPMBX,NETMBX)/DEFPRIV=(TMPMBX,NETMBX) -
/FLAGS=(CAPTIVE)/LGICMD=NL:/NOBATCH /NOINTERACTIVE
$ CREATE/DIRECTORY SYS$SPECIFIC:[DECNET]/OWNER=[376,376]
```

If your requirements differ, add the default account, then modify it.

To start DECnet, use the STARTNET procedure. Issue the command:

```
$ @SYS$MANAGER:STARTNET
```

Two processes will be created: NETACP and REMACP. To verify that
your network is operating properly, enter the NCP commands SHOW
EXECUTOR and SHOW KNOWN CIRCUITS. The executor state should be
on, and the circuit state should be on. If the circuit state is
synchronizing, then your DECnet node is not communicating with a
remote node. This is most often the case on a point-to-point circuit
when the circuit or line parameters are incorrectly defined, or when
the remote node is not on line.

## Defining Remote Nodes

Before remote nodes can be accessed, they must be defined. Two
components for each node must be defined: the node name and node
address. For example:

```
NCP> DEFINE NODE 1.1 NAME BIFF
```

The DEFINE command enters the specified information into your
node's permanent database. A second database, called the volatile
database, is also maintained. To define a node in the volatile database,
use the NCP SET command:

```
NCP> SET NODE 1.2 NAME SKIP
```

A new volatile database is created from the permanent database each time DECnet is brought up.

## Displaying DECnet Information

To display DECnet information, the NCP SHOW command is used. For instance, to see what remote nodes are defined, you'd enter:

NCP> SHOW KNOWN NODES

or

NCP> SHOW NODE *

Some other useful show commands are:

NCP> SHOW EXECUTOR
NCP> SHOW LOGGING MONITOR
NCP> SHOW KNOWN CIRCUITS
NCP> SHOW KNOWN LINES
NCP> SHOW KNOWN LINKS

## Restarting the Network

If you define a new executor, line, or circuit parameters or have network problems, the network might have to be restarted. DECnet is easily restarted by shutting down DECnet and starting it again using STARTNET.

To stop DECnet, use NCP:

NCP> SET EXECUTOR STATE OFF

or

NCP> SET EXECUTOR STATE SHUT

The first command stops DECnet immediately. The second waits for all links to be disconnected.

Next, restart DECnet with the command:

$ @SYS$MANAGER:STARTNET

## NCP Commands

Table 8-9 lists frequently used commands.

## Table 8-9: NCP Commands

| Function | Command |
|---|---|
| Define executor | DEFINE EXECUTOR<br>NAME<br>ADDRESS<br>ROUTING TYPE<br>NONPRIVILIGED<br>USER<br>MAXIMUM<br>ADDRESS |
| Define node name and address | SET/DEFINE NODE area.node<br>NAME name |
| Define a circuit | SET/DEFINE CIRCUIT<br>dev-con-unit |
| Define a line | SET/DEFINE LINE dev-con-unit |
| Display remote<br>node information | SHOW KNOWN NODES<br>SHOW ACTIVE NODES<br>SHOW ADJACENT NODES<br>STATUS |
| Display circuit information | SHOW KNOWN CIRCUITS<br>SHOW ACTIVE CIRCUITS |
| Display line information | SHOW KNOWN LINES<br>SHOW ACTIVE LINES |
| Display executor characteristics | SHOW EXECUTOR<br>CHARACTERISTICS |

## INSTALLING SOFTWARE

All software applications, including VMS updates, must be installed. Installing a software product configures it for your system and makes it available for use. The VMSINSTAL procedure is used to install most software.

VMSINSTAL, located in the SYS$UPDATE directory, is a special command procedure that installs software products that conform to its kit specification. This is true of all Digital software products and most third-party software.

Before using VMSINSTAL, you should:

1. Log into the SYSTEM account.

2. Get all users to log out.

3. Prevent users from logging in:

   $ SET LOGIN/INTERACTIVE=0

4. Read the software product's installation guide.

5. Make required parameter changes in SYSGEN and AUTHORIZE.

6. Make sure you have a backup copy of the system disk.

## Using VMSINSTAL

VMSINSTAL is a command procedure. It can be invoked from any directory with the command:

$ @SYS$UPDATE:VMSINSTAL

When you enter this command, VMSINSTAL will prompt for input parameters after asking one or more vital questions about users (if any are logged in), the network (if it is on), and your system disk backup. Answer yes to all these questions if you want to continue. In practice, it is not advisable to let users stay logged in while you are installing software.

VMSINSTAL will prompt for the following information:

- Distribution volume
- Product name
- Options

A valid distribution volume is any disk, tape, logical name (that equates to a disk or tape), or network node and disk. Some examples are:

DUA0:[PRODUCTS]
$1$MUA1:
BIFF::DUA1:[000000]

Product distribution names are a combination of the product's name and version number. For instance, the product name DTR044 is the kit name for DATATRIEVE Version 4.4. Digital puts its product kit names on the distribution media and in the installation guide.

VMSINSTAL accepts five options, specified by entering a single character. The options are:

- Create an auto-answer file (A)
- Get save set from distribution (G)
- Create a log file (L)
- Access the release notes (N)
- Install product in an alternate root (R)

If you want, you can specify all three of the VMSINSTAL parameters on the invoking command line:

$ @SYS$UPDATE:VMSINSTAL DTR044 MUA0: OPTIONS AL

This command installs DATATRIEVE Version 4.4 from tape drive MUA0 with options A and L.

## MANAGING ACCOUNTS

One of the most important duties the VMS system manager has is creating and maintaining user accounts. Each system user has special needs. It is up to the system manager to determine the access, privilege, and resource requirements of each user account.

The AUTHORIZE utility is used to create and maintain user accounts.

### System Authorization Files

User account information is maintained in three system databases: SYSUAF.DAT, NETPROXY.DAT, and RIGHTSLIST.DAT. These files reside in the SYS$SYSTEM directory.

SYSUAF.DAT is the database that contains local user account information. Each system user has a record in this database that describes his account.

The network proxy file (NETUAF.DAT) is a database containing entries for remote users who have a local account. The database associates a remote user and a system with a local account. The proxy access mechanism permits users to access their files on remote nodes without having to provide access control information, i.e., username and password.

The rights list database is used to associate identifiers with user accounts. For instance, the user's account name can be associated with his user identification code (UIC).

## Default SYSUAF Records

The SYSUAF file comes preconfigured with several records:

**DEFAULT** – The default template record. When creating a new user account, the information that you don't explicitly supply is taken from this record. This record can be modified, but it can't be deleted.

**FIELD** – Default Digital field service account.

**SYSTEM** – Default system manager account. This account has full privileges. This record can be modified, but it can't be deleted.

**SYSTEST** – User test environment account. This account is used to load test the system.

## Creating New Accounts

There are many ways to set up user accounts, but they typically fall into two categories: captive and interactive.

A captive account is for users who require access to a limited number of software resources. This type of account allows the system manager to tightly control the user's access. Captive accounts are most often controlled through a menu system.

An interactive account is for users who need to have interactive use of all (i.e., nonprivileged) system software. In general, interactive accounts are not menu-driven.

Prior to adding a new account, you should determine the following information:

- Username and temporary password
- User identification code
- Account storage device
- Primary applications
- Security requirements

A SYSUAF record has four primary components:

**Identification** – Qualifiers that define the account name, owner, UIC, default device, and directory: /ACCOUNT, /OWNER /DEVICE, DIRECTORY, /LGICMD, and /UIC.

**Limits and Quotas** – Qualifiers that define system resources that can be consumed by the account user: /ASTLM, /BIOLM /CPUTIME, /DIOLM, /ENQLM, /FILLM, /JTQUOTA, /MAXACCTJOBS, /MAXDETACH, /MAXJOBS, /PGFLQUOTA, /PRCLM, /SHRFILLM, /TQELM, /WSDEFAULT, /WSEXTENT, and /WSQUOTA.

**Priority and Privileges** – Qualifiers that define the job processing priority and privileges: /PRIORITY, /QUEPRIORITY /PRIVILEGES, and /DEFPRIVILEGES.

**System Access** – Qualifiers that define primary and secondary login times and flags that define mobility: /ACCESS, /DIALUP, /FLAGS, /INTERACTIVE, /LOCAL, /PRIMEDAYS, and /REMOTE.

There are two methods of adding a new account: by hand and with an ADD USER command procedure. The AUTHORIZE utility is used in both cases. To use AUTHORIZE interactively, enter the following commands:

```
$ SET DEFAULT SYS$SYSTEM
$ RUN AUTHORIZE
```

The AUTHORIZE utility will respond with the UAF> prompt. To add a new account, use the ADD command and supply enough information to make the account unique. Information that you don't explicitly provide will be taken from the DEFAULT account:

```
UAF> ADD ROCK/PASSWORD="ILLNEVERTELL"/UIC=[100,104] –
_UAF> /OWNER="ROCK"/ACCOUNT="ROCK"/DEVICE=USER$DISK –
_UAF> /DIRECTORY=[ROCK]
```

In this example, an account called rock is created with a UIC of [100,104]. The user's default device is USER$DISK (a logical name). Before this account can be used, a directory must be created:

```
$ CREATE/DIRECTORY/OWNER=[ROCK] USER$DISK:[ROCK]
```

A better way to add new accounts to is use a command procedure that prompts you for information. An example command procedure, called ADDUSER.COM, is provided in the SYS$UPDATE directory.

## Modifying User Accounts

The AUTHORIZE command MODIFY is used to change fields in an existing account. For instance, if a user needs additional working set quota, you'd issue the command:

```
UAF> MODIFY username /WSQUOTA=n
```

Here, username is the user's account name, and n is the new working set quota value. You can specify more than one qualifier with the MODIFY command, if required.

If strict security is implemented on your system, you will use the MODIFY command often to enable and disable accounts. To disable an account temporarily, set the DISUSER flag:

```
UAF> MODIFY BYNON /FLAGS=DISUSER
```

To re-enable an account that you have disabled or that has become disabled because of a security violation, you negate the disuser flag:

```
UAF> MODIFY BYNON /FLAGS=NODISUSER
```

## Listing and Showing User Accounts

Use the AUTHORIZE command LIST to create an output file (SYSUAF.LIS) of user records or the SHOW command to display records at your terminal. By default, the LIST command produces a brief report and the SHOW command creates a full report. Use the /BRIEF and /FULL qualifiers to tailor the output as appropriate. Some examples are:

```
$ SHOW * /BRIEF
```

```
$ SHOW SHIPMAN
$ LIST/FULL
```

## Deleting User Accounts

When a user no longer requires access to your system, his account should, for security and housekeeping reasons, be deleted. The AUTHORIZE command REMOVE is used to delete the SYSUAF entry, but there are other tasks that must be done as well.

To remove a user's SYSUAF entry, use the command:

UAF> REMOVE username

Next, if disk quotas are imposed, you must delete the user's disk quota entry with the DISKQUOTA utility. The third step is to remove associated MAIL information by using the MAIL command REMOVE:

```
$ MAIL
MAIL> REMOVE username
```

The final step is to delete the user's files and directory. If the user has files of importance, save them before deleting the account.

## Creating Proxy Database Entries

The proxy login mechanism permits remote users to access systems (on which they have accounts) without having to supply embedded login information. Proxy login is a convenience and a security feature.

To add a proxy database entry, use the AUTHORIZE command ADD/ PROXY. The correct use is:

UAF> ADD/PROXY node::user local_user

where node:: is the name of the remote DECnet node from which the user is authorized to connect, user is the account name on the remote node, and local_user is the name of the user's local account. For example:

UAF> ADD/PROXY CHAZ::BYNON BYNON

This command grants user BYNON on node CHAZ proxy access rights to the local account BYNON.

## AUTHORIZE Commands

Table 8-10 lists the AUTHORIZE commands used to maintain accounts.

### Table 8-10: AUTHORIZE Commands

| Function | Command |
|---|---|
| Create a new account | ADD username [/qual...] COPY username new_username [/qual...] |
| Modify an existing account | MODIFY username /qual RENAME username new_username |
| Modify the default record | DEFAULT /qual [/qual...] |
| Display account information | SHOW username [/qual] LIST [/qual] |
| Delete an account | REMOVE username |
| Create new databases | CREATE/PROXY CREATE/RIGHTS |
| Creating a proxy database entry | ADD/PROXY node::user local_user |
| Creating a rights database entry | ADD/IDENTIFIER=id |
| Controlling access to rights lists identifier | GRANT/IDENTIFIER=id username REVOKE/ID =id username |

## SYSTEM BACKUP

Files must be duplicated to protect data from loss or corruption. You should think of this task as cheap insurance against total disaster. The BACKUP utility is most commonly used to duplicate on-line storage (i.e., your disks).

Generally, the contents of the system disk and any user disks are backed up to magnetic tape for safekeeping. Other media, such as optical disk or removable disks can also be used. After these off-line media contain a backup copy of the on-line files, they should be removed from their drive and stored in a secure location.

### Backup Methods

The BACKUP utility has a number of qualifiers that influence the way it operates and the files it affects. When you use BACKUP, you must make two decisions: what you want to back up, and how you want it backed up. You have the following options:

**Selective** – BACKUP can back up files on a selective basis, according to a specified criteria such as a date, file type, or version number. BACKUP qualifiers (such as /DATE) and file specifications (such as *.TXT) are used to specify the selective files.

**File by file** – BACKUP can copy individual files or entire file directories. In this mode, BACKUP provides file copy facilities (directory creation during copy) that the VAX/VMS COPY command does not.

**Incremental** – An incremental backup saves files created since the most recent backup operation. In general, incremental backups are done by your VAX system manager or operators.

**Physical** – A physical backup operation saves an exact duplicate of a volume. All file structures are ignored. The copy is a bit-by-bit duplicate.

**Image** – An image backup creates a functionally equivalent copy of the original volume. Image backups are typically done on bootable volumes, such as the VAX system disk.

## Volume Initialization and Mounting

In most cases, you will have to initialize a tape or disk volume before you can use it for the first time. Tape volume names can be from one to six characters in length, and disk volume names can be up to 12 characters. Example:

```
$ INITIALIZE MUA0: TAPE
$ INITIALIZE DJA1: BILL_SHIPMAN
```

When you initialize a tape or disk, all files are effectively erased. A volume only needs to be initialized the first time you want to use it, or when you decide the files it contains are no longer needed. Be careful not to initialize a volume that might have files you want to keep.

Before you can use a volume, it must be mounted and writable. For backup purposes, volumes are mostly mounted foreign, i.e., non-Files-11 ODS-2 structured volumes. This is to accommodate BACKUP's special save set format. To mount a tape or disk device as foreign, you'd issue a command such as the following:

```
$ MOUNT/FOREIGN MUA0:
```

or

```
$ MOUNT/FOREIGN DJA1:
```

As of VMS V5, the BACKUP utility will mount the output volume for you if it is not mounted.

## Single File Copy on Disk

The BACKUP copy operation permits you to create an equivalent copy of a disk volume. Unlike the DCL COPY command, BACKUP makes identical copies of the original files and directories, retaining file protection and creation dates.

To copy a single file, enter a command in the format:

```
$ BACKUP file_spec file_spec
```

The first file specification is the source file and the second is the destination. If you specify the destination as simply a directory, BACKUP will assume a wildcard file specification and retain the original name.

For example, to copy your LOGIN.COM file to a directory named [SHIPMAN], you could enter the following command:

$ BACKUP LOGIN.COM [SHIPMAN]

or

$ BACKUP LOGIN.COM [SHIPMAN]LOGIN.COM

If you specify a new file name in the destination file specification, the file will be renamed. For example:

$ BACKUP LOGIN.COM [SHIPMAN]EXAMPLE_LOGIN.COM

## Multifile Copy on Disk

Multiple files can be copied by using wildcards or file lists in the source specification. For example:

$ BACKUP *.TXT [BYNON.MEMOS]
$ BACKUP NOTES.TXT,TRAVEL.TXT,EVENTS.TXT [WILLIS.TEXT]

If the destination directories do not exist, BACKUP will create them for you. This is one of the primary benefits of BACKUP over the DCL COPY command.

## Copying a Directory Tree

To copy an entire directory tree, use the following BACKUP format:

$ BACKUP [directory...]file_spec [directory...]file_spec

All files and directories represented by the ellipsis ([...]) will be copied from the source specification. For example:

$ BACKUP [BYNON...]*.FOR DUA2:[SOURCES.FORTRAN]

or

$ BACKUP USER$DISKS:[SWEET...]*.* USER$DISK2:[*...]

## Saving Disk Files to Tape

When you save files on tape using BACKUP, the output is called a save set. The save set name is always followed by the /SAVE_SET qualifier. You can select any valid VMS file name and type for a save set name.

If you're backing up multiple save sets to a single tape, assign a different name to each save set on the tape. This helps avoid confusion when you restore the files.

This example demonstrates how to back up files from a single directory to a save set on tape:

```
$ MOUNT/FOREIGN MSA0:
 MOUNT-I-MOUNTED, BYNON mounted on _MSA0:
$ BACKUP DUA2:[BYNON.XWIN]*.*;* MSA0:XWIN.BAK/SAVE_SET
```

This command backs up all files in the directory [BYNON.XWIN] to the tape mounted on MSA0:. The save set name is XWIN.BAK.

To back up an entire directory tree, the ellipsis wildcard is used:

```
$ MOUNT/FOREIGN MUA0:
 MOUNT-I-MOUNTED, TAPE mounted on _MUA0:
$ BACKUP DUB0:[SHIPMAN...] MUA0:SHIPMAN.BAK/SAVE_SET
```

This command backs up all files and subdirectories in user Shipman's login directory.

## Restoring Saved Files from Tape

At some point after saving files on tape, you'll need to restore them. This is also done with the BACKUP utility. The procedure is called a tape to disk file restore.

To restore files from a BACKUP tape volume to a disk volume, determine whether you want to restore a single file or an entire save set. Then use the appropriate BACKUP command. The following examples demonstrate the restoration of a single file, as well as the restoration of a BACKUP save set.

```
$ MOUNT/FOREIGN MSA0:
 MOUNT-I-MOUNTED, BYNON mounted on _MSA0:
$ BACKUP MSA0:XWIN.BAK/SAVE_SET -
_$ /SELECT=[BYNON.XWIN]WIDGET1.C *.*
```

This command restores the file WIDGET1.C to the current device and directory. Note that the /SELECT qualifier is used to specify the individual file that is to be restored from the save set.

If you need to restore an entire BACKUP save set to disk, specify the tape drive and the save set name as the source, and the destination disk and directory names. Following the directory name with an ellipsis tells the BACKUP utility that you want files and any subdirectories restored to the root directory:

```
$ MOUNT MUA0: BACKUP
$ BACKUP MUA0:BACKUP.BAK/SAVE_SET BIFF$DUA1:[*...]
```

This command restores all the files and subdirectories in the save set to the original root directory.

## Listing a Backup Save Set

There will be times when you need to know the contents of a BACKUP save set. For example, you might want to restore a few files from a tape, but don't remember the names. By listing the contents of a save set, you can determine the size and name of the files you want to restore.

To get a listing of a BACKUP save set, you must mount the tape containing the save set as a foreign volume. Then enter the BACKUP command with the /LIST qualifier as shown in the example:

```
$ MOUNT/FOREIGN MUA0:
 MOUNT–I–MOUNTED, TAPE mounted on MUA0:
$ BACKUP/LIST *.*/SAVE_SET
```

After information about the backup save set is displayed, each file in the save set will be listed. The save set information includes the directory, file name, file type, version number, size in blocks, and creation date for each file listed.

## Selective Backups

From time to time, you will find it necessary to back up files based on a specific criteria, such as a creation date. Files can be selected by wildcard file specifications, creation date, exclusions, UICs, and expiration dates.

To back up files by creation date, for example, use the /SINCE or /BEFORE qualifiers. If you want to back up all files created or modified since June 1, 1988, for example, use a command such as:

```
$ BACKUP *.*/SINCE=1–JUN–1988 MUA0:MYSTUFF.BAK/SAVE_SET
```

In many cases, you will find it necessary to exclude files from a selected backup. To do so, use the /EXCLUDE qualifier as follows:

```
$ BACKUP *.*/SINCE=1-SEP-1989/EXCLUDE=[*.LOG] -
_$ MUA0:MYSTUFF.BAK/SAVE_SET
```

In this example, all files created since September 1, 1989, except those with a file type of ".LOG", will be backed up to the save set MYSTUFF.BAK.

## Full and Incremental Backups

It's imperative that all system and user information be saved in full on a regular basis, i.e., daily, weekly, or monthly. Each site has different requirements for data integrity. The backup schedule should be based on how much you value your information.

After a full backup of a volume has been made, incremental backup (since the last backup) can be made. The incremental backup process is used to save time and backup media.

A full backup is typically accomplished by making an image copy of each volume. Use the command qualifier /IMAGE to make an image copy of a disk volume. An image save operation copies all files on the source disk, even those marked for delete. You cannot specify an input selection. If you plan to perform incremental backups between image backups, then you must specify the /RECORD qualifier. For example:

```
$ BACKUP/IMAGE/RECORD -
_$ BIFF$DUA0: MUA0:[]APRIL.BAK/SAVE_SET/LABEL=APRIL
```

If you're performing the backup operation with users on the system, you should use the /IGNORE=INTERLOCK qualifier. This qualifier ensures that open files will be saved with as much information as possible. The qualifier is especially useful for files that are always open.

To perform an incremental backup (after an image), use the /SINCE=BACKUP qualifier. This qualifier directs BACKUP to save only those files that have been modified or created since the last BACKUP/ RECORD operation. For example:

```
$ BACKUP/IGNORE=INTERLOCK/RECORD/SINCE=BACKUP -
_$ BIFF$DUA0: MUA0:[]APR4D.BAK/SAVE_SET/LABEL=APR4D
```

Another method of performing an incremental backup is to specify a date with the /SINCE qualifier. For instance, if you perform daily incremental backups and then want to perform a weekly incremental backup, you'd use /SINCE=BACKUP for each daily and /SINCE=date for the weekly:

```
$ BACKUP/IGNORE=INTERLOCK/RECORD/SINCE=3–APR–1989 -
_$ BIFF$DUA0: MUA0:[]APR7W.BAK/SAVE_SET/LABEL=APR7W
```

Note that D and W in the save set and label denote daily and weekly, respectively.

Using a daily/weekly schedule, you can rotate a set of tapes: daily backup set, weekly backup set, and full backup set.

### BACKUP Commands

Table 8-11 lists BACKUP commands by function.

### Table 8-11: BACKUP Commands

| Function | Command |
|---|---|
| BACKUP format | BACKUP [/qual] source destination [/qual] |
| Selective backup | BACKUP/BEFORE=time [/qual...] |
| | BACKUP/CREATED=time [/qual...] |
| | BACKUP/EXCLUDE=file_spec) [qual...] |
| | BACKUP/SINCE=time [qual...] |
| Image backup | BACKUP/IMAGE [qual...] |
| | BACKUP/IMAGE/RECORD [/qual...] |
| | BACKUP/IMAGE/IGNORE=INTERLOCK [qual...] |

## Table 8-11: BACKUP Commands (cont'd)

| Function | Command |
| --- | --- |
| Incremental backup | BACKUP/SINCE=BACKUP [/qual...] |
| Incremental restore | BACKUP/INCREMENTAL [/qual...] |
| Physical backup | BACKUP/PHYSICAL [/ qual...] |
| Listing a save set | BACKUP/LIST source/SAVE_SET |
| Restoring a save set | BACKUP source/SAVE_SET<br>dest [/qual...] |

## MAINTAINING LOG FILES

VMS creates several log files that record useful information about your system. Specifically, they are:

- Accounting log file
- Error log file
- Operator log file

## Accounting Log File

The VMS ACCOUNTING facility collects information about users and their use of system resources. For instance, when a user logs out or prints a document, the pertinent information about these events is logged. You can use this information for:

- Charging for system use.
- Monitoring system security.
- Evaluating how much of the system's resources a user consumes.

The accounting log records the following information:

- Login failures
- Process and subprocess termination

- Detached process termination
- Print jobs
- Batch job termination
- Image activation
- User messages

You can use the SHOW ACCOUNTING command to display the activities being logged.

The SET ACCOUNTING command is used to enable and disable accounting activities. If you're not going to use all of the information that's collected by default, you should disable the activities you don't want. For example, the following commands disable print job accounting and enable image accounting:

```
$ SET ACCOUNTING/DISABLE=PRINT
$ SET ACCOUNTING/ENABLE=IMAGE
```

Accounting information is logged in ACCOUNTNG.DAT, which is located in the SYS$MANAGER directory. Typically, this file is closed out at regular intervals (i.e., daily, weekly, monthly, and so on), and a new file is created. The interval is driven by site requirements, but you shouldn't let it go for more than several months. If your system is heavily used, the accounting log will grow rapidly.

To begin a new accounting file, enter the command:

```
$ SET ACCOUNTING/NEW_FILE
```

The old accounting log can be renamed or purged from the system.

## Accounting Reports

Useful reports can be generated from the accounting log information with the ACCOUNTING utility. Accounting reports are a useful system management tool. The following example would produce a summary report of CPU use, printed pages, and page faults for all system accounts:

```
$ ACCOUNTING/SUMMARY=USER
/REPORT=(PROCESSOR,PAGES,FAULTS)
```

The following information can be reported:

**BUFFERED_IO** – Total buffered IOs
**DIRECT_IO** – Total direct IOs
**ELAPSED** – Total elapsed time
**EXECUTION** – Total images executed
**FAULTS** – Total page faults
**GETS** – Total RMS gets
**PAGE_FILE** – Maximum page file use
**PAGE_READS** – Total page read I/Os
**PAGES** – Total pages printed
**PROCESSOR** – Total processor time consumed
**QIOS** – Total QIOs issued
**RECORDS** – Total records in file (default)
**VOLUMES** – Total volumes mounted
**WORKING_SET** – Maximum working set size

Reports can be summarized by:

**ACCOUNT** – Account name from the UAF
**DATE** – Date of entries
**DAY** – Day of month (1–31)
**HOUR** – Hour of day (0–23)
**IMAGE** – Image name
**JOB** – Name of batch job or print job
**MONTH** – Month of year (1–12)
**NODE** – Remote node name
**PROCESS** – Process type
**QUEUE** – Batch or device queue name
**TERMINAL** – Terminal name
**TYPE** – Type of record (i.e., logout, batch, and so on)
**UIC** – User identification code
**USER** – Username from UAF
**WEEKDAY** – Day of week (i.e., 1=Sunday, 2=Monday, and so on)
**YEAR** – Year of entry

## The Error Log File

When a system error occurs, such as a device failure, the event is logged in the system error log named SYS$ERRORLOG: ERRLOG.SYS. You can display the log information by using the ANALYZE/ ERROR_LOG utility to analyze the file:

$ ANALYZE/ERROR_LOG

Error log information is useful for preventive and corrective maintenance. When checked regularly, the error log can alert you to a potential failure, i.e., a disk going bad. In corrective maintenance situations, the error log can be used as a diagnostic tool. The error log often records events that led to the failure.

## The Operator Log File

The operator log is used to record system events and user requests. The file is called SYS$MANAGER:OPERATOR.LOG, and it records the following information:

- Log initialization
- Device status (i.e., on-line or off-line)
- Operator terminals enabled and disabled
- Volume operations
- User requests
- Changes to system parameters
- Security alarms
- DECnet status

A new operator log is created each time the OPCOM process is started or restarted. Typically, this happens when the system boots. The OPCOM process can be started manually with the command:

$ @SYS$SYSTEM:STARTUP OPCOM

An operator log file can only be printed or displayed at your terminal if it is closed. To print the current log file, you must stop the OPCOM process, rename the OPERATOR.LOG file, then restart OPCOM.

## CONCLUSION

System management is resource management. A perfectly managed VMS system is secure, responsive, and requires little interaction by the system manager. Command procedures should be developed to perform all common tasks.

# Chapter 9

# System Security

A topic that concerns us all is system security. We have important information about ourselves, our customers, our company, or our country stored in a computer system. Some of this information is public knowledge, such as your name and address, but most of it isn't.

The evolution of computers has complicated the task of keeping information secure. The information we store in our computers is easier to access, sort, manipulate, and destroy than the data in computers of the last generation. Unfortunately, as a group, we computer professionals haven't paid enough attention to the potential disasters that could befall our data on today's easy-to-use computers.

Depending on your system and your employer, your security risk could range from the accidental deletion of a file to grave damage to national security. Understanding your security risk is paramount to the protection of your system and the information it maintains. You must know what your threats are before you can plan an adequate defense. Most security problems occur within your own user communities, not by so-called hackers and viruses. Because each site is unique, you must determine your own risks and problems.

System security tasks fall into two categories: preventive and corrective. Preventive measures, the preferred method, address such issues  as physical security, software sources, protection of communication devices, protection of private information, and protection of critical system files. Corrective security measures include plugging security holes, restoring files or disks after they have become corrupt or destroyed, controlling users who are misusing system resources, and protecting your system against skilled hackers bent on breaching security.

This chapter focuses on what you can do to secure your VMS computer systems. We'll discuss positive user identification, internal security, controlled user environments, security policies, and auditing.

## ESTABLISHING A SECURITY POLICY

A security policy outlines potential security problems, security rules, and enforcement. It should be used as a basic tool to guide the assignment of new user accounts, the use of passwords, default file protection, and user access. The security policy also clearly should outline the organization's computer use policy for users. The policy should be distributed to all users, and regular checks of the file system and accounting logs should be made to ensure compliance.

The typical security policy will describe such things as:

- Who should have access to valuable/sensitive information.
- From whom valuable/sensitive information should be protected.
- How valuable/sensitive information should be protected.
- How valuable information will be restored if it gets destroyed or deleted.
- How the system will be physically protected.
- Who should have access to the system and when.
- How users can access the system.
- Who is responsible for system security.

From the above information, the plan can then describe the methods to be used to protect the system and its information, for example:

- Default file and directory protection.
- Application of Access Control Lists.
- User login times and access methods.
- Backups and off-site storage.
- Physical security devices, such as locks and alarms.

- Special devices, such as port controllers, call back units, and encryption.

If the system is isolated from the outside world and has a small user community with similar work interests, then a relatively lax security policy can be employed. On the other hand, if the system is large, has a high public profile, has many different user groups, or contains sensitive information, then the security policy must be more restrictive.

The primary responsibility to comply with the security policy belongs to the users, provided they have a copy of the policy and it has been explained to them. However, the responsibility of ensuring that adequate protection is in place and the enforcement of the security policy belong to the security administrator.

## Friends and Neighbors

When you share a computer system with other people, you must make decisions involving community access. For example, you must decide how much you want the other users to share information. Normally, on a small computer system where users share a strong community of interest, the system manager will make them members of the same group. Under this condition, users can share files at the group level, while individuals can protect files for their own use. On larger systems, where many unrelated user communities exist, the system manager should create different groups.

The security policy should define groups, default group protection, and file sharing between groups. Users should be aware of the group boundaries and the types of files they should protect from group and world access. Most security problems are internal to the organization. The user community must know this.

The heart of VMS system security is the login name and password. If potential outside attackers can be kept off the system, they can cause no damage. For this reason, the security policy must define strict password security rules for systems that can be accessed by modem or network. Each user has the responsibility to defend passwords, but the security administrator is responsible for making sure passwords are protected.

Most users prefer not to change their passwords often, nor do they want to remember difficult-to-guess passwords that are required for adequate protection. So, you must ensure that passwords are aged and that appropriate passwords are used. This is done by defining a password expiration date (30 days for high security, 60-90 days for moderate security) and a minimum password length of at least eight characters. On high security systems, the password generator should be used.

## Auditing as the Ultimate Defense

After implementing a system security policy, some method of enforcement must be applied. This is accomplished, quite simply, by auditing your own controls.

Security auditing is the act of logging events as they occur for later analysis. This task requires forethought and diligence. You must know what your threats are, and you must check your audit trail on a regular basis to ensure security has not been broken. A definition of your known or potential security threats should be included in your security policy. Anticipate potential weaknesses before they become a security breach. Also, let the users know the potential security risks. An informed user is your best defense.

## What Should be Audited?

Auditing must be dictated by the security policy. For example, if the security policy cites user access time as a security concern, then user access times must be audited. Audit only what is necessary, as outlined by your security policy. Unnecessary auditing burdens system performance.

Security auditing should consist of both automated procedures and random checks. For instance, a batch job that runs early each morning could search the accounting database for attempted break-in activity, users who logged in after hours, unusually high CPU consumption, and improper file protection. The results could be sent by electronic mail for you to review when you log in. Random checks to consider are scouting for unauthorized accounts, searching for unfamiliar software in system directories, and looking for unexplained jobs running in batch. Depending on your security requirements, you could have several or several dozen security checks.

The greatest asset you bring to the system is knowledge. The more you know about the system, the better you can protect it.

## How to Handle a Security Breach

A security breach could be internal or external. Your security policy should define what steps will be taken when a security breach is identified.

An internal breach can range from a user deleting a file from which he should have been protected to a user browsing through files and directories for important information, such as employee records or trade secrets. These violations should be handled swiftly. In severe cases, the user's account should be disabled while an investigation takes place.

An external security breach usually starts with a hacker who wishes to expand his skills at your expense. Most often, a hacker will break into your system, snoop through as many files and directories as possible, and leave without causing damage. Most hackers are young, aspiring computer professionals who enjoy the challenge of bypassing security for the fun of using a minicomputer or mainframe. However, there are perpetrators whose sole purpose is to steal information or damage the system.

In the scenario for a break-in, the hacker gets the number for your modem or network from an ex-employee or a network of other hackers. Or the hacker could be the ex-employee, or he could get the access number by random dialing. Most companies have a base number and several sequential numbers after it, i.e., 2100, 2101, 2102, and so on. The hacker then determines what type of operating system you have. VMS is notorious for giving this information away, i.e., Username: = VMS. Then the hacker can attempt a break-in. He tries typical account names until an unprotected account or an obvious password is discovered. He browses though the system at leisure, within the privilege and protection boundaries of the hacked account. Unfortunately, hackers trade phone numbers and account information. If one hacker finds you, dozens will hack.

Most break-ins and attempts are detected by regularly auditing login failures. Many login failures will be logged as someone tries to guess a password, or users will report unexplained login failure messages. VMS reports the time of the last login. This feature should remain enabled. The break-in database logs additional information.

For any security breach, whether the breach occurred or was only attempted, there are several steps you should take to fix the problem.

1. Fly low, stay cool, and face the facts. This means don't do anything stupid, like announce to the world that you've had a break-in and this is what you're going to do about it. Also, don't deny an attack or its importance. Try not to rationalize when things are odd.

2. Identify the perpetrator. This is easy if the hacker is an authorized user and you have adequate alarms set. If you suspect that you have a hacker with an authorized account, enable file auditing on all files. This will simplify identification of the perpetrator. If the system is in a network, inspect the log files that were created at the time of the file access violation. Identifying the unauthorized hacker (someone who does not have an account) is rarely easy, because most sources are anonymous, as from a dial-up line. The only way to catch someone trying to break in is to continue letting him attempt entry while establishing his identity.

3. Prevent security violations of the same kind. For example, if you believe that an authorized user is attempting to break in to other accounts, take the following precautions: Pre-expire all user account passwords, use a password generator for all user accounts, and disable a user account after repeated login failures. If you believe that someone is trying to break in through a dial-up line, shut off the modem and change the phone number. And, make sure the dial-up lines are protected by a system password or modem security device.

If you believe that your system has been infiltrated by a Trojan Horse, virus, data diddler, or worm program, use comprehensive recovery procedures. Back up all important information, and initialize or reformat all your storage devices. If possible, you should boot from an alternate system disk before performing the backup. Operating system software, utilities, and end-user software should then be reloaded from the original distribution. Unless you are certain that backups have not been affected, do not restore from backup media.

## A Way of Life

System security is a 24-hour job. You either have it, or you don't. Take the time to evaluate your security risk. If you don't have a formal security administrator, appoint one. If you don't have a security policy, write one and implement it. Above all, don't take your good fortune for granted, because sooner or later, you'll get burned.

If you require more information on computer security, write or call the National Bureau of Standards' (NBS) Institute for Computer Sciences and Technology (ICST), and request Federal Information Processing Standards Publications List 91 (FIPS PUBS LIST 91) titled "Computer Security Publications." This NBS list contains the names and descriptions of dozens of ICST publications that address computer security. The address is:

Standards Processing Coordinator (ADP)
Institute for Computer Sciences and Technology
Technology Building, B-64
National Bureau of Standards
Gaithersburg, Maryland 20899
(301) 975-2817

## PHYSICAL SECURITY

The most secure computer system is locked in a room with no external connections. There are situations that require this type of security measure, but that's not the norm.

In all cases, however, the primary security of a system relies on good physical security. If you can prevent access to the machine, either by keeping it behind locked doors or by having no external connections (such as networks or modems), you can almost guarantee security. A secure system has no external data connections except for hard-wired terminals (protected by a username and password) kept in locked rooms.

Unfortunately, all VAX systems are accessible through the bootstrap process. An attacker who is allowed access to the machine can reboot the system and enjoy full control. For this reason, you must ensure that the machine itself is not accessible.

The security policy should define the methods and devices used to physically secure the system from tampering and theft. The system manager and operators are responsible for defending the machines, but the security administrator is responsible for ensuring that security controls are properly used.

### Viruses, Worms, Trojan Horses, and Data Diddlers

Another aspect of physical security pertains to the software you load. Any software you load might have security traps added by the developer or by an enemy who might hold the software before you get it. The typical scenario is that the software will load and run correctly, but some part of it contains a breach. When software is run by someone with system privilege or superuser status, the breach is activated. With this type of software, either the machine itself is attacked, or a modification is made to the system to permit the perpetrator to break in.

It is unlikely that this problem would occur with commercial software, but any uncertified software is suspect. Free software available from public bulletin boards or user interest groups is questionable.

The problem with most software attacks is that you cannot usually detect the problem until after the damage is done. Be extremely prudent when adding unknown software to your system. If possible, examine the source code, compile it on the target machine, and test the software in a controlled environment.

A good security policy defines acceptable sources of software and procedures for testing unknown software before it gets loaded on a critical system. Part of this procedure should be to log the source of all software.

The best way to identify a virus is to maintain a checksum database of all executable files. Most computer viruses attach themselves to executable files that run with privileges or superuser status.

## VMS EXTERNAL SECURITY

The greatest problem you face trying to protect your computer system is positive identification. You must know who is using your system. Positive personal identification has been cited in several publications that deal with computer security released by the National Bureau of Standards (NBS). The NBS states that there are three methods to identify an individual:

- By something unique which is known by that person.
- By something unique about that person.
- By something unique which is possessed by that person.

An example of the first method, and that used by a VMS system, is the user password. An example of the second method is biometric identification, such as your fingerprint or retinal capillary patterns. The third method involves a key or the possession of something that grants access, like an automatic teller machine card.

In several publications, the NBS recommends that no single one of these methods be considered secure enough for positive identification. However, two of the three methods can be used in tandem to prove positive identification. For example, a password can be used with a key.

Is VMS secure with only one identifier? Yes and no.

For most environments, a VMS system that's properly maintained is perfectly secure. For others, VMS by itself is a potential disaster.

### User and System Passwords

VMS system security is useless without 100 percent password integrity. Passwords are a VMS system's first line of defense against unauthorized system access. For this reason, strict attention must be paid to the use and maintenance of passwords.

A password is associated with each entry, or account, in the system User Authorization File (SYS$SYSTEM:SYSUAF.DAT) unless explicitly negated. Passwords, which can be one to 31 characters, are stored using a one-way encryption algorithm. The encryption transforms each password into a 64-bit hashed value. After they're encrypted, passwords can't be returned to their original readable form with any publicly known method. For this reason, lost or forgotten passwords must be changed by the system manager.

## Password Tailoring

Using AUTHORIZE, password protection can be tailored to your organization's needs. For instance, the AUTHORIZE qualifier /PWDMINIMUM defines the minimum number of characters to which a password can be set. The default value of six would apply otherwise. If a password is set by the system manager, using AUTHORIZE, the password can be less than the minimum value. The AUTHORIZE qualifier /PWDEXPIRED pre-expires a user's password. A user whose account password has been pre-expired must set a new password when he logs in. You should pre-expire passwords on all new accounts to force the user to set his password.

A password's lifetime can be set by another AUTHORIZE qualifier, /PWDLIFETIME. By default, a password's lifetime is six months. The lifetime established applies to both primary and secondary passwords. The first example below establishes a password lifetime of 45 days, while the latter institutes a password with no expiration date.

```
UAF> MODIFY /PWDLIFETIME="45 -"
UAF> MODIFY /PWDLIFETIME=NONE
```

## Passwords for High-Security Accounts

If you work in a high-security environment, you can prevent users from establishing their own passwords. Most organizations who do this have a security office that assigns passwords to user accounts on a regular schedule. To lock user passwords, use the AUTHORIZE command:

```
UAF> MODIFY /FLAGS=LOCKPWD
```

For additional account security, two passwords can be assigned to an account. This two-key system requires two people to be present to gain access to an account. Each person knows one of the passwords to the account, but not both. Using AUTHORIZE, a second password is established with the command:

```
UAF> MODIFY /PASSWORD=(password1, password2)
```

If you want users to be able to set their own passwords with assurance that password guessing will not compromise the account, use the password generator. The AUTHORIZE qualifier /GENERATE_PASSWORD forces the user to select his password from a generated list. When he enters the DCL command SET PASSWORD, five passwords and a pronunciation table are displayed. The user must choose a password from the list. This method of password implementation is easier, and in some ways more secure, than assigning passwords.

## Password Recommendations

Passwords are sensitive. In essence, they are identical to keys or combinations to locks and must be protected in the same way. Being careless with passwords could be disastrous. In fact, all information about VMS accounts should remain confidential.

Passwords should be relatively long, somewhat nondescriptive and frequently changed. Also, passwords should not be a spouse's name, pet names, phone numbers, car license number or any other information about the user that might be obvious. A password should be at least eight characters to minimize the risk of someone guessing or using another computer to penetrate your system.

Users shouldn't be allowed to share accounts. When an account is shared, it's impossible to pinpoint who violated system security.

Accounts without passwords should be captive. In other words, users of captive accounts should not be able to access DCL or utilities that would allow them to get at system information.

## Implementing a System Password

In some cases, a terminal connected to the VAX might need added protection. For instance, with lines accessed by modem, it's difficult to monitor who is trying to use the system. The system password protects these lines by preventing a login attempt until the system password is entered. Furthermore, until the system password is entered, no information about the system is provided.

The system password is implemented on a line-by-line basis using the command:

$ SET TERMINAL/SYSPWD/PERMANENT TTxn:

Users who log on remotely, through the SET HOST command, can be forced to use the system password by setting bit 19 (hex value 80000) in the system parameter TTY_DEFCHAR2.

The system password itself is created with the command:

$ SET PASSWORD/SYSTEM

That prompts for a password and verification. The system password also can be modified using AUTHORIZE:

UAF> MODIFY/SYSTEM_PASSWORD="new_password"

The SECURITY privilege is required to set or change the system password. It's stored in a separate record of the system User Authorization File, which can't be shown, and the system password has no expiration date.

## VMS Login Protection

By knowing the type of operating system or computer you have, a dial-in and remote access perpetrator has completed the majority of his break-in task. The typical VAX/VMS accounts are SYSTEM, FIELD, ALL-IN-1 and a few others. The experienced perpetrator knows this and immediately tries the most common passwords, such as MANAGER, PASSWORD, SERVICE, A1 and more. So, don't give out that information.

## Login Messages

The first system message that reaches a VMS user logging in is the system announcement message. The translation of the logical name SYS$ANNOUNCE displays when a login sequence is initiated, before the username and password are accepted. Often this message identifies the VAX, as in:

Welcome to VAX/VMS V5.2 at the U.S. Savings Bank

This gives away three important pieces of information, namely the system type, the operating system version and the name of the organization.

A second logical name, SYS$WELCOME, also can be used to provide information to users logging in. The welcome message is the preferred method of providing a welcome message or information about the system. The SYS$WELCOME message isn't displayed until a successful login has been completed.

If you have captive users or users who won't be shown the system welcome message, the AUTHORIZE qualifier /FLAGS=DISWELCOME can be used to disable this feature. In this way, you have full control of the information given out.

## Login Break-In Protection

One excellent security feature of VMS is that it can detect someone trying to hack his way into your system. VMS login break-in protection is controlled by setting up several system parameters that control the number of login retries, break-in threshold, break-in source recognition and the action to be taken when break-in detection is triggered.

The system parameters that control retries are LOGIN RETRY TIMOUT (LGI_RETRY_TMO) and LOGIN RETRY LIMIT (LGI_RETRY_LIM). These parameters control the number of login attempts allowed in succession. This is particularly appropriate for dial-up lines. The default value allows three retries with a time limit of 20 seconds between tries.

Break-in threshold, which is the number of login failures permitted before action is taken, is established with the system parameter LOGIN BREAKIN LIMIT (LGI_BRK_LIM). Login failures are invalid username and password combinations. The default value for LGI_BRK_LIM is five failed login attempts.

When break-in detection is triggered, VMS tracks the source of the break-in based on the system parameter LOGIN BREAKIN TERMINAL (LGI_BRK_TERM). The value of this parameter determines if the username and terminal are to be tracked together or independently. The default value of one has usernames and terminals tracked to-gether, whereas a value of 0 counts failures against usernames only. Tracking just the username is most appropriate for terminal servers, because the terminal line easily can be changed between attempts.

The duration of break-in recognition is set using the system parameter LOGIN BREAKIN TIMEOUT (LGI_BRK_TMO). The default is five minutes, which is sufficient for most situations. This parameter assigns an expiration time to an initial failure on a terminal, username or both. The expiration time is the current system time plus the value LGI_BRK_TMO. Each additional failure adds an additional time of LGI_BRK_TMO.

The more failures logged against a username, terminal or both, the greater the period of time during which failures count toward the number defined by LGI_BRK_LIM. After the expiration arrives, without additional unsuccessful logins occurring, the cumulative failure count returns to zero. A successful login doesn't reset the cumulative failure count.

When a break-in attempt is detected, the action taken is controlled by the parameter LOGIN BREAKIN TERMINAL (LGI_BRK_TERM). If LGI_BRK_TERM is set to 1, no login is permitted from the offending terminal with same username. In other words, only the offending user is locked out from that terminal. If the source is a network user, the remote user will be disallowed from logging in.

Although locking out a terminal line might seem desirable, a problem could occur. On a system using terminal servers, if the parameters are set in a certain manner, all terminal lines could be disabled. This would be only a minor inconvenience in return for a more secure system.

To vary the lockout time, the system parameter LGI_HID_TIM contains a value which is multiplied by a random number. The random number falls between the values of 1 and 1.5. This feature prevents someone from guessing your lockout interval, making it impractical to use another computer to break in.

An additional system parameter LOGIN BREAKIN DISABLE USER (LGI_BRK_DISUSER) can be used to set the DISUSER flag in the system UAF. If a user's account is locked out from this mechanism, the system manager must use AUTHORIZE to change the UAF record. A problem could result in this technique. Repeated break-ins could disable multiple accounts, perhaps all accounts, if the intruder knows all the usernames on the system. If all accounts are disabled, the

SYSTEM account is allowed access to the system from the console terminal.

## VMS SYSTEM INTERNAL SECURITY

Every secure computer system bases its internal protection on a theoretical model. For VMS systems, DEC selected the NIST Secure Reference Model for computing and data storage systems.

The Secure Reference Model defines a computer system in terms of subjects, objects, and a reference database. Subjects are users or jobs, running on the computer system, who desire access to the objects. Objects are tangible, such as memory, files, directories, or peripheral devices.

When a subject requests access to an object, the reference monitor checks its reference database to see if the requested access is permissible.

When a security event occurs, such as an unauthorized attempt to access a file, the reference monitor logs that event in the security audit trail. The security audit trail provides a means to trace attempts to violate system security.

Although a VMS system uses many components to implement the secure model, the most important internal security mechanism is the user identification code (UIC).

## User Identification Code Protection

The UIC is the primary internal VMS protection mechanism. It's an identifier used by the operating system to recognize users and groups of users, and to protect system objects.

A UIC is defined for each user through a field in the system UAF. It can be either numeric or alphanumeric. The numeric UIC is two octal values enclosed in brackets. The values are a group number and a member number, for example:

[130,103]

The first number (130) specifies the group, while the second (103) is the member number. Valid group and member numbers are 1-37776 octal and 0-177776 octal, respectively. The alphanumeric UIC format is specified as one to 31 characters in brackets. Valid characters are A-Z, 0-9, the dollar sign ($), and the underscore (_). Unlike the numeric UIC, an alphanumeric UIC can contain both group and member components, or simply the member, for instance:

[SYSTEM]
[CONSULTANTS,BYNON]

Most user accounts have both a numeric and an alphanumeric UIC. This ensures compatibility with earlier versions of VMS, where only the numeric UIC was available.

## Operations and Users Affected by UIC Protection

UIC protection manages four basic types of operations and four categories of users. The operations are based on the functions a computer can perform on a file, that is, READ, WRITE, EXECUTE, and DELETE. Categories of users include system (i.e., anyone with SYSPRV), group (i.e., anyone in the same UIC group), world (i.e., everyone) and owner (i.e., the owner of the object). UIC protection is applied to system objects, including files, directories, devices, queues, and mailboxes.

UIC protection use is simple. Access is granted or denied on a category-by-category basis. For instance, a file whose UIC protection permits read, write and execute access to the owner only is protected from the world and anyone within the same group.

UIC protection is established using the SET command, as in these examples:

$ SET PROTECTION=(S,O:RW,G,W) ACCOUNTING.DAT
$ SET PROTECTION=W:RWE /DEVICE TXA0:
$ SET PROTECTION=(O:RWE,G:RWE) IDEAS.DIR;1

In the first example, read and write access is granted to the owner, and access to all other categories is denied. The second example shows how to use SET PROTECTION for a device, such as a terminal port. In the third example, directory protection is set for owner and group.

Access to an object through UIC protection is in the order of owner, world, group, and system. The order is based on performance.

Some types of system objects have different interpretations of READ, WRITE, EXECUTE, and DELETE. These are:

### DISK FILES

- READ – Copy, read, or print
- WRITE – Modify or write
- EXECUTE – Run image or command file
- DELETE – Delete
- To write to a file, both read and write access are required.

### DIRECTORY FILES

- READ – List directory
- WRITE – Write or modify directory
- EXECUTE – List files by explicit reference
- Read access grants execute access, so use execute without read to grant access to a file that must be referenced by a complete file specification rather than through a wildcard reference. Also, you need read and write access to create files in a directory.

### DISK AND TAPE VOLUMES

- READ – Read, copy, or print
- WRITE – Write or modify
- EXECUTE – Create and write on volumes
- DELETE – Delete
- Delete and execute don't apply to tapes. Write access to tapes also grants read access.

Default protection is applied to files through the system RMS parameter RMS_FILEPROT. Directories are created, by default, without delete access. Directory protection can be specified at creation time with the CREATE/DIRECTORY command as in:

```
$ CREATE/DIRECTORY/PROTECTION=(S:RE,O:RWED,G,W) dir_spec
```

If not specified, default directory protection is used, or the protection is applied from the next highest directory in the tree.

You can change the protection of a file, and other VMS objects, with the DCL command SET PROTECTION, as in:

$ SET PROTECTION=(S:RWED,O:RWED,G:RWED,W:RWED) file_spec

To change system parameters controlling default protection, use the system parameter RMS_FILEPROT to define default protection:

$ SET PROTECTION=(S:RWED,O:RWED,G:RWED,W:RWED)

DCL provides several commands for listing file protection:

$ DIRECTORY /FULL
$ DIRECTORY /PROTECTION
$ DIRECTORY /SECURITY

## VMS System Privileges

Privileges control the performance of select system activities to certain users. Privilege restrictions protect operating system integrity and the integrity of services provided to the users. They are granted to a user based on need and whether he has the experience to use them without disrupting other users.

Privileges are control operations that can be performed on the system, like mounting or dismounting a disk volume. Privileges are process characteristics assigned initially from a SYSUAF record. Two sets of privileges exist, default and authorized, that are stored as 64-bit masks in the SYSUAF. VMS has 35 privileges. The privileges are divided into seven categories. Each category is classified by the amount of damage its use could cause to the system:

NONE – No privileges.

NORMAL – The minimum privilege needed to use the system effectively (Default: TMPMBX and NETMBX).

GROUP – The ability to affect members of the same UIC group, e.g., GROUP and GRPNAM.

DEVOUR – The potential to consume noncritical systemwide resources, e.g., PRMCEB, PRMGBL, and EXQUOTA.

SYSTEM – The ability to interfere with normal system operation, e.g., ALTPRI, OPER, WORLD, and SECURITY.

FILE – The potential to bypass file protection security, e.g., DIAGNOSE, SYSGBL, and VOLPRO.

**ALL** – The ability to take over or control the system, e.g., SYSPRV, BYPASS, and SETPRV.

## Recommendations for Privileges

Grant minimum privileges. Ninety-nine percent of VMS system users can operate properly with the two default privileges: TMPMBX and NETMBX. If a user or manager doesn't know why a privilege should be granted, it shouldn't be.

Most operators only need OPER privilege or less, and most system manager operations only require SYSPRV and SETPRV. If you have implemented group managers, they need GROUP and GRPPRV.

System managers and system programmers should not work with upper-level privileges such as BYPASS. They can gain extra privileges with the command:

$ SET PROCESS/PRIVILEGE=(priv,priv...)

## Installing Images with Privileges

Images that contain system services that require accelerated privileges can be installed with privilege. Images installed with privilege can be executed by users who don't normally have the privilege to perform operations. In this way, the privilege is granted and controlled by the running program, not by the user.

The operation of installing an executable image with privileges is simple. Use the VMS INSTALL utility, and specify the image name and one or more system privileges:

$ RUN SYS$SYSTEM:INSTALL
INSTALL> imagename /PRIVILEGES=(PRIV,PRIV...)

Privileged images should be installed when the system is booted.

## VMS System Access Control List Protection

A VMS system provides an alternative to the default UIC-based protection, the access control list (ACL). ACL protection doesn't replace UIC protection. ACLs enhance or fine-tune system protection.

ACLs are optional protection set up by users or the system manager. They're flexible because they use natural identifiers, such as UIC and other process characteristics. ACL identifiers are classified UIC identifiers, system-defined identifiers, and general identifiers.

A UIC identifier is numeric, alphanumeric, or hexadecimal in format. System ACL identifiers classify how the user or process is interacting with the system:

**BATCH** ----------------------- Batch process access
**NETWORK** ------------------ Network processes or tasks
**INTERACTIVE** ------------- Interactive processes
**LOCAL** ----------------------- Local terminal access
**DIALUP** ---------------------- Dial-up terminals
**REMOTE** -------------------- Users logged in through network

General identifiers are ones that you add to the rights list for a sundry use, such as people who work in the administrative office. You add identifiers to RIGHTSLIST.DAT with the AUTHORIZE utility:

UAF> CREATE/RIGHTS
UAF> ADD/IDENTIFIER ADMIN
UAF> GRANT/IDENTIFIER ADMIN WILLIS

Here, a new rights list file is created once, the first time. The second command creates, or adds, the new identifier ADMIN. The identifier must be granted to each user who will use it.

## Access Control List Entries

An ACL consists of one or more access control entries (ACEs). An ACE controls access to the object. The capability of using more than one ACE extends the power of the ACL mechanism.

An ACE specifies two items, an identifier and the access. For example, the following ACE grants read, write, and execute access to the object to anyone with the ADMIN identifier:

(IDENTIFIER=ADMIN, ACCESS=READ+WRITE+EXECUTE)

To classify further, there are three ACE types. The identifier ACE controls access for a user or user groups. A security ACE provides notification when specified access is attempted, and the default protection ACE, which is for directory files only, controls default protection applied to files, including subdirectories created in a directory. Table 9-1 lists the ACE options.

## Table 9-1: ACE Options

### Identifier ACE Options:

| | |
|---|---|
| **READ** | Read files, read a disk, and allocate devices. |
| **WRITE** | Read or write a file. |
| **EXECUTE** | Run image or specific reference to a file in a directory. |
| **DELETE** | Delete a file. |
| **CONTROL** | Same privileges as owner (i.e., can modify the ACE). |
| **NONE** | No access to object. |

### Default Protection ACE Options:

| | |
|---|---|
| **DEFAULT** | The ACE is to be applied to all files created in a directory for directory files. |
| **PROTECTED** | The ACE must be deleted specifically with EDIT/ACL or other ACL command. |
| **NOPROPAGATE** | The ACE is not placed on a new version of file. |
| **NONE** | No options apply. |

### Security Alarm ACE Options:

| | |
|---|---|
| **READ** | Notification on attempted READ access |
| **WRITE** | Notification on attempted WRITE access. |
| **EXECUTE** | Notification on attempted EXECUTE access. |
| **DELETE** | Notification on attempted DELETE access. |
| **CONTROL** | Notification on attempted CONTROL access. |
| **SUCCESS** | Notification when access was allowed. |
| **FAILURE** | Notification when access was disallowed. |

The proper ACE format is:

(type[,options][,access_to_grant]

Security ACE example:

(ALARM_JOURNAL=SECURITY,WRITE+DELETE+SUCCESS)

ACL commands:

```
$EDIT/ACL
$SET ACL
$SET DIRECTORY/ACL
$SET DEVICE/ACL
$SET FILE/ACL
$DIRECTORY/SECURITY
```

## File Deletion Security

When files are deleted and blocks become available for use, a problem ensues. If users perform non-RMS file access, they can get to data that still is leftover on the disk. In other words, the disk is open for scavenging.

To avoid this problem, the /ERASE qualifier should be used with the DELETE and PURGE commands. The /ERASE qualifier forces the VMS system to write zeros over the disk space occupied by the file. This process can be automated by redefining the DELETE and PURGE commands with symbols that equate to the commands with the /ERASE qualifiers. These symbols are established in the global login command procedure, SYS$MANAGER:SYLOGIN.COM.

```
$ DEL*ETE:=="DELETE/ERASE"
$ PUR*GE:=="PURGE/ERASE"
```

ERASE ON DELETE can be enabled for a volume with the DCL command:

```
$ SET VOLUME/ERASE_ON_DELETE
```

When you no longer need the information contained on a volume, initialize it with the /ERASE qualifier. The /ERASE qualifier here overwrites all information on the volume. Also, it automatically sets the volume characteristic of ERASE ON DELETE. The default erasure pattern of zeros can be modified by using the information contained in the file SYS$EXAMPLES:DOD_ERAPAT.MAR.

Using the highwater marking feature allows the erasure of blocks added to files when they're extended dynamically. The security pattern is written to this extended area, so that information previously stored won't be recoverable. Highwater marking is enabled for a volume with the DCL command:

$ SET VOLUME/HIGHWATER DUxx:

It's disabled with the qualifier /NOHIGHWATER.

The limitation of all the file and storage erasure techniques is system performance. Considerable processing overhead is incurred using these features. You should carefully think over their value to your system before implementing them.

## CONTROLLED USER ENVIRONMENTS

You might need to completely control the capabilities of certain users on your system. To do so, decide what you will allow them to do and set up a captive environment for them.

AUTHORIZE qualifiers and flags allow you to restrict user access to the system. For instance, the captive flag disallows Ctrl-Y interrupts and user specification of an alternate CLI at login time:

UAF> MODIFY /FLAGS=(CAPTIVE)

Welcome, Mail and New Mail messages also can be disabled:

UAF> MODIFY /FLAGS=(DISMAIL,DISNEWMAIL,-
DISWELCOME,DISREPORT)

To prevent the creation of subprocesses, set the process limit to 0:

UAF> MODIFY /PRCLM=0

This is necessary if you plan to let the user have access to utilities such as MAIL that permit spawning a subprocess.

Passwords can be locked with the MODIFY qualifier /LOCKPWD so users can't change them:

UAF> MODIFY /LOCKPWD

### Captive Login Command Procedures

A simple way to restrict an account is through a login command procedure that is truly captive, that is, it doesn't allow the user access to DCL. The following example shows the use of a login command procedure that allows access to only one image on a VMS system:

```
$ SET NOCONTROL=Y
$ SET NOON
$ RUN PROG
$ LOGOUT/BRIEF
```

A user whose /LGICMD field points him to this command procedure can only run the program and log out.

A second type of command procedure permits restricted access to selected DCL commands:

```
$ SET NOCONTROL=Y
$ SET NOON
$AGAIN:
$ READ/PROMPT="$ " SYS$COMMAND CMD
$ IF CMD .EQS. "ALLIN1" THEN GOTO DOIT
$ IF CMD .EQS. "DECALC" THEN GOTO DOIT
$ IF CMD .EQS. "LOGOUT" THEN GOTO DOIT
$ WRITE SYS$OUTPUT "ILLEGAL COMMAND,TRY AGAIN"
$ GOTO AGAIN
$ DOIT:
$ CMD
$ GOTO AGAIN
```

Additional DCL commands can be allowed by adding more conditional lines. The problem of DCL commands that prompt for input from a terminal can be solved by ASSIGNing a /USER_MODE logical name assignment of SYS$INPUT to SYS$COMMAND prior to using the DCL command.

A second way of restricting a user's environment is to remove commands from a copy of DCLTABLES.EXE. To make the new CLI the user's default, use AUTHORIZE.

The command SET COMMAND/DELETE allows you to remove commands that you don't want the user to access. This is an efficient way to restrict DCL commands. File protection of images invoked with DCL commands must be used to prevent experienced users from using the foreign command feature of DCL to invoke images that aren't in their command table.

## AUDITING AND SURVEILLANCE

Because auditing is your ultimate security defense, let's analyze methods for tracking security violations.

Auditing in the VMS environment is based on two key elements: security alarms and surveillance procedures. Security alarms are events that you request to be recorded. Surveillance procedures are routine jobs set up to monitor system events not protected by security alarms. In each case, the information is recorded for later analysis and corrective action.

Through VMS's SET AUDIT facility, we can log events generated from ACLs, selected types of file access, installation of images, login and logout activity, failed login attempts, and volume mounts and dismounts. All other forms of auditing must be performed through the use of DCL commands, most notably ACCOUNTING, DIRECTORY, SHOW, and MONITOR.

VMS version 5.2 contains many security enhancements, including an audit server. Although the audit server does not improve the overall security of VMS, it does enhance auditing and audit analysis. This is especially true with respect to VAXcluster systems.

By default, security auditing (for VMS versions 5.2 and later) is enabled for a small set of critical event classes. The event audit trail is written to an audit log. The audit server uses an audit server database to oversee security. The database contains information about events to be audited, the location of a security archive file, event timers, and information used to monitor the consumption of system resources. The audit server database is updated with the SET AUDIT command.

Working in conjunction with the audit server is the AUDIT ANALYSIS utility ($ANALYZE/AUDIT). It improves the security administrator's ability to review security events. Prior to VMS V5.2, all security related events were logged in the operator log file. Using the SECAUDIT command procedure, security information could be extracted from the operator's log, but the process was slow.

## Security Alarms

Security alarms are messages sent to the security operator's console when a specific event has taken place. Alarms help you detect a

system break-in attempt or when a valid user is trying to access
an object that doesn't belong to him. For example, security alarms
can be set for:

- Access to selected files or global sections.
- Events requested by an ACL.
- Use of privilege to access a file or global section.
- Installation of images.
- Logins, logouts, and break-in attempts.
- Modification of the system and network UAF.
- Changes to the system or user passwords.
- Modification of the rights database.
- Execution of the SET AUDIT command.
- Volume mount/dismount operations.
- Modification of system parameters.

You select the events to be audited using the command:

$ SET AUDIT/ALARM/ENABLE=(option,option,...)

## Enabling a Security Operator Terminal

Before you enable alarms, you should enable a security operator's
terminal. In general practice, the security terminal should be a
hardcopy device. Use the command:

$ REPLY/ENABLE=SECURITY TXA0:

Any terminal can be enabled as the security operator's terminal.
Security will always go to the operator log file, even if a security
operator terminal hasn't been set up.

## Audit Reduction

Security alarms are effective only when you use the information. If
you enable security alarms on many objects and types of user access,
the operator log file will contain a large volume of alarm information.
The sheer volume of information makes the security audit task
impossible.

To extract security information from the operator log file on VMS
versions 4.0 to 5.1, use the SECAUDIT command procedure, which can

be found in the directory SYS$MANAGER. SECAUDIT has five optional parameters:

P1 – Name of log file to be scanned.
P2 – Username on which to display security alarms.
P3 – Starting date and time of first alarm to be displayed.
P4 – Ending date and time of last alarm to be displayed.
P5 – Selection criteria (same as SET AUDIT command).

Audit reduction for VMS versions 5.2 and later is performed with the AUDIT ANALYSIS utility. It enables you to selectively extract and display information from your security audit log file. Using ANALYZE/AUDIT qualifiers, you can produce reports in a variety of formats. The ANALYZE/AUDIT report format qualifiers are:

/FULL – Produces a full listing.
/BRIEF – Produces a brief one-line listing for each record.
/SUMMARY – Produces a summary of security events.
/BINARY – Creates a binary output file.

Several other qualifiers let you define the reporting period and event types:

/BEFORE – Report records before the specified date.
/SINCE – Report records since the specified date.
/EVENT_CLASS – Report records of the specified event class.

Although it's possible to generate many different reports with the qualifiers listed above, the most common report is the daily report. The best way to implement the daily report is to write a command procedure that runs in batch every evening just before midnight. The following AUDIT/ANALYSIS command generates a daily report:

```
$ ANALYZE/AUDIT/SINCE=TODAYOUTPUT=ddmmmyy.AUDIT -
_$ SYS$MANAGER:SECURITY_AUDIT.AUDIT$JOURNAL
```

If you set up a batch job to produce a daily report, consider mailing the report to your account so you won't forget to read it.

## Accounting Audit Information

The VMS system ACCOUNTING utility provides an excellent source of audit information. It logs information to the file called

SYS$MANAGER:ACCOUNTNG.DAT. It retains information including date and time of login, login source, type of process (i.e., interactive, subprocess, detached, network), CPU time used, I/O time used, and the number of pages printed. For example, to check on users who are using the system after hours, you could create a daily report that lists resources used after normal working hours:

```
$ ACCOUNT/SINCE=1-OCT-1989:18:00/SUMMARY -
_$ /REPORT=(PROCESSOR,PAGES,VOLUMES)
```

| Username | Processor Time | Pages Printed | Volumes Mounted |
|---|---|---|---|
| <login> | 0 00:00:01.36 | 0 | 0 |
| BYNON | 0 41:20:06.41 | 1265 | 3 |
| PCFS$ACCOUNT | 0 00:00:00.00 | 13 | 0 |
| SYSTEM | 0 00:01:03.24 | 0 | 0 |

Obviously, unless you know that BYNON is supposed to be working after hours, you should be suspicious when you look at this report.

## System Surveillance Checks

The active system manager or security manager makes routine checks of system information. This task is important to system security, as only someone who is familiar with the system can spot something wrong. Here's a list of things to check:

- Use the VMS system INSTALL utility to look for unexpected image additions.

- Use the AUTHORIZE utility to look for usernames that you didn't authorize:

```
UAF> SHOW */BRIEF
UAF> SHOW /PROXY
```

- Run VMS ACCOUNTING on a regular basis to measure normal amounts of processing time and use:

```
$ ACCOUNT /REPORT=(PROCESSOR,PAGE...) /SUMMARY
```

- Run ACCOUNTING to check for known users, unknown users, and appropriate hours of system use.

- Review the template command procedures that you use to set up new accounts (ADDUSER.COM on MicroVMS systems).

- Be familiar with all recurring batch jobs and the times they are most likely to run.

- Try to break into user accounts with some of the more obvious password choices.

- Check to see that the users have appropriate default protections in place, especially on directories.

- Implement security alarms from time-to-time to catch system browsers, i.e., people who look through other people's files.

- Keep the rights database up to date. Remove identifiers that aren't in use. Keep current listings:

UAF> REMOVE/ID ADMIN

- Monitor the protection of critical files:

$ DIRECTORY/SECURITY

- Check that your users are logging out at the end of the day or when leaving their desks for a long period. Make periodic physical checks at the end of the day.


## CONCLUSION

It only takes one occurrence of system penetration or one malicious user to lose many man hours of work, valuable or sensitive information, or system resources. When implemented, enforced, and monitored correctly, the security features of VMS are adequate for most organizations.

# Chapter 10

# System Performance Management

In the life of every VAX system, there comes a time when the system bogs down under its load and needs assistance. VAX systems must be tuned to achieve maximum performance under unique situations. In many cases, a VAX system will operate efficiently with no tuning or system parameter changes. It isn't until a VAX system approaches the limits of a resource (memory, I/O, or CPU) that the effects of tuning will be noticed.

This chapter presents some practical tips on system performance management and tuning. Unfortunately, tuning isn't always a cookbook operation. You must devote many hours studying, playing with, and experimenting with VAX systems to fully understand the ramifications of VMS system parameter changes. You have to jump in with both feet and get wet.

Also, you should realize that system tuning isn't a panacea. Tuning is the art of juggling system resources to make up for a deficiency at the expense of another resource. The nature of tuning makes it very easy to get caught in a tuning circle: collecting, changing, testing, collecting, changing, testing, and so on. Know when to quit. Get out of the circle early. There always will be a point in your tuning effort when the work you put in returns little or no results. Remember, your time is valuable, and hardware is getting cheaper every day.

## SYSTEM TUNING

System tuning, quite simply, is adjusting a computer or its workload to make it perform well under specific situations. When initially set up, a VMS system is configured with default system parameters. These default parameters are established by DEC engineers with years of experience using and testing VMS on the whole range of VAX systems. The parameters are a compromise between high performance and resource conservation. Much like a new automobile, which can be tuned to perform better at the expense of gas mileage and pollution, a VMS system can be tuned to take advantage of an abundant resource.

The first phase of any tuning effort is load balancing. Load balancing, also known as resource management, is the process of distributing a system's workload evenly throughout available time. Although this scheduling is often difficult because of the work hours of interactive users, it will always prove to be beneficial to a system.

The second tuning phase is to adjust SYSGEN values initially set up by AUTOGEN. All new VMS operating systems are modified by AUTOGEN. AUTOGEN takes into consideration a number of factors, namely the hardware available and the parameters that you suggest. DEC's conventional wisdom has most system managers believing that tuning is a black art and that the parameters established by AUTOGEN are sufficient. DEC most likely takes this position because many problems occur when gross changes are made by someone who doesn't understand the rules by which to play.

Typically, a newly installed VAX will run just fine on the adjustments made by AUTOGEN. Most VAX systems aren't tuned as soon as the system is brought on line, because there's no information on which to base the tuning. The deficiencies of the system, if any, aren't known.

Another fact that lets AUTOGEN work, in many situations, is that a VMS system is dynamic. A VAX computer operating under VMS will dynamically make parameter changes to itself (on many, but not all, key parameters) as needed. It's important to understand, however, that VMS is a generic operating system. If you want it to perform real-time operations or batch processing, you'll have to tune it for those environments. Tuning VMS for good performance under a particular type of processing load is the only practical reason for tweaking SYSGEN parameters away from their AUTOGEN settings.

Note a few words of wisdom: If your system isn't broken, don't try to fix it. If you don't have a reason to tune your system (i.e., it's sluggish, operational requirements, political pressure, and so on), leave well enough alone. Tuning is not a normal way of life for system managers. It's situational or the last step before acquiring new hardware.

## SYSTEM INFORMATION FOR PERFORMANCE MANAGEMENT

System performance management is a tedious task. It involves data collection and system metrics. Data, or system information, is the basis on which a VMS system is tuned or modified. Without information, system tuning, load balancing, and hardware upgrades are a waste of time and money.

How would a system manager know to increase a user's working set quota to improve system performance if data about that user's process had not been collected? He wouldn't; he'd be guessing. Guessing about system performance problems and acting on that guess is one of the worst mistakes you'll ever make with a VMS system.

Don't guess. Collect data, and collect it consistently.

### Know Your System

One of the most important resources you'll bring to the performance of a system, be it a VAX, MicroVAX, or VAXcluster, is a full understanding of the system's normal workload and use. Understanding how the system is being used and the demands on its available resources allows you to establish performance expectations.

I've found, in many cases, that what was thought to be a performance problem is merely a case of unrealistic expectations. As an example, a programmer who is used to using a moderately loaded VAX 8800 to edit, compile, and link programs will think a single-user MicroVAX 2000 is sluggish. This is the user's expectation of performance, not a performance problem. You can't compare one VAX with another. System metrics are established by comparing work with available resources.

You'll only get to know your system if you collect information about it. Here's a list of items you might like to discover:

- Average number of interactive users.
- Average number of processes.
- Peak use hours.
- Workload characteristics.
- Commonly activated images and command procedures.
- Interactive tasks that can be run in batch mode.
- Tasks that are CPU, memory or I/O intensive.
- Location of page and swap files.
- Typical response times for common tasks.
- Known bottlenecks.
- Jobs waiting in queue.
- System use, including percentage of CPU, page fault and direct I/O rate, memory, disk space, and distribution of users over nodes.

In many cases, you won't be the first to notice a performance or resource problem. Typically, a user complaint will prompt you to begin an investigation. To evaluate the complaint, you must collect the basic facts about the system running at the time of the complaint, for instance:

- Number of users on the system.
- Task response times.
- Whether jobs are deadlocked or waiting (MWAIT, RWSWP, and so on).
- Amount of free memory.

- The direct I/O and page fault rates.
- The percentage of CPU use and the buffered I/O rate.

By collecting this information, you can prove to yourself that a problem exists. After you make this determination, you can start an investigation process to determine the cause and a possible solution.

### The First Look

The key to a successful collection effort is to be selective and collect only what you need. Don't collect information just for the sake of having it; you'll flood yourself with work sifting through it and waste valuable CPU time.

Collect information about key indicators until you notice a problem forming. A good place to start is with the DCL SHOW command. For instance, the SHOW MEMORY command provides a wealth of information about memory use on the running system. In this single display, you can pinpoint major performance problems related to system parameters or the lack of memory. The SHOW MEMORY example (see Screen 10-1) shows a system with very few pages remaining on the free list.

The investigation of this system was prompted by a user's complaint of insufferably slow response. A second look at the display pinpointed the exact problem: process swapping. This system was out of physical memory and was spending most of its processor time performing memory management functions. The interim solution to this machine's problem was to reduce memory management overhead by preventing second-level trimming by the swapper. Thus swapping, which was inevitable anyway, would happen faster.

### The Key to Better Performance

A VAX is memory-oriented. Memory, to a large extent, determines the performance characteristics of the system. Therefore, system memory is a resource you should monitor closely. Memory is the primary resource on which a VAX draws for efficient performance.

Memory management is one of the biggest burdens to a VAX. This

```
$ SHOW MEMORY

    System Memory Resources on 23-MAR-1989 14:15:23.53

    Physical Memory Usage (pages):     Total    Free     In Use    Modified
    Main Memory (4.00Mb)               8192     732      7433      27

    Slot Usage (slots):                Total    Free     Resident  Swapped
    Process Entry Slots                27       11       12        4
    Balance Set Slots                  24       14       10        0

    Fixed-Size Pool Areas (packets):   Total    Free     In Use    Size
    Small Packet (SRP) List            423      91       332       96
    I/O Request Packet (IRP) List 282  175      107      176
    Large Packet (LRP) List            44       33       11        1648

    Dynamic Memory Usage (bytes):      Total    Free     In Use    Largest
    Nonpaged Dynamic Memory            775680   454864   320816    425616
    Paged Dynamic Memory               499712   369120   130592    368448

    Paging File Usage (pages):                  Free     Reservable  Total
    SYS$DISK:[SYS0.SYSEXE]SWAPFILE.SYS          3632     3632        4496
    SYS$DISK:[SYS0.SYSEXE]PAGEFILE.SYS          11157    -8632       20000

Of the physical pages in use, 3449 pages are permanently allocated.
```

## Screen 10-1: SHOW MEMORY display

is easily proven by looking at the cost difference, in time, between a soft page fault and a hard page fault. On a VAX system with one VAX unit of processing (VUP), a soft page fault takes between 0.38 and 0.42 ms. In contrast, a hard page fault takes between 38 ms and 40 ms (about 100 times longer than the soft page fault) or more, depending on the type of disk subsystem in use.

Because of a VAX's memory orientation, a VMS system worries about its memory resources when it drops below various thresholds. Although a memory resource can be far from depleted, a VMS system will become very concerned about giving out what it does have. At the threshold, a VMS system will limit a process' use of memory or expend inordinate amounts of CPU time trying to free memory. This activity occurs even if it's detrimental to overall system performance.

One of your goals in managing the performance of a system is to recognize excessive or detrimental memory management activity and adjust parameters to prevent it. Another VMS problem is that it pays strict attention to what you tell it to do. If you instruct VMS to provide Lee, Bill, or Tamela's process with a working set of 350 pages, 350 pages of memory is all they're going to get. VMS doesn't care that they might need 2,800 pages of memory or that the maximum working set size could be 5,000 pages. It'll just beat the heck out of the VAX paging, because you told it to.

A VAX system manager tames a VMS system by adjusting parameters related to memory use. True, VMS has parameters that direct resources other than memory, but none are as critical as the direction of memory use. We'll discuss many aspects of system tuning throughout this chapter; however, memory management will be the primary emphasis.

## SYSTEM PERFORMANCE INVESTIGATION

The VMS operating system has several excellent tools that can be used to collect system information. As a system manager or operator, you'll need to become familiar with these tools, and take the time to investigate typical CPU use, normal memory consumption, average page faulting rates, and the normal operational modes of your system. Commands as simple as SHOW MEMORY or SHOW SYSTEM can be used to investigate and pinpoint problems.

### The ACCOUNTING Utility

The ACCOUNTING utility is useful for analyzing system use. It will tell you how many people used the system over a given period, what resources were used, and so forth. The information comes from the accounting file SYS$MANAGER:ACCOUNTNG.DAT. In a cluster environment, if you want information specific to each node, individual accounting files must be used. Remember that collecting accounting information itself consumes resources, including CPU, memory, I/O, and disk space. Collect only the information you plan to use.

In a sample ACCOUNTING report (Screen 10-2), we can clearly see that user BYNON consumes the most system resources.

Additional accounting reports would have to be generated to determine if user BYNON is using too much CPU, memory, or I/O

```
$ ACCOUNT/SUM/REPORT=(PRO,DIR,BUFF,FAULT)
```

| Username | Processor Time | Direct I/O | Buffered I/O | Page Faults |
|---|---|---|---|---|
| BYNON | 0 31:57:52.87 | 3990871 | 1120112 | 13214678 |
| DECNET | 0 00:00:17.54 | 173 | 341 | 2980 |
| GUIDES | 0 00:03:55.91 | 1252 | 6272 | 41673 |
| PENDLETON | 0 08:35:50.45 | 414476 | 80573 | 4840040 |
| SHIPMAN | 0 01:26:08.46 | 21851 | 206533 | 648410 |
| STUDENT | 0 00:50:33.53 | 7259 | 25280 | 678031 |
| SYSTEM | 0 02:28:41.91 | 244050 | 172942 | 1372366 |
| T_BYNON | 0 00:14:20.99 | 6961 | 62161 | 153200 |
| WILLIS | 0 00:27:42.08 | 11100 | 36398 | 303256 |

**Screen 10-2: ACCOUNTING report example**

during prime operating time. If so, this user's activity should be balanced over available time.

## The MONITOR Utility

The MONITOR utility provides a gold mine of information about VMS. In general, MONITOR will help you discover the most common resource limitations of your running system. One of the most useful features of MONITOR is its ability to collect and store system information over a period of time. You simply tell MONITOR what data to collect, how often, and for how long. This permits you to analyze the system over an extended period.

Here are some hints about using MONITOR:

Use the DCL command MONITOR IO or MONITOR SYSTEM to observe free memory, i.e., free list size. If little memory is on the free-page list, you might have a memory limitation problem. In our first MONITOR example, the I/O performance of node LIZ (a VAXstation 2000) is monitored and analyzed.

As we can see in Screen 10-3, free list memory is almost nonexistent. Liz's lack of memory is most likely the highest contributing factor to the high I/O and fault rates.

Use the DCL commands MONITOR STATES, MONITOR MODES and MONITOR SYSTEM to observe CPU use. If many of the active

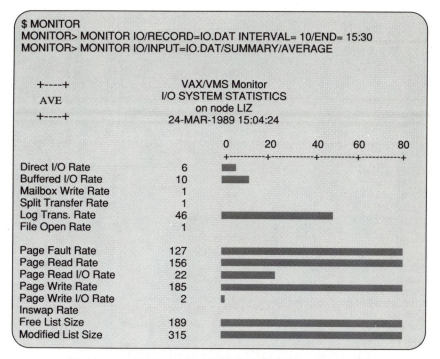

```
$ MONITOR
MONITOR> MONITOR IO/RECORD=IO.DAT INTERVAL= 10/END= 15:30
MONITOR> MONITOR IO/INPUT=IO.DAT/SUMMARY/AVERAGE
```

```
          +----+                    VAX/VMS Monitor
           AVE                   I/O SYSTEM STATISTICS
          +----+                       on node LIZ
                                   24-MAR-1989 15:04:24

                                       0      20     40     60     80
                                       +----------+----------+----------+----------+
Direct I/O Rate              6
Buffered I/O Rate           10
Mailbox Write Rate           1
Split Transfer Rate          1
Log Trans. Rate             46
File Open Rate               1

Page Fault Rate            127
Page Read Rate             156
Page Read I/O Rate          22
Page Write Rate            185
Page Write I/O Rate          2
Inswap Rate
Free List Size             189
Modified List Size         315
```

## Screen 10-3: A MONITOR I/O example

processes are in the computable state, or if CPU use is at or near 100 percent, or if a high percentage of time is spent in kernel mode, you might have a CPU limitation.

In a second MONITOR example (see Screen 10-4), node BIFF was consistently at 100 percent CPU utilization. The MONITOR STATES command was used to report process states on the operational system.

This screen reveals the painfully obvious problem on BIFF: More processes are computable than BIFF can handle. This is determined by the number of processes in the compute queue.

To observe system I/O use, use the DCL command MONITOR IO. Direct I/O is an indication of disk activity, and buffered I/O is an indication of terminal activity. Buffered I/O consumes CPU resources.

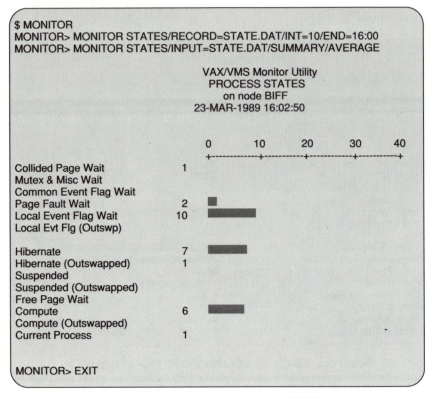

```
$ MONITOR
MONITOR> MONITOR STATES/RECORD=STATE.DAT/INT=10/END=16:00
MONITOR> MONITOR STATES/INPUT=STATE.DAT/SUMMARY/AVERAGE

                                    VAX/VMS Monitor Utility
                                       PROCESS STATES
                                         on node BIFF
                                    23-MAR-1989 16:02:50


                                  0       10      20      30      40
                                  +-------------+-------------+-------------+-------------+
Collided Page Wait               1
Mutex & Misc Wait
Common Event Flag Wait
Page Fault Wait                  2
Local Event Flag Wait           10
Local Evt Flg (Outswp)

Hibernate                        7
Hibernate (Outswapped)           1
Suspended
Suspended (Outswapped)
Free Page Wait
Compute                          6
Compute (Outswapped)
Current Process                  1


MONITOR> EXIT
```

### Screen 10-4: A MONITOR STATES example

## The DCL SHOW Command

The DCL SHOW command is useful for displaying snapshot
information about the system and processes. Use the DCL command
SHOW SYSTEM to display all processes currently running on the
system. This display will show you, at a glance, process states
(helps to locate MWAIT or other resource wait states), process
resource use, process names, and IDs. The sample SHOW SYSTEM
display (see Screen 10-5) shows a system with several outswapped
processes.

Use the DCL command SHOW PROCESS/IDENTIFICATION= n/CONTIN-
UOUS to display information about a specific process, generally a
user or batch job. This information is especially useful for

```
$ SHOW SYSTEM

VAX/VMS V5.1 on node LIZ 23-MAR-1989 14:14:33.81  Uptime  1 00:51:37
Pid    Process Name    State  Pri    I/O         CPU           Page flts      Ph.Mem
0021   SWAPPER         HIB    16     0           0 00:00:12.02  0              0
0042   VUE$BYNON_2     LEF    6      165         0 00:00:17.91  4455           300
0025   JOB_CONTROL     HIBO   10     — swapped out —                          294
0026   NETACP          HIB    10     94          0 00:00:17.86  202            350
0028   REMACP          HIBO   8      — swapped out —                          32
002A   SERVER_0        HIB    6      6988        0 00:07:25.72  8813           1300
002B   BYNON           LEF    4      422         0 00:01:18.94  7576           200
002C   DECW$WM_1       LEF    7      39          0 00:00:20.37  4939           715
002D   DECW$TE_1       LEF    4      2423        0 00:23:31.76  7986           537
0032   EVL             HIB    6      64          0 00:00:03.82  7159           60
0036   BYNON_TWA4      LEF    5      — swapped out —                          99
0037   BYNON_1         HIBO   6      — swapped out —                          121
0038   BYNON_2         CUR    4      278         0 00:00:05.83  1485           300
0039   BYNON_VUE2      LEF    6      199         0 00:00:20.25  7511           300
003A   VUE$BYNON_1     LEF    4      110         0 00:00:09.34  3653           300
```

## Screen 10-5: SHOW SYSTEM display

determining working set parameters. Use the DCL command SHOW MEMORY to display the current status of memory and page and swap file use.

## The AUTHORIZE Utility

The AUTHORIZE utility plays a big part in performance management, for it is here that individual process quotas and limits are established. You should concern yourself with, at a minimum, three factors: working set size, subprocess and job limits, and process priority.

A user's working set size parameters will define the amount of physical memory the process can consume. If a process' working set size is severely limited, the process will place a heavy burden on the entire system by its heavy page fault activity. By the same token, though, don't make user working set sizes artificially large, as this will waste valuable memory.

On a system heavily loaded with users, you should consider limiting the number of subprocesses and jobs that a user can have. Each subprocess a user creates takes up a balance set slot and physical memory.

## Recognizing a Performance Problem

The most obvious tell-tale sign of a performance problem is sluggish response. But, there are better methods of watching and measuring a system's performance. You must start by determining your system's capabilities. You then can watch memory, I/O, and CPU statistics to determine the actual load and health of your system.

Every system is limited by the amount of physical memory it has, its I/O bandwidth, and the CPU's processing power. Each of these resources must be carefully monitored, with precedence given to memory, then I/O, then CPU.

## Memory Performance

Memory statistics that you should be interested in are:

- Page fault rate
- Modified page write rate
- Swap rate
- Free list memory

Page fault rate is the system's total (soft and hard) page fault rate per second. The fault rate that any system can manage is directly related to the CPU's performance and the system's disk I/O bandwidth (for hard faults). As a general rule, many VAX system experts agree that 90 to 100 faults per VUP per second is all that should be expected. A higher fault rate will impose high CPU and I/O overhead. So, as your system begins to reach an unacceptable fault rate level, you must look for ways to reduce it.

The modified page write rate reflects the system's page modification operations. It suggests an I/O activity level attributed to writing pages from the modified page list (MPL) to the system page file. The write rate of the MPL is directly controlled by its size and the system's workload. The write rate is directly imposed on the system's total page fault rate. Thus, it is easy to see that a small MPL could result from excessive faults. Unless you intentionally adjust memory management parameters to favor swapping, in order to make up for a memory deficiency, your system's swap rate should be zero. Swapping is an intense procedure that robs your system's I/O and CPU performance.

If you experience a high page fault rate or swapping, and your system has a generous amount of memory on the free page list (FPL), then your system's memory management parameters are ineffective.

## Disk I/O Performance

Your system's disk I/O performance is affected by direct I/O rate and the effectiveness of ancillary control process (ACP) caching. Direct I/O rate is the number of I/O requests on all your disks.

Unfortunately, there is no concrete rule to follow, when it comes to direct I/O statistics, because the performance of disks and controllers varies so widely. For instance, an RA82 connected to a KDA50 on a MicroVAX II can sustain about 30 I/O operations per second. In contrast, an RD54/RQDX-3 combination achieves only about half as many I/O operations per second.

One method of determining your disk subsystem's performance characteristics is to develop or purchase a performance benchmark program. Such a program provides you with seek rates, access time, latency, data throughput, and the rate at which your system can accept I/O requests.

The disk subsystem's performance is augmented by memory buffers called ACP caches. Your system's overall cache hit rate percentage is an indication of cache effectiveness. When your system is active, expect ACP cache hit rates of 80 percent or more. A lower ACP cache hit rate is a good indication that ACP caches aren't large enough or that your system is suffering from extreme disk fragmentation.

## CPU Performance

Unfortunately, unlike memory or disk I/O, a CPU's performance is always fixed. Much to my disappointment, you can't turn up the clock speed or put in a read-only memory (ROM) hop-up kit. If you have a symmetric multiprocessing (SMP) machine, such as a VAX 6300, you can add another CPU.

An important part of CPU performance management is understanding the source of specific CPU loads. Most of the CPU demand comes from user processes, and some CPU attention is required for memory management tasks and disk I/O. But, there are two other heavy CPU users related directly to VMS: lock management and buffered I/O.

Lock management, which is specified as a system lock rate, is the rate at which the VMS lock manager converts, enqueues, and dequeues resource locks. High lock rates are typically associated with large VAXcluster systems; however, any system that shares many data files among users will produce the same results.

Buffered I/O, which would appear to be an I/O related load, actually manifests as a CPU load. Buffered I/O is directly related to terminal device activity. Therefore, any application that is screen intensive can cause the buffered I/O rate to skyrocket. Also, a heavy user of DECnet can have the same effect.

## When to Load Balance vs. Tuning

Load balancing is a never-ending task. As a proficient system manager, you should continuously investigate methods of spreading out the load. It simply doesn't make sense, from a performance point of view, to beat the bits out of a system for eight hours a day and then let it sit idle for the other 16.

Load balancing is the first part of any tuning effort. This is because a computer system is best geared toward the average work load, not the best- or worst-case workload. Therefore, load balancing should help to average the workload over the available time.

Load balancing should be performed gradually, as the load on the system changes. There are two situations you want to avoid. First, don't wake up one sunny morning and decide you're going to balance the load. Load balancing is performed over time with willing assistance from your users.

Second, don't wait until the last minute. When the system reaches saturation, you're too late. The system needed help weeks ago.

Try to predict what the system load will be and make changes in that direction.

Load balancing is a simple matter of dispersing jobs evenly over the period of available time. This takes the cooperative effort of everyone who uses the system. For example, if you note that a user regularly invokes a long resource-intensive task, ask him to start submitting it as a batch job that will run after hours. Other methods of load balancing include setting primary and secondary login days and/or hours for users, limiting the number of subprocesses a user can create, lowering the number of interactive logins ($SET LOGIN/INTERACTIVE=n), and adjusting the number of concurrent batch jobs that the system will execute (INITIALIZE/ QUEUE/JOB_LIMIT=n).

When your load balancing effort fails to produce results, consider tuning. Tuning a VMS system is rarely required in the major sense of the term, with several exceptions. Tuning is necessary to take advantage of a new system configuration, i.e., a new system, addition of more memory, and so on. Tuning is also essential if you dramatically change the workload by adding users, installing a resource intensive product, or changing primary processing modes. Finally, tuning can be beneficial to system performance when a plentiful resource, such as memory, can be used to make up for a resource bottleneck, such as disk I/O.

## VMS SYSTEM MEMORIES AND THEIR PARAMETERS

To fully understand a VMS system's memory performance characteristics, you must understand the various components.

### Request Packets

A VMS system uses request packets, which are linked lists of memory, to speed up process requests for dynamic memory. Three separate lists are maintained: large request packets (LRP), I/O request packets (IRP), and small request packets (SRP). The packets are used as look-aside lists. When a memory request can't be satisfied from one of the lists, nonpaged pool is allocated.

It's critical that there's always a reasonable free level of request packets. If depleted, a VMS system will spend additional overhead time allocating memory directly from the nonpaged pool. This activity is much slower than simply choosing a packet from one of the linked lists.

The size of the request packets used in each list and the length of the lists are controlled by system parameters. Although the size of the packets is important, it's not as critical as the length of the list, i.e., the number of packets on each list. Typically, the default request packet sizes are fine. In most cases, increasing the packet size only serves to waste memory.

To ensure that a safe level of request packets is available, you should adjust the request packet parameters to achieve the following list levels at your expected peak load:

| Request Packet | System Parameter | Free Level |
|---|---|---|
| SRP | SRPCOUNT | 100 - 120 |
| IRP | IRPCOUNT | 50 - 60 |
| LRP | LRPCOUNT | 25 - 30 |

## Dynamic Memory

VMS maintains two forms of dynamic memory, paged and nonpaged. Nonpaged dynamic memor is used by such facilities as system service routines, device drivers and ACP caching. If nonpaged memory isn't large enough, a VMS system will effectively shut off ACP caching. File system performance will be reduced drastically. Other system functions can suffer too. Your first hard evidence that nonpaged memory is too low will probably be a system message such as:

INSFMEM, insufficient dynamic memory

This message will come when there is not enough memory to load a driver, or it will come from a system service request when the image has disabled resource wait mode. This problem is solved by increasing the value of NPAGEDYN.

Paged dynamic memory is used by processes as a working set cache. Here, working set pages are stored in hopes that when they're needed again, they will already be in memory. If paged dynamic memory is too small, hard paging activity will increase.

Hard page faulting is the biggest performance problem related to memory management. Because program images are loaded from disk through the VMS page fault mechanism, it's impossible to eliminate page faulting. However, any hard page fault activity beyond image activation can and should be eliminated or reduced as much as possible. There are two methods of doing just that: ensure that paged dynamic memory is large enough to cache working set pages faulted out of process working sets, and make user working sets large enough to accommodate their largest (in term of memory consumption) application.

To ensure the best possible performance from the paged and nonpaged memory facilities, you must keep a generous amount of dynamic memory on the free list. Observe the system during peak use times. The following values should be raised until the free levels indicated are reached:

| System Parameter | Free Level |
| --- | --- |
| PAGEDYN | 200,000 |
| NPAGEDYN | 100,000 |

## Page and Swap Files

Page and swap files are a critical system resource. Without them, system virtual memory can't be accomplished. Also, if a system's page and swap file space becomes low, the VMS system will react harshly by putting processes into a resource wait state. With many processes waiting for a resource, especially page file space, the system will bog down or possibly deadlock.

System page file space is allocated to a process dynamically based on a process' virtual writable address space. In addition to a process' use of the page file, facilities such as RMS use it for their virtual memory needs. RMS uses the page file for global buffering of files.

When a process is created, VMS assigns it to a page file. The page file assignment is based on the page file that has the most free space at the time. As of VMS V5, a process can take advantage of multiple page files.

Two problems commonly occur with page files: They become full or fragmented. If a page file becomes full, the VMS system will put all processes assigned to the full page file in a resource wait state. This effectively deadlocks those processes. If a page file becomes fragmented, the system will slow down because of excessive I/O processing.

If disk space permits, a page file should never be more than half used. In other words, page file free space should be greater than page file space in use. An easy method of computing page file size is with the formula PAGEFILE SIZE = (MAXPROCESSCNT * WSMAX). In most cases, two or more page files on separate drives will provide better performance than a single large page file. The number of system page files allowed is controlled by the system parameter PAGFILCNT.

Swap file space is also assigned dynamically as a process requires its use. (Prior to VMS V5, swap file space was statically assigned at process creation time.) The amount of space allocated to a process is based on the working set size of the process.

A swap file that's too small or becomes fragmented affects the system in the same manner as the page file. Swap file space is calculated using the formula SWAPFILE SIZE = (WSQUOTA * BALSETCNT), where WSQUOTA represents the average WSQUOTA size for the system.

## Process Slots

Every system is limited by the number of processes it can manage physically or reasonably. The primary factors in this count are the CPU class, available memory, and workload. In some situations, political or time-sensitive guidelines also apply.

Processes are controlled by two slot counts, process entry slots and balance set slots. Process entry slots dictate the total number of processes permitted on the system at any given time, while the balance set count controls the number of process working sets that can be in physical memory at one time.

A high-process entry slot count will allow a system to be over-loaded. The process entry slot count should reflect the capability and expected workload of the system.

A low-balance set count will cause physical memory to be wasted, regardless of the number of active processes. The balance set count should represent the average number of active processes that will fully use the available memory. In any case, the balance set count must be at least one less than the number of process entry slots to provide a slot for the swapper process (two less in VMS V4, i.e., the null process).

## Swapper Activity and Page Lists

The swapper process is responsible for maintaining a sufficient (as defined by you, the system manager) supply of free memory on your system. It does this by monitoring the number of pages on the FPL. The Free Page List represents the number of memory pages available to processes in the system.

Whenever the FPL drops below the value specified by the SYSGEN parameter FREELIM, the swapper is invoked to shake memory loose from one or more processes. The memory freed by the swapper is put back on the FPL.

There are several methods by which the swapper can recover memory. The first method, known as flushing, involves writing the MPL to the page file; the MPL maintains pages that have been altered since they were faulted into a process' working set. Because of the I/O incurred (both to flush the list and to recover the pages when they're needed again), flushing is detrimental to system performance.

Flushing frequency is determined by two factors: the availability of system memory and the values of the MPW parameters. The MPW parameters should be adjusted to suit available memory and to reduce paging activity. If memory is plentiful, MPL flushing and trimming can be disabled. This is done by setting MPW_HILIMIT below MPW_THRESH.

After MPL flushing and trimming (if not turned off), the swapper will perform first-level trimming of process working sets. First-level trimming is performed on processes whose working sets have grown past their WSQUOTA allotment. In other words, the swapper cashes in on memory loans made against a process' WSEXTENT value. The pages are placed back on the FPL. Process trimming takes place until FREEGOAL pages are on the FPL.

Most often, first-level trimming reduces enough process working set space to reach the swapper's goal. If FREEGOAL is not reached in first-level trimming, the swapper continues by further trimming and/or swapping inactive processes. At this point, second-level trimming also may take place, i.e., processes are trimmed below WSQUOTA to the level defined by the SYSGEN parameter SWPOUTPGCNT.

Second-level trimming is detrimental to system performance. This is because of the additional hard page fault activity that will be incurred by the system as active processes try to regain working set quota memory taken away from them. In all but extremely memory-poor systems, the second-level trimming feature should be disabled. This is done by setting SWPOUTPGCNT equal to WSMAX.

The side effect of disabling second-level trimming is additional swapping when enough memory cannot be scavenged during first-level trimming. Yet, this is okay, because the swapper swaps processes (in their entirety) in and out of the swap file in several large disk I/O operations; a low frequency of swapping is less harmful than second-level trimming. Second-level trimming takes many small pieces of memory from processes, requiring many small I/O operations as the MPL is flushed to the page file. So, a moderate level of swapping is better for system performance than a high level of trimming to prevent swapping.

## SYSTEM RESPONSE PARAMETERS

A VMS system implements several parameters that affect its multiprocessing characteristics. The most important of these is the system parameter QUANTUM. QUANTUM specifies a period of time, measured in 10-ms units, that a process gets to run in the CPU before releasing it to another process. The ideal QUANTUM value provides a process with just enough time to get its computing work accomplished before having to perform I/O.

QUANTUM should be adjusted for the type of processing you perform on your system. If you seek good response for interactive users, QUANTUM should be lower than the default. If you operate in a batch-oriented environment, the value of QUANTUM should be increased slightly. The default QUANTUM value (i.e., 20) is adequate for the typical mixed-mode system. Decreasing QUANTUM will increase CPU use at a certain point because of context switching, i.e., the CPU spends more time switching processes in and out of context for processing than it does on actual work.

One of the anomalies of VMS, which mainly affects memory management, is dormant processes. A dormant process can't get CPU time because one or more higher priority processes is hogging the CPU. The problem is not that the lower priority process is not being serviced (because that's the way it's supposed to be), but that the dormant process is tying up potentially critical resources. For instance, the dormant process can have a large chunk of memory allocated, or it can have a lock on one or more records in a file. Memory management is affected by dormant processes because memory management functions occur at quantum end. If a high priority process hogs the CPU, quantum end is never reached.

To combat the problems associated with dormant processes, two special SYSGEN parameters were implemented: DORMANTWAIT and PIXSCAN. PIXSCAN is used to force a priority boost of a dormant process after PIXSCAN seconds, allowing locks to be released and memory to be trimmed. When a process lays dormant for DOR-MANTWAIT, its working set may be decremented by WSDEC pages. The PIXSCAN boost is only required for one quantum.

## Automatic Working Set Adjustment
The second mechanism that affects process performance is called the automatic working set adjustment (AWSA). AWSA is a set of parameters that defines how memory will be allocated. The automatic working set adjustment is a very delicate part of the

VMS memory management scheme. If the memory management parameters are handled improperly, you'll cause more harm than good. Always record your system's initial settings, and measure system performance before and after making adjustments.

The AWSA mechanism allows a VAX system to be dynamic, robbing Peter to pay Paul, you might say. This is important, if physical memory is a limited resource. One of the functions of AWSA is to trim process working sets when memory becomes scarce or when it's not actively in use. Memory use is detected by a process' page faulting activity.

There are two AWSA parameters that control working set incrementing and decrementing: page fault rate low (PFRATL) and page fault rate high (PFRATH). When a process' page faulting reaches the level defined by PFRATH, its working set will be incremented by the amount specified in the working set increment (WSINC). Working set decrementing begins when a process' page fault rate falls below the value of PFRATL. Working sets are decremented by the amount specified in WSDEC. To keep the system from trimming working sets, set the parameters PFRATL and WSDEC to 0.

I recommend that you don't shut off voluntary working set trimming. Trimming working sets, when a process has temporarily reduced its requirement, or becomes inactive, is the best way to recoup memory for other processes. Remember, the purpose of memory management is to share what's available.

To make a system respond rapidly to a process' need for memory, lower the value of PFRATH and increase the value of WSINC. In this way, a larger quantity of memory will be allocated each time it's needed, and the process will receive the memory sooner. This technique also will decrease CPU overhead related to memory management. Note, however, that this should only be done on a memory rich system.

The following parameter values are recommended for systems with sufficient memory:

| <u>System Parameter</u> | <u>Value</u> |
|---|---|
| PFRATH | 10-50 |
| PFRATL | 1 |
| WSINC | 300-600 |
| WSDEC | 10-20 |

Note that these values are no where near the conservative setting established by AUTOGEN. The reason is quite clear: If you have the memory, use it. If you don't have a generous amount of free memory (under load), you should stay with the parameters predicated by AUTOGEN, or tighten the belt.

## Process Working Set Quotas

Directly related to the AWSA is the process working set itself. A process' working set is the physical pages of memory allocated to it for its work. The limits of a process working set are defined by the user authorization file (UAF) parameters WSDEFAULT, WSQUOTA and WSEXTENT.

WSDEFAULT is the initial amount of memory a process is allocated when created. WSDEFAULT is typically set to a low value (less than 200).

If a process needs more memory than WSDEFAULT, it will be allowed to expand to the value defined by WSQUOTA. Typically, the value of WSQUOTA should be set to the requirements of the user's most frequently used applications. For instance, if a user spends most of his time using a word processor that could demand a working set of 1,398 pages, you might set WSQUOTA to 1,100. You should never exceed the highest demand of the user's largest application. If you do so, when memory becomes scarce, first-level trimming would be ineffective.

If memory is available and the process' page fault rate still demands more memory, the process will be allowed to borrow memory up to the final limit, WSEXTENT. This is how you can ensure that a hungry application will get all the memory it wants, if the memory is available. For example, WSEXTENT could be set to a value between 1,400 and 1,450 to accommodate the user's application.

It's imperative that each account have its working set values set correctly. It only takes one process, with poor working set performance, to hard page fault your VAX into mush.

## FILE SYSTEM PERFORMANCE

One of the best investments you can make in your system is to spend a little time tuning, balancing, and maintaining the file system. There are three important aspects to your file system: the number of spindles (disk drives) and controllers, contiguous storage, and buffering and caching.

### Input/Output Throughput

The number of spindles and controllers your system has will have an impact on the system's I/O performance. This makes sense, because two drives can read and write twice as much data as one. The average access time of two drives is potentially twice that of a single drive. So, the first rule to better disk I/O performance on any VAX system is to spread the load evenly over multiple disk volumes. The same holds true for the disk controllers. A controller managing two drives will perform better than the same controller with four drives. Systems based on hierarchical storage controllers (i.e., VAXclusters) should have their drives evenly balanced among the available HSCs.

### Fragmentation

There's also the issue of contiguous storage, or lack of it, called fragmentation. It's the bane of every VMS system. A fragmented file system is detrimental to system performance. You can't prevent it, but you can fix it.

There are three parts to the fragmentation problem. First, there's file fragmentation, which are files with multiple noncontiguous file extensions. The second fragmentation problem is record fragmentation, which is dead space left in an indexed file when records are deleted, called empty buckets. Finally, there's page file fragmentation. Page file fragmentation comes about when your system's page files are too small.

The page file is a critical resource. System performance degradation will occur when page file use exceeds 50 percent. This is because it becomes difficult to find contiguous blocks to allocate to a demanding process.

The size of a system's page files depends greatly on the number of users and their applications. However, a few guidelines always apply:

- Use multiple page files of equal size, if possible.
- Locate page files on low use disks.
- Always make page files contiguous. The page file size can be computed using PAGEFILE SIZE = (MAXPROCESSCNT * WSMAX). The number of system page files is controlled by the system parameter PAGFILCNT.

A disk fragmentation problem can be solved by performing a full backup and restore or by using a disk defragmentation utility. Record fragmentation is fixed with the CONVERT/RECLAIM utility.

## RMS Buffering and ACP Caches

RMS buffering, or more precisely global buffering, defines the number of buffers that can be shared by multiple processes accessing a file. Buffering is defined on a file-by-file basis, using the $SET FILE/GLOBAL_BUFFER command or through the use of the file definition language (FDL) utility. RMS buffering is needed to achieve good performance on shared data files, especially when a data file is accessed by three or more processes at once.

Ancillary control process caches are portions of paged dynamic memory used to buffer or cache directories, file headers, file IDs, and so on. The ACP maintains the following caches:

- Quota cache
- Extent cache
- Directory cache
- File Header cache
- File ID cache

Of these, the directory and file header caches are the most important to file system performance.

The directory cache is memory allocated by the extended QIO processor (XQP) to cache directory file information. This cache permits the XQP to perform directory searches without actually having to read the disk. On volumes that have multiple subdirectory levels and many files in a single directory, such as ALL-IN-1 disks, the directory cache will play an important role in overall file system performance.

Directory searching, during a file open operation, represents a substantial amount of system overhead. On an active system with many users, the file open rate will easily exceed eight to 10 file opens per second. If directory information isn't cached properly, these file opens will incur many additional direct file I/O operations.

There are three system parameters that affect directory caching: ACP_DIRCACHE, ACP_MAXREAD, and ACP_DINDXCACHE.

The parameter ACP_DIRCACHE defines the number of directory blocks for each volume that can be cached by the XQP. Each block consumes 512 bytes from paged dynamic memory. The ACP_DIRCACHE should be large enough to hold all of the most commonly used directory files.

The ACP_DINDXCACHE parameter defines the number of file control blocks that can be maintained by the XQP for directory files. This cache is used to keep open as many directory files as possible. Make this parameter large enough to keep open the most actively used directory files. Each directory entry requires 180 bytes of nonpaged dynamic memory.

The parameter ACP_MAXREAD controls the maximum number of blocks that will read into the directory cache. This parameter should be set slightly larger than the average directory file size in blocks.

The file header cache is used by the XQP to keep from having to read a file header from disk when the file is opened or when a window control block needs to be updated. This cache has a significant impact on system performance.

The file header cache is controlled by the system parameter ACP_HDRCACHE. Each entry in the cache requires 512 bytes of paged dynamic memory. The size of the cache will determine the number of file headers that can be cached. It should be large enough so that all of the most commonly accessed files can have their headers cached, plus 32-40 for miscellaneous open files.

A final note on ACP caching: Because file header and directory caching is performed in paged dynamic memory, you must ensure that there's enough memory from which to allocate the cache. The size of paged dynamic memory is controlled by the system parameter PAGEDYN. If PAGEDYN is too small, the cache will be set very small. The result of this error will effectively be no caching at all. To monitor caching activity, use the DCL command $MONITOR/FILE_SYSTEM_CACHE.

## ADJUSTING SYSTEM PARAMETERS

VMS is a complex operating system. As such, it has an elaborate set of rules and parameters that govern it. Making matters even worse, many of these system parameters interact. Changing certain parameters will drastically affect seemingly unrelated components.

Two facilities exist to adjust and change system parameters, SYSGEN and AUTOGEN. The SYSGEN utility is used to change system parameters directly. Using it for system performance purposes is highly discouraged.

The AUTOGEN utility automates the parameter changing process. AUTOGEN is a command procedure that collects information from the running system and uses this data to adjust SYSGEN parameters. Optionally, AUTOGEN overrides its computed SYSGEN values with values provided in a user-defined parameter file, SYS$SYSTEM: MODPARAMS.DAT.

The benefit of using AUTOGEN, versus changing parameters directly with SYSGEN, is that although you might not be a VAX system internals expert, AUTOGEN is. AUTOGEN understands what parameters work together. For example, if you want to decrease the parameter MAXPROCESSCNT, AUTOGEN understands that

BALSETCNT always should lag MAXPROCESSCNT by at least one and makes this adjustment for you.

The easiest and safest tuning effort you can make is to execute AUTOGEN to adjust SYSUAF working set parameters, using the AUTHORIZE utility. Adequate working set parameters can be established by monitoring a process' consumption of memory. Use the DCL command SHOW PROCESS/CONTINUOUS/ID=n to watch a process in execution. Remember that a working set can't grow larger than the SYSGEN value for WSMAX. If larger working sets are required, increase this parameter.

## CONCLUSION

Load balancing and tuning are slow processes. Adjustments should be made gradually and the results compared against known statistics. You must plan to spend time monitoring the system, after making modifications, to evaluate the results. The best method of evaluating tuning success is to monitor the system under a reproduceable workload or by monitoring various programs under fixed workload conditions. Your system is balanced successfully if it remains steadily busy throughout the day, with few peaks and valleys of activity.

# DCL Commands

This appendix section lists each major DCL command and a brief description of its function. Not all DCL commands are presented here. For a complete list and description, refer to the *VAX/VMS DCL Dictionary*.

**= (Assignment statement)**   Assigns an expression to a symbol.

symbol =[=] expression
symbol(bit_position,size] =[=] expression

**:= (Assignment statement)**   Assigns a string expression to a symbol.

symbol :=[=] string
symbol[offset,size] :=[=] string

**@ file_spec [p1 p2...p8]**   Executes a DCL command procedure.
QUALIFIER:
/OUTPUT=file_spec

**ACCOUNTING file_spec[,...]**   Invokes the ACCOUNTING utility to collect and report accounting information.

QUALIFIERS:

| | | | |
|---|---|---|---|
| /ACCOUNT | /ADDRESS | /BEFORE | /BINARY |
| /ENTRY | /FULL | /IDENTIFICATION | /IMAGE |
| /JOB | /LOG | /NODE | /OUTPUT |
| /OWNER | /PRIORITY | /PROCESS | /QUEUE |
| /REJECTED | /REMOTE_ID | /REPORT | /SINCE |
| /SORT | /STATUS | /SUMMARY | /TERMINAL |
| /TITLE | /TYPE | /UIC | /USER |

**ALLOCATE device_name: [logical_name]**   Provides exclusive use of a device and, optionally, establishes a logical name for that device. While a device is allocated, other users may access the device until you DEALLOCATE it or log out.

QUALIFIERS:
/GENERIC

**ANALYZE/CRASH_DUMP file_spec**   Invokes the system DUMP ANALYZER utility for analysis of a system dump file.

**ANALYZE/DISK_STRUCTURE device:**   Invokes the ANALYZE/ DISK_STRUCTURE utility to check the readability and validity of Files-11 Structure Level 1 and Files-11 Structure Level 2 disk volumes, and to report errors and inconsistencies.

**ANALYZE/ERROR_LOG [/qualifier(s)][file_spec[,...]]**   Invokes the ERRORLOG REPORT FORMATTER to selectively report the contents of an error log file.

**ANALYZE/IMAGE file_spec[,...]**   Analyzes the contents of an executable image or a shareable image, and checks for obvious errors.

**ANALYZE/MEDIA device:**   Invokes the BAD BLOCK LOCATOR utility, which analyzes block-addressable devices and records the location of blocks that cannot reliably store data.

**ANALYZE/OBJECT file_spec[,...]**   Analyzes the contents of an object file and checks for any obvious errors.

**ANALYZE/PROCESS_DUMP dump_file**   Invokes the VMS DEBUGGER for analysis of a process dump file that was created when an image failed during execution. You must use the /DUMP qualifier with the RUN or SET PROCESS command to generate a dump file.

**ANALYZE/RMS_FILE file_spec[,...]**   Invokes the ANALYZE /RMS_FILE utility to inspect and analyze the internal structure of a Record Management Services file.

**APPEND input_file_spec[,...] output_file_spec**   Adds the contents of one or more input files to the end of a file.

QUALIFIERS:

| | | | |
|---|---|---|---|
| /ALLOCATION | /BACKUP | /BEFORE | /BY_OWNER |
| /CONFIRM | /CONTIGUOUS | /CREATED | /EXCLUDE |
| /EXPIRED | /EXTENSION | /LOG | /MODIFIED |
| /NEW_VERSION | /READ_CHECK | /SINCE | /WRITE_CHECK |

**ASSIGN equivalence_name logical_name**   Equates a logical name to a physical device name, file specification, or another logical name.

**ASSIGN/MERGE**   Merges the contents of one queue with another.

**ASSIGN/QUEUE**   Assigns a logical queue to a device queue.

**ATTACH [process_name]**   Enables you to transfer control from the current process to another process created by you.

QUALIFIER:
/IDENTIFICATION

**BACKUP input_spec output_spec**   Invokes the BACKUP utility to perform one of the following file operations:
- Copy disk files.
- Save disk files as a save set (a single data file) on a disk or magnetic tape volume.
- Restore files from a save set.
- Compare files.
- Display information about files contained in a save set.

QUALIFIERS:

| | | | |
|---|---|---|---|
| /BACKUP | /BEFORE | /BLOCK_SIZE | /BRIEF |
| /BUFFER_COUNT | /COMMENT | /COMPARE | /CONFIRM |
| /CRC | /CREATED | /DELETE | /DENSITY |
| /EXCLUDE | /EXPIRED | /FAST | /FULL |
| /GROUP_SIZE | /IGNORE | /IMAGE | /INCREMENTAL |
| /INITIALIZE | /INTERCHANGE | /JOURNAL | /LABEL |
| /LIST | /LOG | /MODIFIED | /NEW_VERSION |
| /OVERLAY | /OWNER_UIC | /PHYSICAL | /PROTECTION |
| /RECORD | /REPLACE | /REWIND | /SAVE_SET |
| /SELECT | /SINCE | /TRUNCATE | /VERIFY |
| /VOLUME | | | |

**CALL label [p1 p2...p8]**   Transfers command procedure control to a labeled subroutine in the procedure.

QUALIFIER:
/OUTPUT

**CANCEL [process_name]**   Cancels a scheduled wake_up request for the specified process.
QUALIFIER:
/IDENTIFICATION

**CLOSE logical_name**   Used to close a file opened for input/ output with the OPEN command, and deassigns the logical name created for the file.
QUALIFIERS:
/ERROR                    /LOG

**CONNECT virtual_terminal_name**   Connects a physical terminal to a virtual terminal connected to another process.
QUALIFIERS:
/CONTINUE                 /LOGOUT

**CONTINUE**   Resumes execution of a DCL command, program, or command procedure interrupted by pressing <CTRL/Y> or <CTRL/ C>. You can abbreviate the CONTINUE command to the letter C.

**COPY input_file_spec[,...] output_file_spec**   Creates a new file from one or more existing files.  The COPY command can be used to:
  • Copy an input file to an output file, optionally changing its name and location.
  • Copy a group of input files to a group of output files.
  • Concatenate two or more files into a single new file.
QUALIFIERS:
| /ALLOCATION | /BACKUP | /BEFORE | /BY_OWNER |
| /CONCATENATE | /CONFIRM | /CONTIGUOUS | /CREATED |
| /EXCLUDE | /EXPIRED | /EXTENSION | /LOG |
| /MODIFIED | /OVERLAY | /PROTECTION | /READ_CHECK |
| /REPLACE | /SINCE | /TRUNCATE | /VOLUME |
| /WRITE_CHECK | | | |

**CREATE file_spec**   Creates one or more sequential disk files from records that follow in the input stream (i.e., the keyboard, a modem, and so on). To terminate input and close the file, enter <CTRL/Z>.

QUALIFIERS:
/LOG              /OWNER_UIC              /PROTECTION              /VOLUME

## CREATE/DIRECTORY directory_spec[,...]   Creates a new directory or subdirectory for cataloging files.

QUALIFIERS:
/LOG          /OWNER_UIC      /PROTECTION      /VERSION_LIMIT      /VOLUME

## CREATE/FDL=fdl_file_spec [file_spec]   Invokes the FILE DEFINITION LANGUAGE utility to use the specifications in a definition file to create a new (i.e., empty) data file.

QUALIFER:
/LOG

## DEALLOCATE device_name:   Releases a previously allocated device to the pool of available devices.

QUALIFER:
/ALL

## DEASSIGN logical_name[:]   Deletes logical name assignments made with the ALLOCATE, ASSIGN, DEFINE, or MOUNT command.

QUALIFERS:
| /ALL | /EXECUTIVE_MODE | /GROUP |
| /JOB | /PROCESS | /SUPERVISOR_MODE |
| /SYSTEM | /TABLE | /USER_MODE |

## DEASSIGN/QUEUE logical_queue_name[:]   Deassigns a logical queue from its printer or terminal queue assignment and stops the associated logical queue.

## DEBUG   Invokes the debugger.

## DEFINE logical_name equivalence_name[,...]   Creates a logical name entry and assigns it an equivalence string, or a list of equivalence strings, to the specified logical name.

QUALIFIERS:
| /CHARACTERISTIC | /EXECUTIVE_MODE | /FORM |
| /GROUP | /JOB | /KEY |
| /LOG | /NAME_ATTRIBUTES | /PROCESS |
| /SUPERVISOR_MODE | /SYSTEM | /TABLE |
| /TRANSLATION_ATTRIBUTES | /USER_MODE | |

## DEFINE/KEY key_name string   Associates a character string and a set of attributes with a function key.

QUALIFIERS:

| | | | |
|---|---|---|---|
| /ECHO | /ERASE | /IF_STATE | /LOCK_STATE |
| /LOG | /SET_STATE | /TERMINATE | |

**DELETE file_spec[,...]**   Deletes one or more files from a mass device.

QUALIFIERS:

| | | | |
|---|---|---|---|
| /BACKUP | /BEFORE | /BY_OWNER | /CONFIRM |
| /CREATED | /ERASE | /EXCLUDE | /EXPIRED |
| /LOG | /MODIFIED | /SINCE | |

**DELETE/CHARACTERISTIC characteristic_name**   Deletes the definition of a queue characteristic that was previously established with the DEFINE/CHARACTERISTIC command.

**DELETE/ENTRY=(queue_entry_number[,...])**
**queue_name[:]**   Deletes one or more job entries from the named queue.

**DELETE/KEY key_name**   Deletes a key definition established by the DEFINE/KEY command.

QUALIFIERS:

| | | |
|---|---|---|
| /ALL | /LOG | /STATE |

**DELETE/QUEUE queue_name[:]**   Deletes the specified queue from the system.

**DELETE/SYMBOL symbol_name**   Removes a symbol definition from a local or global symbol table or removes all symbol definitions in a symbol table.

QUALIFIERS:

| | | | |
|---|---|---|---|
| /ALL | /GLOBAL | /LOCAL | /LOG |

**DEPOSIT location=data[,...]**   Overwrites the contents of a specified location or series of locations in virtual memory. The DEPOSIT and EXAMINE commands are used primarily when debugging programs interactively.

QUALIFIERS:

| | | | |
|---|---|---|---|
| /ASCII | /BYTE | /DECIMAL | /HEXADECIMAL |
| /LONGWORD | /OCTAL | /WORD | |

**DIFFERENCES master_file_spec [revision_file_spec]**   Compares the contents of two disk files and creates a listing of those records that do not match.

QUALIFIERS:

| | | |
|---|---|---|
| /CHANGE_BAR | /COMMENT_DELIMITER | /IGNORE |
| /MATCH | /MAXIMUM_DIFFERENCES | /MERGED |
| /MODE | /NUMBER | /OUTPUT |
| /PARALLEL | /SEPARATED | /SLP |
| /WIDTH | /WINDOW | |

**DIRECTORY  [file_spec[,...]]**   Provides a list of files or information about a file or group of files.

QUALIFIERS:

| | | | |
|---|---|---|---|
| /ACL | /BACKUP | /BEFORE | /BRIEF |
| /BY_OWNER | /COLUMNS | /CREATED | /DATE |
| /EXCLUDE | /EXPIRED | /FILE_ID | /FULL |
| /GRAND_TOTAL | /HEADING | /MODIFIED | /OUTPUT |
| /OWNER | /PRINTER | /PROTECTION | /SECURITY |
| /SELECT | /SINCE | /SIZE | /TOTAL |
| /TRAILING | /VERSIONS | /WIDTH | |

**DISCONNECT**   Disconnects a physical terminal from a virtual terminal that has been connected to a process. The virtual terminal, and its associated process, will remain on the system when the physical terminal is disconnected from it.

QUALIFIER:
/CONTINUE

**DISMOUNT device_name[:]**   Dismounts a disk or magnetic tape volume that was previously mounted with a MOUNT command.

QUALIFIERS:

| | | | |
|---|---|---|---|
| /ABORT | /CLUSTER | /UNIT | /UNLOAD |

**DUMP file_spec [,...]**   Displays the contents of files or volumes in ASCII, decimal, hexadecimal, or octal representation.

QUALIFIERS:

| | | | |
|---|---|---|---|
| /ALLOCATED | /BLOCKS | /BYTE | /DECIMAL |
| /FILE_HEADER | /FORMATTED | /HEADER | /HEXADECIMAL |
| /LONGWORD | /NUMBER | /OCTAL | /OUTPUT |
| /PRINTER | /RECORDS | /WORD | |

**EDIT/ACL file_spec**   Invokes the access control list editor to create or update access control list information for a specified object.

QUALIFIERS:

| | | | |
|---|---|---|---|
| /JOURNAL | /KEEP | /MODE | /OBJECT | /RECOVER |

**EDIT/EDT file_spec**   Invokes the EDT text editor. The /EDT qualifier is not required, as EDT is the default editor.

QUALIFIERS:

| | | |
|---|---|---|
| /COMMAND | /CREATE | /JOURNAL |
| /OUTPUT | /READ_ONLY | /RECOVER |

**EDIT/FDL file_spec**   Invokes the file definition language editor to create or modify an FDL file.

QUALIFIERS:

| | | | |
|---|---|---|---|
| /ANALYSIS | /CREATE | /DISPLAY | /EMPHASIS |
| /GRANULARITY | /NOINTERACTIVE | /NUMBER_KEYS | /OUTPUT |
| /PROMPTING | /RESPONSES | /SCRIPT | |

**EDIT/TPU file_spec**   Invokes the TEXT PROCESSING utility. To invoke TPU with the EDT emulator  interface, define the logical TPUSECINI to point to the section file for the EDT interface as follows: $ DEFINE TPUSECINI EDTSECINI

QUALIFIERS:

| | | | |
|---|---|---|---|
| /COMMAND | /CREATE | /DISPLAY | /JOURNAL |
| /OUTPUT | /READ_ONLY | /RECOVER | /SECTION |

**EOD**   Signals the end of an input stream when a command, program or utility is reading data from an input device other than a terminal.

**EXAMINE  location[:location]**   Displays the contents of virtual memory.

QUALIFIERS:

| | | | |
|---|---|---|---|
| /ASCII | /BYTE | /DECIMAL | /HEXADECIMAL |
| /LONGWORD | /OCTAL | /WORD | |

**EXIT [status_code]**   Terminates the current command procedure. If the command procedure was executed from within another command procedure, control will return to the calling procedure.

**GOSUB label**   Transfers command procedure control to a labeled subroutine.

**GOTO label**   Transfers control to a labeled statement in a command procedure.

**HELP**   Invokes the HELP utility to display information about a VMS command or topic.

QUALIFIERS:

| /INSTRUCTIONS | /LIBLIST | /LIBRARY | /OUTPUT |
| /PAGE | /PROMPT | /USERLIBRARY | |

**IF expression THEN command**   Tests the value of a logical expression and executes the command following the THEN keyword if the test is true.

**IF expression THEN command ELSE command ENDIF**   Tests the value of a logical expression and executes the commands following the THEN keyword if the test is true. If the test is false, the commands following the ELSE clause are executed. The command must be written as follows:

```
$ IF expression
$  THEN [command]
$      command
$       .
$       .
$  ELSE [command]
$      command
$       .
$       .
$ ENDIF
```

**INITIALIZE  device_name[:] volume_label**   Formats and writes a label on a mass storage volume.

QUALIFIERS:

| /ACCESSED | /BADBLOCKS | /CLUSTER_SIZE | /DATA_CHECK |
| /DENSITY | /DIRECTORIES | /ERASE | /EXTENSION |
| /FILE_PROTECTION | /GROUP | /HEADERS | /HIGHWATER |
| /INDEX | /LABEL | /MAXIMUM_FILES | /OVERRIDE |
| /OWNER_UIC | /PROTECTION | /SHARE | /STRUCTURE |
| /SYSTEM | /USER_NAME | /VERIFIED | /WINDOWS |

**INITIALIZE/QUEUE  queue_name[:]**   Creates and initializes queues. This command is used to create and assign names and attributes to queues. When creating a batch queue, the qualifier /BATCH is required.

QUALIFIERS:

| | | |
|---|---|---|
| /BASE_PRIORITY | /BATCH | /BLOCK_LIMIT |
| /CHARACTERISTICS | /CPUDEFAULT | /CPUMAXIMUM |
| /DEFAULT | /DISABLE_SWAPPING | /ENABLE_GENERIC |
| /FORM_MOUNTED | /GENERIC | /JOB_LIMIT |
| /LIBRARY | /ON | /OWNER_UIC |
| /PROCESSOR | /PROTECTION | /RECORD_BLOCKING |
| /RETAIN | /SCHEDULE | /SEPARATE |
| /START | /TERMINAL | /WSDEFAULT |
| /WSEXTENT | /WSQUOTA | |

**INQUIRE symbol_name [prompt]**   Provides interactive assignment of a value for a local or global symbol in a command procedure.

QUALIFIERS:

| | | |
|---|---|---|
| /GLOBAL | /LOCAL | /PUNCTUATION |

**LIBRARY library_file_spec [input_file_spec[,...]]**   Invokes the LIBRARIAN utility to create, modify, or describe macro, object, help, text, or shareable image library.

QUALIFIERS:

| | | |
|---|---|---|
| /BEFORE | /COMPRESS | /CREATE |
| /CROSS_REFERENCE | /DATA | /DELETE |
| /EXTRACT | /FULL | /GLOBALS |
| /HELP | /HISTORY | /INSERT |
| /LIST | /LOG | /MACRO |
| /MODULE | /NAMES | /OBJECT |
| /ONLY | /OUTPUT | /REMOVE |
| /REPLACE | /SELECTIVE_SEARCH | /SHARE |
| /SINCE | /SQUEEZE | /TEXT |
| /WIDTH | | |

**LINK file_spec[,...]**   Invokes the LINKER to link object modules into a VMS program image.

QUALIFIERS:

| | | |
|---|---|---|
| /BRIEF | /CONTIGUOUS | /CROSS_REFERENCE |
| /DEBUG | /EXECUTABLE | /FULL |
| /HEADER | /INCLUDE | /IMAGE |
| /LIBRARY | /MAP | /PROTECT |
| /SHAREABLE | /SYMBOL_TABLE | /SYSLIB |
| /SYSSHR | /SYSTEM | /TRACEBACK |
| /USERLIBRARY | /OPTIONS | /SELECTIVE_SEARCH |

**LOGOUT**   Terminates an interactive terminal session with VMS.

QUALIFIERS:

| | | |
|---|---|---|
| /BRIEF | /FULL | /HANGUP |

**MACRO  file_spec[,...]**   Invokes the VAX/VMS MACRO ASSEMBLER to assemble MACRO assembly language source programs.

QUALIFIERS:

| /CROSS_REFERENCE | /DEBUG | /DISABLE |
|---|---|---|
| /ENABLE | /LIBRARY | /LIST |
| /OBJECT | /SHOW | /UPDATE |

**MAIL [file_spec] [recipient_name]**  Invokes the personal MAIL utility, which is used to send messages to, and receive messages from, other users of the system.

QUALIFIERS:

| /SUBJECT | /EDIT | /SELF |
|---|---|---|

**MERGE input_file_spec1,input_file_spec2[,...]**
**output_file_spec**  Invokes the SORT utility to combine up to 10 similarly sorted input files. The input files to be merged must be in sorted order before invoking MERGE.

QUALIFIERS:

| /ALLOCATION | /BUCKET_SIZE | /CHECK_SEQUENCE |
|---|---|---|
| /COLLATING_SEQUENCE | /CONTIGUOUS | /DUPLICATES |
| /FORMAT | /INDEXED_SEQUENTIAL | /KEY |
| /OVERLAY | /RELATIVE | /SEQUENTIAL |
| /SPECIFICATION | /STABLE | /STATISTICS |

**MESSAGE  file_spec[,...]**  Invokes the MESSAGE utility to compile message definition files.

QUALIFIERS:

| /FILE_NAME | /LIST | /OBJECT | /SYMBOLS | /TEXT |
|---|---|---|---|---|

**MONITOR [class_name[,...]]**  Invokes the MONITOR utility to monitor various classes of system performance data. Data can be analyzed from a running system or from a previously created recording file.

You can execute a single MONITOR request, or enter MONITOR interactive mode to execute a number of requests. The interactive mode is accessed by entering the MONITOR command with no parameters or qualifiers.

A MONITOR request is terminated by entering <CTRL/C> or <CTRL/Z>. Pressing <CTRL/C> causes MONITOR to enter interactive mode, while <CTRL/Z> returns control to DCL.

PARAMETERS:

| BALL_CLASSES | CLUSTER | DECNET | DISK |
|---|---|---|---|
| DLOCK | FCP | FILE_SYSTEM_CACHE | IO |
| LOCK | MODES | PAGE | POOL |
| PROCESSES | SCS | STATES | SYSTEM |

QUALIFIERS:

| /BEGINNING | /BY_NODE | /COMMENT | /DISPLAY |
|---|---|---|---|
| /ENDING | /FLUSH_INTERVAL | /INPUT | /INTERVAL |
| /NODE | /RECORD | /SUMMARY | /VIEWING_TIME |

CLASS NAME QUALIFIERS:

| /ALL | /AVERAGE | /CPU | /CURRENT |
|---|---|---|---|
| /ITEM | /MAXIMUM | /MINIMUM | /PERCENT |
| /TOPBIO | /TOPCPU | /TOPDIO | /TOPFAULT |

## MOUNT device_name[:][,...] [volume_label[,...]]
[logical_name[:]]   Invokes the MOUNT utility to make a disk or tape volume available for use.

QUALIFIERS:

| /ASSIST | /ACCESSED | /AUTOMATIC |
|---|---|---|
| /BIND | /BLOCKSIZE | /CACHE |
| /CLUSTER | /COMMENT | /CONFIRM |
| /COPY | /DATA_CHECK | /DENSITY |
| /EXTENSION | /FOREIGN | /GROUP |
| /HDR3 | /INITIALIZE | /LABEL |
| /MESSAGE | /MOUNT_VERIFICATION | /OVERRIDE |
| /OWNER_UIC | /PROCESSOR | /PROTECTION |
| /QUOTA | /REBUILD | /RECORDSIZE |
| /SHADOW | /SHARE | /SYSTEM |
| /UNLOAD | /WINDOWS | /WRITE |

## ON condition THEN dcl_command   Defines the DCL command to be executed when a command or program executed within a command procedure encounters an error condition or is interrupted by the user pressing <CTRL/Y>.

## OPEN logical_name[:] file_spec   Opens a file for input/output. The OPEN command assigns a logical name to the file and places the name in the process logical name table.

QUALIFIERS:

| /APPEND | /ERROR | /READ | /SHARE | /WRITE |
|---|---|---|---|---|

## PATCH file_spec   Invokes the PATCH utility to patch an executable image, shareable image, or device driver image.

QUALIFIERS:

| /ABSOLUTE | /JOURNAL | /NEW_VERSION | /OUTPUT |
|---|---|---|---|
| /UPDATE | /VOLUME | | |

## PHONE [phone_command]   Invokes the PHONE utility. PHONE enables you to communicate with other users on your system or any other VMS system connected to your system via DECnet.

QUALIFIERS:
/SCROLL                    /SWITCH_HOOK                    /VIEWPORT_SIZE

## PRINT file_spec[,...]   Queues up one or more files for printing.

QUALIFIERS:

| | | | |
|---|---|---|---|
| /AFTER | /BACKUP | /BEFORE | /BURST |
| /BY_OWNER | /CHARACTERISTICS | /CONFIRM | /COPIES |
| /CREATED | /DELETE | /DEVICE | /EXCLUDE |
| /EXPIRED | /FEED | /FLAG | /FORM |
| /HEADER | /HOLD | /IDENTIFY | /JOB_COUNT |
| /LOWERCASE | /MODIFIED | /NAME | /NOTE |
| /NOTIFY | /OPERATOR | /PAGES | /PARAMETERS |
| /PASSALL | /PRIORITY | /QUEUE | /REMOTE |
| /RESTART | /SETUP | /SINCE | /SPACE |
| /TRAILER | /USER | | |

## PURGE [file_spec[,...]]   Deletes all but the highest versions of the specified files.

QUALIFIERS:

| | | | |
|---|---|---|---|
| /BACKUP | /BEFORE | /BY_OWNER | /CONFIRM |
| /CREATED | /ERASE | /EXCLUDE | /EXPIRED |
| /KEEP | /LOG | /MODIFIED | /SINCE |

## READ logical_name[:] symbol_name   The READ command inputs a single record from the specified input file and assigns the contents of the record to the specified symbol name.

QUALIFIERS:

| | | | | |
|---|---|---|---|---|
| /DELETE | /END_OF_FILE | /ERROR | /INDEX | /KEY |
| /MATCH | /NOLOCK | /PROMPT | /TIME_OUT | |

## RECALL [command_specifier]   Recalls previously entered commands for reprocessing or correcting.

QUALIFIERS:
/ALL                    /ERASE

## RENAME  input_file_spec[,...] output_file_spec   Modifies the file specification in an existing disk file or disk directory.

QUALIFIERS:

| | | | |
|---|---|---|---|
| /BACKUP | /BEFORE | /BY_OWNER | /CONFIRM |
| /CREATED | /EXCLUDE | /EXPIRED | /LOG |
| /MODIFIED | /NEW_VERSION | /SINCE | |

## REPLY ["message"]   Allows a system operator to communicate with system users.

QUALIFIERS:

| | | | |
|---|---|---|---|
| /ABORT | /ALL | /BELL | /BLANK_TAPE |
| /DISABLE | /ENABLE | /INITIALIZE_TAPE | /LOG |
| /NODE | /NOTIFY | /PENDING | /SHUTDOWN |
| /STATUS | /TEMPORARY | /TERMINAL | /TO |
| /URGENT | /USERNAME | /WAIT | |

**REQUEST "message"**   Writes a message on the system operator's terminal, and optionally requests a reply.

QUALIFIERS:

| | |
|---|---|
| /REPLY | /TO |

**RETURN [status_code]**   Terminates a GOSUB statement and returns control to the command following the calling GOSUB command.

**RUN**   Used to perform the following functions:
- Place an image into execution in the process (see Image).
- Create a subprocess or detached process to run a specified image (see Process).

**SEARCH file_spec[,...] search_string[,...]**   Searches one or more files for the specified strings and lists all the lines containing occurrences of the strings.

QUALIFIERS:

| | | | |
|---|---|---|---|
| /EXACT | /EXCLUDE | /FORMAT | /HEADING |
| /LOG | /MATCH | /NUMBERS | /OUTPUT |
| /REMAINING | /STATISTICS | /WINDOW | |

**SET ACCOUNTING**   Enables or disables logging various accounting activities in the system accounting log file SYS$MANAGER:ACCOUNTING.DAT. The SET ACCOUNTING command is also used to close the current accounting log file, and to open a new one with a higher version number.

QUALIFIERS:

| | | |
|---|---|---|
| /DISABLE | /ENABLE | /NEW_FILE |

**SET ACL object_name**   Allows you to modify the access control list of a VMS object.

QUALIFIERS:

| | | | |
|---|---|---|---|
| /ACL | /AFTER | /BEFORE | /BY_OWNER |
| /CONFIRM | /CREATED | /DEFAULT | /DELETE |
| /EDIT | /EXCLUDE | /JOURNAL | /KEEP |
| /LIKE | /LOG | /MODE | /NEW |
| /OBJECT_TYPE | /RECOVER | /REPLACE | /SINCE |

**SET AUDIT**   Enables or disables security auditing.

QUALIFIERS:
| | | | |
|---|---|---|---|
| /ALARM | /DISABLE | /ENABLE | /FAILURE_MODE |

**SET BROADCAST=(class_name[,...])**   Allows you to block out various terminal messages from being broadcast to your terminal.

**SET COMMAND [file_spec[,...]]**   Invokes the COMMAND DEFINITION utility to add, delete, or replace commands in your process command table or a specified command table file.

QUALIFIERS:
| | | | |
|---|---|---|---|
| /DELETE | /LISTING | /OBJECT | /OUTPUT |
| /REPLACE | /TABLE | | |

**SET [NO]CONTROL[=(T,Y)]**   Defines whether or not control will pass to the command line interpreter when <CTRL/Y> is pressed and whether process statistics will be displayed when <CTRL/T> is pressed.

**SET DAY**   Used to reset the default day type specified in the user authorization file for the current day.

QUALIFIERS:
| | | | |
|---|---|---|---|
| /DEFAULT | /LOG | /PRIMARY | /SECONDARY |

**SET DEFAULT device_name:directory_spec**   Changes the default device and/or directory specification. The new default is used with all subsequent file operations that do not explicitly include a device or directory name.

**SET DEVICE device_name[:]**   Establishes a printer or terminal as a spooled device, or sets the error logging status for a device.

QUALIFIERS:
| | | | |
|---|---|---|---|
| /AVAILABLE | /DUAL_PORT | /ERROR_LOGGING | /LOG | /SPOOLED |

**SET DIRECTORY directory_spec[,...]**   Modifies directory characteristics.

QUALIFIERS:
| | | |
|---|---|---|
| /BACKUP | /BEFORE | /BY_OWNER |
| /CONFIRM | /CREATED | /EXCLUDE |
| /EXPIRED | /LOG | /MODIFIED |
| /OWNER_UIC | /SINCE | /VERSION_LIMIT |

**SET DISPLAY** When DECwindows is installed, this command is used to define the display server.

QUALIFIERS:

| | | | |
|---|---|---|---|
| /CREATE | /NODE | /TRANSPORT | /PERMANENT |

**SET FILE file_spec[,...]** Modifies file characteristics.

QUALIFIERS:

| | | |
|---|---|---|
| /BACKUP | /BEFORE | /BY_OWNER |
| /CONFIRM | /CREATED | /DATA_CHECK |
| /END_OF_FILE | /ENTER | /ERASE_ON_DELETE |
| /EXCLUDE | /EXPIRATION_DATE | /EXTENSION |
| /GLOBAL_BUFFER | /LOG | /NODIRECTORY |
| /OWNER_UIC | /PROTECTION | /REMOVE |
| /SINCE | /STATISTICS | /UNLOCK |
| /TRUNCATE | /VERSION_LIMIT | |

**SET HOST node_name** Connects your terminal to another processor in a DECnet network or to an asynchronous terminal port.

QUALIFIERS:

| | | | |
|---|---|---|---|
| /LOG | /DTE | /DUP | /HSC |

**SET KEY** Changes the current key definition state. Keys are defined by the DEFINE/KEY command.

QUALIFIERS:

| | |
|---|---|
| /LOG | /STATE |

**SET LOGINS** Defines the number of users who may gain access to the system. This command also displays the current interactive level.

QUALIFIER:

/INTERACTIVE

**SET MAGTAPE device_name[:]** Defines default characteristics to be associated with a magnetic tape device for subsequent file operations.

QUALIFIERS:

| | | |
|---|---|---|
| /DENSITY | /END_OF_FILE | /LOG |
| /LOGSOFT | /REWIND | /SKIP |
| /UNLOAD | | |

**SET MESSAGE [file_spec]** Allows you to specify the format of messages, or to override or supplement system messages.

QUALIFIERS:

| | | | | |
|---|---|---|---|---|
| /DELETE | /FACILITY | /IDENTIFICATION | /SEVERITY | /TEXT |

**SET [NO]ON**   Controls command interpreter error checking. If SET NOON is in effect, the command interpreter will ignore errors in a command procedure and continue processing.

**SET OUTPUT_RATE[=delta_time]**   Defines the rate at which output will be written to a batch job log file.

**SET PASSWORD**   Permits users to change their password to a VMS account.

QUALIFIERS:
| | | |
|---|---|---|
| /GENERATE | /SECONDARY | /SYSTEM |

**SET PRINTER printer_name[:]**   Defines characteristics for line printer.

QUALIFIERS:
| | | | |
|---|---|---|---|
| /CR | /FALLBACK | /FF | /LA11 |
| /LA180 | /LOWERCASE | /LOG | /LP11 |
| /PAGE | /PASSALL | /PRINTALL | /TAB |
| /TRUNCATE | /UNKNOWN | /UPPERCASE | /WIDTH |
| /WRAP | | | |

**SET PROCESS [process_name]**   Modifies execution characteristics associated with the named process for the current login session. If a process is not specified, changes are made to the current process.

QUALIFIERS:
| | | |
|---|---|---|
| /CPU | /DUMP | /IDENTIFICATION |
| /NAME | /PRIORITY | /PRIVILEGES |
| /RESOURCE_WAIT | /RESUME | /SUSPEND |
| /SWAPPING | | |

**SET PROMPT[=string]**   Defines a new DCL prompt for your process. The default prompt is a dollar sign ($).

QUALIFIER:
/CARRIAGE_CONTROL

**SET PROTECTION[=(code)] file_spec[,...]**   Modifies the protection applied to a particular file or to a group of files. The protection of a file limits the access available to various groups of system users.

When used without a file specification, it establishes the default protection for all the files subsequently created during the login session.

It also may be used to modify the protection of a nonfile-oriented device.

QUALIFIERS:

| /CONFIRM | /LOG | /PROTECTION | /DEFAULT | /DEVICE |

**SET QUEUE queue_name**   Used to modify the current status or attributes of a queue, or to change the current status or attributes of a job that is not currently executing in a queue.

QUALIFIERS:

| /BASE_PRIORITY | /BLOCK_LIMIT | /CHARACTERISTICS |
|---|---|---|
| /CPUDEFAULT | /CPUMAXIMUM | /DEFAULT |
| /DISABLE_SWAPPING | /ENABLE_GENERIC | /ENTRY/ |
| FORM_MOUNTED | /JOB_LIMIT | /OWNER_UIC |
| /PROTECTION | /RECORD_BLOCKING | /RETAIN |
| /SCHEDULE | /SEPARATE | /WSDEFAULT |
| /WSEXTENT | /WSQUOTA | |

**SET RESTART_VALUE=string**   Defines a test value for restarting portions of batch job after a system failure.

**SET RIGHTS_LIST id_name[,...]**   Allows you to modify the process or system rights list.

QUALIFIERS:

| /ATTRIBUTES | /DISABLE | /ENABLE |
|---|---|---|
| /IDENTIFICATION | /PROCESS | /SYSTEM |

**SET RMS_DEFAULT**   Used to set default values for the multiblock and multibuffer counts, network transfer sizes, prologue level, and extend quantity used by Record Management Services for various file operations.

QUALIFIERS:

| /BLOCK_COUNT | /BUFFER_COUNT | /DISK |
|---|---|---|
| /EXTEND_QUANTITY | /INDEXED | /MAGTAPE |
| /NETWORK_BLOCK_COUNT | /PROLOG | /RELATIVE |
| /SEQUENTIAL | /SYSTEM | /UNIT_RECORD |

**SET SYMBOL**   Controls access to local and global symbols within command procedures.

QUALIFIER:

| /SCOPE |

**SET TERMINAL [device_name[:]]**   Modifies interpretation of various terminal characteristics.

QUALIFIERS:

| | | |
|---|---|---|
| /ADVANCED_VIDEO | /ALTYPEAHD | /ANSI_CRT |
| /APPLICATION_KEYPAD | /AUTOBAUD | /BLOCK_MODE |
| /BRDCSTMBX | /BROADCAST | /CRFILL |
| /DEC_CRT | /DEVICE_TYPE | /DIALUP |
| /DISCONNECT | /DISMISS | /DMA |
| /ECHO | /EDIT_MODE | /EIGHT_BIT |
| /ESCAPE | /FALLBACK | /FRAME |
| /FORM | /FULLDUP | /HALFDUP |
| /HANGUP | /HARDCOPY | /HOSTSYNC |
| /INQUIRE | /INSERT | /LFFILL |
| /LINE_EDITING | /LOCAL_ECHO | /LOWERCASE |
| /MANUAL | /MODEM | /NUMERIC_KEYPAD |
| /OVERSTRIKE | /PAGE | /PARITY |
| /PASTHRU | /PERMANENT | /PRINTER_PORT |
| /PROTOCOL | /READSYNC | /REGIS |
| /SCOPE | /SET_SPEED | /SECURE_SERVER |
| /SIXEL_GRAPHICS | /SOFT_CHARACTERS | /SPEED |
| /SWITCH | /SYSPASSWORD | /TAB |
| /TTSYNC | /TYPE_AHEAD | /UNKNOWN |
| /UPPERCASE | /WIDTH | /WRAP |

**SET TIME[=time]**   Resets the system time to be used with all time-dependent activities in the VMS operating system.

**SET UIC uic**   Establishes a new default user identification code (UIC).

**SET [NO]VERIFY [=([NO]PROCEDURE, [NO]IMAGE)]**
Controls whether command and data lines, in a command procedure, are displayed as they are processed.

**SET VOLUME device_spec[:][,...]**   Modifies the characteristics of a mounted Files-11 volume.

QUALIFIERS:

| | | |
|---|---|---|
| /ACCESSED | /DATA_CHECK | /ERASE_ON_DELETE |
| /EXTENSION | /FILE_PROTECTION | /HIGHWATER_MARKING |
| /LABEL | /LOG | /MOUNT_VERIFICATION |
| /OWNER_UIC | /PROTECTION | /REBUILD |
| /RETENTION | /UNLOAD | /USER_NAME |
| /WINDOWS | | |

**SET WORKING_SET**   Sets the default working set size for the current process, or sets an upper limit to which the working set size can be changed by an image that the process executes.

QUALIFIERS:

| | | | | |
|---|---|---|---|---|
| /ADJUST | /EXTENT | /LIMIT | /LOG | /QUOTA |

**SHOW ACCOUNTING**   Displays items for which accounting is enabled.

QUALIFIER:
/OUTPUT

**SHOW ACL**   Permits you to display the access control list (ACL) of a VMS object.

QUALIFIER:
/OBJECT_TYPE

**SHOW AUDIT**   Supplies a display that identifies enable security auditing  features and the events that they will report.

QUALIFIER:
/OUTPUT

**SHOW BROADCAST**   Displays message classes that are currently being affected by the SET BROADCAST command.

QUALIFIER:
/OUTPUT

**SHOW DEFAULT**   Displays the current default device and directory specification, along with any equivalence strings that have been defined.

**SHOW DEVICES [device_name[:]]**   Displays the status of a device on the running VMS system.

QUALIFIERS:
| | | |
|---|---|---|
| /ALLOCATED | /BRIEF | /FILES |
| /FULL | /MOUNTED | /OUTPUT |
| /SYSTEM | /WINDOWS | /SERVED |

**SHOW ENTRY [entry_number,...]**   Displays information about a user's batch or print jobs.

QUALIFIERS:
| | | |
|---|---|---|
| /BATCH | /BRIEF | /BY_JOB_STATUS |
| /DEVICE | /FILES | /FULL |
| /GENERIC | /OUTPUT | /USER_NAME |

**SHOW ERROR**   Displays an error count for all devices with an error count greater than 0.

QUALIFIERS:
| | |
|---|---|
| /FULL | /OUTPUT |

**SHOW KEY [key_name]**   Displays the key definition for the specified key.

QUALIFIERS:
/ALL          /BRIEF          /DIRECTORY          /FULL          /STATE

**SHOW LOGICAL [logical_name[:],[...]]**   Displays logical names from one or more logical name tables, or displays the equivalence strings assigned to the specified logical names.

QUALIFIERS:
| | | |
|---|---|---|
| /ACCESS_MODE | /ALL | /DESCENDANTS |
| /FULL | /GROUP | /JOB |
| /OUTPUT | /PROCESS | /STRUCTURE / |
| SYSTEM | /TABLE | |

**SHOW MAGTAPE device_name[:]**   Displays the characteristics and status of a specified magnetic tape device.

QUALIFIER:
/OUTPUT

**SHOW MEMORY**   Displays availability and use of memory related resources.

QUALIFIERS:
| | | |
|---|---|---|
| /ALL | /FILES | /FULL |
| /OUTPUT | /PHYSICAL_PAGES | /POOL |
| /SLOTS | | |

**SHOW NETWORK**   Displays node information about the DECnet network of which your host processor is a member.

QUALIFIER:
/OUTPUT

**SHOW PRINTER device_name[:]**   Displays characteristics defined for a system printer.

QUALIFIER:
/OUTPUT

**SHOW PROCESS [process_name]**   Displays information about a process and any of its subprocesses.

QUALIFIERS:
| | | |
|---|---|---|
| /ACCOUNTING | /ALL | /CONTINUOUS |
| /IDENTIFICATION | /MEMORY | /OUTPUT |
| /PRIVILEGES | /QUOTAS | /SUBPROCESSES |

**SHOW PROTECTION** Displays the file protection that will be applied to all new files created during the current login session.

**SHOW QUEUE [queue_name]** Displays information about queues and the jobs currently in queue.

QUALIFIERS:

| | | |
|---|---|---|
| /ALL | /ALL_JOBS | /BATCH |
| /BRIEF | /BY_JOB_STATUS | /DEVICE |
| /GENERIC | /FILES | /FULL |
| /FORM | /SUMMARY | /OUTPUT |
| /CHARACTERISTICS | | |

**SHOW QUOTA** Displays the disk quota that is currently authorized for a specific user on a specific disk.

QUALIFIERS:

| | |
|---|---|
| /DISK | /USER |

**SHOW RMS_DEFAULT** Displays the default multiblock count, multibuffer count, network transfer size, prologue level, and extend quantity that Record Management Services will use for file operations.

QUALIFIER:
/OUTPUT

**SHOW STATUS** Displays status information for the current process.

**SHOW SYMBOL [symbol_name]** Displays the value of a local or global symbol.

QUALIFIERS:

| | | | |
|---|---|---|---|
| /ALL | /GLOBAL | /LOCAL | /LOG |

**SHOW SYSTEM** Displays a list of processes currently running on the system.

QUALIFIERS:

| | | |
|---|---|---|
| /BATCH | /FULL | /NETWORK |
| /OUTPUT | /PROCESS | /SUBPROCESS |

**SHOW TERMINAL [device_name[:]]** Displays the characteristics of a specified terminal.

QUALIFIERS:

| | |
|---|---|
| /OUTPUT | /PERMANENT |

**SHOW TIME** Displays the current system date and time.

**SHOW TRANSLATION logical_name** Searches logical name
tables for a specified logical name, then returns the first
equivalence name of the match found.
QUALIFIER:
/TABLE

**SHOW USERS [username]** Displays a list of users currently
using the system, their terminal names, usernames, and their
process identification codes.
QUALIFIER:
/OUTPUT

**SHOW WORKING_SET** Displays the current working set
limit, quota, and extent assigned to the current process.
QUALIFIER:
/OUTPUT

**SORT input_file_spec[,...] output_file_spec** Invokes the SORT
utility to reorder records in a file into a defined sequence.
QUALIFIERS:
| | | |
|---|---|---|
| /COLLATING_SEQUENCE | /DUPLICATES | /KEY |
| /PROCESS | /SPECIFICATION | /STABLE |
| /STATISTICS | /WORK_FILES | /FORMAT |

OUTPUT FILE QUALIFIERS:
| | | |
|---|---|---|
| /ALLOCATION | /BUCKET_SIZE | /CONTIGUOUS |
| /FORMAT | /INDEXED_SEQUENTIAL | /OVERLAY |
| /RELATIVE | /SEQUENTIAL | |

**SPAWN [command_string]** Creates a subprocess to the current
process.
QUALIFIERS:
| | | |
|---|---|---|
| /CARRIAGE_CONTROL | /CLI | /INPUT |
| /KEYPAD | /LOG | /LOGICAL_NAMES |
| /NOTIFY | /OUTPUT | /PROCESS |
| /PROMPT | /SYMBOLS | /TABLE |
| /WAIT | | |

**START/QUEUE queue_name** Starts or restarts the specified
queue.

**STOP process_name** Specifies the name of a process to be
deleted from the system. If the /IDENTIFICATION qualifier is used,
the process name is ignored.

QUALIFIER:
/IDENTIFICATION

## STOP/QUEUE queue_name[:]   The STOP/QUEUE command
causes the specified queue to pause.

QUALIFIERS:
| /ABORT | /ENTRY | /MANAGER |
| /NEXT | /REQUEUE | /RESET |

## SUBMIT file_spec[,...]   Enters command procedures into a batch
queue.

QUALIFIERS:
| /AFTER | /BACKUP | /BEFORE | /BY_OWNER |
| /CHARACTERISTICS | /CLI | /CONFIRM | /CPUTIME |
| /CREATED | /DELETE | /EXCLUDE | /EXPIRED |
| /HOLD | /IDENTIFY | /KEEP | /LOG_FILE |
| /MODIFIED | /NAME | /NOTIFY | /PARAMETERS |
| /PRINTER | /PRIORITY | /QUEUE | /REMOTE |
| /RESTART | /SINCE | /USER | /WSDEFAULT |
| /WSEXTENT | /WSQUOTA | | |

## SYNCHRONIZE [job_name]   Places the process issuing the
command into a wait state until the specified job completes
execution.

QUALIFIERS:
| /ENTRY | /QUEUE |

## TYPE file_spec[,...]   Displays the contents of a file or group of
files on the current output device (normally your terminal screen).

QUALIFIERS:
| /BACKUP | /BEFORE | /BY_OWNER |
| /CONFIRM | /CREATED | /EXCLUDE |
| /EXPIRED | /MODIFIED | /OUTPUT |
| /PAGE | /SINCE | |

## UNLOCK file_spec[,...]   Makes accessible a file that was made
inaccessible by being improperly closed.

QUALIFIERS:
| /CONFIRM | /LOG |

## WAIT delta_time   Places the current process in a wait state until
a specified period of time has passed.

## WRITE logical_name expression[,...]   Writes the specified data
record to the output file indicated by the logical name.

QUALIFIERS:
| /ERROR | /SYMBOL | /UPDATE |

# Lexical Functions

The following are VMS lexical functions and a brief description of each. Parameters for the lexicals are listed after the function name. Parentheses are required whether or not the lexical function requires parameters.

### F$CVSI(bit_position,width,string)
Used to extract bit fields from a character string. The result is converted to a signed integer value.

**Example:**
```
$ B[0,8] = %X42
$ SHOW SYMBOL B
B = "B"
$ XYZ = F$CVSI(0,4,B)
$ SHOW SYMBOL X
X = 2   Hex = 0000002  Octal = 00000000002
```

### F$CVTIME(input_time,output_time,field)
Converts absolute or combination time to the format "yyyy-mm-dd hh:mm:ss.cc". The F$CVTIME function can also be used to return information about an absolute, combination, or delta time string.

**Example:**
```
$ DATE = F$TIME()
$ SHOW SYMBOL DATE
DATE = "14-APR-1989 08:36:13.11"
$ DATE = F$CVTIME(DATE)
$ SHOW SYMBOL DATE
DATE = "1989-04-13 08:36:13.11"
```

```
$ DAY = F$CVTIME(F$TIME(),,"WEEKDAY")
$ SHOW SYMBOL DAY
NEXT = "Friday"
```

### F$CVUI(bit_position,width,string)

Extracts bit fields from a character string and converts the result to an unsigned integer value.

**Example:**
```
$ X[0,32] = %X2B
$ SHOW SYMBOL X
X = "+"
$ Y = F$CVUI(0,4,X)
$ SHOW SYMBOL Y
X = 11   Hex = 0000000B  Octal = 000013
```

### F$DIRECTORY()

Returns the default directory name as a character string. The F$DIRECTORY function has no arguments.

**Example:**
```
$ SAVE_DIR = F$DIRECTORY()
$ SET DEFAULT SYS$SYSTEM
$ DEFINE/USER_MODE SYS$INPUT SYS$COMMAND
$ RUN AUTHORIZE
   .
   .
   .
$ SET DEFAULT 'SAVE_DIR'
```

### F$EDIT(string,edit_list)

Used to edit a character string based on the parameters specified in the edit_list.

**Edit_list:**

| COLLAPSE | COMPRESS | LOWERCASE |
|----------|-----------|-----------|
| TRIM | UNCOMMENT | UPCASE |

**Example:**
```
$ STRING = " this string has        tabs      in      it "
$ SHOW SYMBOL STRING
STRING = "this string has        tabs      in      it "
$ STRING = F$EDIT(STRING, "COMPRESS, TRIM, UPCASE")
$ SHOW SYMBOL STRING
STRING = "THIS STRING HAS TABS IN IT"
```

### F$ELEMENT(element_number,delimiter,string)

Extracts an element from a character string in which the elements are separated by some specified delimiter.

**Example:**
```
$ MNTH = "JAN,FEB,MAR,APR,MAY,JUN,JUL,AUG,SEP,OCT,NOV,DEC"
$ INQUIRE MONTH "Enter the month (MMM): "
$ CNT = 0
```

```
$VERIFY_MONTH_LOOP:
$ MONTH_LABEL = F$ELEMENT(CNT,",",DAY_LIST)
$ IF MONTH_LABEL .EQS. "," THEN GOTO ERROR
$ IF MONTH .EQS. MONTH_LABEL THEN GOTO 'MONTH_LABEL'
$ CNT = CNT +1
$ GOTO VERIFY_MONTH_LOOP
$
$JAN:
  .
  .
  .
$FEB:
  .
  .
```

## F$ENVIRONMENT(item)

Returns information about the DCL command environment.

**Items:**

| | | |
|---|---|---|
| CAPTIVE | CONTROL | DEFAULT |
| DEPTH | INTERACTIVE | KEY_STATE |
| MAX_DEPTH | MESSAGE | NOCONTROL |
| ON_CONTROL_Y | ON_SEVERITY | OUTPUT_RATE |
| PROCEDURE | PROMPT | PROMPT_CONTROL |
| PROTECTION | SYMBOL_SCOPE | VERIFY_IMAGE |
| VERIFY_PROCEDURE | | |

**Example:**
```
$ SAVE_MESS = F$ENVIRONMENT("MESSAGE")
$ SET MESSAGE/NOFACILITY/NOIDENT/NOTEXT/NOSEVERITY
  .
  .
  .
$ SET MESSAGE'SAVE_MESSAGE'
$ SAVE_PROT = F$ENVIRONMENT("PROTECTION")
$ SET PROTECTION=(S:RWED,O:RWED,G,W)/DEFAULT
  .
  .
  .
$ SET PROTECTION=('SAVE_PROT')/DEFAULT
```

## F$EXTRACT(offset,length,string)

Extracts a substring from a given character string.

**Example:**
```
$ DATE = F$EXREACT(0,11,F$TIME())
$ WRITE SYS$OUTPUT "Today is ''DATE'"
Today is 14-APR-1989
```

## F$FAO(control_string[,arg1,arg2...arg15])

Calls the $FAO system service to convert a specified control string to formatted ASCII. This function may be used to:

- Insert variable character string data into an output string.
- Convert integer values to ASCII and substitute the result into the output string.

**Example:**
```
$ A = " DIE"
$ B = " AND"
$ C = " PAY"
$ D = " TAXES"
$ PHRASE = F$FAO("ALL I HAVE TO DO IS !4(AS)",A,B,C,D)
$ SHOW SYMBOL PHRASE
$ PHRASE = "ALL I HAVE TO DO IS DIE AND PAY TAXES"
```

## F$FILE_ATTRIBUTES(file_spec,item)

Returns attribute information for the specified file.

**Items:**

| | | | | | | | | | | |
|---|---|---|---|---|---|---|---|---|---|---|
| ALQ | BDT | BKS | BLS | CBT | CDT | CTG | DEQ | DID | DVI | EDT |
| EOF | FID | FSZ | GRP | KNOWN | MBM | MRN | MRS | NOA | NOK | ORG |
| PRO | PVN | RAT | RCK | RDT | RFM | RVN | UIC | WCK | | |

**Example:**
```
$ ORGANIZATION = F$FILE_ATTRIBUTES("SYSUAF.DAT","ORG")
$ SHOW SYMBOL ORGANIZATION
ORGANIZATION = "IDX"
```

## F$GETDVI(device,item)

Calls the $GETDVI system service to return an item of information on a specified device. This function allows a process to obtain information for a device to which the process has not necessarily allocated or assigned a channel.

**Items:**

| | | |
|---|---|---|
| ACPPID | ACPTYPE | ALL |
| ALLOCLASS | ALT_HOST_AVAIL | ALT_HOST_NAME |
| ALT_HOST_TYPE | AVL | CCL |
| CLUSTER | CONCEALED | CYLINDERS |
| DEVBUFSIZ | DEVCHAR | DEVCHAR2 |
| DEVCLASS | DEVDEPEND | DEVDEPEND2 |
| DEVNAM | DEVSTS | DEVTYPE |
| DIR | DMT | DUA |
| ELG | ERRCNT | EXISTS |
| FOD | FOR | FREEBLOCKS |
| FULLDEVNAM | GEN | HOST_AVAIL |
| HOST_COUNT | HOST_NAME | HOST_TYPE |
| IDV | LOCKID | LOGVOLNAM |
| MAXBLOCK | MAXFILES | MBX |
| MNT | MOUNTCNTNET | NEXTDEVNAM |
| ODV | OPCNT | OPR |
| OWNUIC | PID | RCK |
| RCT | REC | RECSIZ |
| REFCNT | REMOTE_DEVICE | RND |
| ROOTDEVNAM | RTM | SDI |
| SECTORS | SERIALNUM | SERVED_DEVICESHR |
| SPL | SPLDEVNAM | SQD |
| STS | SWL | TRACKS |
| TRANSCNT | TRM | TT_ALTYPEAHD |
| TT_ANSICRT | TT_APP_KEYPAD | TT_AUTOBAUD |
| TT_AVO | TT_BLOCK | TT_BRDCSTMBX |
| TT_CRFILL | TT_DECCRT | TT_DIALUP |

| TT_DISCONNECT | TT_DMA | TT_DRCS |
|---|---|---|
| TT_EDIT | TT_EDITING | TT_EIGHTBIT |
| TT_ESCAPE | TT_FALLBACK | TT_HALFDUP |
| TT_HANGUP | TT_HOSTSYNC | TT_INSERT |
| TT_LFFILL | TT_LOCALECHO | TT_LOWER |
| TT_MBXDSABL | TT_MECHFORM | TT_MECHTAB |
| TT_MODEM | TT_MODHANGUP | TT_NOBRDCST |
| TT_NOECHO | TT_NOTYPEAHD | TT_OPER |
| TT_PAGE | TT_PASTHRU | TT_PHYDEVNAM |
| TT_PRINTER | TT_READSYNC | TT_REGIS |
| TT_REMOTE | TT_SCOPE | TT_SECURE |
| TT_SETSPEED | TT_SIXEL | TT_TTSYNC |
| TT_WRAP | UNIT | VOLCOUNT |
| VOLNAM | VPROT | WCK |

Volume Shadowing items:
SHDW_CATCHUP_COPYING
SHDW_FAILED_MEMBER
SHDW_MASTER
SHDW_MASTER_NAME
SHDW_MEMBER
SHDW_MERGE_COPYING
SHDW_NEXT_MBR_NAME

Example:
```
$ INQUIRE DISK "Disk name"
$ DISK = DISK - ":"
$ ON WARNING THEN STOP
$ TRA = F$GETDVI(DISK,"TRACKS")
$ SEC = F$GETDVI(DISK,"SECTORS")
$ CYL = F$GETDVI(DISK,"CYLINDERS")
$ BLK = F$GETDVI(DISK,"MAXBLOCK")
$ WRITE SYS$OUTPUT "Disk ''DISK': has:"
$ WRITE SYS$OUTPUT "'TRA' tracks,"
$ WRITE SYS$OUTPUT " ''SEC' sectors per track, and"
$ WRITE SYS$OUTPUT " ''CYL' cylinders,"
$ WRITE SYS$OUTPUT " for a total of ''BLK' blocks."
```

## F$GETJPI(pid,item)

Calls the $GETJPI system service to return accounting, status, and identification information on a specified process.

Items:

| ACCOUNT | APTCNT | ASTACT | ASTCNT |
|---|---|---|---|
| ASTEN | ASTLM | AUTHPRI | AUTHPRIV |
| BIOCNT | BIOLM | BUFIO | BYTCNT |
| BYTLM | CPULIM | CPUTIM | CURPRIV |
| DFPFC | DFWSCNT | DIOCNT | DIOLM |
| DIRIO | EFCS | EFCU | EFWM |
| ENQCNT | ENQLM | EXCVEC | FILCNT |
| FILLM | FINALEXC | FREP0VA | FREP1VA |
| FREPTECNT | GPGCNT | GRP | IMAGECOUNT |
| IMAGNAME | IMAGPRIV | INQUAN | JOBPRCCNT |
| LOGIN | LOGINTIM | MEM | MODE |
| MSGMASK | MASTER_PID | OWNER | PAGEFLTS |
| PAGFILCNT | PAGFILLOC | PGFLQUOTA | PHDFLAGS |
| PID | PPGCNT | PRCCNT | PRCLM |
| PRCNAM | PRI | PRIB | PROCPRIV |

| | | | |
|---|---|---|---|
| SITESPEC | STATE | STS | SWPFILLOC |
| TERMINAL | TMBU | TQCNT | TQLM |
| UIC | USERNAME | VIRTPEAK | VOLUMES |
| WSAUTH | WSAUTHEXT | WSEXTENT | WSPEAK |
| WSQUOTA | WSSIZE | | |

**Example:**
```
$ WRITE SYS$OUTPUT F$GETJPI(20,"PRCNAM")
NULL
$ WRITE SYS$OUTPUT F$GETJPI(20,"AUTHPRI")
0
```

## F$GETQUI(function,[item],[object_id],[flags])

Invokes the $GETQUI system service to return information about
queues and jobs.

**Example:**
```
$ SIZE = F$GETQUI("DISPLAY_ENTRY", "JOB_SIZE", 124)
$ SHOW SYMBOL SIZE
64
$ IF F$GETQUI("DISPLAY_QUEUE", "QUEUE_STOPPED", "SYS$BATCH") -
  THEN WRITE SYS$OUTPUT "SYS$BATCH IS STOPPED!"
```

## F$GETSYI(item [,node])

Calls the $GETSYI system service to return status and identification
information about the running system or about a node in the
VAXcluster, if your system is a VAXcluster.

**Items:**

| | |
|---|---|
| ARCHFLAG | BOOTTIME |
| CHARACTER_EMULATED | CPU |
| DECIMAL_EMULATED | D_FLOAT_EMULATED |
| F_FLOAT_EMULATED | G_FLOAT_EMULATED |
| PAGEFILE_FREE | PAGEFILE_PAGE |
| SID | SWAPFILE_FREE |
| SWAPFILE_PAGE | VERSION |

**VAXcluster items:**

| | | |
|---|---|---|
| ACTIVECPU_CNT | AVAILCPU_CNT | ERRORLOGBUFFERS |
| CLUSTER_FSYSID | CLUSTER_FTIME | CLUSTER_MEMBER |
| CLUSTER_NODES | CLUSTER_QUORUM | CLUSTER_VOTES |
| NODENAME | NODE_AREA | NODE_CSID |
| NODE_HWTYPE | NODE_HWVERS | NODE_NUMBER |
| NODE_QUORUM | NODE_SWINCARN | NODE_SWTYPE |
| NODE_SWVERS | NODE_SYSTEMID | NODE_VOTES |
| SCS_EXISTS | | |

**Example:**
```
$ WRITE SYS$OUTPUT F$GETSYI ("NODENAME")
BIFF
$ WRITE SYS$OUTPUT F$GETSYI ("SID")
134217778
```

### F$IDENTIFIER(identifier,conversion_type)

Converts an identifier to its integer equivalent, or vice versa. An identifier is a name or number that identifies a category of users of a data resource. The system uses identifiers to determine user access to a system resource.

**Example:**
```
$ UIC = F$IDENTIFIER("BYNON","NAME_TO_NUMBER")
$ SHOW SYMBOL UIC
UIC = 4194305  Hex = 00400001  Octal = 0002000000001
$ MY_UIC = F$FAO("!%U",UIC)
$ SHOW SYMBOL MY_UIC
MY_UIC = [100,001]
```

### F$INTEGER(expression)

Returns the integer value of the result of the specified expression.

**Example:**
```
$ X = "99"
$ Y = F$INTEGER(X - "-1")
$ SHOW SYMBOL Y
Y = 199 Hex=000000C7 Octal=00000000307
```

### F$LENGTH(string)

Returns the length of a specified character string.
```
Example:
WRITE SYS$OUTPUT F$LENGTH("123")
3
```

### F$LOCATE(substring,string)

Locates a character or character substring within a string and returns its offset within the string. If the character or character substring is not found, the function returns the length of the string that was searched.

**Example:**
```
WRITE SYS$OUTPUT F$LOCATE("3","123")
2
```

### F$MESSAGE(status_code)

Returns a character string containing the message associated with a system status code.

**Example:**
```
$ ERROR = F$MESSAGE(%X2A)
$ SHOW SYMBOL ERROR
ERROR = "%SYSTEM-E-ABORT, Abort"
```

## F$MODE()

Returns a character string displaying the mode in which a process is executing. The F$MODE function has no arguments.

**Example:**
```
$ IF F$MODE() .EQS. "NETWORK" THEN EXIT
```

## F$PARSE(file_spec[,related_spec][,field][,parse_type])

Calls the $PARSE record management service to parse a file specification and return either its expanded file specification or a particular file specification field that you have specified.

**Example:**
```
$ FILE = F$PARSE("SYSTARTUP_V5.COM",,,,"SYNTAX_ONLY")
$ SHOW SYMBOL FILE
FILE = "SYS$SYSROOT:[SYSMGR]SYSTARTUP_V5.COM;5
```

## F$PID(context_symbol)

This function returns a process identification number (PID), and updates the context symbol to point to the current position in the system's process list.

**Example:**
```
$ CONTEXT = ""
$PID_LOOP:
$ PID = F$PID(CONTEXT)
$ IF PID .EQS. ""
$  THEN
$    EXIT
$  ELSE
$    WRITE SYS$OUTPUT PID
$    GOTO LOOP
$ ENDIF
```

## F$PRIVILEGE(priv_states)

Returns a value of true or false depending on whether your current process privileges match the privileges listed in the parameter argument.

**Example:**
```
$ BYPASS = F$PRIVILEGE("BYPASS")
$ SHOW SYMBOL BYPASS
BYPASS = "FALSE"
```

## F$PROCESS()

Obtains the current process name as a character string. The F$PROCESS function requires no arguments.

**Example:**
$ WRITE SYS$OUTPUT F$PROCESS()
SHIPMAN

## F$SEARCH(file_spec[,stream_id])

Calls the $SEARCH record management service to search a directory and return the full file specification for a specified file.

**Example:**
$SEARCH_LOOP:
$ FILE = F$SEARCH("SYS$MANAGER:*.COM")
$ IF FILE .EQS. ""
$   THEN
$     EXIT
$   ELSE
$     WRITE SYS$OUTPUT FILE
$     GOTO SEARCH_LOOP
$ ENDIF

## F$SETPRV(priv_states)

Returns a list of keywords indicating current user privileges. In addition, this function may be used to call the $SETPRV system service to enable or disable specified user privileges. The return string indicates the status of the user privileges before any changes have been made with the F$SETPRV function.

**Example:**
$ PRIV = F$SETPRV("NETMBX,TMPMBX,SYSPRV")
$ SHOW SYMBOL PRIV
PRIV = "NETMBX,TMPMBX,NOSYSPRV")

## F$STRING(expression)

Returns the character string equivalent of the result of the specified expression.

**Example:**
$ TEN = 10
$ TWENTY = F$STRING(10 + TEN)
$ SHOW SYMBOL TWENTY
TWENTY = "20"

## F$TIME()

Returns the current date and time string. The F$TIME function has no arguments.

**Example:**
$ WRITE SYS$OUTPUT F$TIME()
14-APR-1989 10:57:49.10

### F$TRNLNM(logical_name [,table] [,index] [,mode] [,case] [,item])

Translates a logical name to its equivalence name string, or returns the requested attributes of the logical name. The equivalence string is not checked to determine if it is a logical name or not.

**Items:**

| | | |
|---|---|---|
| ACCESS_MODE | CONCEALED | CONFINE |
| CRELOG | LENGTH | MAX_INDEX |
| NO_ALIAS | TABLE | TABLE_NAME |
| TERMINAL | VALUE | |

**Example:**
```
$ OLD_DIR = F$TRNLNM("USER$DISK")+F$DIRECTORY()
  .
  .
  .
$ SET DEFAULT 'OLD_DIR'
```

### F$TYPE(symbol_name)

### Returns the data type of a symbol.

**Example:**
```
$ X=1
$ WRITE SYS$OUTPUT F$TYPE(X)
INTEGER
$ X="HELLO"
$ WRITE SYS$OUTPUT F$TYPE(X)
STRING
```

### F$USER()

Returns the user identification code (UIC), in named format, for the current user. The F$USER function has no arguments.

**Example:**
```
$ WRITE SYS$OUTPUT F$USER()
[BYNON]
```

### F$VERIFY([procedure_value] [,image_value])

Returns an integer value which indicates whether procedure verification mode is currently on or off. If used with arguments, the F$VERIFY function can turn verification mode on or off. You must include the parentheses after the F$VERIFY function, whether or not you specify arguments.

**Example:**
```
$ VERIFY = F$VERIFY(0)
  .
  .
  .
$ IF VERIFY .EQ. 1 THEN SET VERIFY
```

# DCL Operators

The following table lists the logical expression operators that can be used in DCL statements.

## DCL Operators

| Operator | Evaluation Precedence | Description |
|----------|-----------------------|-------------|
| + | 1 | Indicates a positive number. |
| - | 1 | Indicates a negative number. |
| / | 2 | Divides two numbers. |
| * | 2 | Multiplies two numbers. |
| + | 3 | Adds two numbers or concatenates two character strings. |
| - | 3 | Subtracts two numbers or character strings. |
| .EQS. | 4 | Tests two character strings for equality. |
| .GES. | 4 | Tests for first string being greater than or equal to the second. |
| .GTS. | 4 | Tests for the first character string being greater than the second. |
| .LES. | 4 | Tests the first character for being less than or equal to the second. |
| .LTS. | 4 | Tests the first character string for being less than the second. |

## DCL Operators (cont'd.)

| Operator | Evaluation Precedence | Description |
|----------|-----------------------|-------------|
| .NES. | 4 | Tests two character strings for being not equal. |
| .EQ. | 4 | Tests two numbers for equality. |
| .GE. | 4 | Tests the first number for being greater than or equal to the second. |
| .GT. | 4 | Tests the first number for being greater than the second number. |
| .LE. | 4 | Tests the first number for being less than or equal to the second number. |
| .LT. | 4 | Tests the first number for being less than the second. |
| .NE. | 4 | Tests two numbers for not being equal. |
| .NOT. | 5 | Logically negates a value. |
| .AND. | 6 | Logically ANDs two numbers. |
| .OR. | 7 | Logically ORs two numbers. |

# VT Terminal Function Keys, Control Keys, and Escape Sequences

## Terminal Function and Control Keys

| Key | Function Performed |
| --- | --- |
| <RETURN> | Inputs data or a command string typed at the terminal to the computer. All commands and data that you type at the terminal must be followed by <RETURN> or the computer will never see the information. |
| <DELETE> | Rubs out errors as you are typing a command. If you hold the <DELETE> key down, it will continue to erase characters on the current line from right to left. |
| <TAB> | Moves the cursor to the next tab stop position. If pressed while in an editing session, this key will move the text element before the cursor to the next tab stop. |

# Terminal Function and Control Keys (cont'd.)

| Key | Function Performed |
| --- | --- |
| <HOLD SCREEN> | Toggles output to the display ON/OFF. It provides the same functionality as the <CTRL/S> and <CTRL/Q> keys. |
| <CTRL/A> | Allows you to insert, rather than overstrike, characters on a DCL command line that you are editing. |
| <CTRL/B> or <Up Arrow> | Displays DCL commands that you have previously entered into the system. |
| <CTRL/C> or <F6> | Interrupts the command currently being processed or the program being executed. |
| <CTRL/E> | Positions the cursor at the end of the line. |
| <CTRL/H> | Positions the cursor at the beginning of the line. |
| <CTRL/I> | Duplicates the function of the <TAB> key. |
| <CTRL/O> | Alternately suppresses and continues the display of output at the terminal. |
| <CTRL/Q> | Resumes (toggles on) output to the display after a <CTRL/S> has been pressed. |
| <CTRL/R> | Retypes the current input line and repositions the cursor at the end of the retyped line. |
| <CTRL/S> | Suspends (toggles off) output to the display until <CTRL/Q> is pressed. |
| <CTRL/T> | Displays process statistics. |
| <CTRL/U> | Discards the current input line and performs a carriage return. |
| <CTRL/W> | Refreshes the screen. |
| <CTRL/X> | Flushes the type-ahead buffer. |
| <CTRL/Y> | Interrupts command or program execution and returns control to the DCL command line interpreter. |
| <CTRL/Z> or <F10> | Indicates end of file for data entered from the terminal. |
| <Down Arrow> | Recalls the next command in the recall buffer. |

## SELECTING A CHARACTER SET

DEC's VT terminals have three character sets from which to choose:
U.S. (default), U.K., and GRAPHIC. The U.S. and U.K. character sets are
identical with the exception of the number sign/pound sign. The
GRAPHICS character set displays an assortment of line drawing
characters and special symbols.

The following table lists escape sequences for changing character sets:

| Character Set | Escape Sequence |
|---------------|-----------------|
| US (ASCII)    | <ESC>(B         |
| UK National   | <ESC>(A         |
| GRAPHIC       | <ESC>(0         |

## CURSOR MOVEMENT

DEC's VT series terminals support a rich set of commands for
positioning the cursor. This table lists these escape sequences.
(Substitute the character n for the number of lines or character
positions. If you omit n, the command will default to 1.)

| Escape Sequence | Cursor Function |
|-----------------|-----------------|
| <ESC>[M         | Moves cursor up (scrolls within defined scrolling region) |
| <ESC>[nA        | Moves cursor up (no scrolling) |
| <ESC>D<LF>      | Moves cursor down (scrolls within defined scrolling region) |
| <ESC>[nB        | Moves cursor down (no scrolling) |
| <ESC>[nC        | Moves the cursor to the right |
| <ESC>[nD        | Moves the cursor to the left |
| <ESC>E          | Positions the cursor at the beginning of the next line |
| <ESC>[r;cH      | Positions the cursor at row r and column c |
| <ESC>7          | Saves the cursor's column position and character attributes |
| <ESC>8          | Restores the cursor's column position and character attributes |

## SCREEN ERASING

The following table defines those escape sequences that allow you to
clear a specified position on the display. After erasing screen text, the
cursor will be where erasing completed.

| Escape Sequence | Erase Screen Function |
|---|---|
| <ESC>[0K | Erase from the cursor to the end of the line |
| <ESC>[1K | Erase from the beginning of the line to the cursor |
| <ESC>[2K | Erase the entire line |
| <ESC>[0J | Erase from the cursor to the end of the screen |
| <ESC>[1J | Erase from the bottom of the screen to the cursor |
| <ESC>[2J | Erase the entire screen |

## SCROLLING REGIONS

A scrolling region is a horizontal portion of the display in which text scrolls. Text lines above and below the scrolling region are protected from the scrolling text; they remain stationary. The following table lists those escape sequences used to define scrolling regions.

| Escape Sequence | Scrolling Function |
|---|---|
| <ESC>[t;br | Define a scrolling region with the top line = t and the bottom line = b |
| <ESC>[?6h | Set cursor position 0,0 equal to the upper left corner of the scrolling region |
| <ESC>[?6l | Set cursor position 0,0 equal to the upper left corner of the defined scrolling region |

## DISPLAY CHARACTERISTICS

The following table defines the escape sequences that allow you to modify display characteristics.

| Escape Sequence | Display Characteristic Functions |
|---|---|
| <ESC>[0m | Normal characteristics (reset) |
| <ESC>[1m | Bold characters |
| <ESC>[4m | Underline characters |
| <ESC>[5m | Blinking characters |
| <ESC>[7m | Reverse video characters |
| <ESC>#3 | Double height characters (top half) |
| <ESC>#4 | Double height characters (bottom half) |
| <ESC>#5 | Single width characters (default) |
| <ESC>#6 | Double width characters |

## TERMINAL CHARACTERISTICS

This table defines the escape sequences that permit you to set various terminal attributes.

| Escape Sequence | Terminal Characteristic Functions |
|---|---|
| <ESC>[?3l | Set terminal to 132-column mode |
| <ESC>[?3h | Set terminal to 80-column mode |
| <ESC>H | Set tab stop at current column position |
| <ESC>[g | Clear tab stop at current column |
| <ESC>[3g | Clear all tab stops |

# System Generation Parameters

This is a list of each VMS SYSGEN parameter and a brief description of its function.

**ACP_BASEPRIO**
Ancillary control process (ACP) base priority.

**ACP_DATACHECK**
Data verification for ACP I/O operations.

**ACP_DIRCACHE**
The number of blocks in the file directory cache.

**ACP_DINDXCACHE**
Controls the size of the directory index cache to minimize directory file access overhead.

**ACP_EXTCACHE**
The number of cached disk extents.

**ACP_EXTLIMIT**
The maximum fraction of disk extents to cache in tenths of a percent.

**ACP_FIDCACHE**
Number of cached file identification slots.

### ACP_HDRCACHE
Number of blocks in the file header cache.

### ACP_MAPCACHE
Number of blocks in bitmap cache. This value sets the number of pages for caching bit map blocks.

### ACP_MAXREAD
Maximum number of blocks to read at once for directories.

### ACP_MULTIPLE
Specifies that separate ACPs are to be created for each volume.

### ACP_QUOCACHE
Specifies the number of quota file entries to cache.

### ACP_REBLDSYS
Indicates whether the system disk should be rebuilt if it was improperly dismounted.

### ACP_SHARE
Permits sharing of ancillary control process code, which enables the creation of a global section for the first ACP used, so that succeeding ACPs may share its code.

### ACP_SWAPFLGS
Enables swapping of ACPs.

### ACP_SYSACC
Defines the number of directory file control blocks that will be cached for system access disks.

### ACP_WINDOW
Default window size for system volumes.

### ACP_WORKSET
ACP working set in pages (0 indicates maximum).

### ACP_WRITEBACK
Deferred cache writeback enable.

### ACP_XQP_RES
Controls whether or not the XQP is memory-resident. The default of 1 denotes that the XQP is memory-resident.

**ALLOCLASS**
Determines the system allocation class.

**BALSETCNT**
Indicates the number of working sets permitted to be concurrently resident in memory.

**BJOBLIM**
Maximum number of batch jobs allowed in the system at any time.

**BORROWLIM**
Desired free list length that must exist to allow processes to grow past their WSQUOTA.

**BUGCHECKFATAL**
Specifies that all continuable bugchecks will turn into fatal BUGCHECKS.

**BUGREBOOT**
Enables automatic reboot on bugcheck.

**CLISYMTBL**
Sets the size of the command interpreter symbol table.

**CRDENABLE**
Enables detection and logging of memory customer runable diagnostics (CRD) errors.

**DEADLOCK_WAIT**
Number of seconds a lock must wait before a deadlock search is initiated.

**DEFMBXBUFQUO**
Default buffer quota for mailboxes.

**DEFMBXMXMSG**
Default maximum Mailbox message size.

**DEFMBXNUMMSG**
Default number of messages for Mailbox creation.

**DEFPRI**
Default priority for job initiations.

**DEFQUEPRI**
Establishes the scheduling priority for jobs entered in batch queues when no explicit scheduling priority is specified by the submitter.

## DISK_QUORUM
The name of the cluster quorum disk.

## DISMOUMSG
Enables/disables operator notification of volume dismounts.

## DORMANTWAIT
Specifies (in seconds) the amount of time that may elapse without a significant event before the system treats a low-priority computable process as a dormant process for scheduling purposes.

## DUMPBUG
Enables system dump on bugcheck.

## DUMPSTYLE
Specifies the desired method for taking system dumps when the system BUGCHECKs.

## ERRORLOGBUFFERS
Specifies the amount of physical memory reserved for system error log entries. If too low, attempts to write messages to the error log file may fail. If ERRORLOGBUFFERS is too high, pages will be wasted by error log buffers.

## EXPECTED_VOTES
Indicates the maximum number of votes that may be present in the cluster. This value is used to derive the number of votes that must be present for the VAXcluster to function (i.e., achieve quorum).

## EXTRACPU
Sets the number of 10 millisecond units to be allowed as an extension when CPU time expires.

## FREEGOAL
Specifies the number of free pages that the swapper will attempt to make available when correcting for free list size less than FREELIM.

## FREELIM
Indicates the minimum number of pages that must remain free on the free page list.

## GBLPAGES
Sets the size of the global page table and the limit for the total number of global pages that can be created.

### GBLPAGFIL
Establishes the maximum number of global pages with page file backing store that can be created.

### GBLSECTIONS
Defines the maximum number of global sections that can be made known to the system by allocating the necessary storage for the GST entries.

### GROWLIM
The desired free list length that must exist to allow processes to grow past WSQUOTA.

### IJOBLIM
Sets the maximum number of interactive jobs allowed in the system at any time.

### INTSTKPAGES
Establishes the size of the interrupt stack in pages.

### IRPCOUNT
Determines the number of I/O packets to be preallocated and linked together for fast allocation and deallocation.

### IRPCOUNTV
Number of packets to which the IRP list may be extended.

### KFILSTCNT
Sets the maximum number of known file lists that can be made known to the system.

### LGI_BRK_TERM
If set, this parameter causes the terminal name to be part of the association string for the terminal mode of break-in detection.

### LGI_BRK_DISUSER
If set, this parameter turns on the DISUSER flag in the user authorization file (UAF) record when an attempted break-in is detected, thus permanently locking out that account.

### LGI_BRK_LIM
Specifies the number of failures that may occur at login time before the system will take action against a possible break-in.

## LGI_BRK_TMO
Designates the number of seconds that a user, terminal, or node is permitted to attempt a login before the system assumes that a break-in attempt is occurring and evasive action is required.

## LGI_HID_TIM
Specifies the number of seconds that evasive action will persist following the detection of a possible break-in attempt. The evasive action consists of refusing to allow any logins during this period even if a valid username and password are entered.

## LGI_PWD_TMO
Period of time, in seconds, a user has to correctly enter the system password on a terminal on which the system password is in effect.

## LGI_RETRY_TMO
Specifies the number of seconds allowed between login retry attempts after a login failure.

## LGI_RETRY_LIM
Specifies the number of retry attempts allowed for users attempting to login over dial-up lines.

## LNMPHASHTBL
Sets the size of process logical name hash table.

## LOCKDIRWT
Determines the portion of lock manager directory that will be handled by this system.

## LOCKIDTBL
Establishes the size of lock ID table.

## LOCKIDTBL_MAX
Establishes the maximum size of the lock ID table.

## LONGWAIT
Sets the number of one-second units that need to have elapsed. LONGWAIT processes are the most eligible from which to attempt to recover pages when a shortage is detected.

## LRPCOUNT
Number of large request packets to allocate to the large request packets (LRP) look-aside list.

## LRPCOUNTV
Number of LRP's to which the LRP list may be extended.

## LRPSIZE
Number of bytes to allocate to an LRP.

## MAXBUF
Maximum number of bytes that can be transferred in one buffered I/O request.

## MAXPROCESSCNT
Establishes the maximum number of processes on the system.

## MAXQUEPRI
Determines the highest scheduling priority that can be assigned to jobs entered in batch queues without the submitter process having OPER or ALTPRI privilege.

## MAXSYSGROUP
The highest value (decimal) that a group number can have and still be classified as a system user identification code (UIC) group member.

## MINWSCNT
Sets the minimum number of fluid pages (i.e., pages not locked in the working set) required for the execution of a process. This value, plus the size of the process header, constitutes the minimum working set size.

## MOUNTMSG
Enables operator notification of volume mounts.

## MPW_HILIMIT
Sets the threshold at which to begin writing modified pages.

## MPW_IOLIMIT
Number of outstanding I/Os to the modified page writer. For VMS V5.0, the modified page writer can have up to 127 I/Os outstanding.

## MPW_LOLIMIT
Sets the threshold at which modified page writing will normally stop.

## MPW_LOWAITLIMIT
Establishes the threshold at which processes in the miscellaneous wait state MPWBUSY are allowed to resume. This parameter increases

system performance for fast processors with large memories by reducing the amount of time processes spend in the MPWBUSY wait state.

### MPW_THRESH
Sets the lower limit threshold stopping the use of the modified page writer from being used as the primary mechanism to recover memory.

### MPW_WAITLIMIT
Establishes the threshold of when to put a process into resource wait if it is generating a modified page and the size of the modified list is greater than this parameter.

### MPW_WRTCLUSTER
Specifies the number of pages to attempt to write from the modified page list as a single contiguous I/O transfer to disk.

### MSCP_BUFFER
Specifies the amount of memory (in pages) to be allocated to the mass storage control protocol (MSCP) server's local buffer area. The buffer area is the space used by the server to transfer data between client systems and local disks.

### MSCP_CREDITS
Sets the maximum number of outstanding I/O requests that can be active from each client system.

### MSCP_LOAD
Controls the loading of the MSCP server during a system boot.

### MSCP_SERVE_ALL
Controls the serving of disks during a system boot.

### MULTIPROCESSING
Controls loading of the system synchronization image.

### MVTIMEOUT
Mount verification timeout.

### NISCS_CONV_BOOT
Controls whether or not a conversational boot is permitted during a remote system boot.

## NISCS_LOAD_PEA0
Controls whether the network interconnect system communication services (NI–SCS) port driver PEDRIVER is loaded during system boot. By default, the driver is not loaded.

## NISCS_PORT_SERV
Supplies flag bits for PEDRIVER port services. Bits 0 and 1 set (decimal value 3) enables data checking. All other bits are reserved for future use.

## NJOBLIM
Maximum number of network jobs allowed in the system at any time.

## NPAGEDYN
Determines the number of bytes to allocate for the nonpaged dynamic pool.

## NPAGEVIR
Determines the number of bytes to which the nonpaged pool may be extended.

## PAGEDYN
Determines the number of bytes to allocate for the paged dynamic pool.

## PAGFILCNT
Determines the maximum number of paging files that can be made known to the system.

## PAMAXPORT
Sets the maximum number of computer interconnect (CI) ports that the CI port driver will poll for broken port-to-port virtual circuits or a failed remote node.

## PANOPOLL
Used to supress CI polling for ports. If set, a system will not discover that another system has shut down or powered down promptly and will not discover a new system that has booted.

## PANUMPOLL
The number of ports to poll each interval.

## PAPOLLINTERVAL
Sets the time between poll initiates.

## PAPOOLINTERVAL
Time between check for SYSAPs waiting for pool.

## PASANITY
Controls whether the port sanity timer is enabled to permit remote systems to detect a system that has been hung at IPL 7 or above for 99 seconds.

## PASTDGBUF
The number of DG buffers to queue for START handshake.

## PASTIMOUT
Timeout period between START retries.

## PFCDEFAULT
Specifies the maximum number of pages that will be read from sections not specifying a cluster factor.

## PFRATH
Sets the upper page fault rate threshold for automatic working set size incrementing.

## PFRATL
Establishes the lower page fault rate threshold for automatic working set size decrementing.

## POOLPAGING
Enables paging of pageable dynamic pool.

## PQL_DASTLM
Default number of pending asynchronous system traps (AST) available to a process.

## PQL_MASTLM
Minimum number of pending ASTs available to a process.

## PQL_DBIOLM
Default number of buffered I/O requests outstanding available to a process.

## PQL_MBIOLM
Minimum number of buffered I/O requests outstanding available to a process.

## PQL_DBYTLM
Default number of bytes allowed in any single buffered I/O request.

**PQL_MBYTLM**
Minimum number of bytes allowed in any single buffered I/O request.

**PQL_DCPULM**
Default CPU time limit.

**PQL_MCPULM**
Minimum CPU time limit.

**PQL_DDIOLM**
Default number of direct I/O requests outstanding available to a process.

**PQL_MDIOLM**
Minimum number of direct I/O requests outstanding available to a process.

**PQL_DFILLM**
Default number of open files available to a process.

**PQL_MFILLM**
Minimum number of open files available to a process.

**PQL_DPGFLQUOTA**
Default paging file quota.

**PQL_MPGFLQUOTA**
Minimum paging file quota.

**PQL_DPRCLM**
Default number of sub-processes available to a process.

**PQL_MPRCLM**
Minimum number of sub-processes available to a process.

**PQL_DTQELM**
Default number of timer queue entries available to a process.

**PQL_MTQELM**
Minimum number of timer queue entries available to a process.

**PQL_DWSDEFAULT**
Default working set default size.

**PQL_MWSDEFAULT**
Minimum working set default size.

**PQL_DWSQUOTA**
Default working set quota.

**PQL_MWSQUOTA**
Minimum working set quota.

**PQL_DWSEXTENT**
Default working set extent.

**PQL_MWSEXTENT**
Minimum working set extent.

**PQL_DENQLM**
Default enqueue limit.

**PQL_MENQLM**
Minimum enqueue limit.

**PQL_DJTQUOTA**
Quota allocated to the jobwide logical name table when it's created.

**PQL_MJTQUOTA**
Quota allocated to the jobwide logical name table on its creation.

**PRCPOLINTERVAL**
Minimum interval between system communication services (SCS)
polls.

**PROCSECTCNT**
The guaranteed number of process sections that can be created.

**QDSKINTERVAL**
Establishes the disk quorum polling interval in seconds.

**QDSKVOTES**
Specifies the number of votes contributed by a quorum disk in a
VAXcluster.

**QUANTUM**
Maximum amount of processor time a process can receive while
other processes are waiting.

**REALTIME_SPTS**
Number of system page table (SPT) entries to preallocate for use
by real time processes connecting to devices via the connect to
interrupt driver.

### RECNXINTERVAL
Period during which attempts are made to restore a lost connection between cluster members.

### RESHASHTBL
Size of resource hash table.

### RJOBLIM
Maximum number of remote terminal jobs allowed in the system at any time. This parameter is sampled when remote ancillary control process (REMACP) is started.

### RMS_DFMBC
Default multiblock count.

### RMS_DFMBFSDK
Default multibuffer count for sequential disk operations.

### RMS_DFMBFSMT
Default multibuffer count for magtape operations.

### RMS_DFMBFSUR
Default multibuffer count for unit record devices.

### RMS_DFMBFREL
Default multibuffer count for relative files.

### RMS_DFMBFIDX
Default multibuffer count indexed files.

### RMS_DFMBFHSH
Default multibuffer count hashed.

### RMS_DFNBC
Determines the default message size in disk blocks to be used when performing DECnet file transfer operations.

### RMS_EXTEND_SIZE
Default extend quantity for Record Management Services (RMS) files.

### RMS_FILEPROT
Default file protection.

### RMS_GBLBUFQUO
Specifies the number of global buffers that may be allocated on the system at any one time.

**RMS_PROLOGUE**
Default prologue level for RMS files.

**SAVEDUMP**
If the dump file is saved in the page file, save it until it is analyzed.

**SBIERRENABLE**
Enables synchronous backplane interconnect (SBI) error detection and logging.

**SCSBUFFCNT**
Buffer Descriptor Table entries.

**SCSCONNCNT**
Connect Descriptor Table entries.

**SCSFLOWCUSH**
System communication service (SCS) flow control cushion.

**SCSMAXDG**
System communication service (SCS) maximum datagram size.

**SCSMAXMSG**
System communication service (SCS) maximum sequenced message size.

**SCSNODE**
The system communication service (SCS) system node name.

**SCSRESPCNT**
Response Descriptor Table entries.

**SCSSYSTEMID**
Low longword of the SCS system ID.

**SCSSYSTEMIDH**
High 16 bits of the 48 bit SCS system ID.

**SETTIME**
Forces entry of time at system boot.

**SHADOWING**
A Boolean value that specifies the type of disk class driver that is loaded on the system.

## SMP_CPUS
Identifies which secondary processors, if available, are to be booted into the multiprocessing system.

## SMP_LNGSPINWAIT
Identifies certain shared resources in a multiprocessing system that take longer to become available than allowed for by the SMP_SPINWAIT parameter.

## SMP_SANITY_CNT
Establishes, in 10-millisecond clock ticks, the timeout interval for each CPU in a multiprocessing system.

## SMP_SPINWAIT
Establishes, in 10-microsecond intervals, the amount of time a CPU normally waits for access to a shared resource. This process is called spinwaiting.

## SPTREQ
The minimum number of system page table (SPT) entries required for mapping various system components.

## SRPCOUNT
Number of small request packets to allocate to the small request packet (SRP) look-aside list.

## SRPCOUNTV
Number of SRPs to which the small request packet (SRP) list may be extended.

## SRPSIZE
Number of bytes to allocate to an small request packet (SRP).

## SWPFILCNT
Establishes the maximum number of swapfiles that can be made known to the system.

## SWPOUTPGCNT
Sets the number of pages to which to attempt to reduce a working set before starting the outswap.

## SYSMWCNT
Establishes the number of pages for the working set containing the currently resident pages of pageable system space.

### TAPE_MVTIMEOUT
The time in seconds that a mount verification attempt will continue on a given magnetic tape volume.

### TIMEPROMPTWAIT
Sets the amount of time to wait for the time of day when booting.

### TTY_SCANDELTA
Sets the interval for polling terminals for dial-up and hang-up events.

### TTY_SPEED
Systemwide default speed for terminals. Low byte is transmit; high byte is receive or 0 indicating the receive speed is the same as the transmit speed. See $TTDEF for baud rates.

### TTY_RSPEED
Default receive speed. Setting to zero implies that TTY_SPEED controls both transmit and receive.

### TTY_BUF
Default terminal line width.

### TTY_DEFCHAR
Default terminal characteristics and page length. See $TTDEF for bits.

### TTY_DEFCHAR2
Default terminal characteristics (second longword). See $TT2DEF for bits.

### TTY_TYPAHDSZ
Size of the terminal type-ahead buffer.

### TTY_ALTYPAHD
Alternate type-ahead buffer size.

### TTY_ALTALARM
Number of remaining characters when an XOFF is sent when using alternate typeahead buffer.

### TTY_DMASIZE
Minimum size of packet required to do a direct memory access (DMA) operation within the terminal driver.

## TTY_CLASSNAME
Two-character prefix used in looking up the terminal class driver when booting.

## TTY_PROT
Default terminal allocation protection.

## TTY_OWNER
Specifies the owner user identification code (UIC) against which the terminal protection is set.

## TTY_DIALTYPE
Flags for dial-up.

## TTY_SILOTIME
Timeout on input silo interrupts for DMF32.

## TTY_TIMEOUT
Sets the number of seconds before a process associated with a disconnected terminal is deleted.

## TTY_AUTOCHAR
Sets the character the terminal driver echoes when autobaud completes successfully.

## UDABURSTRATE
One less than the maximum number of longwords the host is willing to allow per NPR transfer. Zero implies the port should use its own default value.

## UAFALTERNATE
Tells SYSINIT to make a logical name redirecting SYSUAF to SYSUAFALT.

## VAXCLUSTER
Loads the code to support a VAX cluster whenever SCS support is present.

## VIRTUALPAGECNT
Determines the total number of pages that can be mapped for a process, which can be divided in any fashion between P0 and P1 space.

## VOTES
Number of votes held by the system that can contribute to the quorum.

## WINDOW_SYSTEM
Specifies the windowing system to be used on a workstation.

## WRITESYSPARAMS
Parameters were modified during SYSBOOT and will be written out to VAXVMSSYS.PAR by STARTUP.COM.

## WSDEC
Sets the number of pages to decrease the working set to compensate for a page fault rate below the lower threshold.

## WSINC
Sets the number of pages to increase the working set size to compensate for a high page fault rate.

## WSMAX
Determines the systemwide maximum size of a process working set regardless of process quota.

## WS_OPA0
Enables OPA0 output to the QVSS screen for a VAX workstation.

## XFMAXRATE
Limits the data transfer rate that can be set for a DR32. The larger the value, the faster the transfer rate.

# VMS Privileges

## ACNT

Allows creation of processes, including detached and subprocesses in which the collection of accounting information is disabled.

## ALLSPOOL

Allows a process to allocate a spooled device. Usually given to symbionts only.

## ALTPRI

Allows a process to raise rather than just lower its priority. In combination with group or world privilege, a process could raise or lower the priorities of other processes in the same group or anyone respectively.

## BUGCHK

Allows a process to make bugcheck entries in the error logs. Used by VAX/VMS system routines.

## BYPASS

Allows a process to bypass normal file protection for READ, WRITE, EXECUTE or DELETE operations.

## CMEXEC

Allows a user to change processor mode to executive during which time it can execute change mode to kernel system service. To knowledgeable users, this privilege grants access to all VAX instructions and data structures.

### CMKRNL
For knowledgeable users, allows access to all data structures and use of instructions.

### DETACH
Allows the creation of a detached process with a user identification code different from the creator. The process could have any UIC including one in the system group.

### DIAGNOSE
Allows a user to run online diagnostics and read all messages as they are sent to the error log file.

### EXQUOTA
Allows a user to ignore the restriction of blocks that can be specified on one or more disk volumes for them.

### GROUP
Allows a process to suspend, resume, delete, set priority, wake, schedule wakeup, cancel wakeup, force exit, and get job process information on processes in user identification code group. In addition, it can affect queue entries for group jobs and change process characteristics with the SET PROCESS command.

### GRPNAM
Allows insertion and removal of entries in the group logical name table.

### GRPPRV
Allows a process system access to files, change file ownership, and change the protection of files within the same user identification code group.

### LOG_IO
Allows QIO logical I/O requests allowing reading of any logical blocks on a file structured device such as a disk. Such operations are not required for nonfile structured devices.

### PHY_IO
Allows QIO physical level requests to device drivers or to devices.

**MOUNT**
Allows QIO mount volume operations done by system routines, such as the mounting of the system disk.

**NETMBX**
A privilege granted to all users that allows indirect creation of mailboxes across a network.

**OPER**
Allows a process to reply to user's requests, broadcast messages to terminals, create or delete operator's consoles, open and close the operator's log file, set devices spooled, and create and control print and batch queues.

**PFNMAP**
Allows a process to directly reference physical pages of memory without contention.

**PRMCEB**
Allows creation of permanent common event flag clusters in nonpaged pool.

**PRMGBL**
Allows creation of permanent global sections.

**PRMMBX**
Allows creation of permanent mailboxes.

**PSWAPM**
Allows a process to make itself nonswappable.

**READALL**
Allows read and control access to all files.

**SECURITY**
Allows setting of the system password and enabling and disabling of security audits.

**SETPRV**
Allows a process to give itself any privilege or create other processes with all privileges.

**SHARE**
Allows a process to assign channels to devices allocated to other users, such as print symbionts.

**SHMEM**
Allows the creation of global sections and mailboxes in multiported memory.

**SYSGBL**
Allows the creation of system global sections.

**SYSLCK**
Allows locking of system resources (system disk) with the $ENQ system service.

**SYSNAM**
Allows addition and deletion of entries in the system logical name table.

**SYSPRV**
Allows system access to objects.

**TMPMBX**
Allows creation to temporary mailboxes, a privilege usually granted to all users.

**VOLPRO**
Allows a user to initialize a volume with any user identification code owner, override the expiration date on any tape or disk, use the /FOREIGN qualifier to mount a disk or tape.

**WORLD**
Affects all other process for the operations shown under group.

**ABORT** An exception that occurs when executing an instruction that sometimes leaves the registers and memory in a state such that the instruction can't be restarted. (D)

This term also is used when referring to the abnormal termination of a program.

**ABSOLUTE ADDRESS** A binary number assigned to each permanent memory location. (D)

**ABSOLUTE TIME** A positive number that expresses the exact time, i.e., year, month, day, hour, seconds, and ticks. (D)

**ACCESS** In computer terminology, a verb meaning to get, to find, or to look up the contents of, to gain admittance to, or to obtain the use of. Access of data may be direct, random, or sequential.

**ACCESS CONTROL** Validating login, connect requests (DECnet), and file-access requests to determine if they can be accepted. (D)

**ACCESS CONTROL LIST** A list composed of entries that define the types of access that can be granted or denied to users of an object. Generally, the object is a device, directory, file, or mailbox. (D)

**ACCESS CONTROL LIST ENTRY** An entry in an access control list that specifies identifiers and access rights to the object. (D)

**ACCESS MODE** Any of the four processor modes in which VAX software executes. Four modes are available in the VMS access scheme. Listed in order from most to least privileged, they are kernel (mode 0), executive (mode 1), supervisor (mode 2), and user (mode 3). When in kernel mode, the software executing has complete control of the system. When in any other mode, the processor cannot execute privileged instructions. (D)

**ACCESS VIOLATION** An attempt to reference an address that has not been mapped in to virtual memory, or an attempt to reference an address that is not accessible in the current access mode. For instance, attempting to address a kernel privileged address while in the user access mode would result in an access violation. (D)

**ACCOUNT**  The VMS entity used to permit access to the computer system. You must have an account, or be able to log into an account, to be able to access and use the computer. An account is a unit of system ACCOUNTING. (D)

**ACCOUNT NAME**  A name specified by the system manager in the UAF to identify a given account. Statistics on the user resources consumed by a job are accumulated and charged to the account name. An exception to this rule involves disk quota, which is charged to the user's UIC. (D)

**ACCOUNT NUMBER**  A pair of numbers that identifies an authorized system user. The format of an account number (also known as a user identification number) is [group,member]. (D)

**ACCUMULATOR**  A hardware register that stores data used for logic or arithmetic operations. (D)

**ADDRESS**  A hexadecimal (base 16) number used by VMS and user-supplied software that identifies a storage location in the system. Addresses may be virtual or physical.

**ADDRESS SPACE**  The set of all possible addresses available to a given process. Address space may be virtual or physical. (D)

**ADDRESSING MODE**  The way an operand is specified in an instruction statement, e.g., literal, indexed, or register deferred.

**AGGREGATE**  A collection of related items (data) that can be referred to individually or collectively.

**ALARM**  A message sent to the operator's terminal in response to a security event.

**ALLOCATE**  The distribution of computer resources.

**ALLOCATION**  The act of reserving a given hardware device for the exclusive use of a given process. If you want to allocate a tape drive so you can copy disk files onto a magnetic tape, you enter a DCL command such as ALLOCATE MUA0:. You may only allocate a device when that device is not already allocated to another user or process. If you attempt to allocate a previously allocated device, VMS returns an error message informing you that the device is already allocated to another user. (D)

**ALPHANUMERIC CHARACTER**  A standard ASCII decimal digit (0 through 9), an upper or lowercase alphabetic character, the dollar sign ($), or the underscore (_) character. Alphanumeric characters are valid for filenames, account names and user passwords.

**ALPHANUMERIC USER IDENTIFICATION**  A UIC that consists of either a member identifier or a group and member identifier specified in alphanumeric form. In an alphanumeric UIC, both the group and member identifiers may be up to 31 characters long and must contain at least one alphabetic character. (D)

**AMERICAN STANDARD CODE FOR INFORMATION INTERCHANGE
(ASCII)** This code is the standard used by DEC computers like the VAX to represent
alphabetic and numeric characters and other special symbols. Each ASCII character is
an eight-bit binary number. Contrast with Extended Binary Coded Decimal Code
(EBCDIC), the representation used on IBM hardware.

**ANCILLARY CONTROL PROCESS (ACP)** A VMS process that interfaces a
VAX I/O device driver with the user software requiring the use of the device. If your
program writes data to magnetic tape, the program will access the magtape ancillary
control process (MTAACP) in the process of transferring and writing data to the
tape drive. The Files-11 ancillary control process (F11ACP) handles read/write
operations on VAX Files-11 structured disks. (D)

**ASSEMBLER** A language processor that translates a series of assembly language
statements into an object program called an object module.

**ASSEMBLY LANGUAGE** A low-level programming language that uses
machine-oriented mnemonic statements. MACRO-32 is the assembly language
used on VMS systems.

**ASSIGNMENT STATEMENT** A statement that defines a symbol name to be
used in place of a numeric value or a character string. Symbols may be defined
as synonyms for system commands; they may also serve as variables in DCL
command procedures.

**ASYNCHRONOUS SYSTEM TRAP (ACP)** A software generated interrupt to
a user-defined routine. An AST enables a process to be notified of an event. (D)

**AUDITING** Logging an event that has security implications.

**AUTHORIZATION FILE** A file containing an entry for each user of the system.
Each entry identifies the user name, quotas, privileges, user identification code,
and access time. Same as SYSUAF and user authorization file. (D)

**BALANCE SET** The group of all working sets resident in the physical memory
of a VAX CPU. Any process whose working set is a member of the balance set
has a memory requirement that balances or can be fulfilled with available
physical memory. (D)

**BANDWIDTH** The range of operating frequencies assigned to a channel or system.

**BASE PRIORITY** The processing priority established in and assigned from the user
authorization file when a process is created. In VMS, priorities range from 0 to 15 for
interactive processes, and from 16 to 31 for real-time processes. The higher the base
priority of a process, the more rapidly (i.e., the more attention it will be paid by the
CPU) the process will be executed. With sufficient privilege, you can alter the base
priority of a running process. (D)

**BATCH PROCESSING**  The processing mode in which you submit a job to the computer through a batch queue, using the DCL SUBMIT command. Your job will execute when the jobs preceding it in the queue have completed. In the batch mode, you do not have two-way communication with the computer system. Your commands are submitted to the system as a file.

**BINARY**  Pertaining to base 2 numeric representation. The decimal number 7 is represented as 111 in the binary numbering system.

**BIT**  Contraction for binary digit. May indicate a single character in a binary number, or the smallest unit of capacity for information storage in a computer system.

**BLOCK**  The smallest independently addressable unit of data that a given device can transfer in any one I/O operation. On VAX disk devices, a block is defined as 512 contiguous bytes of disk space. (D)

**BOOT BLOCK**  Defined as block number zero on a VMS disk. It contains the program (VMB.EXE) that begins the sequence of initializing the processor, loading VMS into memory and starting up the operating system. (D)

**BOOTSTRAP**  The process of initializing or starting up a CPU. Loading the CPU with operating software.

**BREAK-IN ATTEMPT**  An attempted breach of security in which an outsider tries to penetrate a computer system. Break-in attempts can take many forms but are often perpetrated by unauthorized individuals who try to penetrate a computer system by dialing in and attempting to guess valid usernames and passwords.

**BUCKET**  A storage structure used in indexed files to store and transfer units of data. A bucket is one to 32 disk blocks long and may only contain an entire record. (D)

**BUFFER**  A temporary storage area used to contain text or data.

**BUG**  A computer malfunction or software error.

**BUGCHECK**  The internal diagnostic service provided by VMS. When VMS detects an internal system failure, it logs the error in a file. If the failure is of sufficient severity, it is referred to as a Fatal Bugcheck Error and results in the failure or crash of the system. (D)

**BUS**  A flat ribbon cable used to connect computer system components. (D)

**BYTE**  Eight consecutive bits of data starting on an addressable boundary. The bits are numbered from the right, 0 through 7. One byte will store an ASCII character.

**CACHE** A small, high-speed memory located between the VAX processor and its slower main memory. The cache contains instructions or data recently used by the processor. It also anticipates and fetches the next several bytes of data or instructions that will be used. Because the cache typically has a 90 percent accuracy or hit rate, it increases data transfer and memory speed. (D)

**CARRIER SENSE** A signal provided by an Ethernet transceiver to indicate that one or more nodes on the network is currently transmitting.

**CAPTIVE ACCOUNT** A type of VMS account that limits the activities of a user. The account works by locking the user into a command procedure during login. The user is restricted to the menu of commands provided in the captive account. Captive accounts are often employed to allow users to perform privileged tasks like system backup without granting them these privileges to use for their own purposes. (D)

**CENTRAL PROCESSING UNIT (CPU)** The portion of a computer system that contains the arithmetic, logical and control circuits needed for the interpretation and execution of instructions. (D)

**CHANNEL** A path connecting a user process to a physical device in a computer system. Programmers assign system channels to the input and output devices to which they wish their programs to communicate.

**CLUSTER** The basic unit of space allocation on a VMS disk. It consists of a number of contiguous blocks. It is also defined as the number of pages that are brought into memory during a single paging operation. (D)

**COAXIAL CABLE** A two-conductor cable in which one conductor completely wraps the other to provide shielding.

**COLLISION** Multiple network transmissions broadcast simultaneously on the same channel. The result is a garbled transmission.

**COMMAND** An instruction that directs the command interpreter to perform a given task. The instruction may be typed in at a terminal or entered by invoking a command procedure. In VMS, commands are generally issued in Digital Command Language, a set of English verbs.

**COMMAND FILE** See Command Procedure.

**COMMAND LINE INTERPRETER (CLI)** A system procedure that accepts commands, examines them for validity and syntax, and directs the computer to execute the commands. The default command line interpreter for VMS systems is the Digital Command Language (DCL) interpreter. (D)

**COMMAND PROCEDURE** A file, usually created by a computer user, containing a predefined series of commands and data that the command line interpreter will accept and process. By using a command procedure, you avoid typing each individual command, data element, and response. Command procedures can be invoked interactively with the DCL @ statement, or they can be submitted to the batch processor. (D)

**COMMAND STRING** A DCL command verb and any parameters and qualifiers associated with it. (D)

**COMPILER** A programming language processor that translates high-level statements from a source program into a machine-readable object module. Programs written in languages like FORTRAN and PASCAL must be compiled before they can be linked and executed.

**CONCATENATE** To link together or join, as in a chain. Records and files may be concatenated.

**CONDITIONAL STATEMENT** A statement that determines the truth value of a condition using Boolean logic.

**CONSOLE COMMAND LANGUAGE (CCL)** A series of instructions that can be entered into the VAX console subsystem via the operator's console during a conversational bootstrap, or at other times when it's necessary to communicate with the console subsystem. The CCL gives the operator the ability to halt the processor, examine the contents of virtual or physical memory locations, deposit information into virtual or physical memory, and perform various other tasks. CCL is invoked differently on the various VAX processors. On the 11/750, the processor is halted with a command at the operator console, and the CCL prompt of three right angle brackets (>>>) is displayed. (D)

**CONSOLE SUBSYSTEM** The manual control unit integrated into a VAX CPU. The console includes a microprocessor and an interface to the operator console. It permits the operator to start and halt the system, run diagnostics, and monitor system operation. (D)

**CONTIGUOUS** Consecutively numbered, physically adjacent units. In computer terminology, this refers to data elements. As an unrelated example, the lower 48 United States are considered to be contiguous.

**CONTINUATION CHARACTER** A hyphen entered at the end of a line of a long command string. It indicates that the command string is to be continued on the next line rather than being submitted to the computer via the <RETURN> key. The first character of a line succeeding a line ended with a hyphen is a slash (/). (D)

**CONTROL CHARACTER** Any character having an ASCII value of less than 32. Included are such characters as backspace (CTRL/H or ASCII 8), bell (CTRL/G or ASCII 7) and escape (ESC or ASCII 27).

**CONTROL STATUS REGISTER (CSR)** A hardware register for the control/ status of a device or controller. A CSR exists in the processor's I/O space. (D)

**CURSOR** A flashing block or bar of light that appears on the screen of a video terminal. It indicates where the next character entered will be displayed on the screen.

**CYBERPHOBIA** The fear of computers.

**CYLINDER** The set of corresponding tracks on all the recording surfaces of a disk. If a disk has five recording surfaces, cylinder one consists of the first or outermost track on each of the recording surfaces. This concept is easy to remember if you consider that each cylinder contains tracks located at the same radius on each recording surface.

**DATA** A general term used to denote raw or processed information in the form of letters, numbers and symbols. On a VMS system, data is stored in fields within records within files.

**DATA ELEMENT** A single item of information.

**DATA FILE** A specific file that contains related data stored in the fields of records.

**DEBUG** To detect, locate, and correct errors from a computer program, or to find and repair malfunctions in computer hardware.

**DEBUGGER** An interactive VMS utility that permits you to display and modify variables in a program as the program is being executed, or to step through a program line-by-line to locate and correct programming errors. (D)

**DECnet** Digital Equipment Corporation software that enables DEC computer users to access information and resources on remote computer systems via telecommunication lines. (D)

**DEFAULT** The action taken by a computer system or program if no specific command or response is given; the device or file that is referred to by the system unless you specify another one; the assumption of predetermined values or actions.

**DEFAULT DISK** The disk on a VAX system that stores all your files when you do not explicitly state a different device name in your file specifications. Your default disk is established in the user authorization file entry for your account. (D)

**DELIMITER** A character that organizes or separates individual elements of a file specification or character string. Periods, commas, colons, and semicolons are examples of delimiters.

**DETACHED PROGRAM** A VMS program that operates without a terminal. A detached program cannot communicate with a user until it is attached to a terminal. (D)

**DEVICE**  The general name for any physical or logical entity connected with a computer and capable of transmitting, receiving or storing data. Terminals and modems are called communication devices, while disk and tape drives are known as mass storage devices.

**DEVICE INDEPENDENCE**  The characteristic of a system, file, or program that allows it to operate on any type of device. In the case of VMS programs and files, device independence is achieved through the use of logical names. (D)

**DEVICE NAME**  The name used in a file specification or program to identify a device on which information is stored. In Digital terminology, a device name consists of a mnemonic code. The code takes the form ddcu: where dd is the device type, c is the controller identifier, u is the unit number, and the colon is a terminator. A logical name like SYS$INPUT that is equated to a physical device like your terminal is also considered to be a device name. (D)

**DIGITAL COMMAND LANGUAGE (DCL)**  The standard VMS command interpreter and the collection of valid English-like keywords or verbs that it interprets and acts upon. (D)

**DIRECT I/O**  An I/O operation in which the operating system locks the pages containing the associated buffer in memory for the duration of the transfer. (D)

**DIRECTORY**  A master file with a file type of .DIR that catalogs your files on a given device; it can also be a file used to locate subsidiary files on a volume. A directory contains the file name, file type, version number, protection code, and other internal information for each file it catalogs. (D)

**DIRECTORY NAME**  The field in a file specification that identifies the directory in which a given file is listed. In VMS, a directory name can consist of up to nine alphanumeric characters. The name begins with a left bracket ([) and is terminated with a right bracket (]). When you create a directory, the default file type and extension .DIR;1 are automatically supplied by VMS. (D)

**DISK**  A flat circular platter or stack of platters coated with a magnetizable substance. Data is stored on the platter or platters by the selective magnetization of portions of the surface. The data is read from and written to these rapidly spinning surfaces by movable read/write heads. Because of the speed at which the disk rotates and the speed at which the read/write heads can be positioned, disk drives are considered to be high-speed random-access mass storage devices.

**DISK QUOTA**  The number of blocks of disk space that the files in your account may occupy. Your disk quota will normally include a permanent quota and an overdraft amount. Disk quota is established by the DISKQUOTA utility which is run by the system manager. If you exceed your quota, you will be unable to create new files or add to existing ones. Try to delete obsolete files on a regular basis, as disk space is almost always at a premium on computer systems. (D)

**DISK SCAVENGING** Any method of obtaining data from a disk that is presumed to have been erased.

**DOWN–LINE LOAD** To send a copy of a system image (operating system) to the memory of a target (requesting) node.

**DRIVE** The portion of a mass storage device upon which the media (magnetic tape reel, disk, or disk pack) is mounted. The drive contains the electromechanical units that rotate the media. These units also perform the reading and writing of data from or onto the media.

**DRIVER** A software component that handles physical I/O to a device.

**DUMP** The printing out of all or part of the contents of a storage device or of the physical memory of a computer system. The only way a programmer can read the contents of an executable program (.EXE) file is by dumping the file. (D)

**ECHO** The display of characters on a terminal screen or hardcopy media as they are entered at the keyboard. Characters are echoed by default on a VMS system except when you are entering or changing your password.

**EDIT** To create or modify the form or format of data; to revise text material; to invoke a Digital editor such as EDT, TPU, SLP, SOS or TECO.

**EDITOR** A program used to create or modify files. The default VMS editor is EDT.

**END-NODE** A nonrouting DECnet node. (D)

**EQUIVALENCE NAME** The string associated with a logical name in a logical name table. This equivalence name can be another logical name or a device name. For instance, the equivalence name DUA0: (a device name) could be equated with USER$DISK (a logical name). (D)

**ERROR MESSAGE** The message returned by VMS when an action you have directed to take place fails. (D)

**EVASIVE ACTION** A method used by VMS to respond to break-in attempts. It takes place after several login failures because of incorrect password specification by a specific source. After evasive action is initiated, the offending source is locked out of the system for a variable period of time.

**EVENT** In VMS, the occurrence of an activity or the change in the status of a process which affects that process. Because VMS is event-driven, when an event relative to a process is reported to the VMS scheduler, the ability of that process to execute or continue execution may be affected. (D)

**EXECUTE** To perform a routine or carry out an instruction; to run a program or executable image.

**EXECUTABLE IMAGE** An image that can be run within the context of a process. When the command is given to run an executable image, the image is read into a process from an executable image (.EXE) file. The process then runs the image. (D)

**EXECUTIVE** The collection of VMS software that controls and monitors the functioning of the operating system. (D)

**EXECUTIVE MODE** The second most privileged VMS processor access mode (mode 1). The executive mode is the access mode in which most VMS system services are executed. (D)

**EXTENSION** An alternate name for the file type in a file specification. On a disk, an extension is defined as the amount of space that is added to the end of a file when a new addition to the file exceeds the allocated length of the file. (D)

**EXTENT** Contiguous disk space containing a file or a portion of a file. An extent may consist of one or more clusters. (D)

**FIELD** A specified number of contiguous character positions capable of holding a single element of data. A field is a subdivision of a record.

**FILE** An organized collection of related data stored on a tape or disk volume. In most cases, files will consist of a number of records, each of which contains a number of fields. The use of records and files aids in the logical and coherent storage of data.

**FILE NAME** The portion of a file specification preceding the file type. It gives the file a logical name. (D)

**FILE SPECIFICATION** The unique identification of a file on a mass storage volume. It describes the physical location of the file as the file name and file type identifiers. A complete file specification will include the node name, the device name, directory name, file name, file type, and version number. File specifications have the format:
NODE::DEVICE:[DIRECTORY]FILENAME.TYPE;VERSION NUMBER
Each complete file specification must be unique; there can be only one occurrence of any particular full file specification at any one time. You usually need only concern yourself with the filename, file type and version number. (D)

**FILES-11** DEC's name for the disk structure used by its RSX-11 and VMS operating systems. On-Disk Structure 1 (ODS-1) is used by RSX-11, while the more sophisticated On-Disk Structure 2 (ODS-2) is the default disk structure used by VMS. ODS-1 is upwardly compatible with ODS-2 (i.e., VMS can read a disk with ODS-1 structure), but the RSX-11 operating system cannot read an ODS-2 structured volume. (D)

**FILE TYPE** The portion of a file specification that follows the file name and precedes the file extension. The file type often describes the nature or use of the file. (D)

**GATEWAY**  A device or computer used to provide a connection between two individual packet switching networks. (D)

**GENERAL REGISTER**  Any of the 16 VAX registers used as the operands of the native mode instruction set. (D)

**GLOBAL SYMBOL**  Any symbol defined by an assignment statement that will be recognized by any command procedure executed in any account on a system. (D)

**GOLD KEY**  The <PF1> key on the LK201 keyboard. (D)

**GROUP**  In the VMS file protection scheme, a group is one of the four classes of users definable to a VMS system. Specifically, a group is a set of users who have access to each other's directories and the files contained within them. (D)

**GROUP IDENTIFIER**  The group of characters in a two-part alphanumeric user identification code entry. Users who share the same group identifier are said to be in the same UIC group. (D)

**GROUP NUMBER**  The first group of digits in a numeric user identification code. Users who share the same group number are considered to be in the same UIC group. (D)

**HALF DUPLEX**  A method of bidirectional data transmission in which two-way communication is possible by transmitting one way at a time.

**HARDCOPY**  Printed computer output, produced by a line printer or hardcopy terminal.

**HARDWARE**  The physical devices and equipment associated with a computer system. Contrast with software, or the operating system and programs used within the system.

**HELP FILE**  A text file associated with the VMS HELP command. You can add entries to the HELP file supplied with the VMS operating system. The HELP file can provide up to eight levels of information beneath each main topic. (D)

**HIGH-LEVEL LANGUAGE**  A programming language that consists of English-like statements. This type of language is generally machine-independent. Each high-level program statement is translated into several machine language instructions when the program is compiled and linked.

**HIGHWATER MARKING**  A technique that monitors the extent of a disk file (how much space it occupies) and prevents the owner of the file from reading the allocated disk space beyond the extent. The extent of a file is considered to be its highwater mark; any space allocated beyond the extent is protected against disk scavenging by the VMS erase-on-allocate feature. (D)

**IMAGE** Procedures and data bound together by the LINKER; often the end result of compiling and linking a program on the system. VMS supports three kinds of images, i.e., executable (e.g. executable program), shared and system. (D)

**IMAGE ACTIVATOR** The VMS procedures that ready an image for execution within a process. The image activator invokes memory management facilities to enable paging and mapping the image's virtual pages to physical pages. (D)

**IMAGE PRIVILEGES** The privileges assigned to an image when it is installed by the image activator. These privileges are generally derived from the user authorization file, although the system manager can install an image with special privileges if this is desirable. (D)

**INPUT** The process of transferring external data into main memory or an intermediate storage device. Input is also defined as the data that is transferred.

**INPUT/OUTPUT** Input, output, or both. Commonly referred to as I/O.

**INTERACTIVE** A mode of system operation. In the interactive mode, you are in two-way communication with the system through the use of a terminal. The opposite of the interactive mode is the batch mode of operation.

**INTERRECORD GAP** A blank space deliberately placed between individual records on a magnetic tape. It is used by the read/write head of the tape drive to sense the end of one record and the beginning of the next one.

**INTERRUPT** An event other than a program instruction that changes the normal flow of execution of a program or process. Usually an interrupt is external to the program or process executing when the interrupt occurs. An interrupt can be generated by a device or by system software.

**INVOKE** To call up or run a program or compiler, or to execute a command procedure with the @ symbol. (D)

**JOB** From the standpoint of VMS, a job is the accounting unit equated with a process. Because certain processes can spawn or create subprocesses, a job can contain a number of processes. Jobs are classified as batch or interactive. When you log into the system, an interactive job is created to handle your requests and processes. If you submit a program to a batch queue for processing, a batch job is created. (D)

**JOB CONTROLLER** The VMS process that establishes the process context of a job, handles the LOGIN and LOGOUT facilities, maintains accounting records, and terminates processes. (D)

**KERNEL MODE** This is mode 0, the most privileged access mode in which VMS software executes. The most privileged services of VMS, such as the pager and I/O drivers, run in the kernel mode. (D)

**KEYPAD**  On a LK201 keyboard, the two groups of keys to the right of the main keyboard. (D)

**KEYWORD**  In Digital Command Language, a valid command, option, or qualifier. (D)

**LINE EDITOR**  A text editor that allows you to add to, modify, or delete information from a file on a line-by-line basis.

**LINKER**  The VMS facility that creates an executable program image from one or more object modules output by a compiler or assembler. The linking process involves the establishment of virtual addresses for portions of the image, acquisition of system services referenced by the program, and accumulation of data that will be needed for image execution. Using the LINKER, you can link a VAX BASIC object program with a MACRO-32 object program and end up with an executable program containing both the BASIC and MACRO-32 object modules. (D)

**LOCAL AREA NETWORK (LAN)**  A privately owned communication system that offers high-speed access to the attached resources.

**LOCAL SYMBOL**  Any symbol defined by an assignment statement that is recognized only within the DCL command procedure in which it has been defined. Contrast with global symbol. (D)

**LOGICAL NAME**  A name that you specify as a substitute for a file specification or a portion of a file specification. You can assign logical names to frequently used devices or files to save keystrokes or provide device independence. (D)

**LOGICAL NAME TABLE**  This is an area in the system containing the set of logical names and equivalence names for a particular process, a particular group, or for the entire system. (D)

**LOGIN**  The procedure of initiating communication with a computer system from a terminal.

**LOGOUT**  The act of terminating a terminal session with a computer system.

**LOGIN FILE**  Also referred to as LOGIN.COM, the command procedure that executes automatically whenever you log in to the system or submit a batch job. It is used to tailor your account environment to meet your needs. You can write your own LOGIN.COM or the system manager can assign a preset LOGIN.COM to your account in the user authorization file. (D)

**LONGWORD**  32 bits or four contiguous bytes beginning on a byte boundary. The longword is the unit required for addressing virtual space in a 32-bit computer like the VAX. (D)

**MACHINE LANGUAGE** A computer program expressed in binary numbers. An executable image consists of machine language instructions.

**MACRO** A statement that requests a language processor such as MACRO-32 to generate a predefined series of instructions. The use of macros can save an assembly language programmer a great deal of time. For example, division is done in assembly language by repetitive subtraction. Using the macro DIV, the programmer does not have to write the subtraction routine to perform a division operation.

**MAGNETIC TAPE** A mass storage media consisting of tape coated with a metallic oxide. Data can be recorded and stored in the form of magnetically polarized spots on this tape. Although information on magnetic tape cannot be accessed as rapidly as data on disks, it is a far less expensive media. Files stored on disks are often copied or backed up to magnetic tape for archival storage and safekeeping.

**MAILBOX** A software data structure used as a record-oriented device for sharing data between processes. (D)

**MASS STORAGE DEVICE** A hardware device capable of reading and writing large amounts of data on mass storage media such as magnetic tape reels, disk packs, or floppy disks.

**MEMBER IDENTIFIER** The entry in a one-part alphanumeric user identification code (UIC) or the second half of a two-part alphanumeric UIC. It uniquely identifies the user who has been assigned the code. (D)

**MEMBER NUMBER** The second number in a numeric user identification code. (D)

**MEMORY MANAGEMENT** The VMS functions that include page mapping and protection within the processor and the VMS pager, swapper and image activator. (D)

**MINICOMPUTER** Any general purpose, multiuser digital computer in the low-to-average price range.

**MOUNT** To physically place a disk pack or magnetic tape on a drive, ready the drive for operation, and place the drive online. Also, to issue the MOUNT command in order to logically associate a volume with the hardware unit onto which it has been physically mounted. (D)

**NETWORK** A collection of individual but interconnected computer systems linked by a communication protocol such as DECnet. Networked computer systems can share files and other resources with each other.

**NIBBLE** Half of a byte; either the low-order or high-order four bits of a byte.

**NODE** An individual computer system within a network. Each system can communicate with some or all of the other computers in the network, depending on the communications protocol and the configuration of the network.

**NODE SPECIFICATION**  A portion of a file specification that identifies the location of a particular computer, or node, within a computer network. Node specifications are terminated with two colons (::). (D)

**NULL PROCESS**  This is a VMS process that accumulates idle computer time for accounting purposes. It functions at the lowest priority within the system and occupies one entire priority class. (D)

**NUMERIC**  Pertaining to numbers or to representation by means of numbers. In field definition, a numeric field is one in which only numbers may be stored.

**OBJECT MODULE**  Designated by the file type .OBJ, an object module is the binary output from a program compiler or assembler. This output is input to the LINKER. An object module is not readable or executable. (D)

**OFF–LINE**  Refers to peripheral equipment or devices not currently under direct control of the computer system.

**OPEN ACCOUNT**  A VMS account that doesn't require a password for login. (D)

**OPERATING SYSTEM**  An organized collection of techniques and procedures that control the overall operation of a computer system. In other words, the operating system acts as a supervisor. It is supplied by the computer vendor as a portion of the system software. On Digital's VAX computers, the operating system is called Virtual Memory System (VMS).

**OPERATOR'S CONSOLE**  Usually the hardcopy terminal designated as the system operator's terminal (OPA0:), but it can be any terminal designated as an operator console by the DCL command REPLY/ENABLE. It's possible to respond to OPCOM messages and to start up and shut down the computer system from any terminal designated as the operator's console. A temporary operator's terminal can be disabled with the DCL REPLY/DISABLE command. (D)

**OWNER**  In the VMS file protection scheme, the owner is the member of a group to whom a file belongs. (D)

**P1 THROUGH P8**  A value passed on the DCL command line to a command procedure that is equated to a symbol from P1 through P8. (D)

**PAGE**  The basic unit used by VMS for establishing working set sizes, transferring data between memory and disk storage, and for memory mapping. A page consists of 512 contiguous byte locations beginning on an even 512 byte boundary. (D)

**PAGE FAULT**  An exception that occurs when a page that is not currently within a process working set is referenced. When a page fault occurs in a process, the process is suspended until the system writes used pages back out to the disk and replaces them by reading in the pages that the process' working set requires. (D)

**PAGE FAULT CLUSTER**  The number of 512-byte pages that are read into memory or back out to the disk during each page fault. (D)

**PAGER**  One of the VMS memory management facilities, the pager is a set of privileged kernel mode instructions that reads in a required page cluster when a page fault occurs. This permits the image that generated the page fault to resume execution. Note that in VMS a process can page only against itself. Thus, a page fault generated by one user's process cannot affect the working set of another user's process. (D)

**PAGING**  The action of bringing pages of an executing process into physical memory when the process image is first activated, or when requested by a page fault.

**PARAMETER**  The object of a command; the noun associated with a DCL command verb within a command string. A parameter can be a symbol value passed to a command procedure, a word defined by DCL, or a file specification. In the DCL command string PRINT MYFILE.DAT for example, MYFILE.DAT is a parameter.

**PARSE**  To break a command string into its individual elements so it can be interpreted. When a command string is parsed, it is broken into the DCL command verb, its parameters, and qualifiers.

**PASSWORD**  The protective keyword associated with an account.

**PERIPHERAL**  A hardware device, in a computer system, that is not a functional part of the CPU, e.g., printer, disk drive and so on.

**PHYSICAL ADDRESS**  The address used by VMS to identify a specific location in physical memory or on a disk drive. (D)

**PHYSICAL MEMORY**  The tangible memory boards or modules within a computer containing data and instructions that the computer can directly fetch and execute; also elements of the operating system or any other data that the processor must manipulate in order to function. Physical memory is also referred to as main memory.

**PRIORITY**  A numeric rank assigned to an image, process or account to determine its precedence in obtaining system resources such as CPU time or disk access. In VMS, processing priorities range from 0 to 15 for interactive processes, and from 16 to 31 for real-time processes. VMS can dynamically raise and lower the priority of processes, but it cannot lower a process' priority beneath the base priority established in the user authorization file. (D)

**PRIVILEGES**  In VMS, the 35 keywords that identify special system functions that can be granted or denied to system users. Privileges are categorized by their potential to affect the computer system or its resources. They are granted or denied in a manner consistent with the needs of users and the need to maintain the integrity of the system. (D)

**PROCESS**  The basic entity that can be scheduled by VMS. A process provides the context in which an image executes. A process includes software and hardware contexts and an address space. (D)

**PROCESS PAGE TABLE**  This is the table that the system uses to map and locate the pages of virtual memory used by a process. One such table is present for each active process in the system. (D)

**PROCESS SPACE**  The lowest-addressed half of virtual address space. It consists of 2-GB of addresses divided into two 1-GB regions. Data and process instructions are resident in this process space. (D)

**PROGRAM**  A complete sequence of instructions and routines necessary to solve a problem on a computer system.

**PROGRAM REGION**  The bottom half of process space, or the P0 region. This 1-GB region contains the image currently being executed by a process and user code that the image has called.

**PROMPT**  A word, words, or symbol used by the computer system as a cue to assist you in making a response, or to inform you that the system is waiting for a response.

**PROTECTION CODE**  In VMS, specifies what type of access different categories of users can have to a file. Four types of access (i.e., read, write, execute, and delete) may be granted or denied to four categories of users (i.e., system, owner, group, and world). An additional type of access, control, can be specified in an access control list.

**QUALIFIER**  A portion of a command added to a given DCL command verb. It modifies the verb or command parameter by specifying one of several options. For example, if you issue the DIRECTORY command with the /SIZE qualifier (DIRECTORY/SIZE), the /SIZE qualifier will indicate to the DCL interpreter that you want to know the size (in blocks) of a file. (D)

**QUANTUM**  A specified minimum time that a process remains in memory before it is eligible to be swapped out. It also indicates the maximum amount of time that a process can execute before another process is given its share of execution time. (D)

**QUEUE**  A waiting line in the computer system. The system has special areas set aside for input, output, and special device queues. With sufficient user privilege, you can create, start, modify, stop, and delete specific queues. A typical queue on a VMS system is SYS$BATCH, the default batch queue.

**QUEUE MANAGER**  A VMS system program that provides orderly processing of batch and print jobs. (D)

**QUOTA** The total amount of a reusable system resource that a job is permitted to use during a given period of time. Quotas are established in the user authorization file. They can be used to set limits on working set size, virtual address space, and CPU time consumable by a process. (D)

**RANDOM ACCESS** A technique by which the computer can find one data element as rapidly as any other, regardless of its specific location in storage, without requiring a sequential search.

**RANDOM ACCESS MEMORY (RAM)** A read/write memory device.

**RECORD** A meaningful collection of related information (data elements) organized into fields and treated as a single unit by the computer. Records are composed of fields; one or more records make up a data file.

**RECORD LOCKING** The ability to control access to an indexed or relative file record when that file is being accessed by more than one user.

**RECORD MANAGEMENT SERVICES (RMS)** A set of system routines that open, close, read from, extend, and delete files. When you invoke a DCL command that deletes files, such as the PURGE command, RMS is the system service that performs the file deletion. (D)

**REGISTER** A storage location in the computer system CPU that is not considered to be a portion of main memory. Registers are accessible by programmers and the VMS operating system.

**RESOURCE** A physical portion of the computer system such as a tape drive or memory; a reusable operating system-specific entity such as working set size or maximum virtual page count.

**RESPONSE TIME** The time that elapses between when you press <Return> after entering data or a command into the computer, and your receipt of output from the computer. Response time on VMS systems is affected by the number of users on the system, the jobs that are running, and the availability of system devices.

**REVERSE VIDEO** A reverse of the normal video contrast. If the default is amber lettering on a black screen, reverse video makes the lettering appear in black on amber. The EDT editor and some user programs use reverse video to highlight text or information.

**RIGHTS DATABASE** A file that lists users and special identifiers associated with them. This associative file is used in the access control list system. (D)

**RIGHTS LIST** In the access control list system, a list associated with each process that contains all the identifiers that the process holds. (D)

**RWED** Refers to the VMS file access scheme of read, write, execute and delete.

**SCROLLING**  On a video terminal, the process that makes new information appear at the bottom of the screen. Simultaneously, the old information is pushed up until it disappears at the top of the screen.

**SECURE TERMINAL SERVER**  An optional VMS feature that ensures that you can only log in to a terminal that has already been logged out. To log in to a terminal that is protected with the secure server, you must first press the <BREAK> key. This will automatically halt any process that might be executing from the terminal and log the terminal out. This technique is a deterrent to password grabber programs. (D)

**SEQUENTIAL ACCESS**  A method of accessing records in a file by reading them in the order in which they appear in the file. Records on a reel of magnetic tape are stored and accessed sequentially by the tape drive. Compared to random access, sequential access is slow and inefficient.

**SOFTWARE**  The sum total of assemblers, compilers, programs, utilities, and commands available within a computer system. System software includes system specific utilities and subprograms, as well as the operating system used by the processor.

**SOURCE PROGRAM**  A program written in an assembly or high-level language. A source program must be assembled or compiled and then linked before it can be executed by a computer.

**SPOOLING**  A method of using a high-speed mass storage device as an intermediate buffer to hold data passing from a low-speed device, such as a terminal, to memory, or from memory to a line printer.

**STRING**  A specific sequence of characters. The characters and words in a DCL command are often referred to as a command string.

**SUBDIRECTORY**  A directory file that is cataloged in a higher-level directory in an account. It lists additional files that belong to the owner of the directory. In VMS, a subdirectory is denoted by a period preceding its name. The subdirectory name is concatenated to the name of the higher-level directory that lists it.

**SUBPROCESS**  A process created or spawned by a parent process. The creator process owns the subprocess; the subprocess shares the quotas and limits imposed on the creator process. After a subprocess is spawned, you have no further control over its execution. Subprocesses may be created or spawned with the DCL SPAWN command. When the creating process exits the system, all of its subprocesses are deleted. (D)

**SUBROUTINE**  In a program, a routine that can be called and used by another routine to accomplish a specific task.

**SUPERVISOR MODE**  In the access mode scheme, the third most privileged mode (mode 2). The DCL command line interpreter runs in the supervisor mode. (D)

**SWAPPER**  The swapper performs memory scheduling and execution throughout the computer system. Based on priorities and the degree of system usage, the swapper removes processes from the balance set (swaps them out), creates shells for new processes, and enters processes that have been waiting for execution into the balance set. (D)

**SWAPPING**  The act of sharing memory resources between several processes by writing an entire working set to secondary storage (swapping out) and reading another working set into physical memory (swapping in).

**SYMBIONT**  A system process that transfers record-oriented data to or from mass storage devices such as disk drives. The system symbionts are functions of spooling and queuing. An example of a symbiont is the print symbiont, which transfers a print file from disk to the line printer. (D)

**SYMBOL**  A user-defined name that can be equated to a command, character string or arithmetic value through the DCL ASSIGN statement. A symbol must be defined or given a meaning so that it can be used.

**SYNTAX**  The structure of expressions in a language or a command language; the rules governing the structure of a programming language or the form that a command must follow to be valid.

**SYSGEN**  Refers to the VMS system generation program, used to configure a new VMS system or to modify the parameters and characteristics of an operating VAX system. (D)

**SYSTEM**  In the VMS file protection scheme, system is the most privileged of the system, owner, group and world categories. The system category includes user identification codes [1,0] through [1,10] and is used by VMS, system managers, and system operators. System also refers to a combination of personnel, material, facilities and equipment that work together to achieve a goal or perform a function. A system includes its methods and procedures, and may be comprised of a number of subsystems. (D)

**SYSTEM IMAGE**  The image that is read into the VAX front-end processor from disk or tape when the system is booted and started up. This image contains a subset of the VMS operating system and is used to load the remainder of VMS, and initialize and start up the computer system. (D)

**SYSTEM PASSWORD**  A password that must be entered at a terminal before the system will initiate the login procedure and display the username prompt. (D)

**SYSTEM REGION**  The low-addressed half of system space or the third quarter of overall virtual address space. Virtual addresses contained in the system region can be shared between processes. They include such entities as individual process page tables. (D)

**SYSTEM SERVICES**  These are user-callable procedures provided by VMS. They include memory management, logical name, change mode, I/O and process control services. Most system services are provided and executed for users by VMS, but some services are available for and may be called and used by application programmers. (D)

**SYSTEM SPACE**  The top half of virtual address space, consisting of the system common region and the reserved region. (D)

**TERMINAL**  A peripheral device used for interactive communication with a computer. It consists of a typewriter-like keyboard and a printer or video screen.

**THROUGHPUT**  A measure of computer system efficiency; the rate at which work can be input, processed and output by a computer.

**TIMESHARING**  A scheme in which each user of a computer system is allocated a fair share of computer time and resources in rotation.

**USER IDENTIFICATION CODE (UIC)**  A code consisting of two numbers or two alphanumeric identifiers enclosed in brackets and separated by a comma in the form [group,member]. An alphanumeric UIC may optionally consist of a single member identifier. The UIC identifies the group and member of a given user or file and is used by VMS to permit or deny file access. (D)

**USER MODE**  In the access mode scheme, the user mode (mode 3) is the fourth, or least privileged mode. User processes are run in this mode. (D)

**USERNAME**  The name associated with your account that you type at a terminal to log in to the system. (D)

**UTILITY**  A general purpose program or facility provided by an operating system to perform common or generic tasks. On a VMS system, functions like PHONE, MAIL and SORT are considered to be utilities.

**VERSION NUMBER**  The numeric field that follows the file type and terminates a file specification. It begins with a semicolon and is followed by a number. Each time a new version of a given file is created, the system automatically assigns it a new version number incremented by one. This number uniquely identifies a file, as no two duplicate file specifications can have the same version number. (D)

**VIRTUAL ADDRESS**  This is a 32-bit integer that identifies the location of a given byte in virtual address space. When needed, the VMS memory management system will translate a virtual address to a physical address within the memory of the computer. (D)

**VIRTUAL ADDRESS EXTENSION (VAX)**  A high performance, multiprocessing computer system based on a 32–bit architecture. VAX is made by Digital Equipment Corporation. (D)

**VIRTUAL ADDRESS SPACE**  The set of all virtual addresses that are available within VMS. It can be conceived of as a linear array of 4,294,967,296-byte addresses. (D)

**VIRTUAL MEMORY** The set of storage locations on disk and in physical memory that is referred to by virtual addresses. For the user, the storage locations on disk appear to be located in physical memory, and can be used as such. The maximum size of virtual memory in a computer system is contingent upon available physical memory and the amount of disk space that can be used to store virtual memory addresses. (D)

**VIRTUAL MEMORY SYSTEM (VMS)** The operating system for VAX computer systems. (D)

**VOLUME** The largest logical unit of the file structure. Examples of volumes are disk packs and reels of magnetic tape. (D)

**WILDCARD CHARACTER** An asterisk (*) or percent sign (%) that is used within or in place of a file name, file type, directory name or version number in a file specification to indicate *all* for the given field or portion of the field. (D)

**WORD** 16 bits or two contiguous bytes beginning on a byte boundary. This is the unit required for addressing locations in a PDP-11 or other 16-bit computer. (D)

**WORKING SET** The number of pages in physical memory to which a process can refer without incurring a page fault. The larger the working set size, the fewer page faults that the process will generate. However, as working set sizes increase, the number of processes in the balance set decreases. VMS permits the establishment of a minimum working set size, a working set quota, and a maximum size to which a working set can grow as long as it does not interfere with other processes. You can obtain a display of your current working set size by issuing the DCL command SHOW WORKING_SET. (D)

**WORLD** In the system, owner, group, world scheme, world refers to all users of the system, including the system manager, operators and members of an owner's group as well as members of other groups. (D)

# Index

## W

## X

Bynon, David W. and Shannon, Terry C. *Introduction to VAX/VMS (Second Edition)*. Professional Press, Inc., 1987.
> An end-user guide to the VMS operating system, this book explores the VMS user environment, DCL, command procedures, and many VMS utilities.

Jones, Oliver. *Introduction to the X Window System*. Prentice-Hall, 1989.
> This book explores all aspects of the MIT X Window System. Detailed are the X Window System environment, its use, the X protocol, and application programming using Xlib.

Madnick, Stuart E. and Donovan, John J. *Operating Systems*. McGraw-Hill Book Company, 1974.
> The book is a complete text on operating system techniques and implementations. It discusses all aspects of computer operating system design, including device management, processor management, and memory management.

Marotta, Robert E. ed. *The Digital Dictionary (Second Edition)*. Digital Equipment Corporation, 1986.
> A dictionary of technical and DEC-specific terms.

McNamera, John E. *Technical Aspects of Data Communications (Second Edition)*. Digital Equipment Corporation, 1982.
> This book takes a close look at the hardware and software systems used in data communications. Digital's DDCMP protocol is explained in detail, along with common CCITT standards.

Peters, J.F., III. *The Art of Assembly Language Programming VAX-11*. Reston Publishing Company, Inc., 1985.
> An extensive text on the instruction set and assembly language of the VAX-11 CPU. The author addresses all aspects of programming with MACRO-32, including a detailed description of the VAX registers and control mechanisms.

Tanenbaum, Andrew S. *Computer Networks*. Prentice-Hall, Inc., 1981.
> The book presents a comprehensive study of the ISO reference model. Several popular networks are introduced, including DECnet, SNA, ARPANET, and X.25.

The following Digital VMS Version 5.0, VMS Version 5.1, and VMS Version 5.2 guides were referenced:

*Guide to VMS System Security*. Digital Equipment Corporation, June, 1989.

*VMS DECwindows User's Guide*. Digital Equipment Corporation, December 1988.

*VMS General User's Manual*. Digital Equipment Corporation, April 1988.

*VMS Guide to System Performance Management*. Digital Equipment Corporation, April 1988.

*VMS Guide to VAXclusters*. Digital Equipment Corporation, April, 1989.

*VMS System Manager's Manual*. Digital Equipment Corporation, April 1988.

The following National Bureau of Standards (now National Institute for Standards and Technology) computer security publications were referenced:

*Guidelines for ADP Physical Security and Risk Management*. FIPS PUB 31, NBS, June 1974.

*Guidelines on User Authentication Techniques for Computer Network Access Control*. FIPS PUB 83, NBS, September 1980.

*Standard on Password Usage*. FIPS PUB 112, NBS, May 1985.